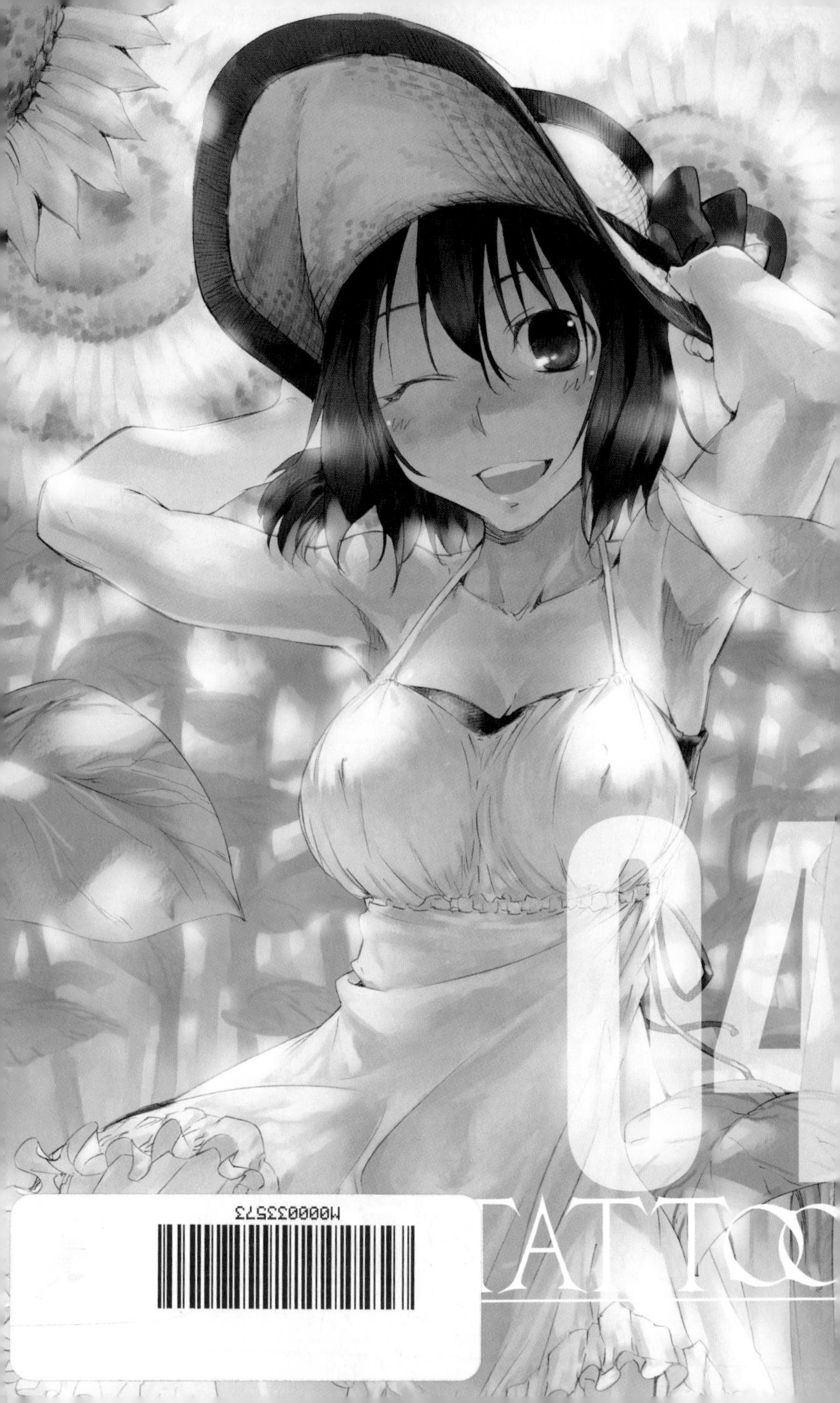
04
TATTO

ABOO TATTOO

04

CONTENTS

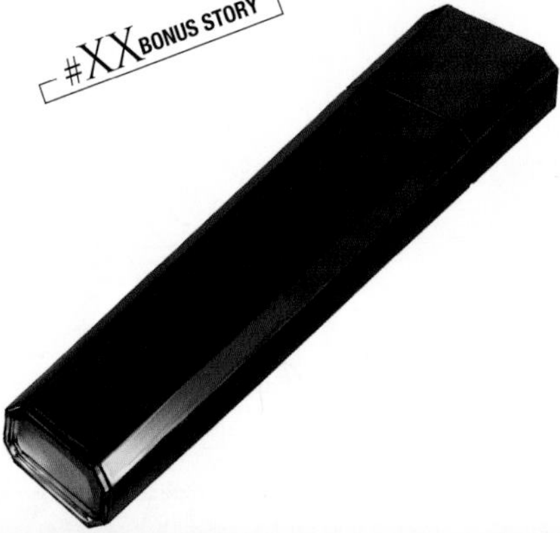

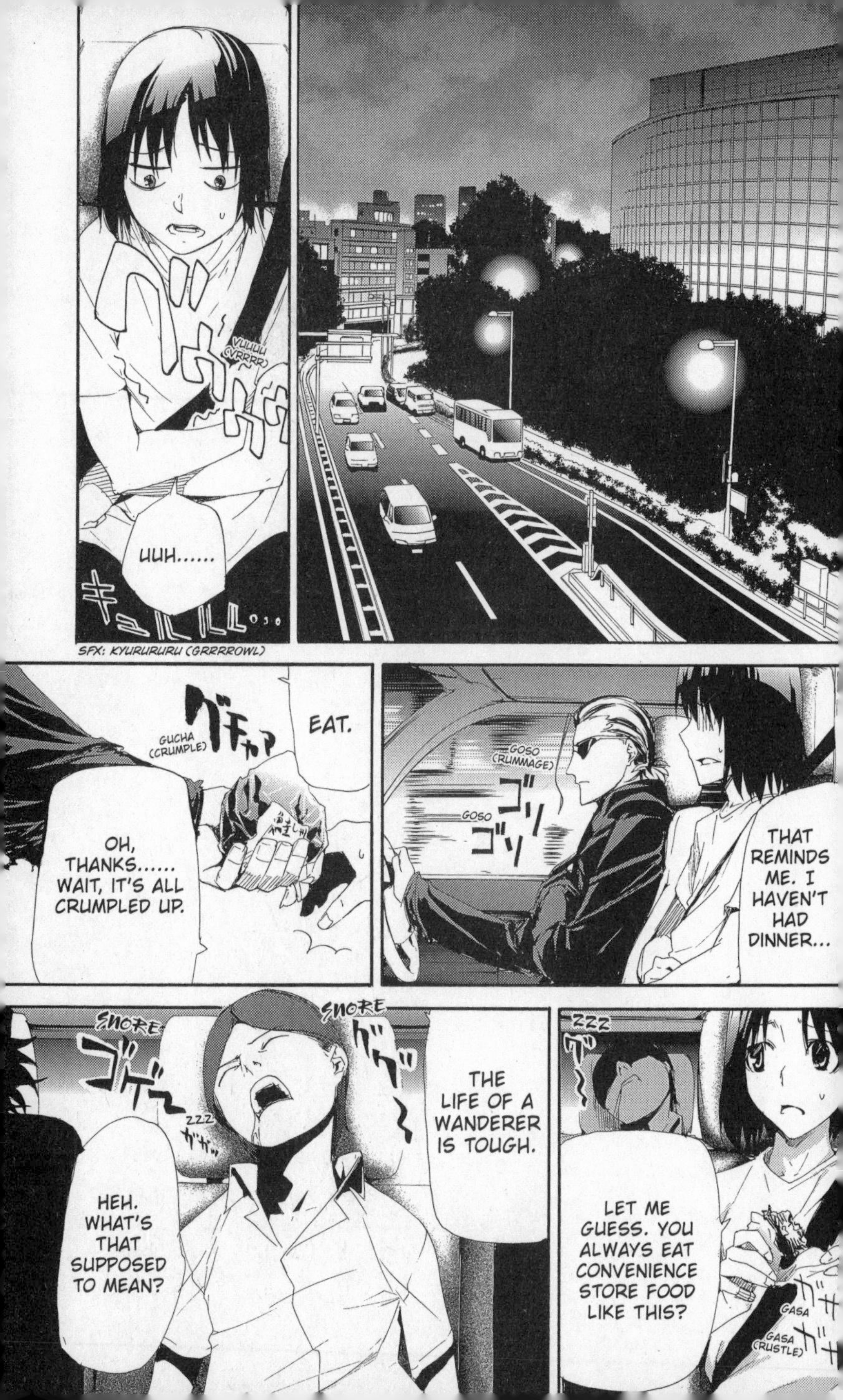
VUUUU (VRRRR)
UUH......
SFX: KYURURURU (GRRRROWL)
GOSO (RUMMAGE)
GOSO
THAT REMINDS ME. I HAVEN'T HAD DINNER...
EAT.
GUCHA (CRUMPLE)
OH, THANKS...... WAIT, IT'S ALL CRUMPLED UP.
ZZZ
LET ME GUESS. YOU ALWAYS EAT CONVENIENCE STORE FOOD LIKE THIS?
GASA
GASA (RUSTLE)
SNORE
SNORE
ZZZ
THE LIFE OF A WANDERER IS TOUGH.
HEH. WHAT'S THAT SUPPOSED TO MEAN?

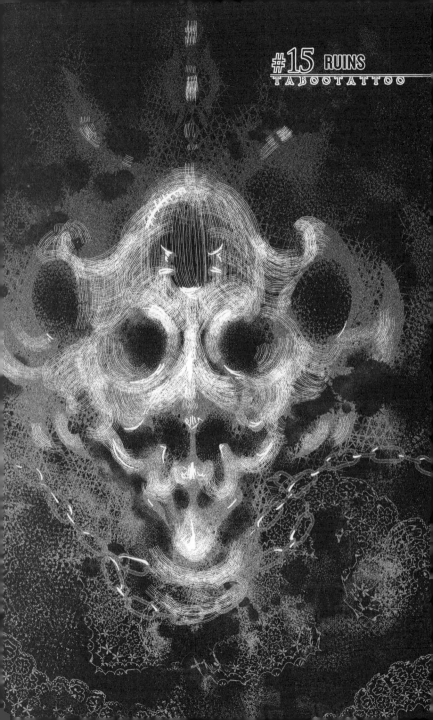

#15 RUINS
TABOOTATTOO

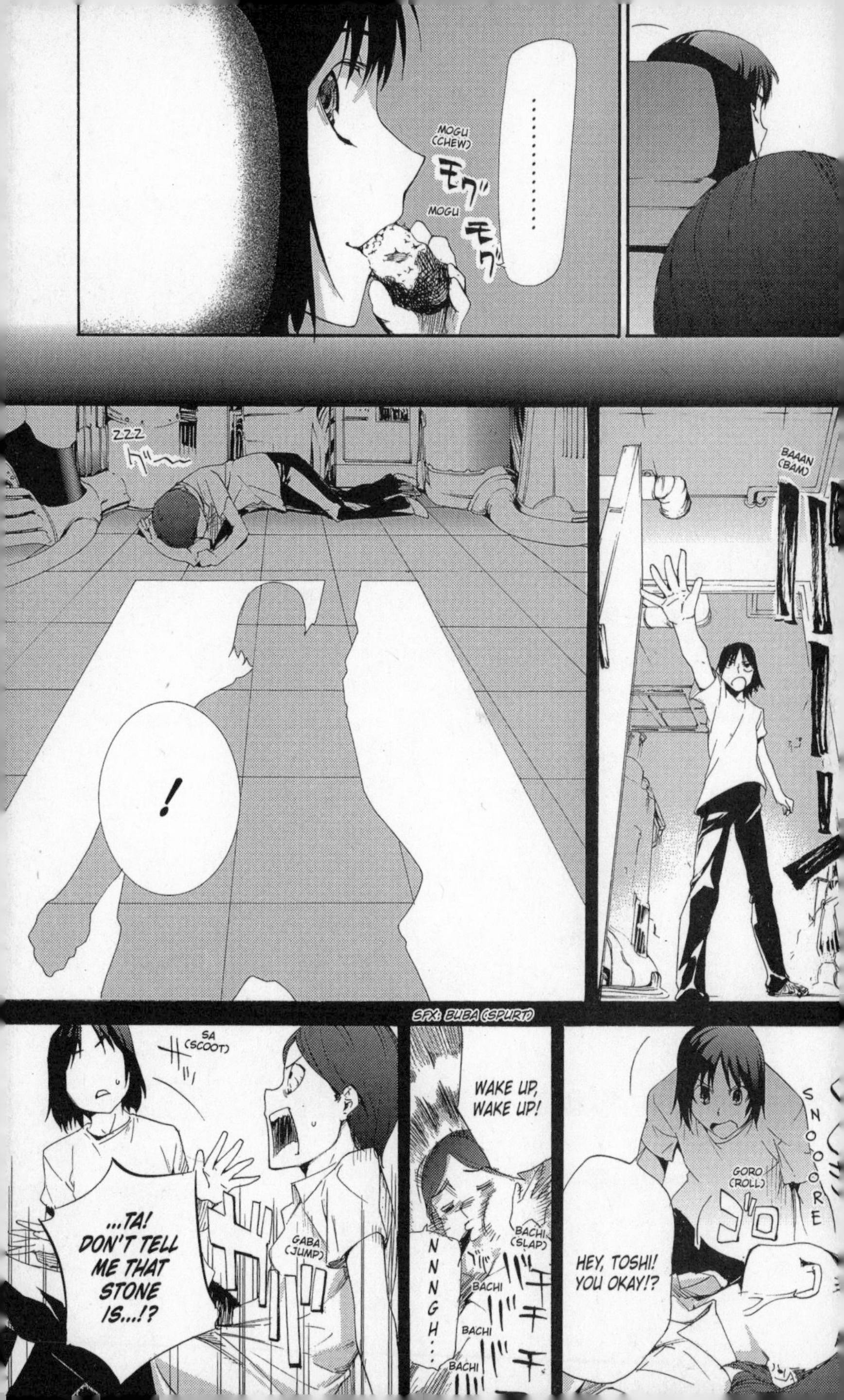
......
MOGU (CHEW)
モグ
MOGU
モグ
BAAAN (BAM)
ZZZ
!
SFX: BUBA (SPURT)
SNOOORE
GORO (ROLL)
ゴロ
HEY, TOSHI! YOU OKAY!?
WAKE UP, WAKE UP!
BACHI (SLAP)
NNNGH...
BACHI
BACHI
BACHI
SA (SCOOT)
...TA! DON'T TELL ME THAT STONE IS...!?
GABA (JUMP)

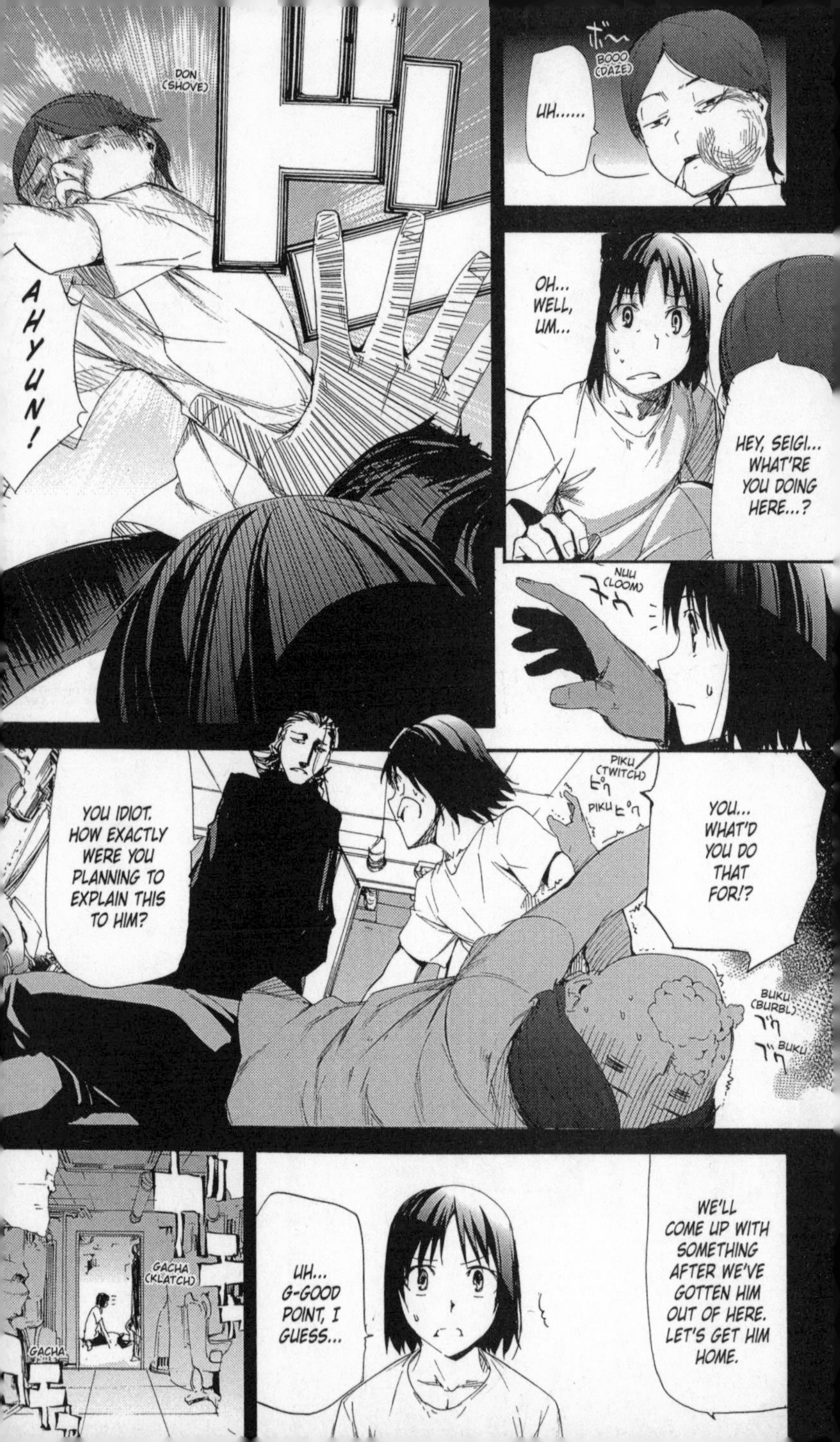
BOOO (DAZE)
UH......
HEY, SEIGI... WHAT'RE YOU DOING HERE...?
OH... WELL, UM...
NUU (LOOM)
DON (SHOVE)
AHYUN!
YOU... WHAT'D YOU DO THAT FOR!?
PIKU (TWITCH)
PIKU
BUKU (BURBL)
BUKU
YOU IDIOT. HOW EXACTLY WERE YOU PLANNING TO EXPLAIN THIS TO HIM?
WE'LL COME UP WITH SOMETHING AFTER WE'VE GOTTEN HIM OUT OF HERE. LET'S GET HIM HOME.
UH... G-GOOD POINT, I GUESS...
GACHA (KLATCH)
GACHA

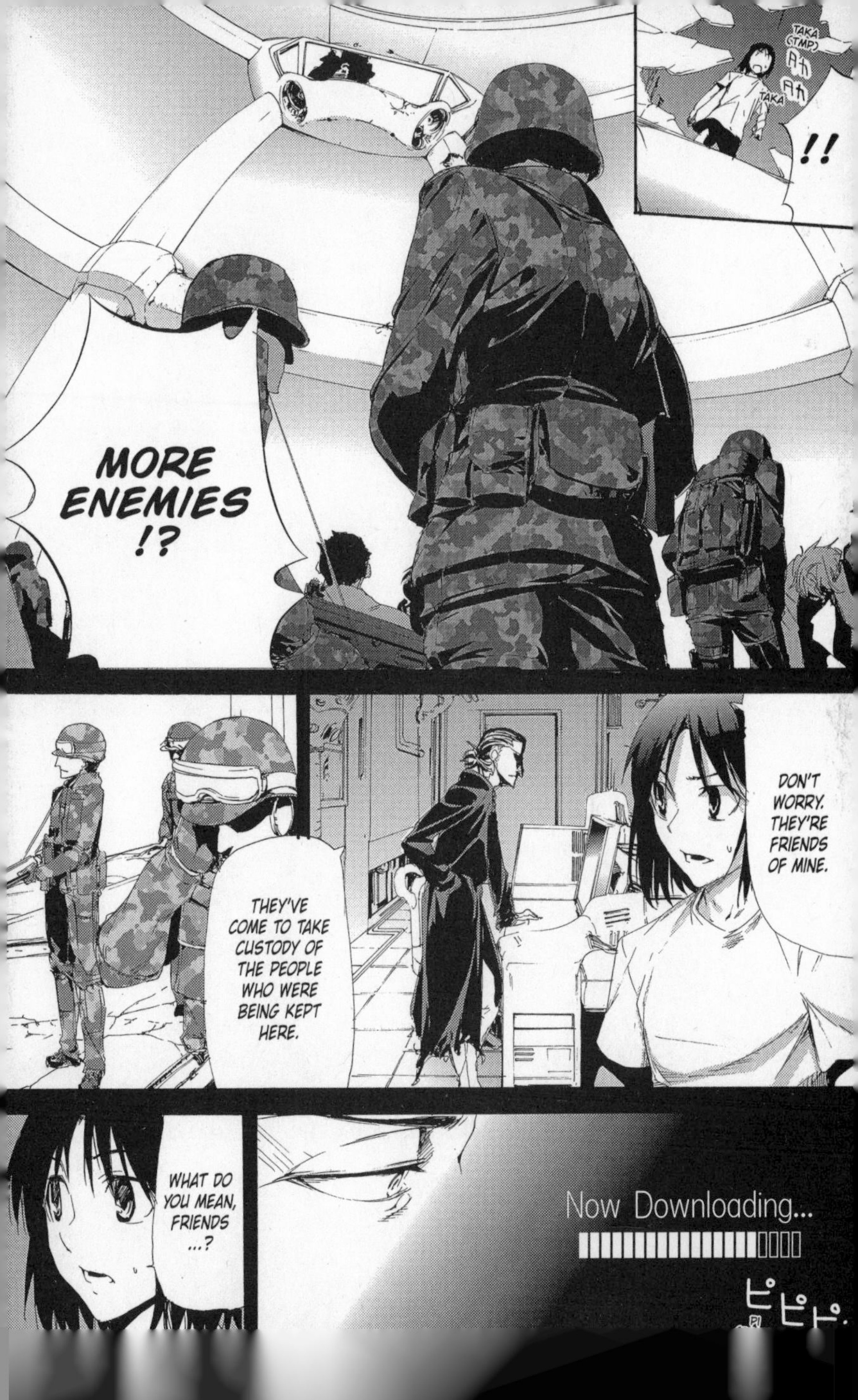
TAKA (TMP)
TAKA
!!
MORE ENEMIES!?
DON'T WORRY. THEY'RE FRIENDS OF MINE.
THEY'VE COME TO TAKE CUSTODY OF THE PEOPLE WHO WERE BEING KEPT HERE.
Now Downloading...
ピピピ
WHAT DO YOU MEAN, FRIENDS...?

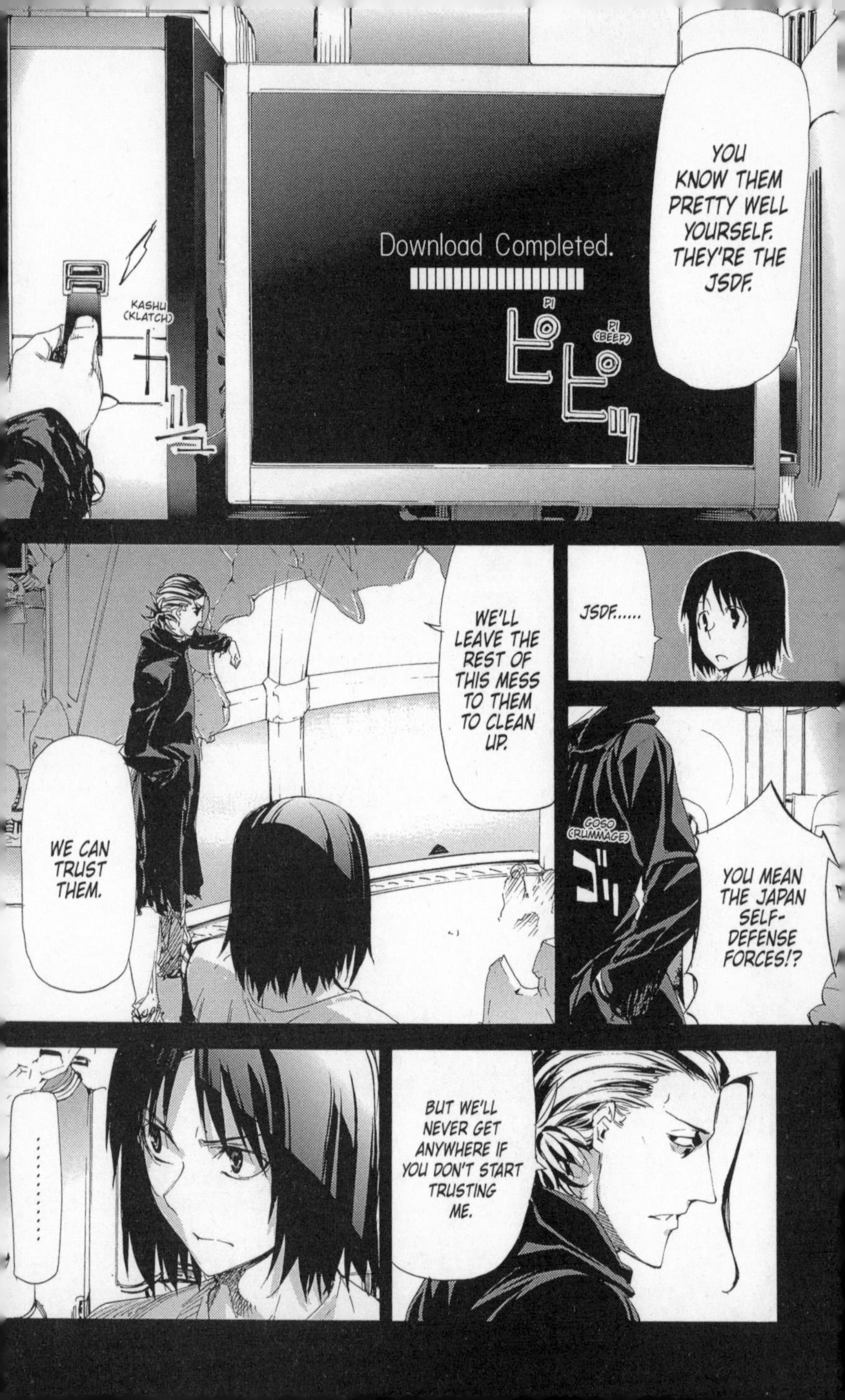
YOU KNOW THEM PRETTY WELL YOURSELF. THEY'RE THE JSDF.
Download Completed.
PI PI (BEEP)
KASHU (KLATCH)
JSDF......
GOSO (RUMMAGE)
YOU MEAN THE JAPAN SELF-DEFENSE FORCES!?
WE'LL LEAVE THE REST OF THIS MESS TO THEM TO CLEAN UP.
WE CAN TRUST THEM.
BUT WE'LL NEVER GET ANYWHERE IF YOU DON'T START TRUSTING ME.
......

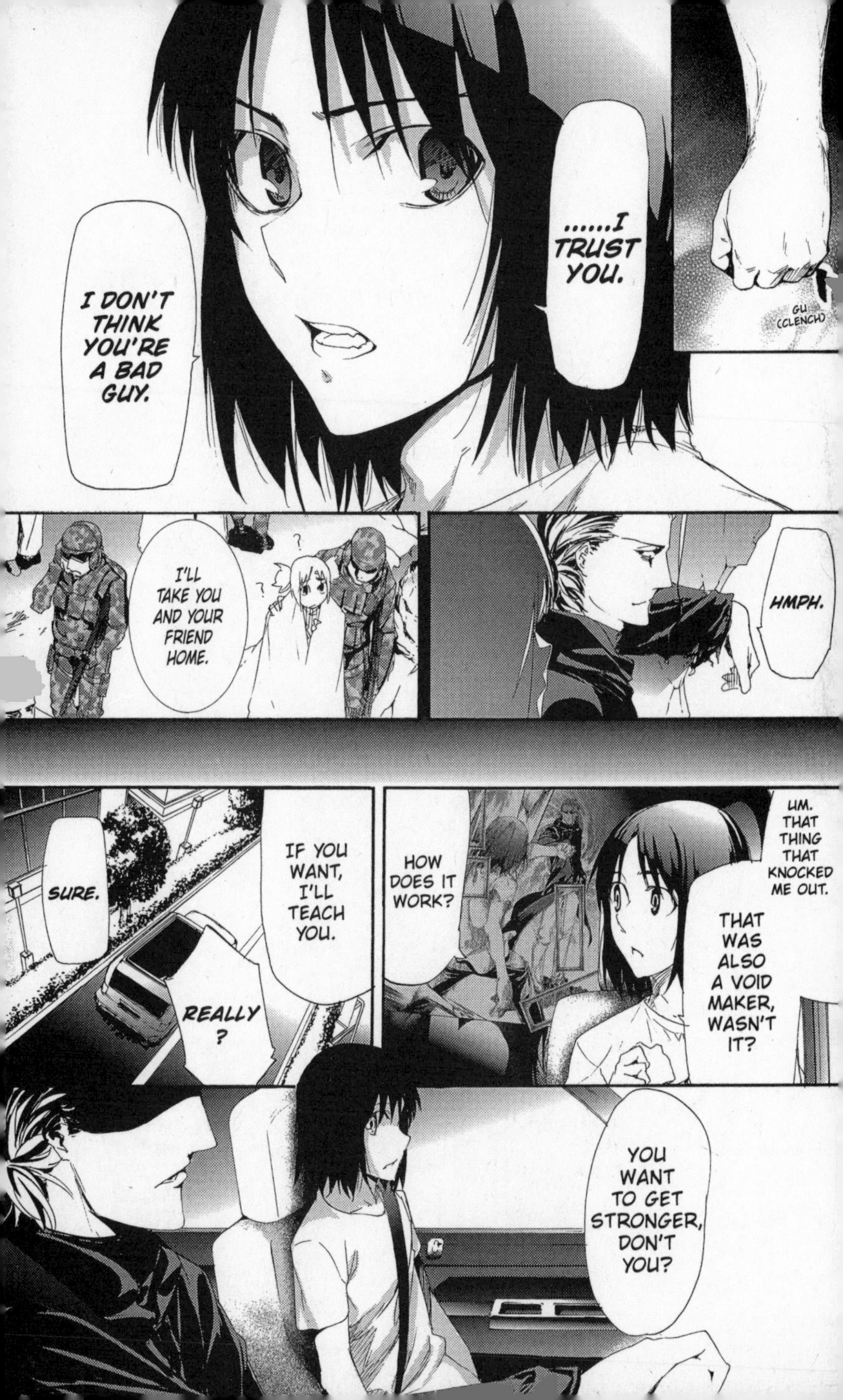
GU (CLENCH)
......I TRUST YOU.
I DON'T THINK YOU'RE A BAD GUY.
HMPH.
I'LL TAKE YOU AND YOUR FRIEND HOME.
UM. THAT THING THAT KNOCKED ME OUT.
THAT WAS ALSO A VOID MAKER, WASN'T IT?
HOW DOES IT WORK?
IF YOU WANT, I'LL TEACH YOU.
REALLY?
SURE.
YOU WANT TO GET STRONGER, DON'T YOU?

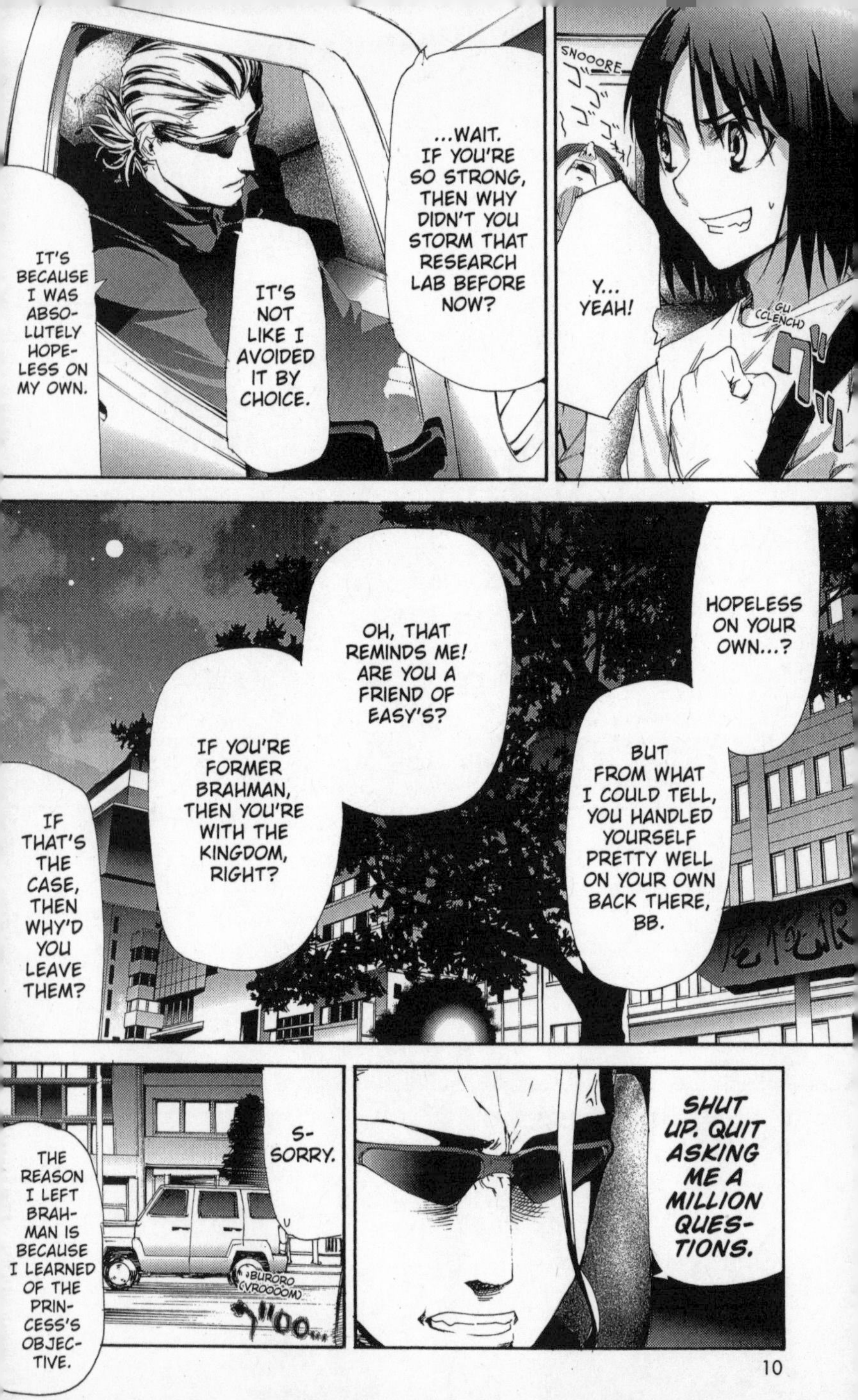
SNOOORE
Y... YEAH!
GU (CLENCH)
...WAIT. IF YOU'RE SO STRONG, THEN WHY DIDN'T YOU STORM THAT RESEARCH LAB BEFORE NOW?
IT'S NOT LIKE I AVOIDED IT BY CHOICE.
IT'S BECAUSE I WAS ABSOLUTELY HOPELESS ON MY OWN.
HOPELESS ON YOUR OWN...?
BUT FROM WHAT I COULD TELL, YOU HANDLED YOURSELF PRETTY WELL ON YOUR OWN BACK THERE, BB.
OH, THAT REMINDS ME! ARE YOU A FRIEND OF EASY'S?
IF YOU'RE FORMER BRAHMAN, THEN YOU'RE WITH THE KINGDOM, RIGHT?
IF THAT'S THE CASE, THEN WHY'D YOU LEAVE THEM?
SHUT UP. QUIT ASKING ME A MILLION QUESTIONS.
S-SORRY.
BURORO (VROOOOM)
THE REASON I LEFT BRAHMAN IS BECAUSE I LEARNED OF THE PRINCESS'S OBJECTIVE.

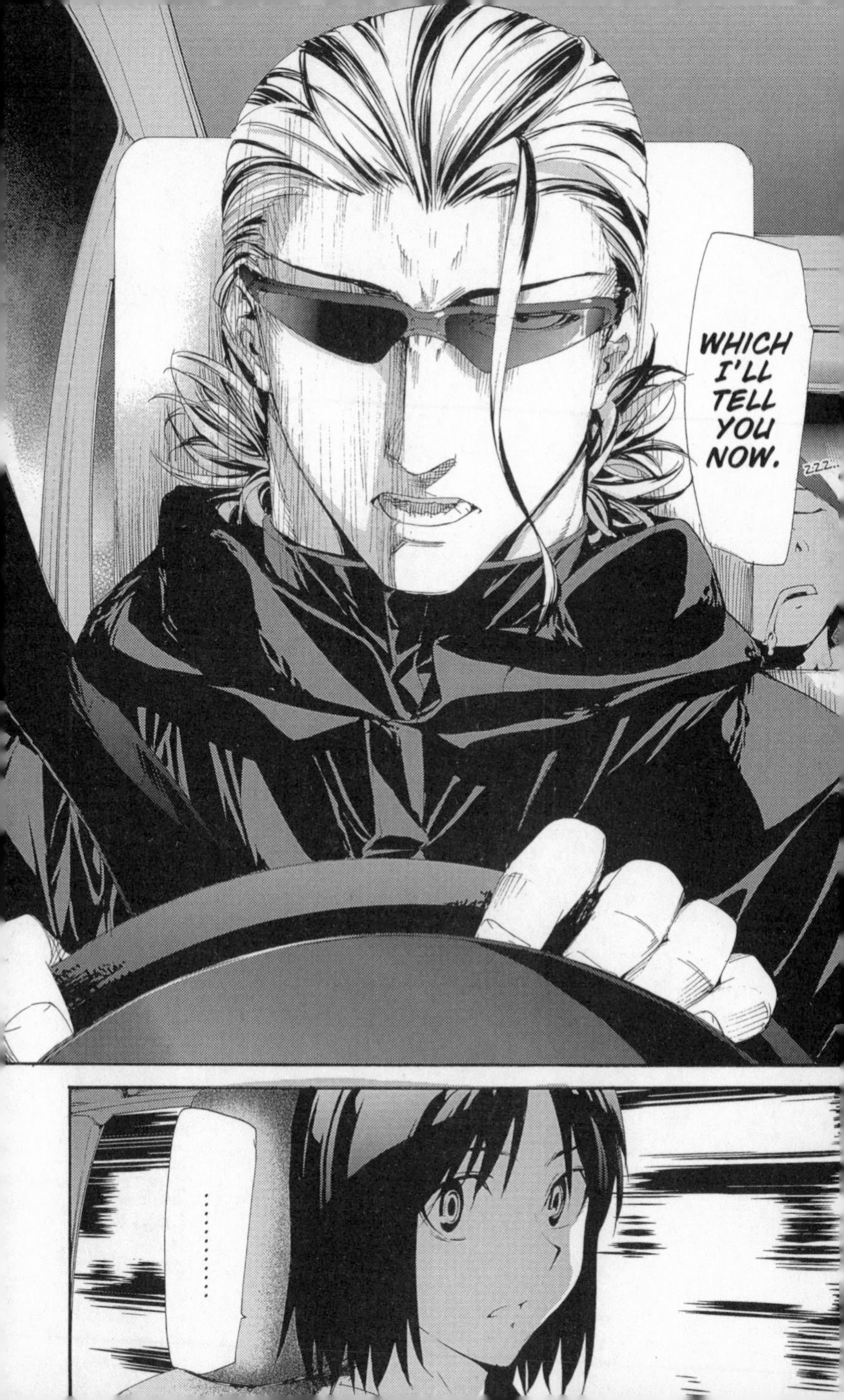
WHICH I'LL TELL YOU NOW.
ZZZ...
....

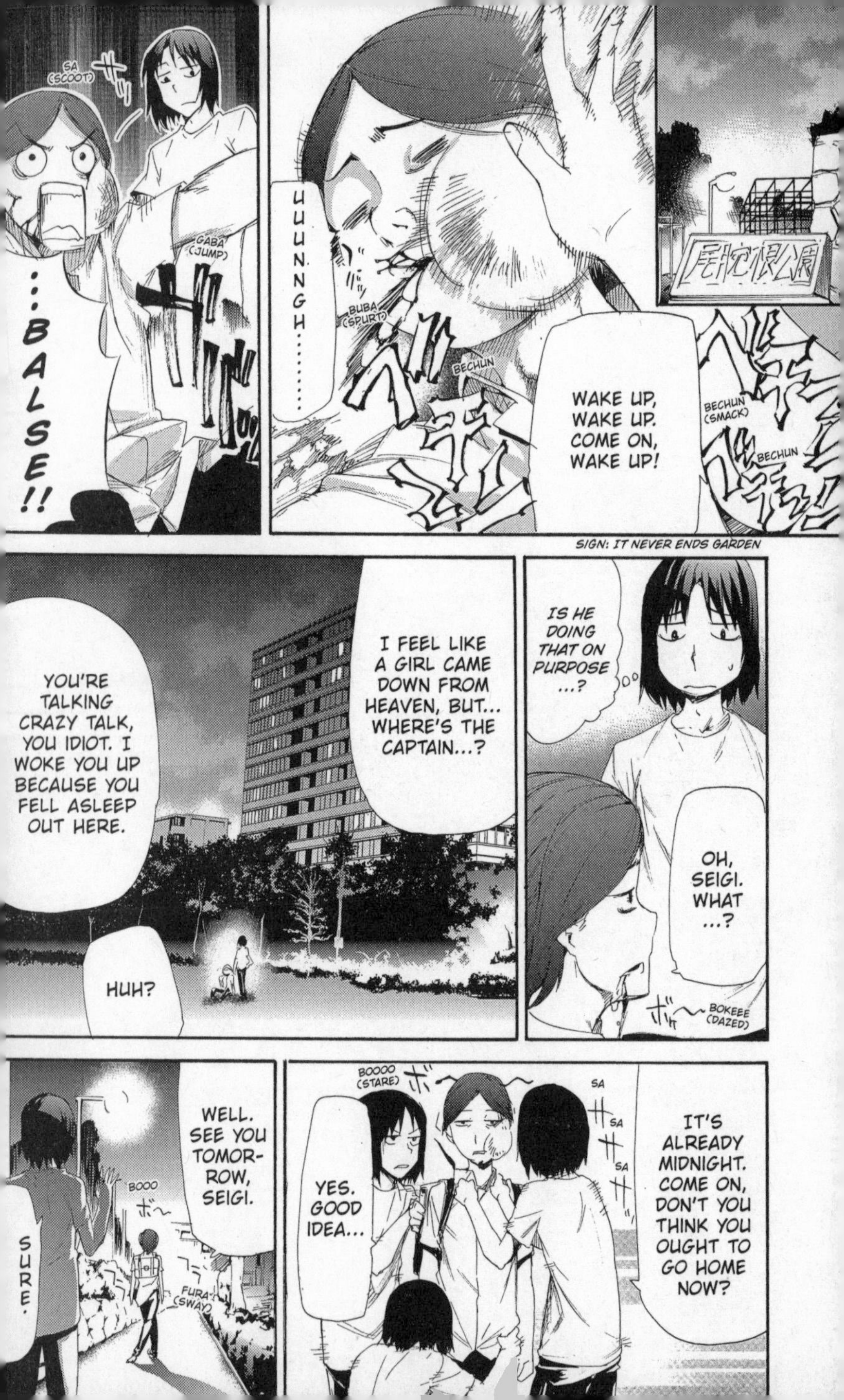
WAKE UP, WAKE UP. COME ON, WAKE UP!
BECHUN (SMACK)
BECHUN
UUUNNGH......
BUBA (SPURT)
BECHUN
SA (SCOOT)
GABA (JUMP)
...BALSE!!
IS HE DOING THAT ON PURPOSE ...?
OH, SEIGI. WHAT ...?
BOKEEE (DAZED)
I FEEL LIKE A GIRL CAME DOWN FROM HEAVEN, BUT... WHERE'S THE CAPTAIN...?
YOU'RE TALKING CRAZY TALK, YOU IDIOT. I WOKE YOU UP BECAUSE YOU FELL ASLEEP OUT HERE.
HUH?
BOOOO (STARE)
IT'S ALREADY MIDNIGHT. COME ON, DON'T YOU THINK YOU OUGHT TO GO HOME NOW?
SA
SA
SA
YES. GOOD IDEA...
WELL. SEE YOU TOMOR-ROW, SEIGI.
BOOO
FURA (SWAY)
SURE.
SIGN: IT NEVER ENDS GARDEN

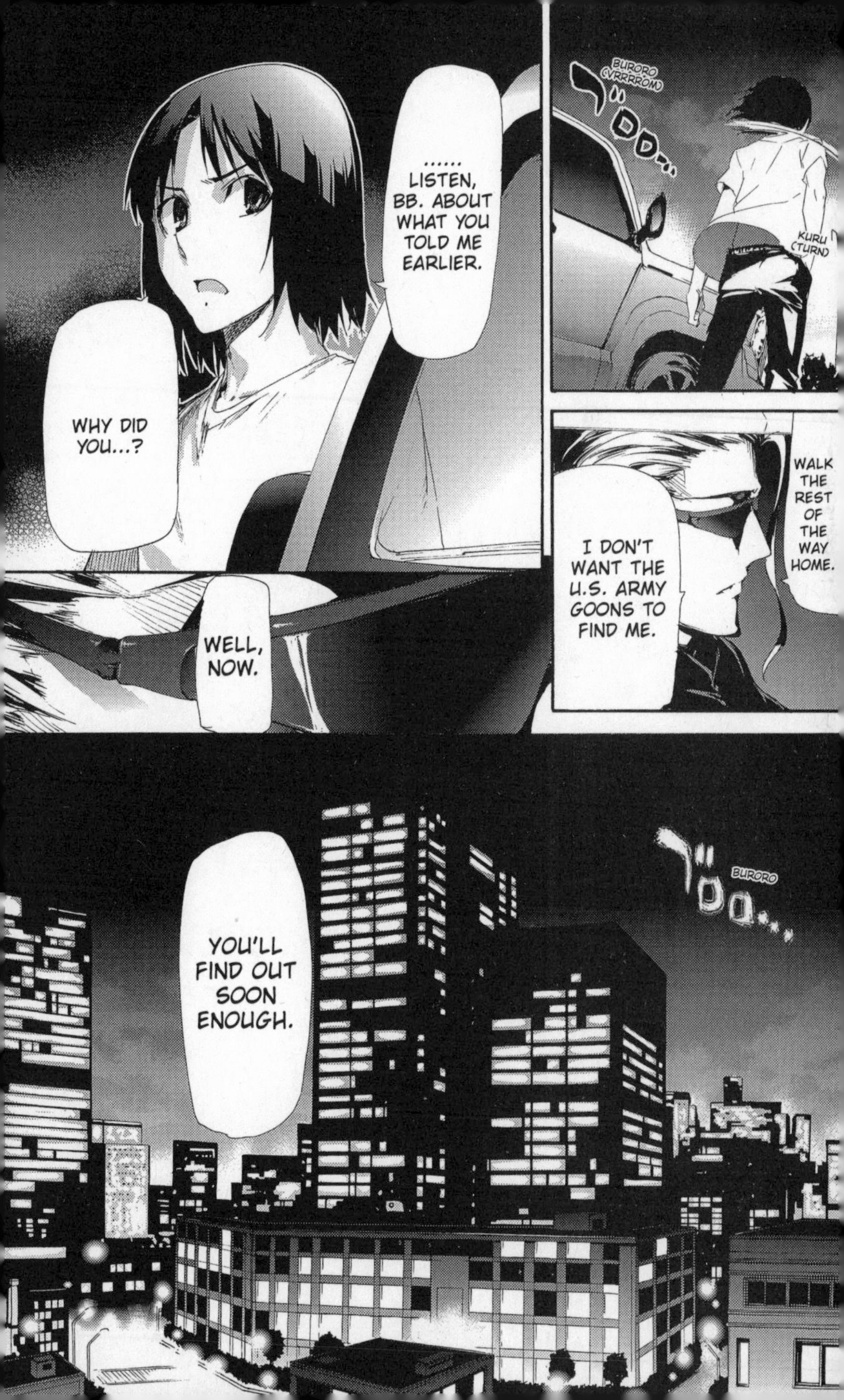
BURORO (VRRRROM)
KURU (TURN)
WALK THE REST OF THE WAY HOME.
I DON'T WANT THE U.S. ARMY GOONS TO FIND ME.
...... LISTEN, BB. ABOUT WHAT YOU TOLD ME EARLIER.
WHY DID YOU...?
WELL, NOW.
BURORO
YOU'LL FIND OUT SOON ENOUGH.

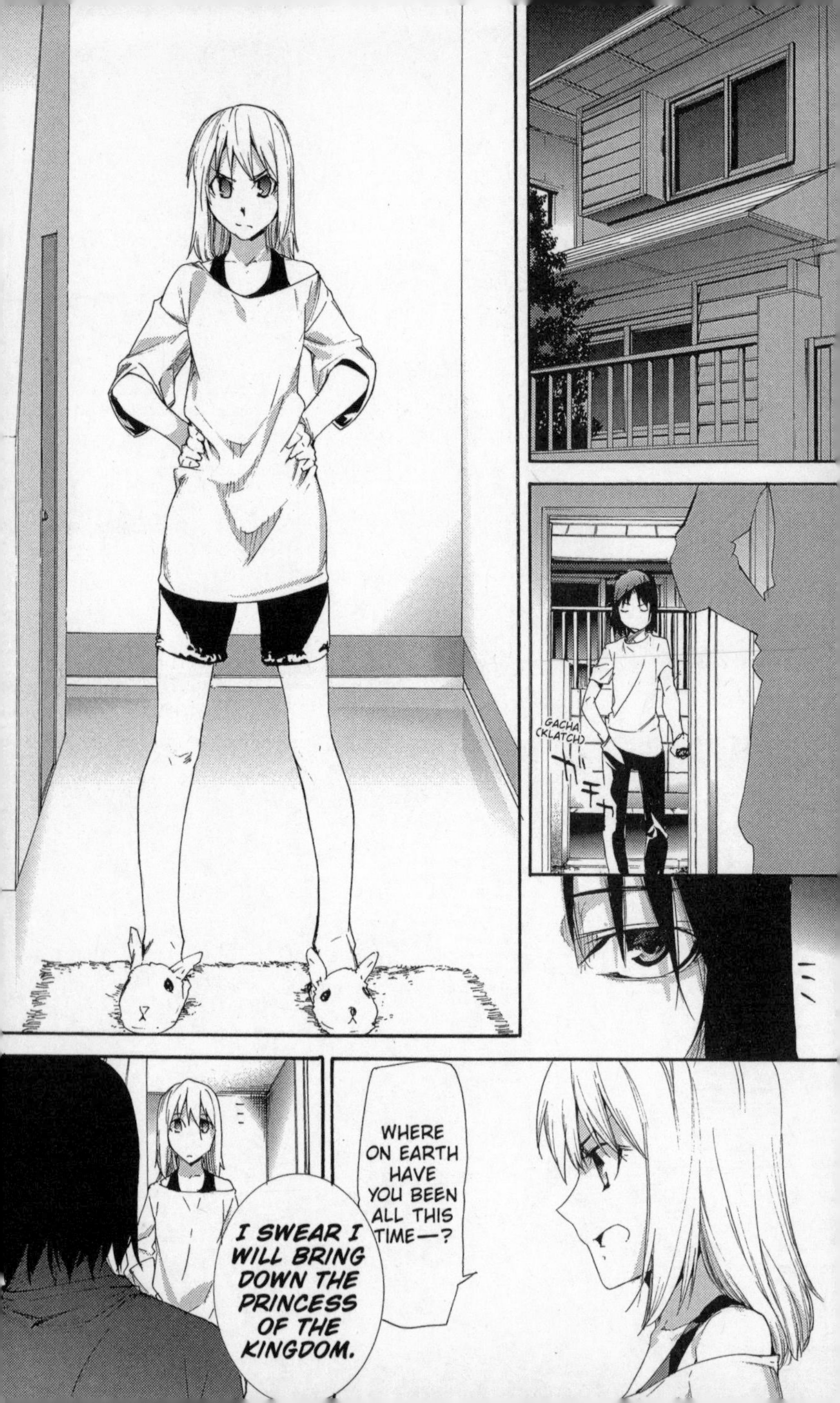
GACHA (KLATCH)
WHERE ON EARTH HAVE YOU BEEN ALL THIS TIME—?
I SWEAR I WILL BRING DOWN THE PRINCESS OF THE KINGDOM.

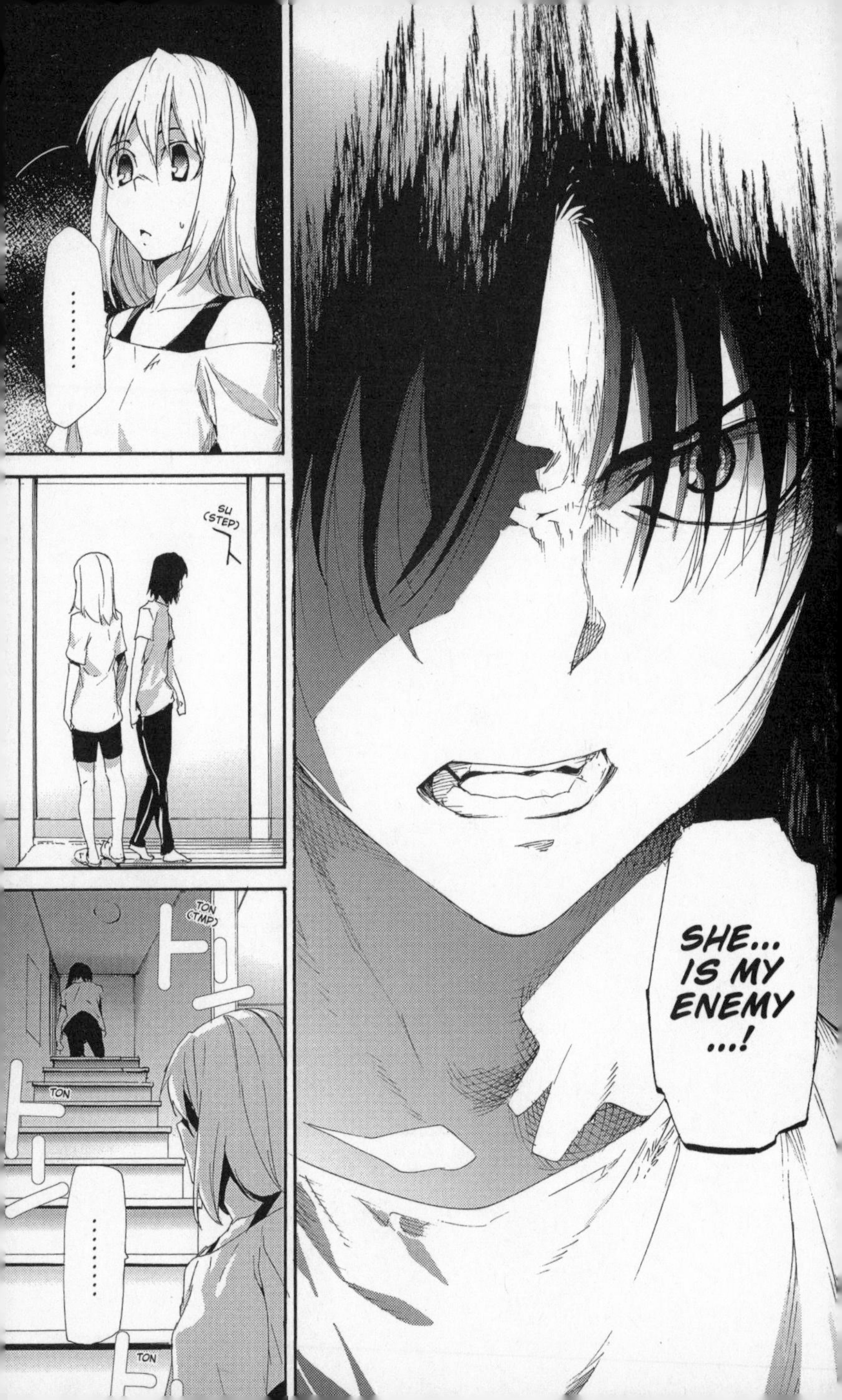
SHE... IS MY ENEMY ...!
......
SU (STEP)
TON (TMP)
TON
......
TON

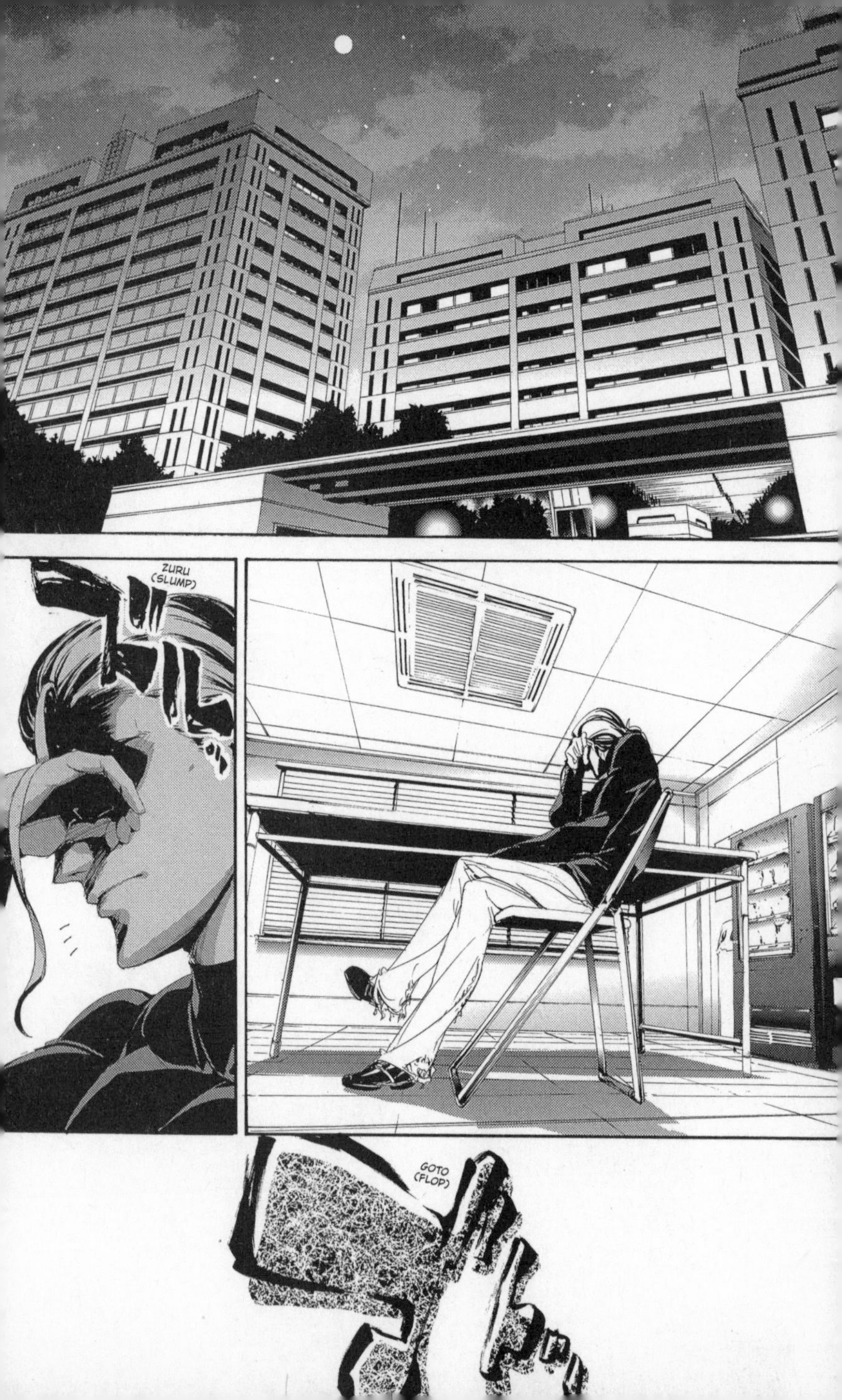
ZURU (SLUMP)
GOTO (FLOP)

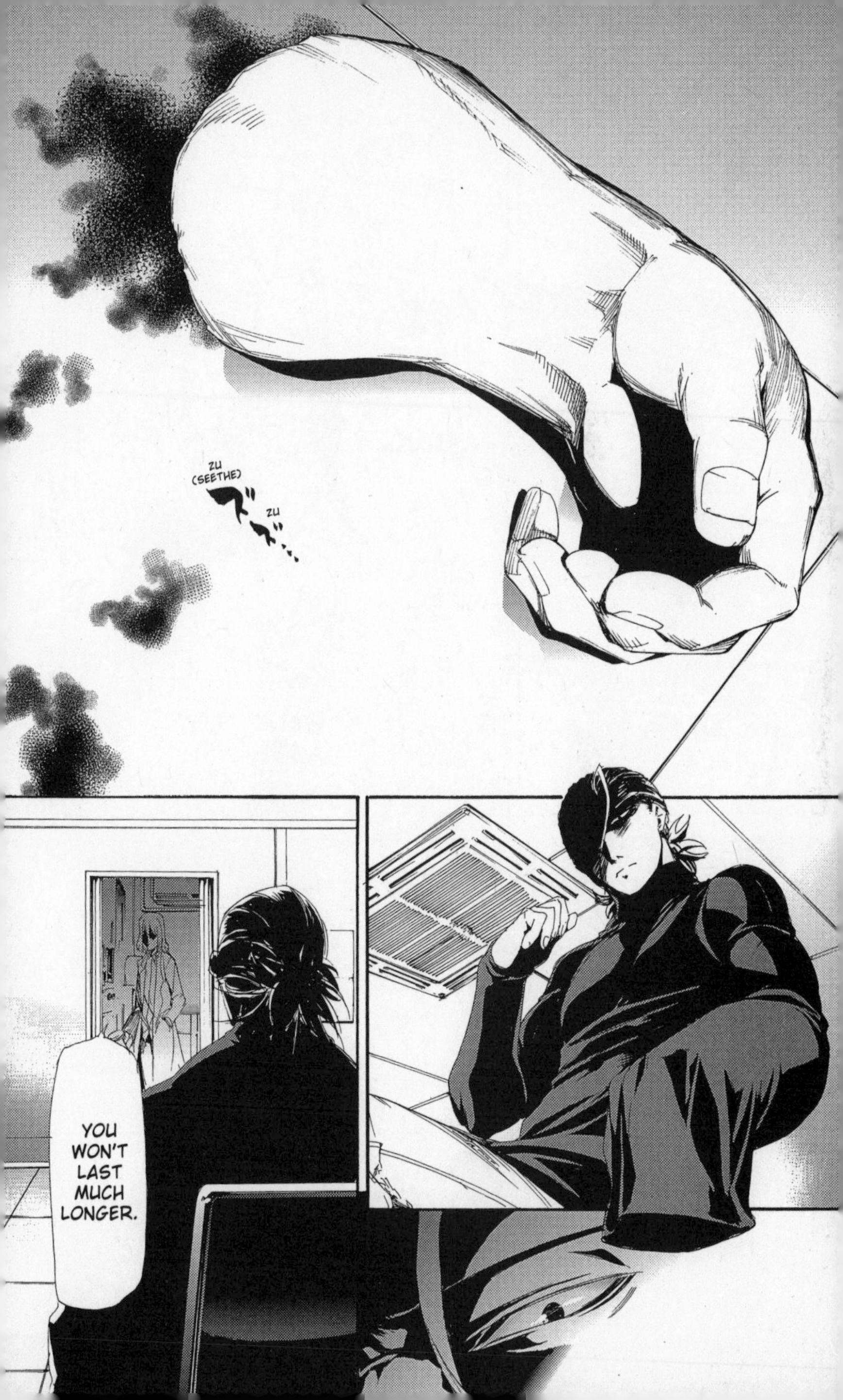
ZU (SEETHE)
ZU
YOU WON'T LAST MUCH LONGER.

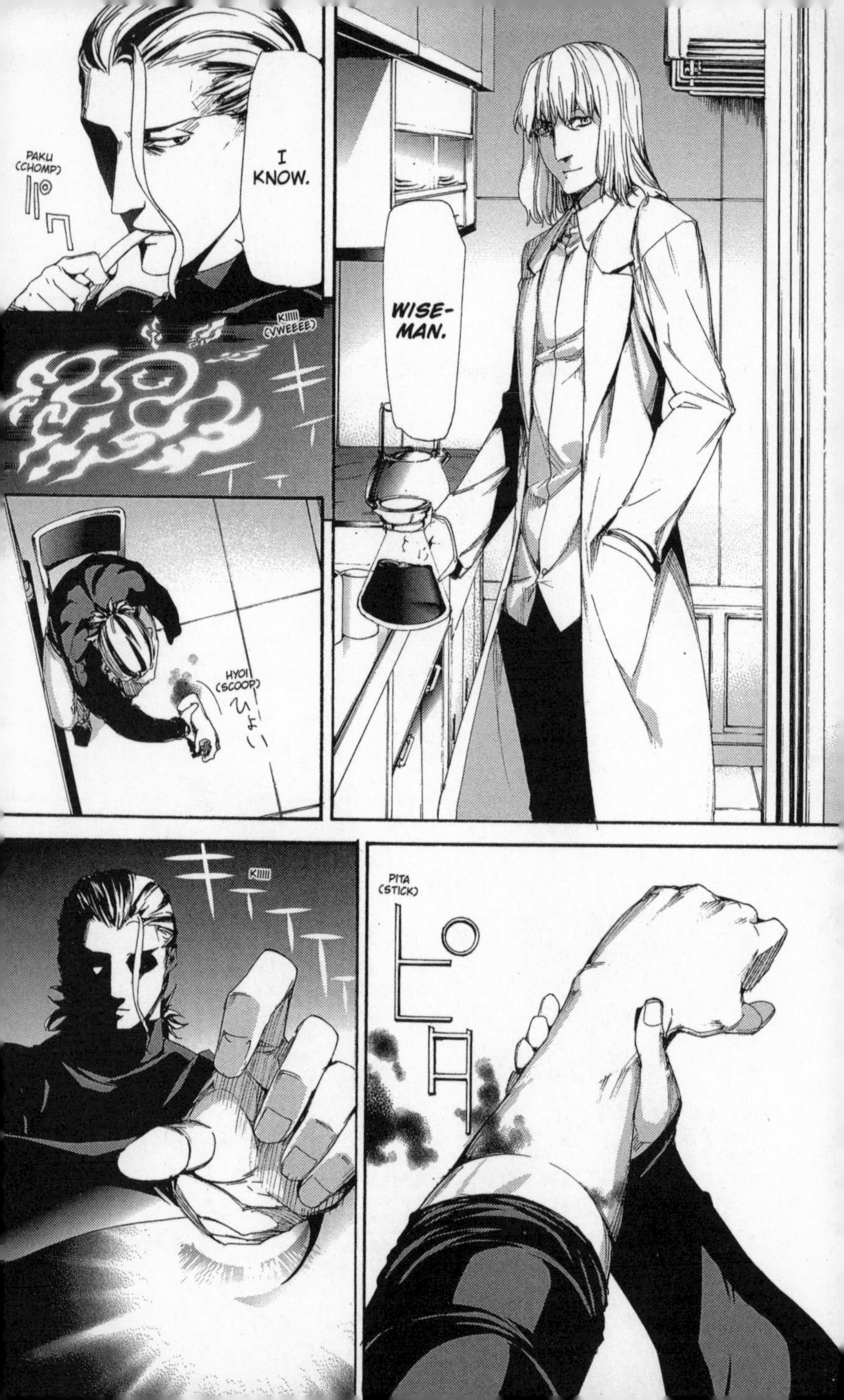
WISE-MAN.
I KNOW.
PAKU (CHOMP)
パク
KIIII (VWEEEE)
HYOI (SCOOP)
ひょい
PITA (STICK)
ピタ
KIIII

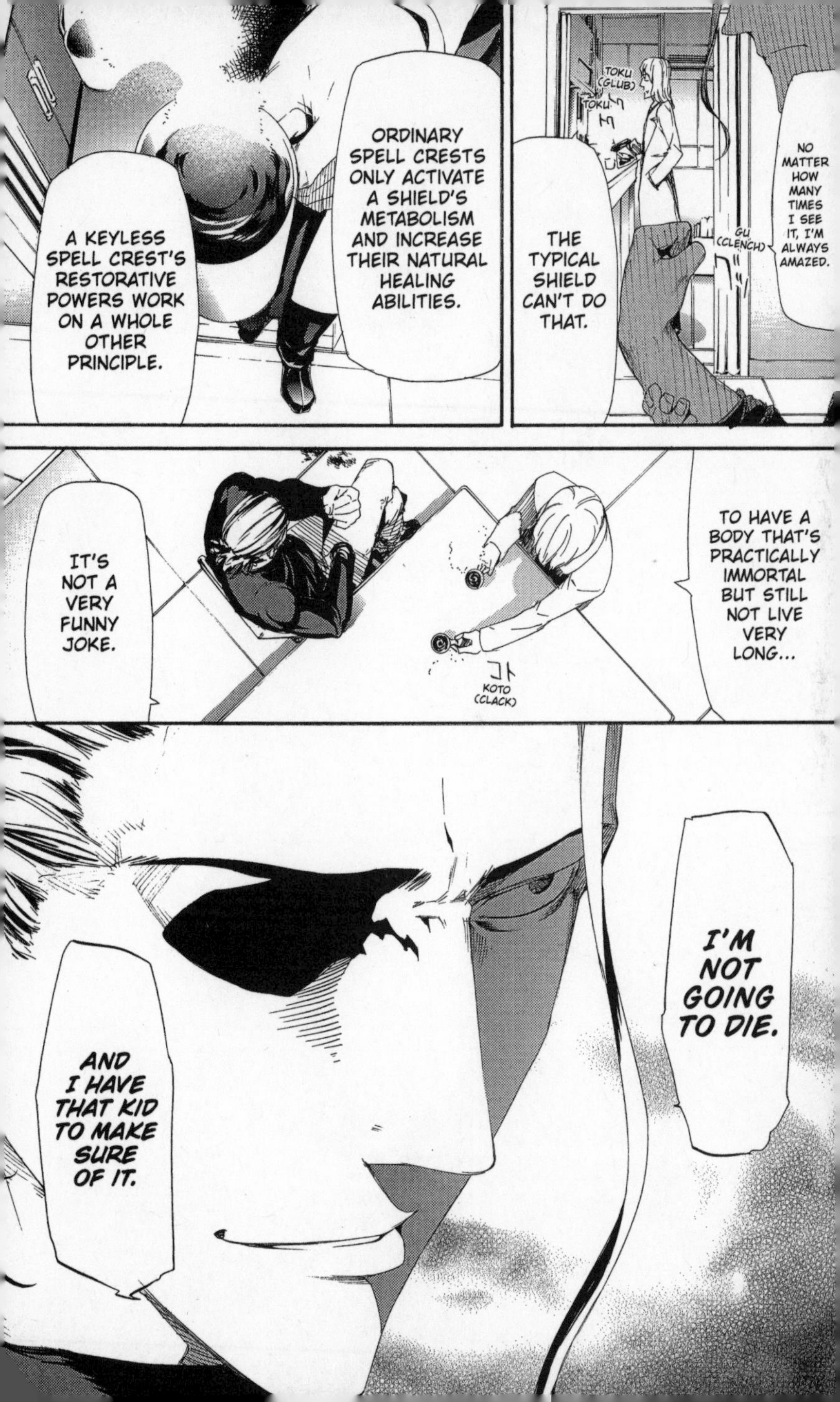
NO MATTER HOW MANY TIMES I SEE IT, I'M ALWAYS AMAZED.
TOKU (GLUB) TOKU
GU (CLENCH)
THE TYPICAL SHIELD CAN'T DO THAT.
ORDINARY SPELL CRESTS ONLY ACTIVATE A SHIELD'S METABOLISM AND INCREASE THEIR NATURAL HEALING ABILITIES.
A KEYLESS SPELL CREST'S RESTORATIVE POWERS WORK ON A WHOLE OTHER PRINCIPLE.
TO HAVE A BODY THAT'S PRACTICALLY IMMORTAL BUT STILL NOT LIVE VERY LONG...
KOTO (CLACK)
IT'S NOT A VERY FUNNY JOKE.
I'M NOT GOING TO DIE.
AND I HAVE THAT KID TO MAKE SURE OF IT.

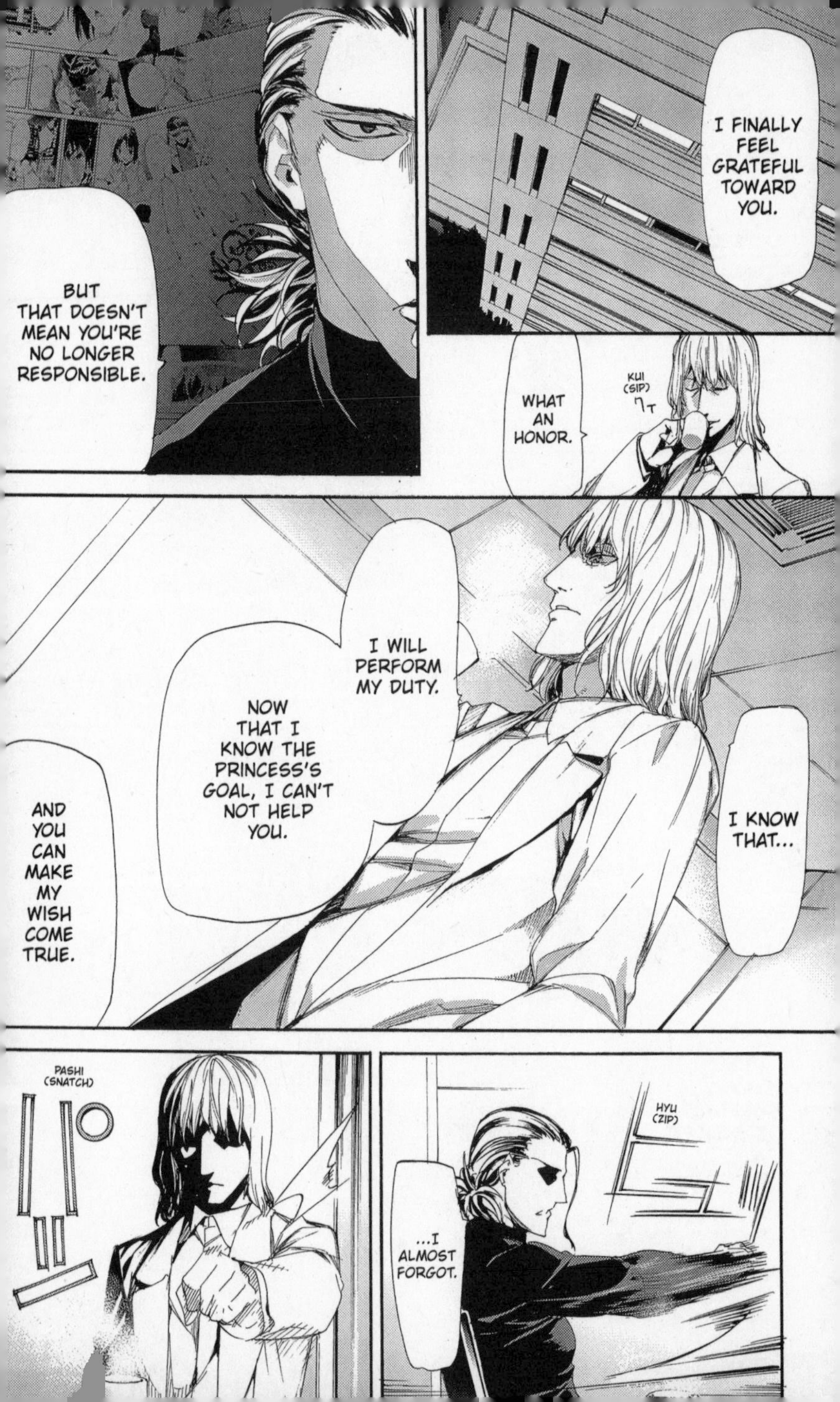
I FINALLY FEEL GRATEFUL TOWARD YOU.
KUI (SIP)
WHAT AN HONOR.
BUT THAT DOESN'T MEAN YOU'RE NO LONGER RESPONSIBLE.
I KNOW THAT...
I WILL PERFORM MY DUTY.
NOW THAT I KNOW THE PRINCESS'S GOAL, I CAN'T NOT HELP YOU.
AND YOU CAN MAKE MY WISH COME TRUE.
HYU (ZIP)
...I ALMOST FORGOT.
PASHI (SNATCH)

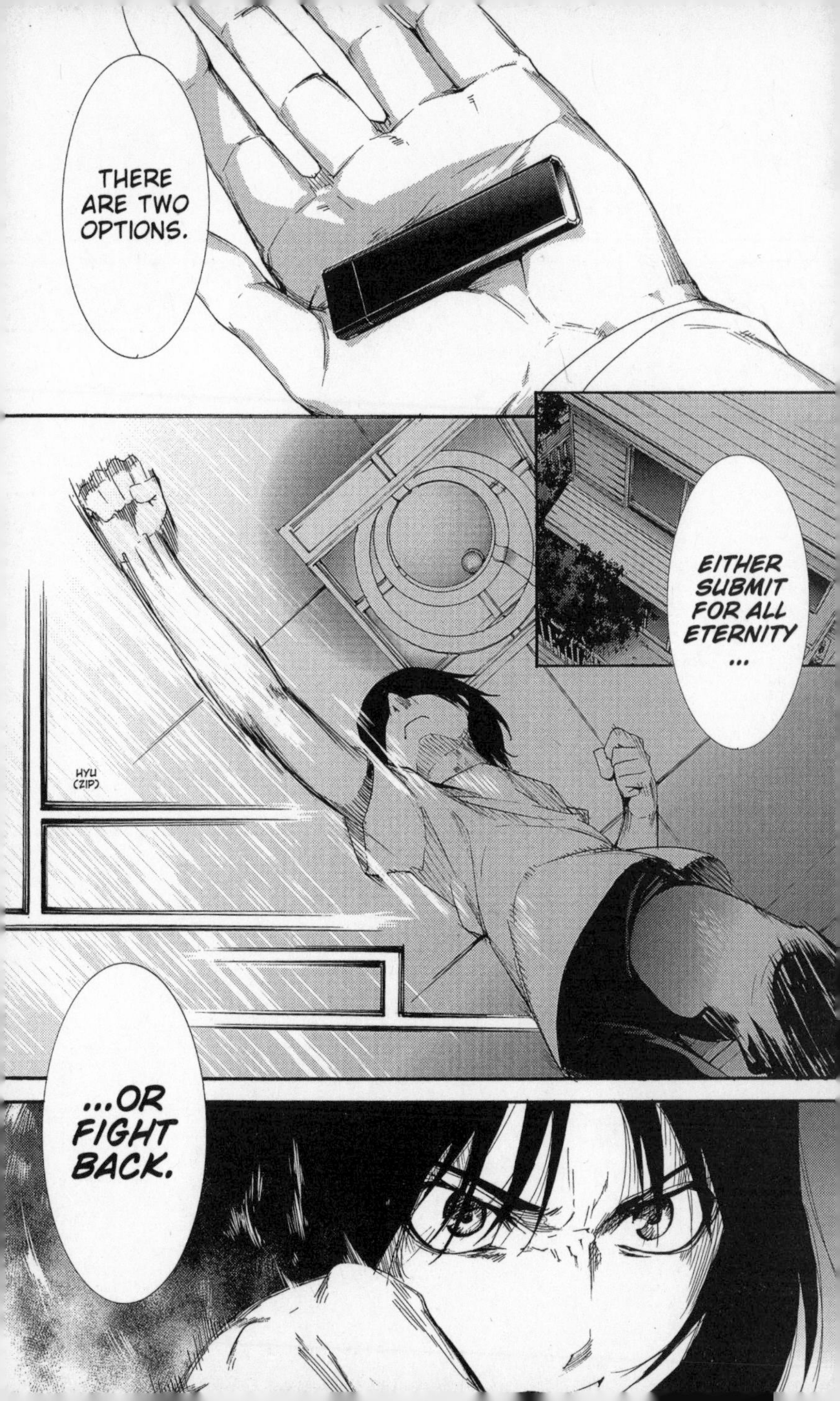
THERE ARE TWO OPTIONS.
EITHER SUBMIT FOR ALL ETERNITY ...
HYU (ZIP)
...OR FIGHT BACK.

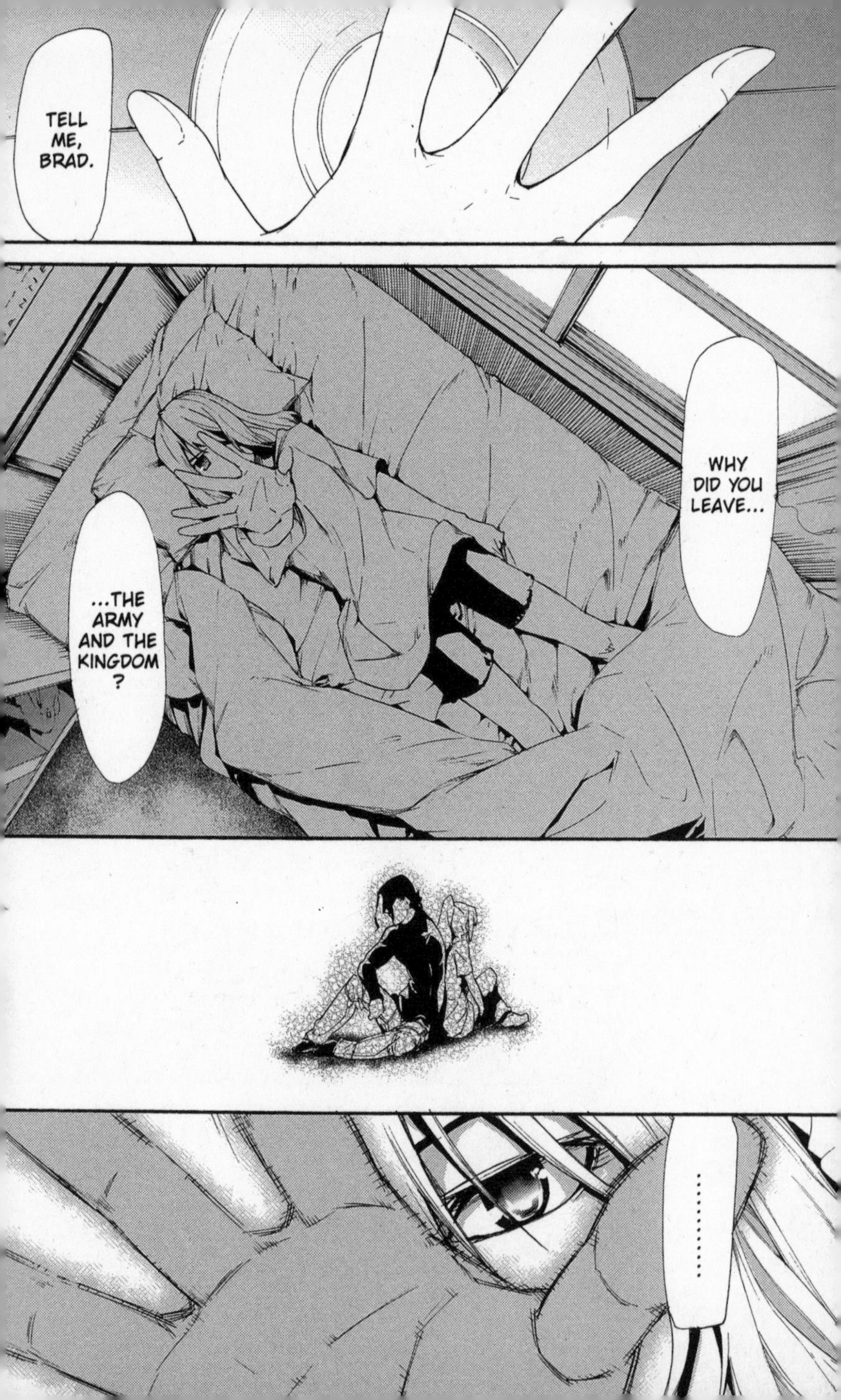
TELL ME, BRAD.
WHY DID YOU LEAVE...
...THE ARMY AND THE KINGDOM?
....

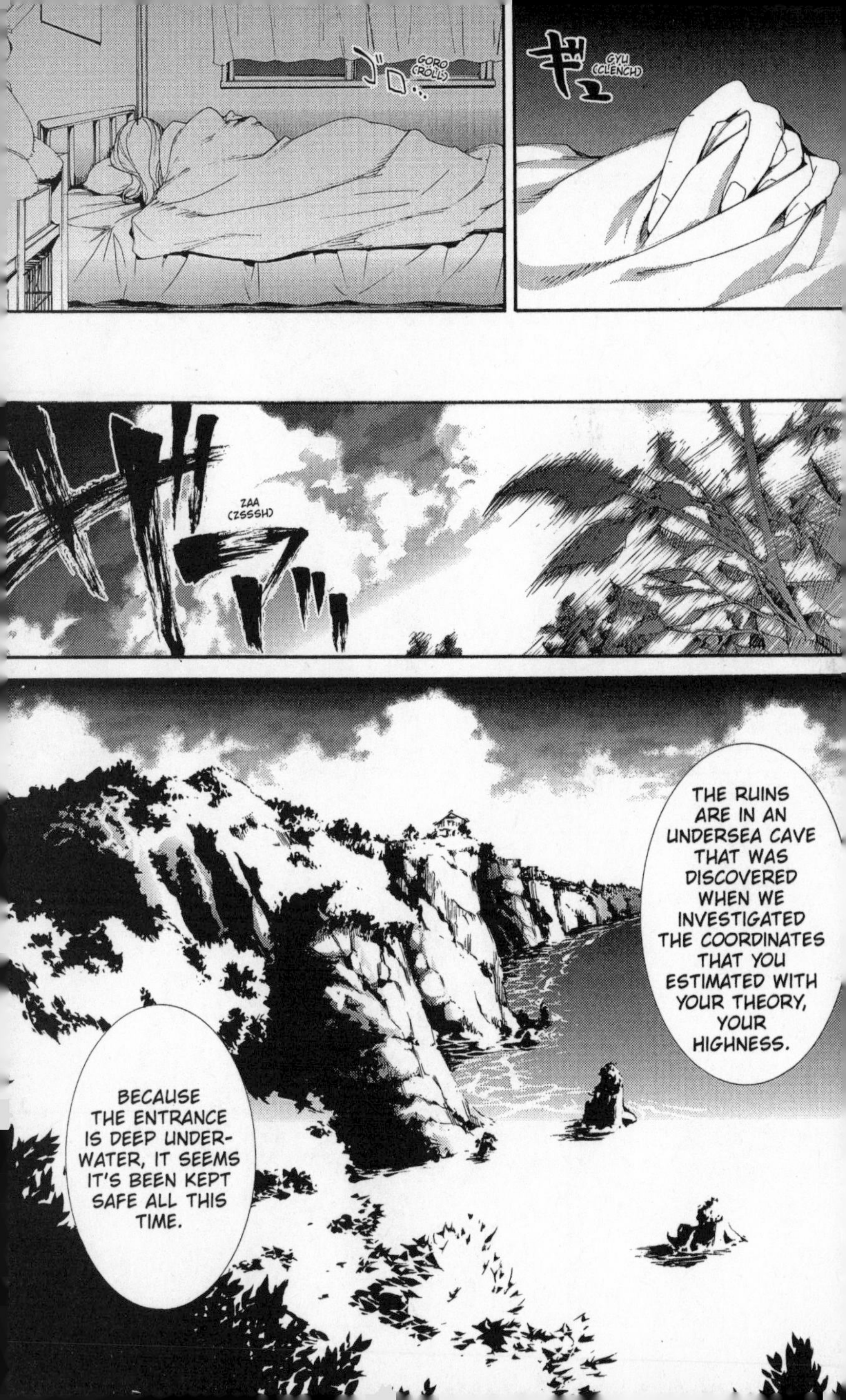
ギュ
GYU (CLENCH)
ゴロ…
GORO (ROLLS)
ZAA (ZSSSH)
THE RUINS ARE IN AN UNDERSEA CAVE THAT WAS DISCOVERED WHEN WE INVESTIGATED THE COORDINATES THAT YOU ESTIMATED WITH YOUR THEORY, YOUR HIGHNESS.
BECAUSE THE ENTRANCE IS DEEP UNDER-WATER, IT SEEMS IT'S BEEN KEPT SAFE ALL THIS TIME.

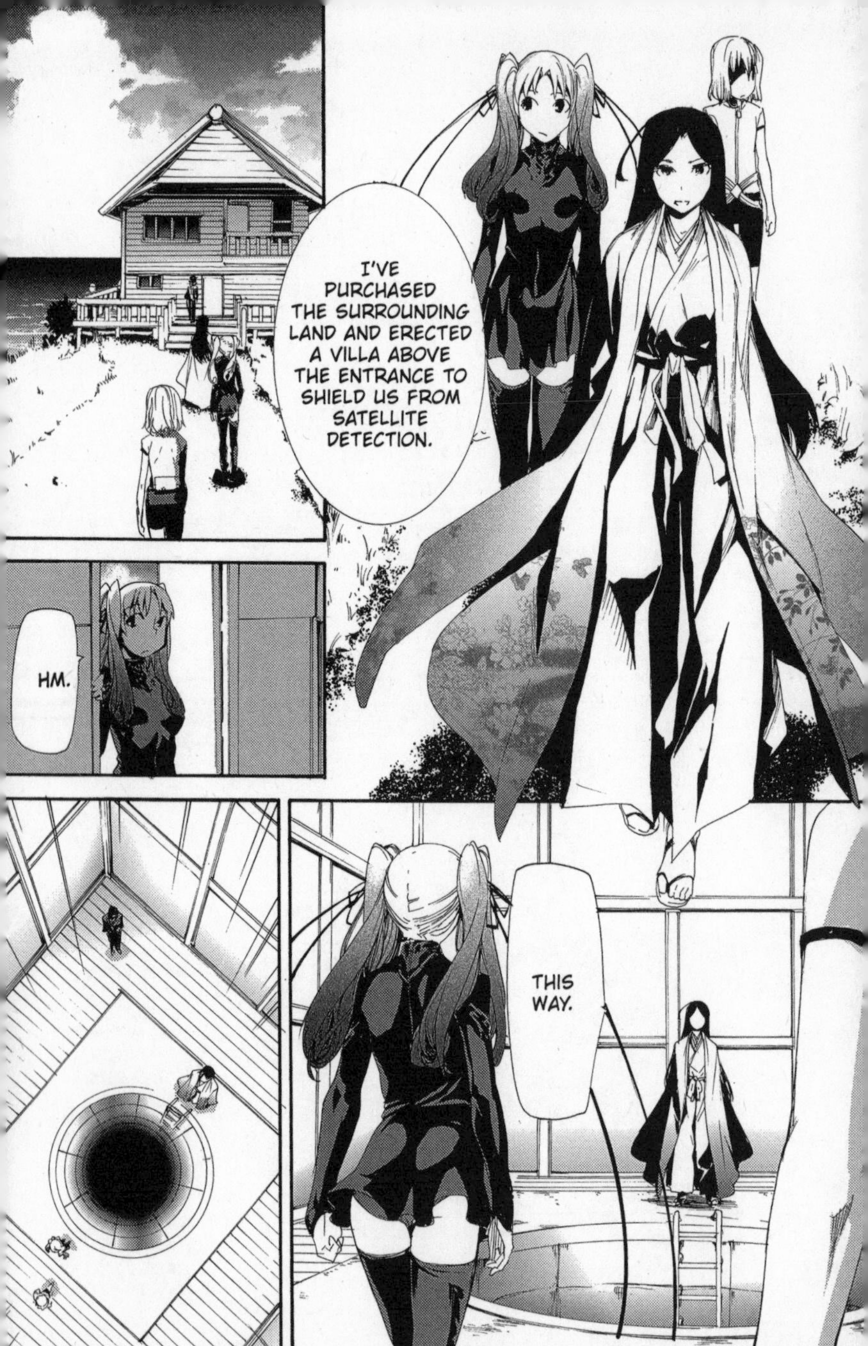
I'VE PURCHASED THE SURROUNDING LAND AND ERECTED A VILLA ABOVE THE ENTRANCE TO SHIELD US FROM SATELLITE DETECTION.
HM.
THIS WAY.

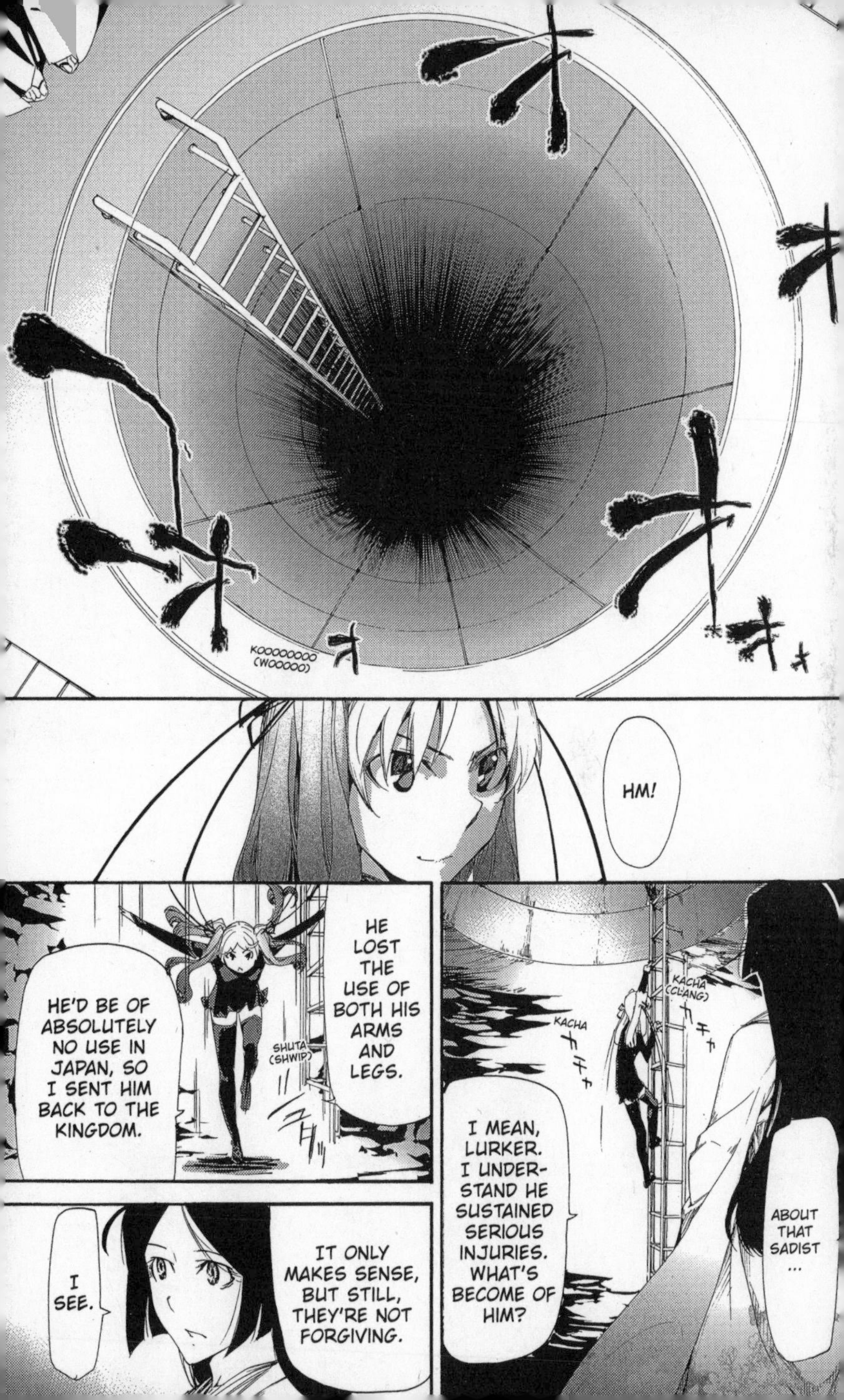
KOOOOOOOO (WOOOOO)
HM!
ABOUT THAT SADIST ...
I MEAN, LURKER. I UNDERSTAND HE SUSTAINED SERIOUS INJURIES. WHAT'S BECOME OF HIM?
KACHA (CLANG)
KACHA
HE LOST THE USE OF BOTH HIS ARMS AND LEGS.
SHUTA (SHWIP)
HE'D BE OF ABSOLUTELY NO USE IN JAPAN, SO I SENT HIM BACK TO THE KINGDOM.
IT ONLY MAKES SENSE, BUT STILL, THEY'RE NOT FORGIVING.
I SEE.

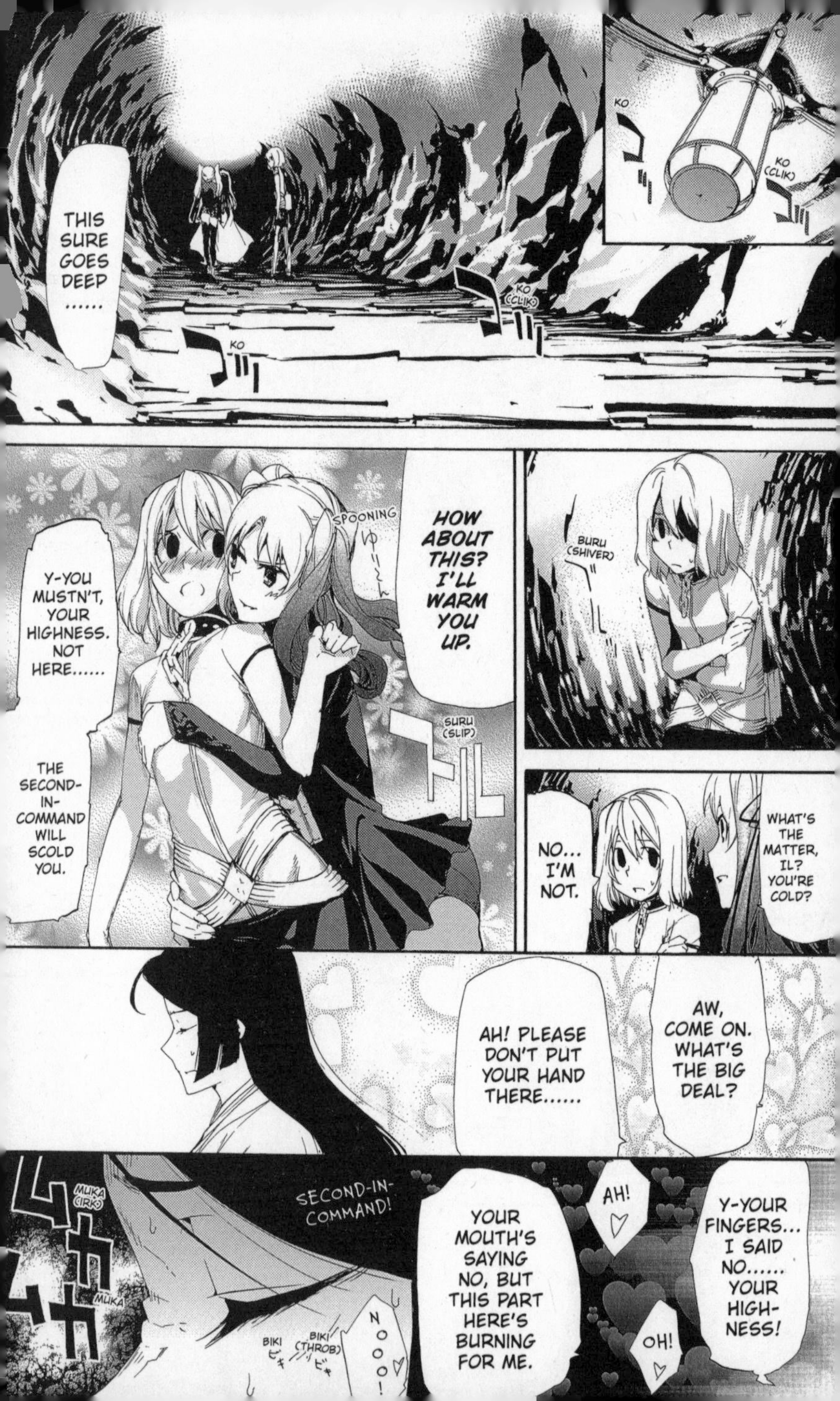
KO
KO (CLIK)
KO (CLIK)
THIS SURE GOES DEEP......
KO
BURU (SHIVER)
WHAT'S THE MATTER, IL? YOU'RE COLD?
NO... I'M NOT.
HOW ABOUT THIS? I'LL WARM YOU UP.
SPOONING
Y-YOU MUSTN'T, YOUR HIGHNESS. NOT HERE......
SURU (SLIP)
THE SECOND-IN-COMMAND WILL SCOLD YOU.
AW, COME ON. WHAT'S THE BIG DEAL?
AH! PLEASE DON'T PUT YOUR HAND THERE......
Y-YOUR FINGERS... I SAID NO...... YOUR HIGH-NESS!
AH!
OH!
YOUR MOUTH'S SAYING NO, BUT THIS PART HERE'S BURNING FOR ME.
NOOOO!
SECOND-IN-COMMAND!
BIKI BIKI (THROB)
MUKA (IRK)
MUKA

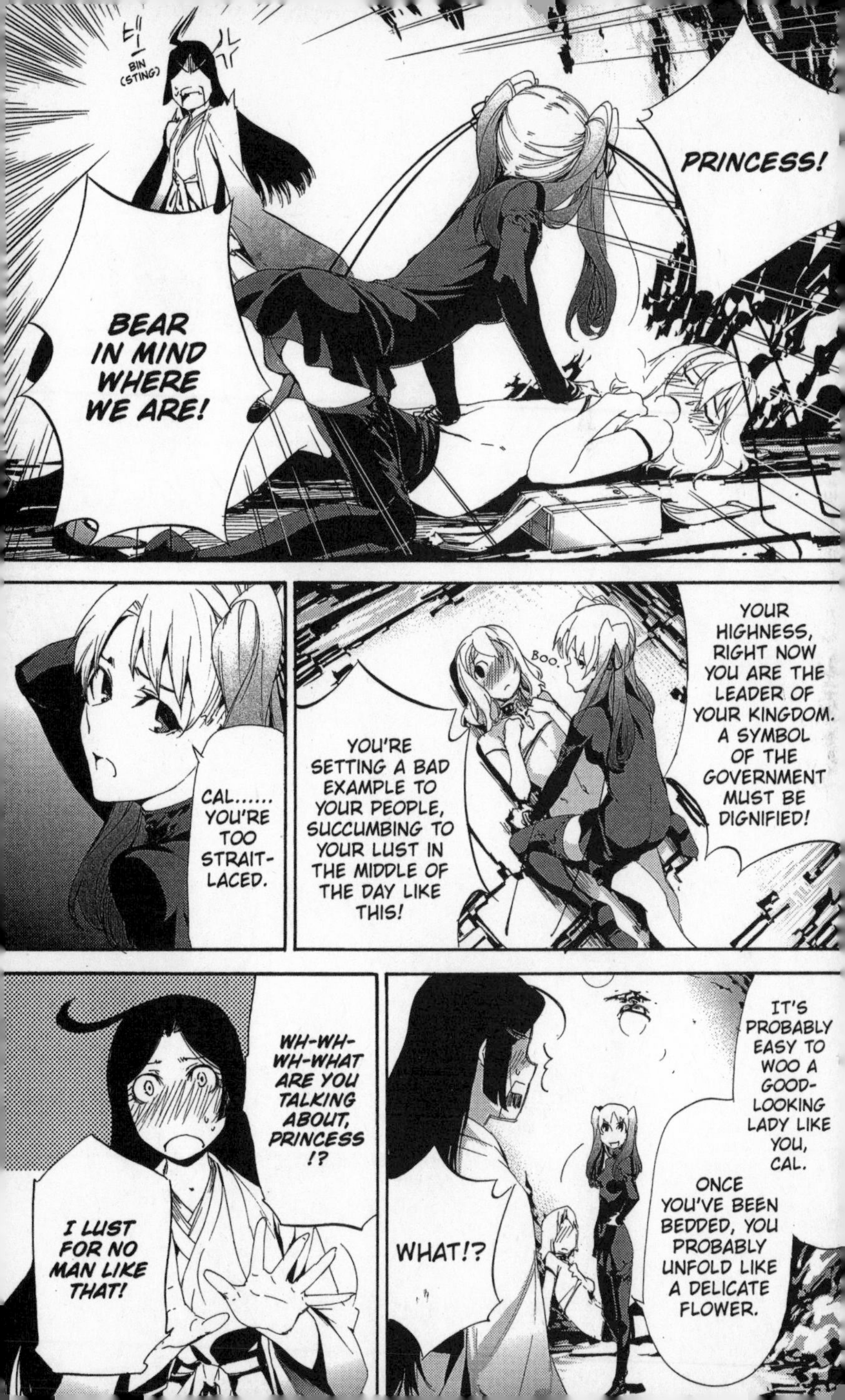
PRINCESS!
BEAR IN MIND WHERE WE ARE!
빈
BIN (STING)
YOUR HIGHNESS, RIGHT NOW YOU ARE THE LEADER OF YOUR KINGDOM. A SYMBOL OF THE GOVERNMENT MUST BE DIGNIFIED!
BOO.
YOU'RE SETTING A BAD EXAMPLE TO YOUR PEOPLE, SUCCUMBING TO YOUR LUST IN THE MIDDLE OF THE DAY LIKE THIS!
CAL...... YOU'RE TOO STRAIT-LACED.
IT'S PROBABLY EASY TO WOO A GOOD-LOOKING LADY LIKE YOU, CAL.
ONCE YOU'VE BEEN BEDDED, YOU PROBABLY UNFOLD LIKE A DELICATE FLOWER.
WHAT!?
WH-WH-WH-WHAT ARE YOU TALKING ABOUT, PRINCESS!?
I LUST FOR NO MAN LIKE THAT!

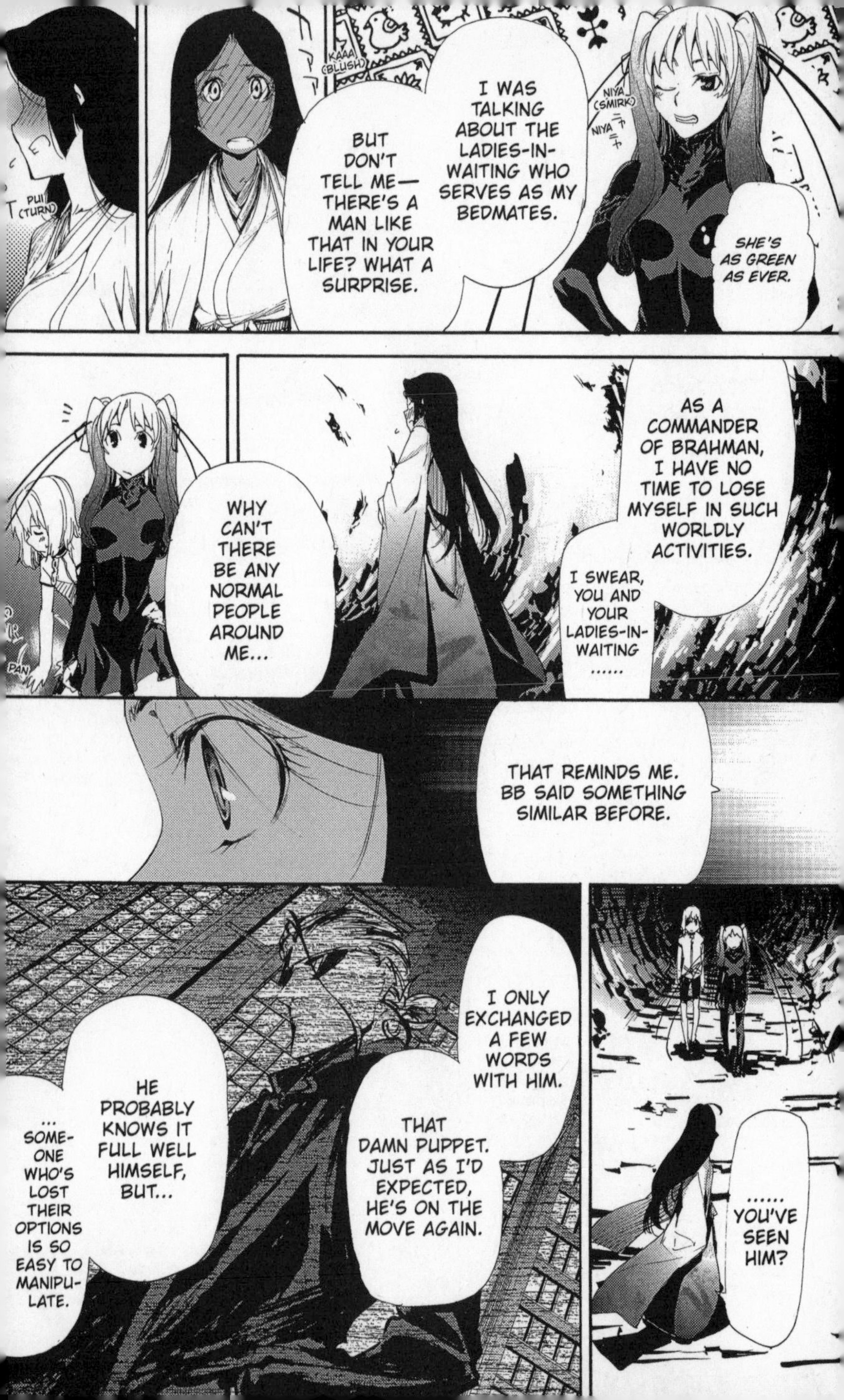
I WAS TALKING ABOUT THE LADIES-IN-WAITING WHO SERVES AS MY BEDMATES.
NIYA NIYA (SMIRK)
SHE'S AS GREEN AS EVER.
KAAA (BLUSH)
BUT DON'T TELL ME— THERE'S A MAN LIKE THAT IN YOUR LIFE? WHAT A SURPRISE.
PUI (TURN)
AS A COMMANDER OF BRAHMAN, I HAVE NO TIME TO LOSE MYSELF IN SUCH WORLDLY ACTIVITIES.
I SWEAR, YOU AND YOUR LADIES-IN-WAITING ......
WHY CAN'T THERE BE ANY NORMAL PEOPLE AROUND ME...
DAN
THAT REMINDS ME. BB SAID SOMETHING SIMILAR BEFORE.
...... YOU'VE SEEN HIM?
I ONLY EXCHANGED A FEW WORDS WITH HIM.
THAT DAMN PUPPET. JUST AS I'D EXPECTED, HE'S ON THE MOVE AGAIN.
HE PROBABLY KNOWS IT FULL WELL HIMSELF, BUT...
... SOME-ONE WHO'S LOST THEIR OPTIONS IS SO EASY TO MANIPU-LATE.

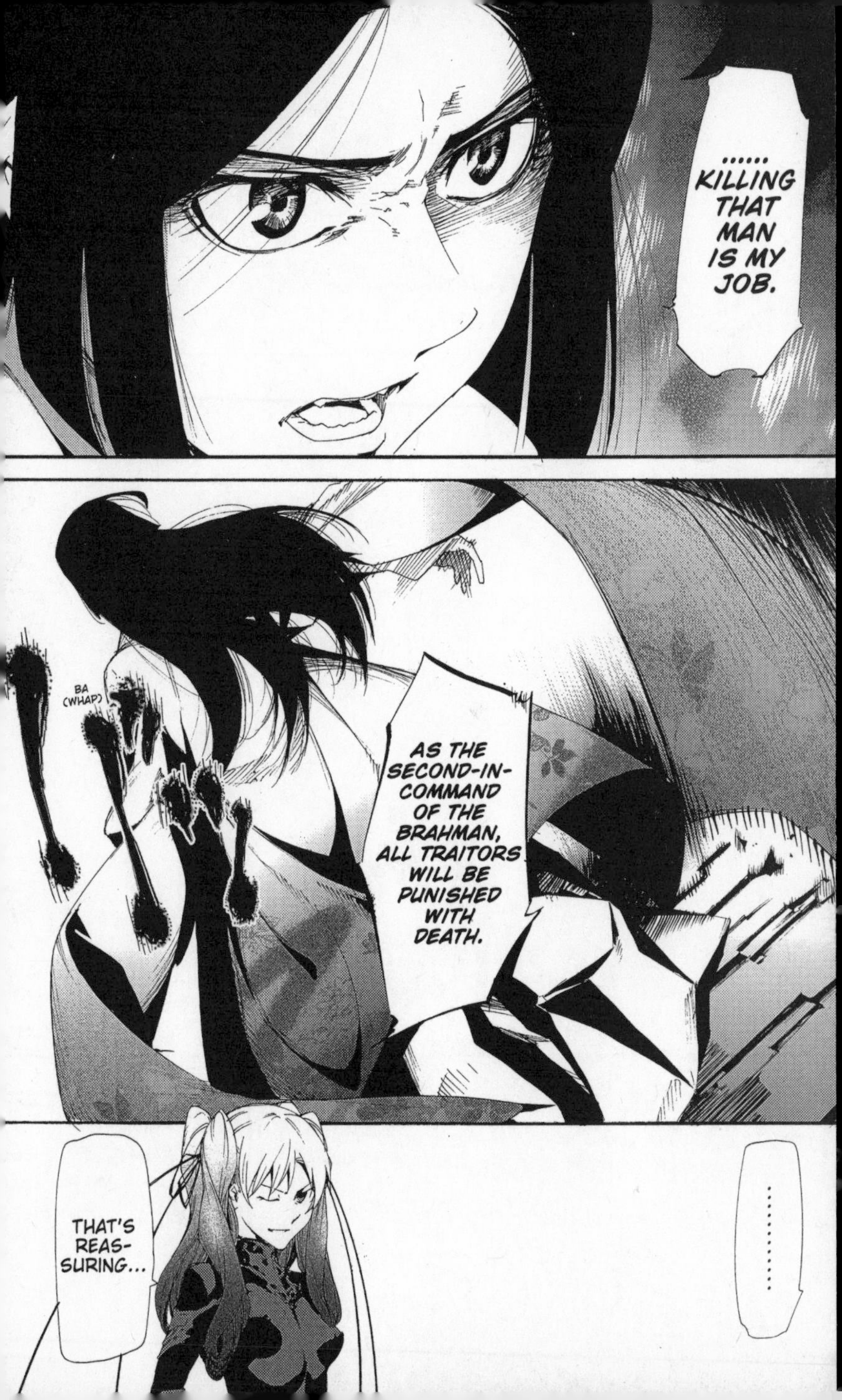
......
KILLING THAT MAN IS MY JOB.
AS THE SECOND-IN-COMMAND OF THE BRAHMAN, ALL TRAITORS WILL BE PUNISHED WITH DEATH.
BA (WHAP)
....
THAT'S REAS-SURING...

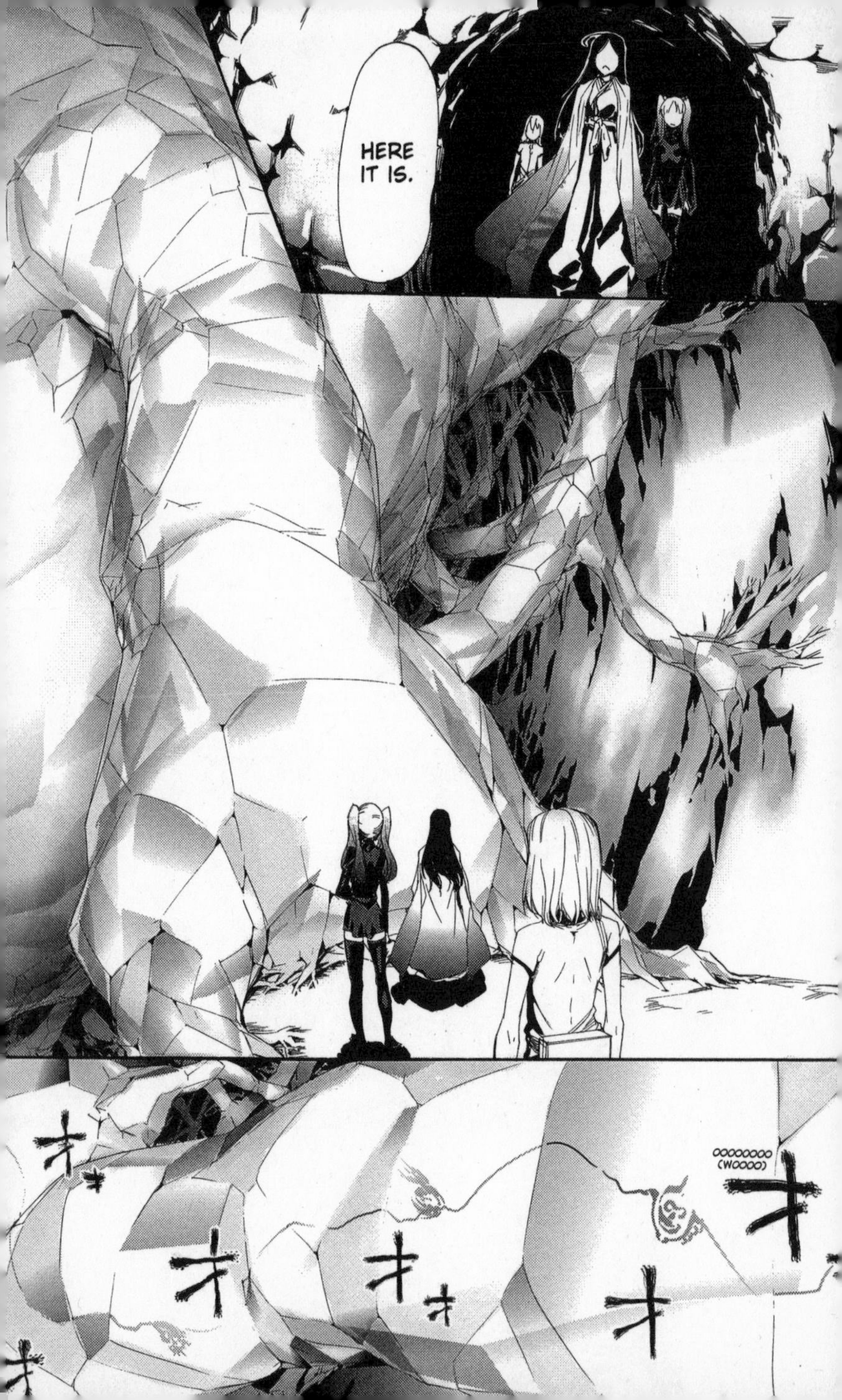
HERE IT IS.
OOOOOOOO (WOOOO)
オオオオオオオオ

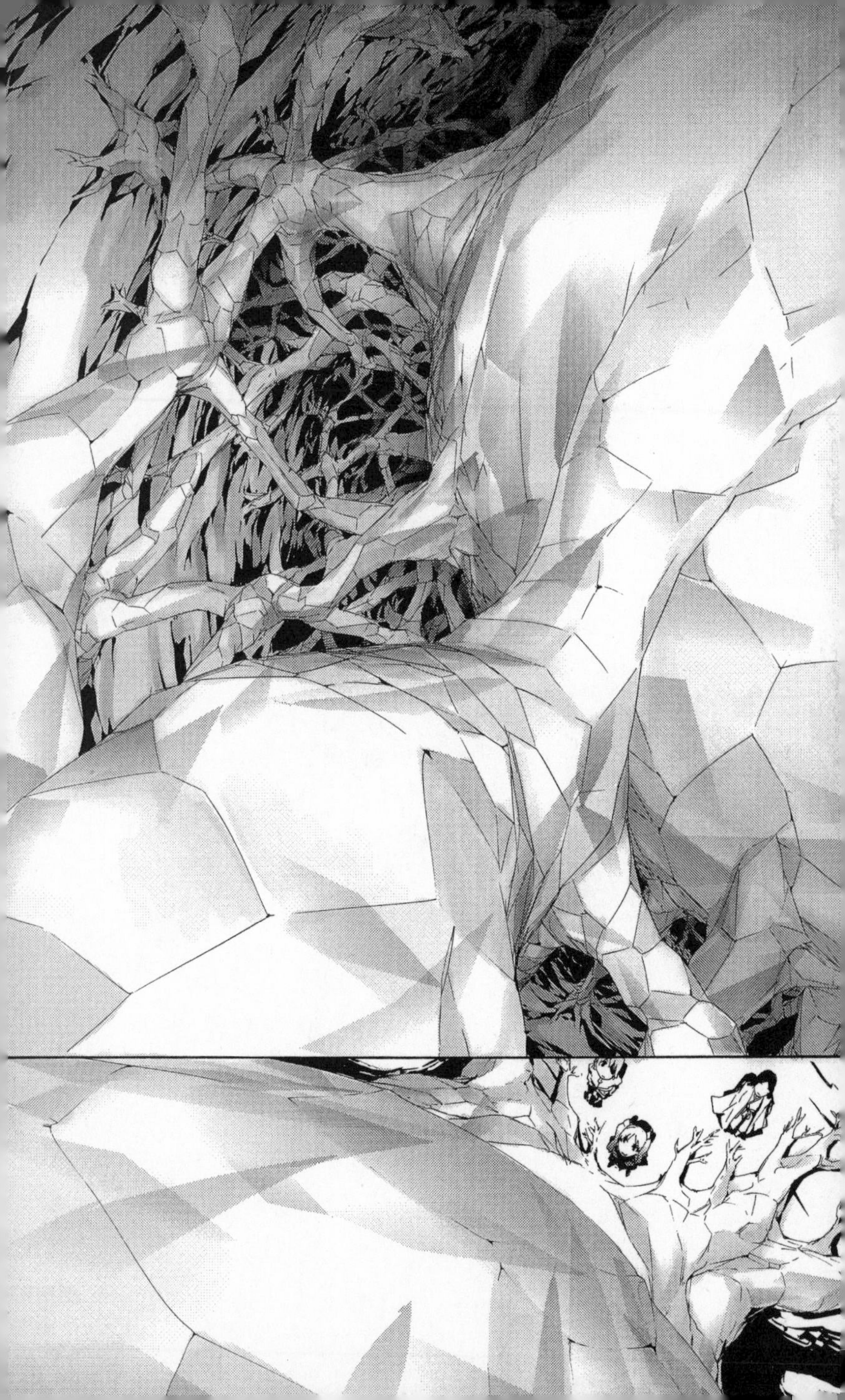

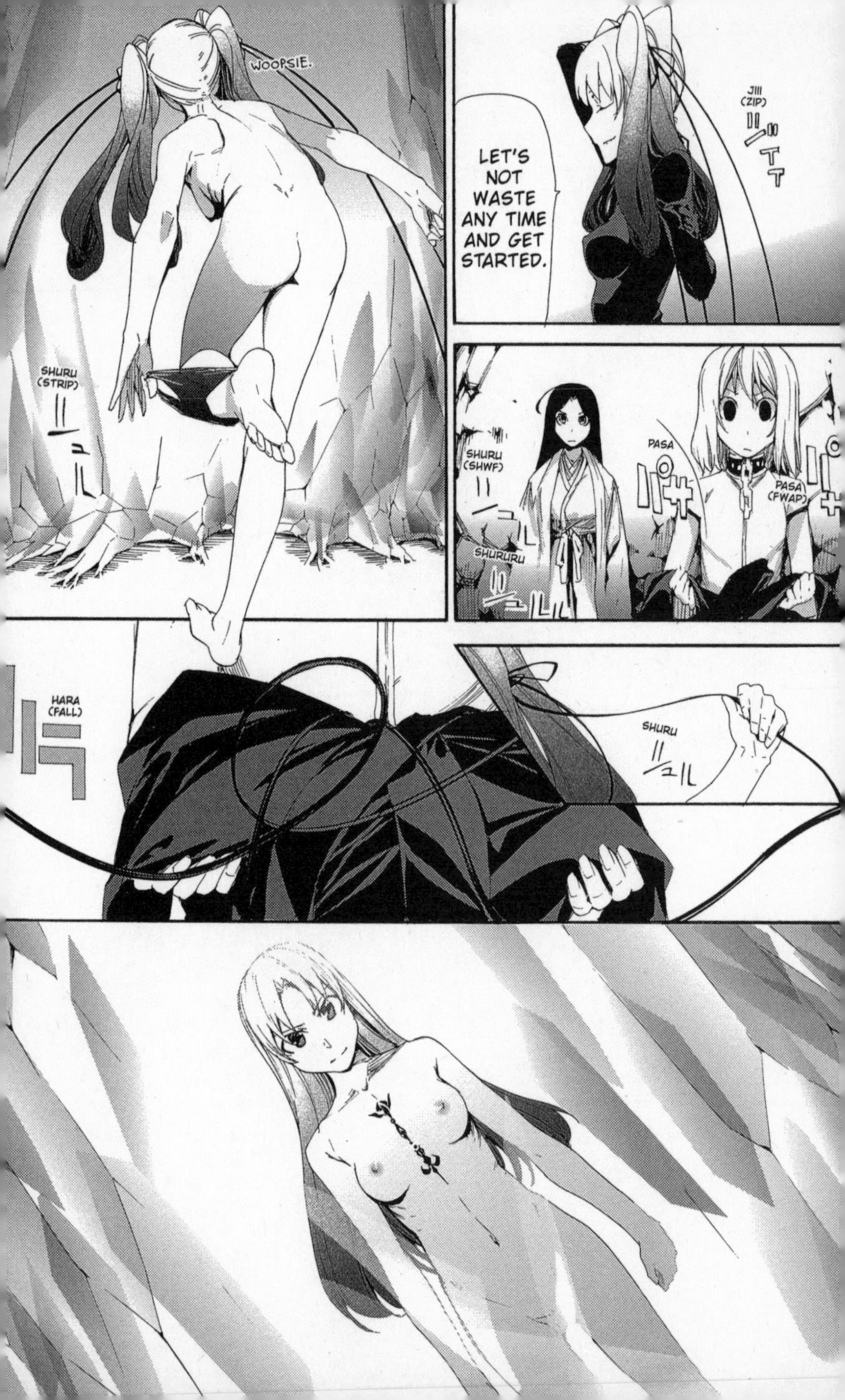
LET'S NOT WASTE ANY TIME AND GET STARTED.
JIII (ZIP)
PASA (FWAP)
PASA
SHURU (SHWF)
SHURURU
WOOPSIE.
SHURU (STRIP)
SHURU
HARA (FALL)

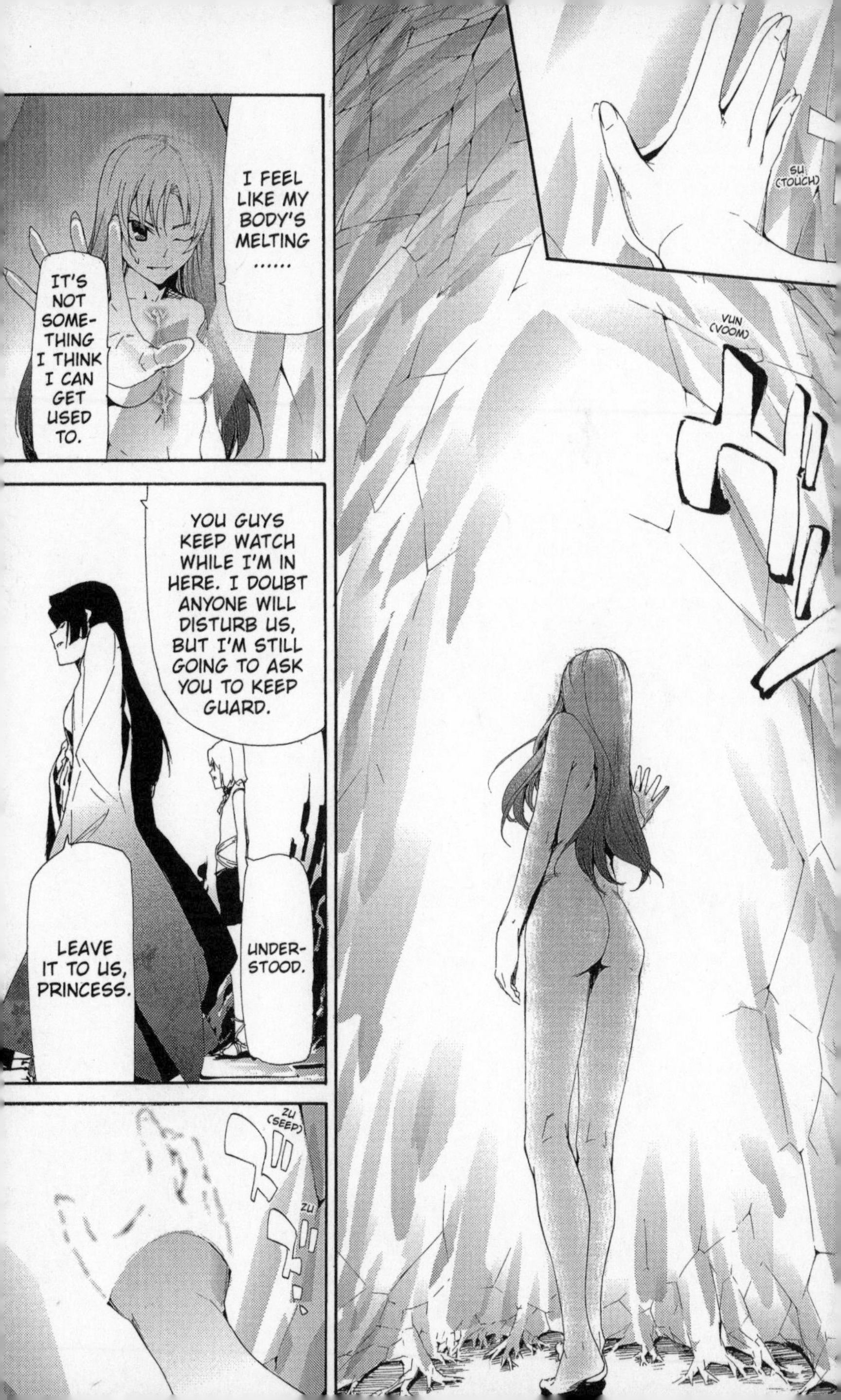
SU
(TOUCH)
VUN
(VOOM)
I FEEL LIKE MY BODY'S MELTING ......
IT'S NOT SOME-THING I THINK I CAN GET USED TO.
YOU GUYS KEEP WATCH WHILE I'M IN HERE. I DOUBT ANYONE WILL DISTURB US, BUT I'M STILL GOING TO ASK YOU TO KEEP GUARD.
UNDER-STOOD.
LEAVE IT TO US, PRINCESS.
ZU
(SEEP)
ZU

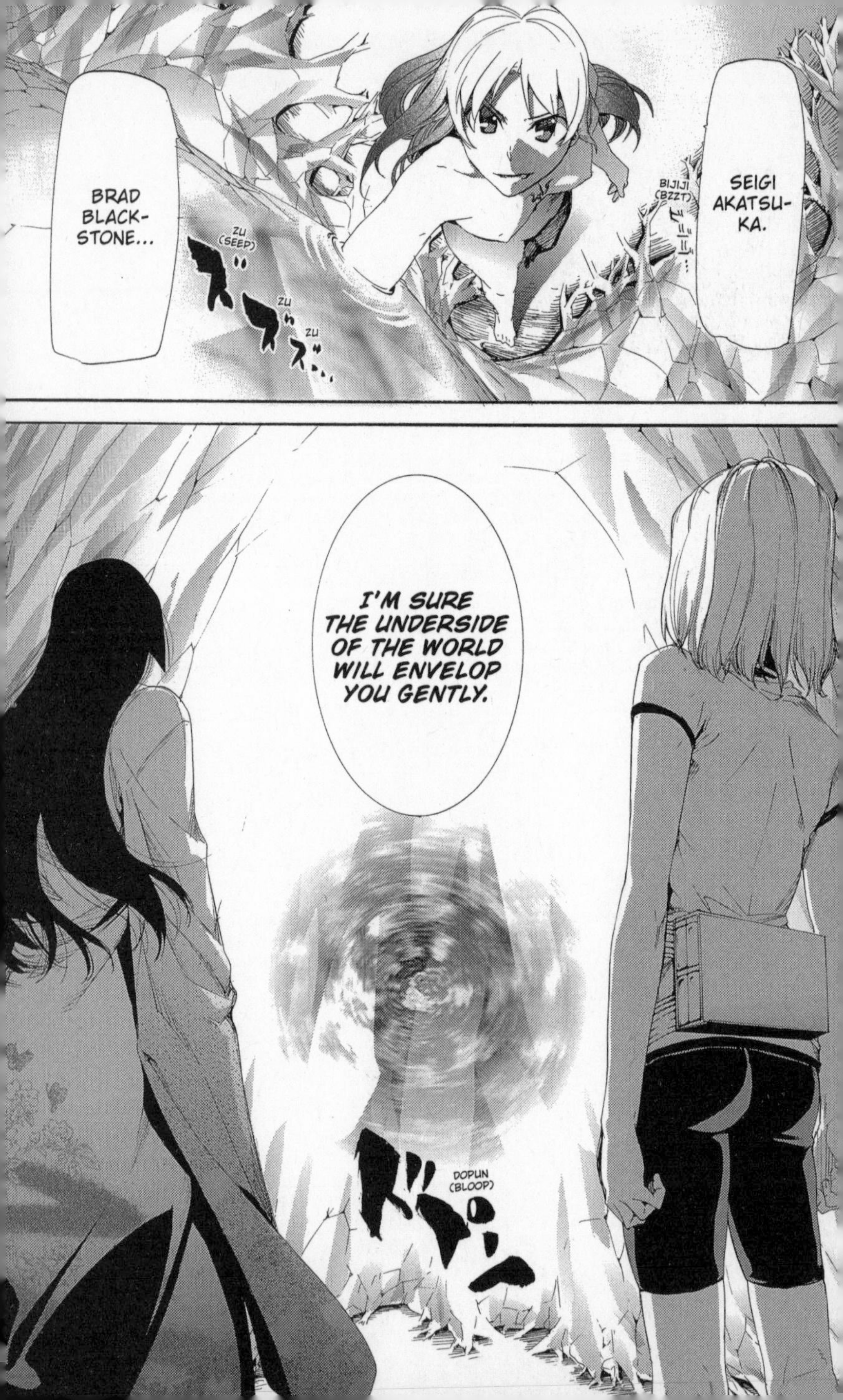
BIJIJI (BZZT)
SEIGI AKATSUKA.
BRAD BLACKSTONE...
ZU (SEEP)
ZU
ZU
I'M SURE THE UNDERSIDE OF THE WORLD WILL ENVELOP YOU GENTLY.
DOPUN (BLOOP)

TABOO TATTOO

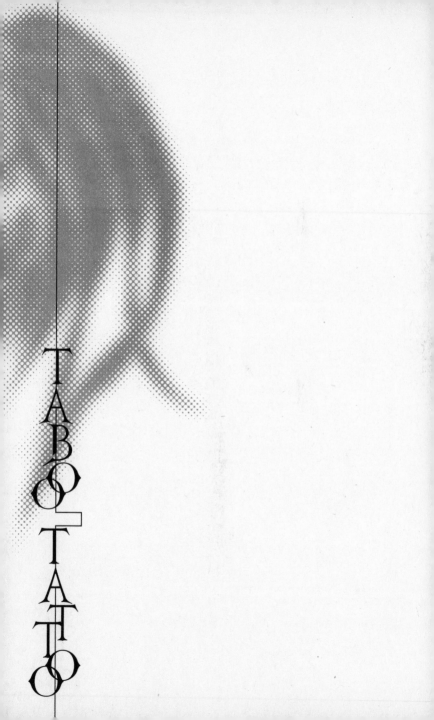

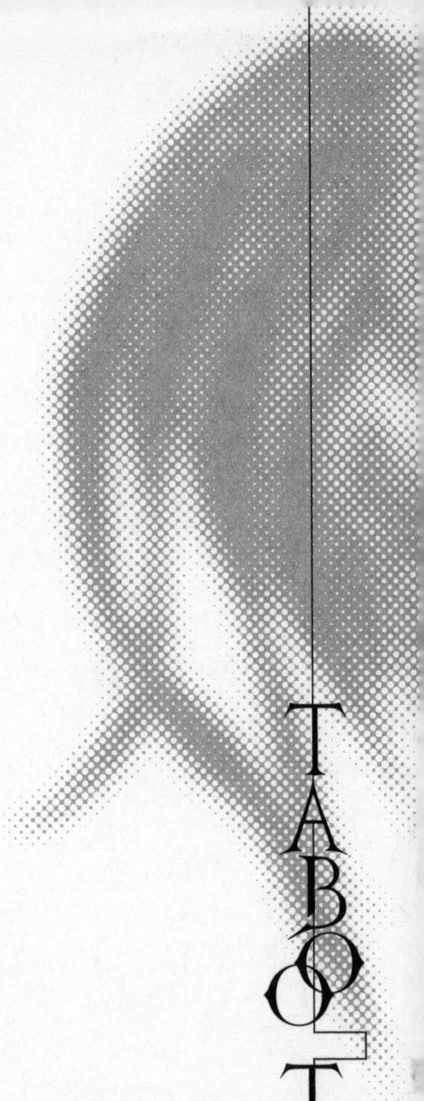

TABOO TATTOO

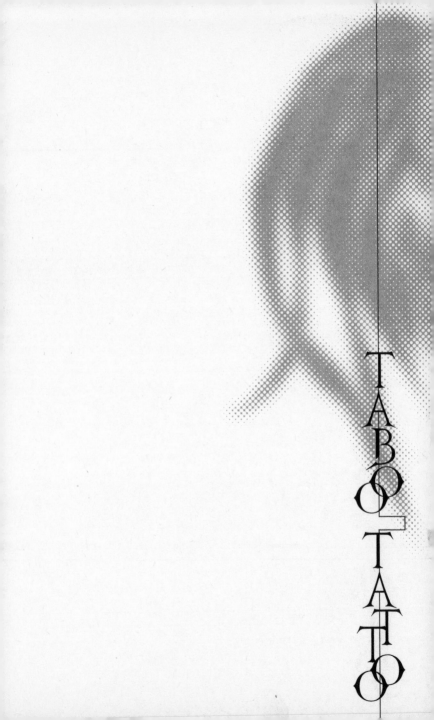

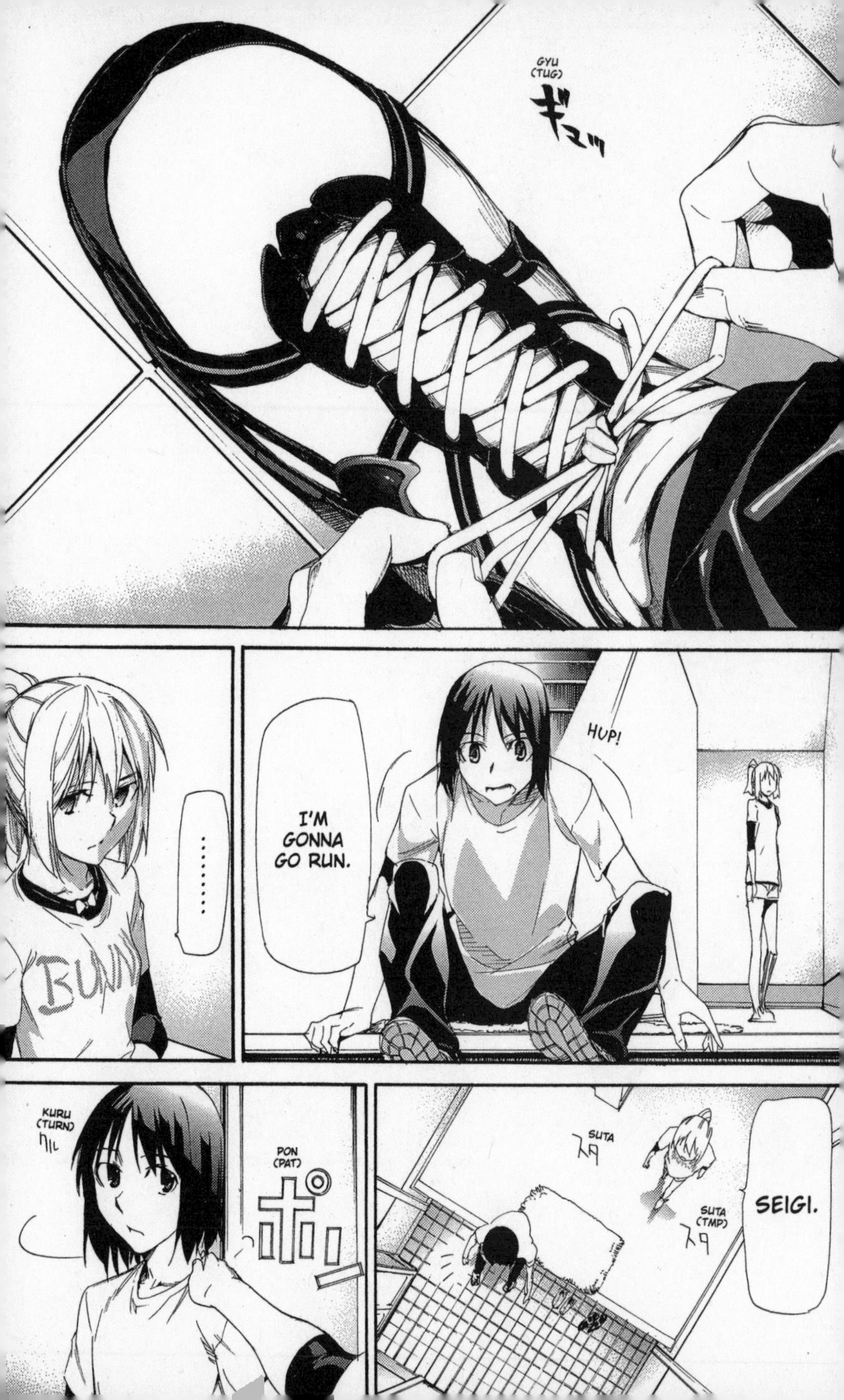
GYU (TUG)
ギュッ
HUP!
I'M GONNA GO RUN.
......
SEIGI.
SUTA
スタ
SUTA (TMP)
スタ
PON (PAT)
ポン
KURU (TURN)
クル

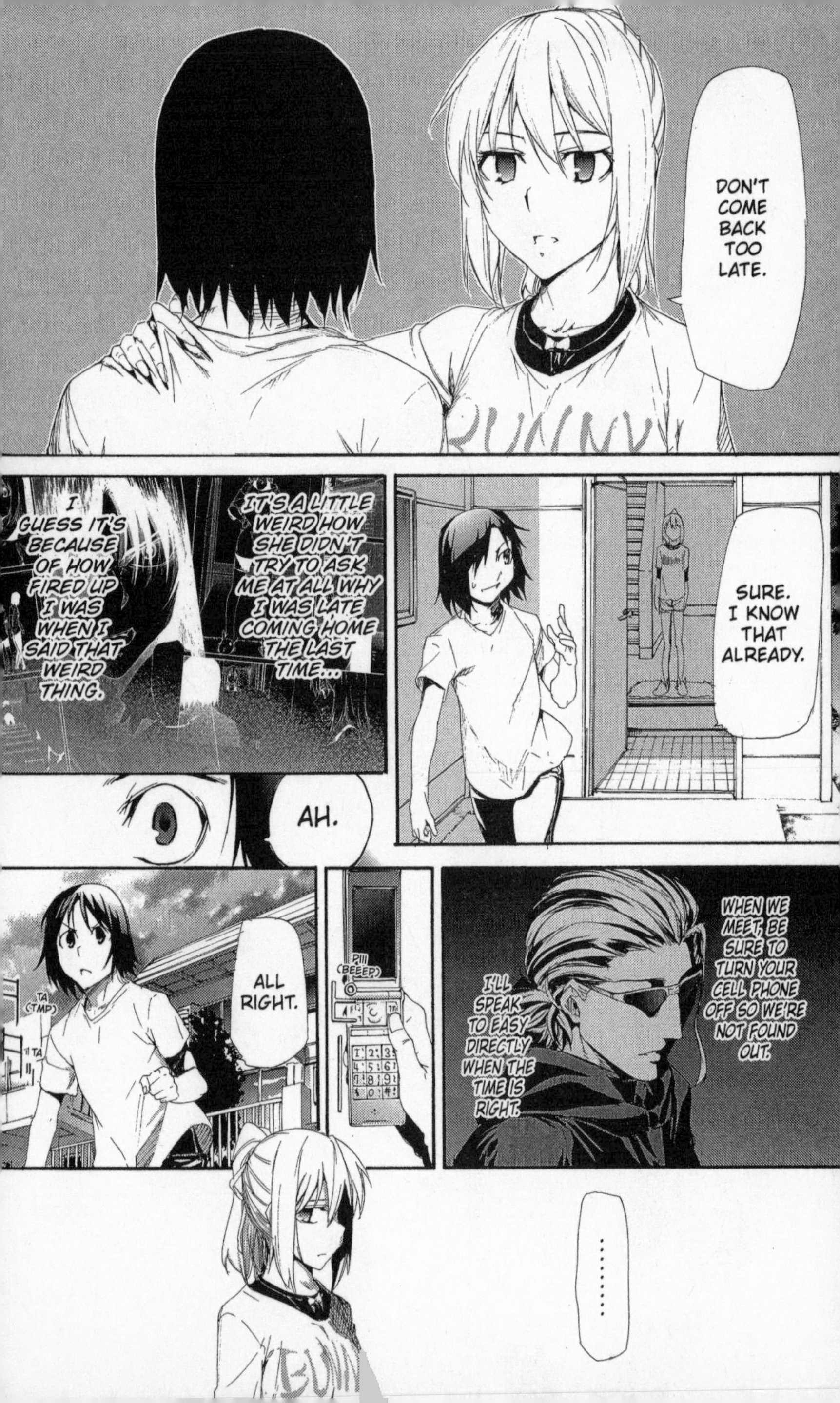
DON'T COME BACK TOO LATE.
SURE. I KNOW THAT ALREADY.
IT'S A LITTLE WEIRD HOW SHE DIDN'T TRY TO ASK ME AT ALL WHY I WAS LATE COMING HOME THE LAST TIME...
I GUESS IT'S BECAUSE OF HOW FIRED UP I WAS WHEN I SAID THAT WEIRD THING.
AH.
WHEN WE MEET, BE SURE TO TURN YOUR CELL PHONE OFF SO WE'RE NOT FOUND OUT.
I'LL SPEAK TO EASY DIRECTLY WHEN THE TIME IS RIGHT.
PIII (BEEEP)
ALL RIGHT.
TA (TMP)
TA
......

#16 REUNION

TABOOTATTOO

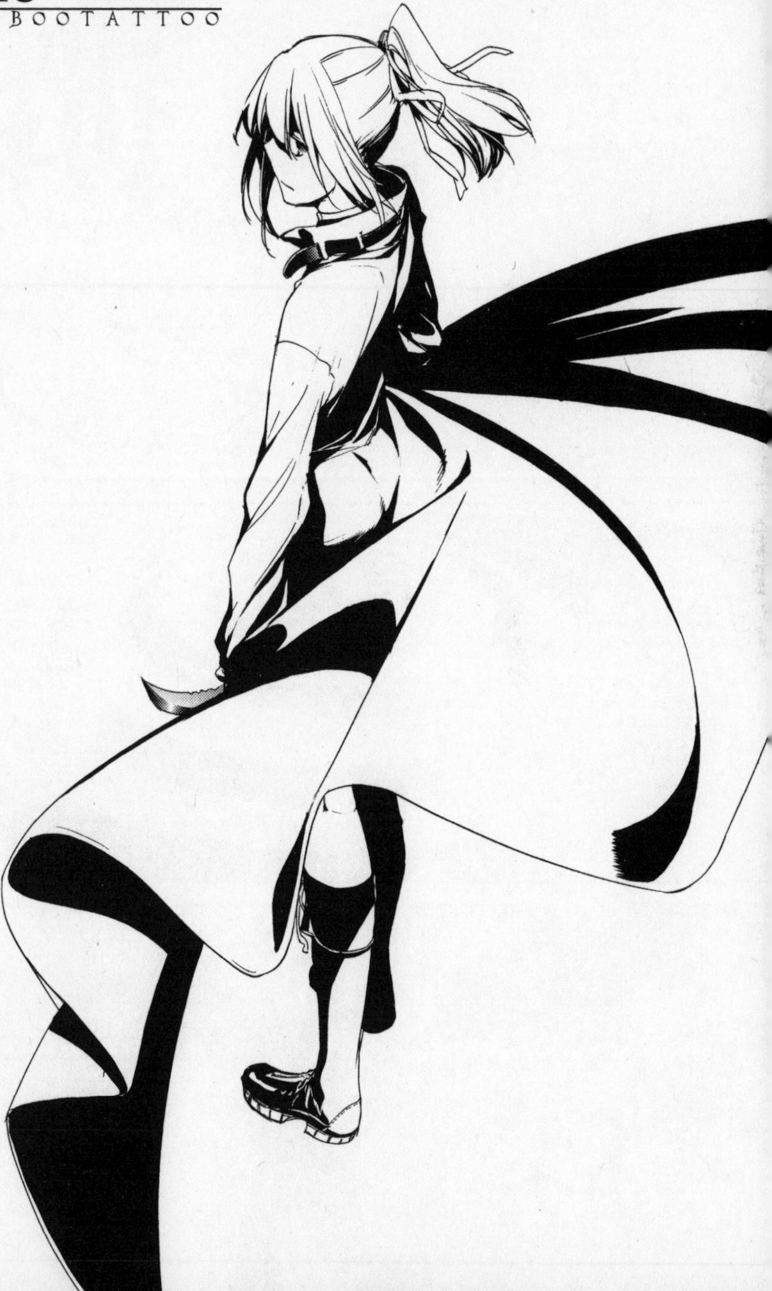

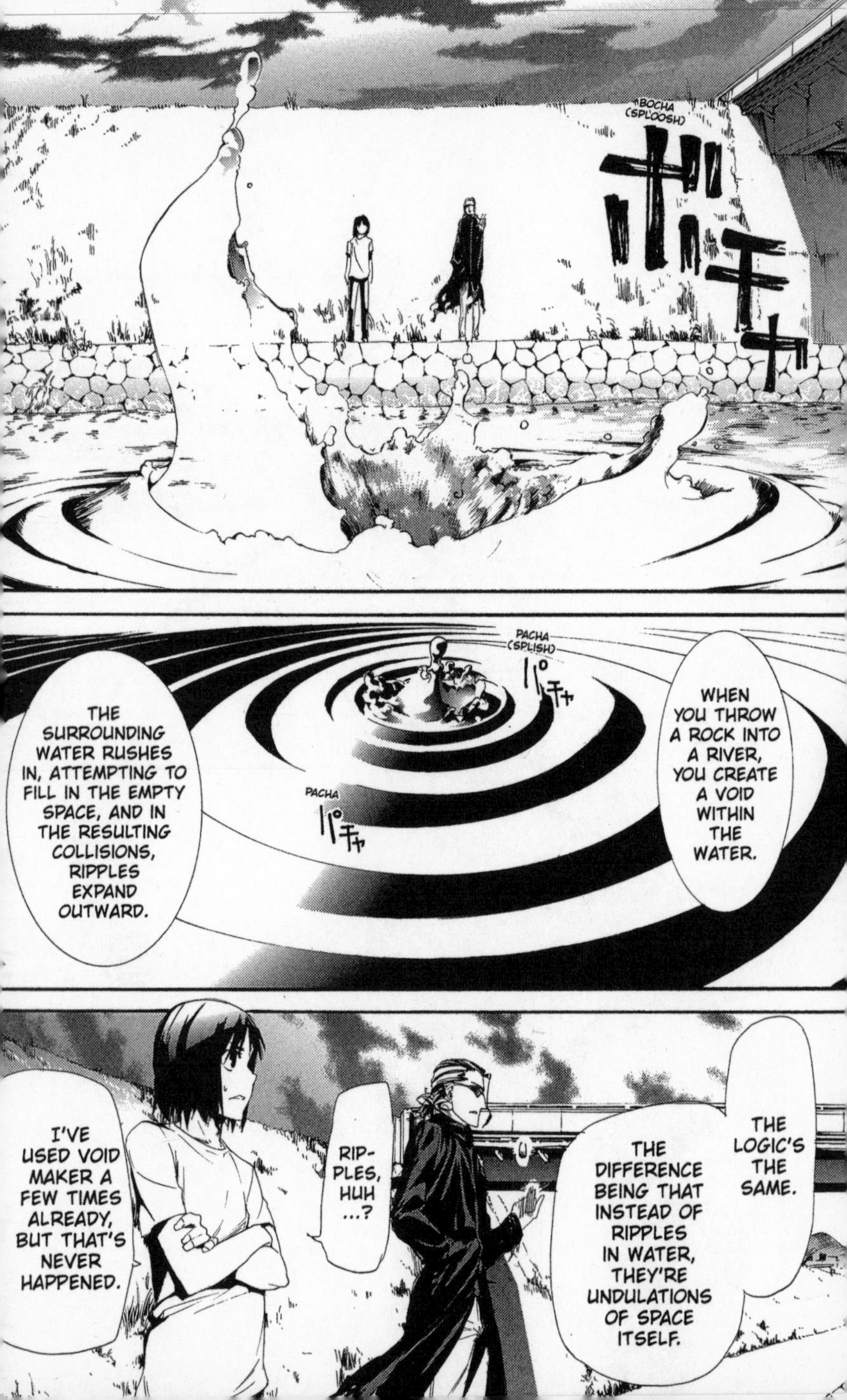
BOCHA (SPLOOSH)
ボチャ
PACHA (SPLISH)
パチャ
WHEN YOU THROW A ROCK INTO A RIVER, YOU CREATE A VOID WITHIN THE WATER.
PACHA
パチャ
THE SURROUNDING WATER RUSHES IN, ATTEMPTING TO FILL IN THE EMPTY SPACE, AND IN THE RESULTING COLLISIONS, RIPPLES EXPAND OUTWARD.
THE LOGIC'S THE SAME.
THE DIFFERENCE BEING THAT INSTEAD OF RIPPLES IN WATER, THEY'RE UNDULATIONS OF SPACE ITSELF.
RIP-PLES, HUH ...?
I'VE USED VOID MAKER A FEW TIMES ALREADY, BUT THAT'S NEVER HAPPENED.

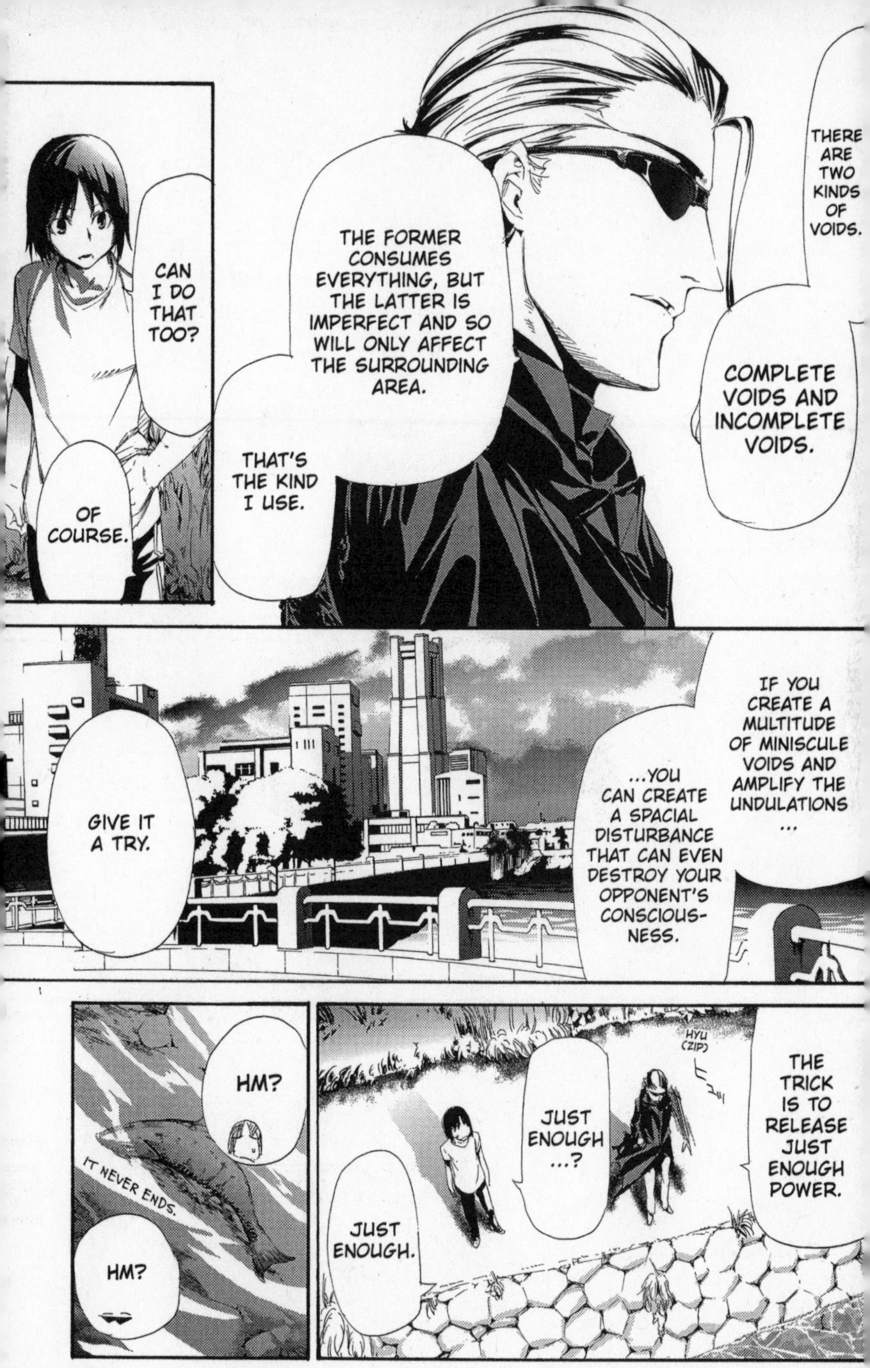
THERE ARE TWO KINDS OF VOIDS.
COMPLETE VOIDS AND INCOMPLETE VOIDS.
THE FORMER CONSUMES EVERYTHING, BUT THE LATTER IS IMPERFECT AND SO WILL ONLY AFFECT THE SURROUNDING AREA.
THAT'S THE KIND I USE.
CAN I DO THAT TOO?
OF COURSE.
IF YOU CREATE A MULTITUDE OF MINISCULE VOIDS AND AMPLIFY THE UNDULATIONS ...
...YOU CAN CREATE A SPACIAL DISTURBANCE THAT CAN EVEN DESTROY YOUR OPPONENT'S CONSCIOUS-NESS.
GIVE IT A TRY.
THE TRICK IS TO RELEASE JUST ENOUGH POWER.
HYU (ZIP)
JUST ENOUGH ...?
JUST ENOUGH.
HM?
IT NEVER ENDS.
HM?

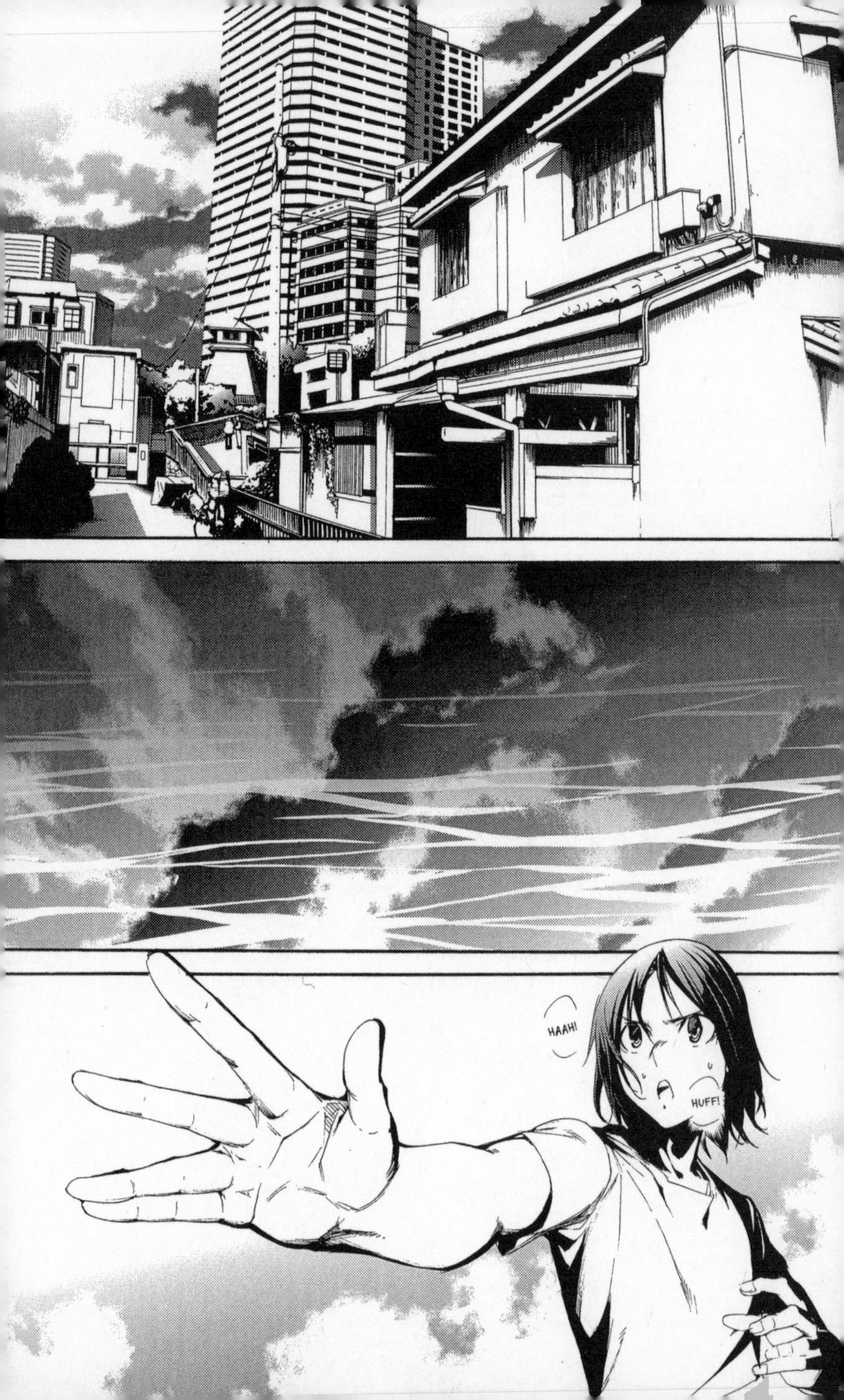
HAAH!
HUFF!

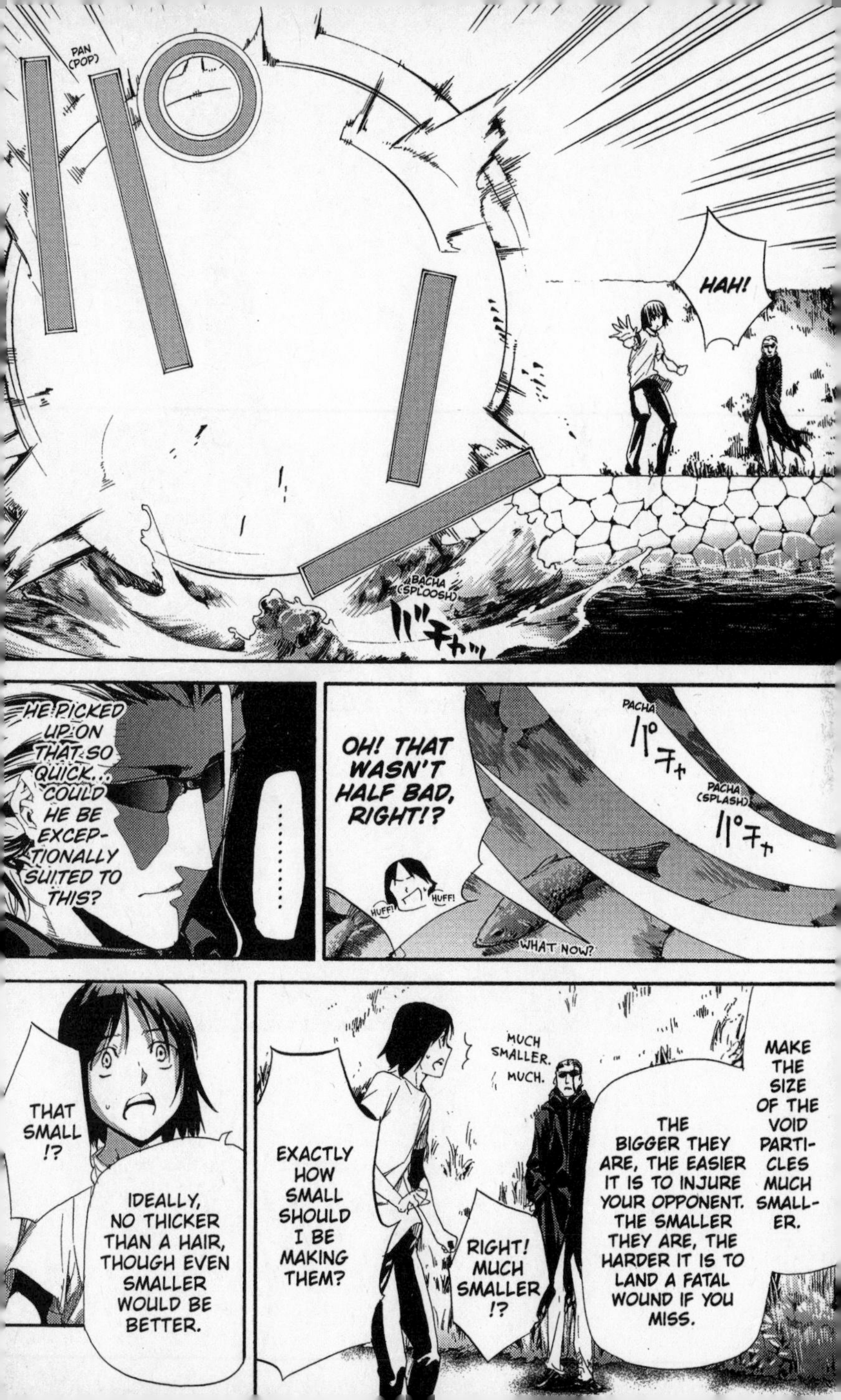
HAH!
PAN (POP)
BACHA (SPLOOSH)
PACHA
PACHA (SPLASH)
OH! THAT WASN'T HALF BAD, RIGHT!?
HUFF! HUFF!
WHAT NOW?
......
HE PICKED UP ON THAT SO QUICK... COULD HE BE EXCEPTIONALLY SUITED TO THIS?
MAKE THE SIZE OF THE VOID PARTICLES MUCH SMALLER.
THE BIGGER THEY ARE, THE EASIER IT IS TO INJURE YOUR OPPONENT. THE SMALLER THEY ARE, THE HARDER IT IS TO LAND A FATAL WOUND IF YOU MISS.
MUCH SMALLER. MUCH.
RIGHT! MUCH SMALLER!?
EXACTLY HOW SMALL SHOULD I BE MAKING THEM?
IDEALLY, NO THICKER THAN A HAIR, THOUGH EVEN SMALLER WOULD BE BETTER.
THAT SMALL!?

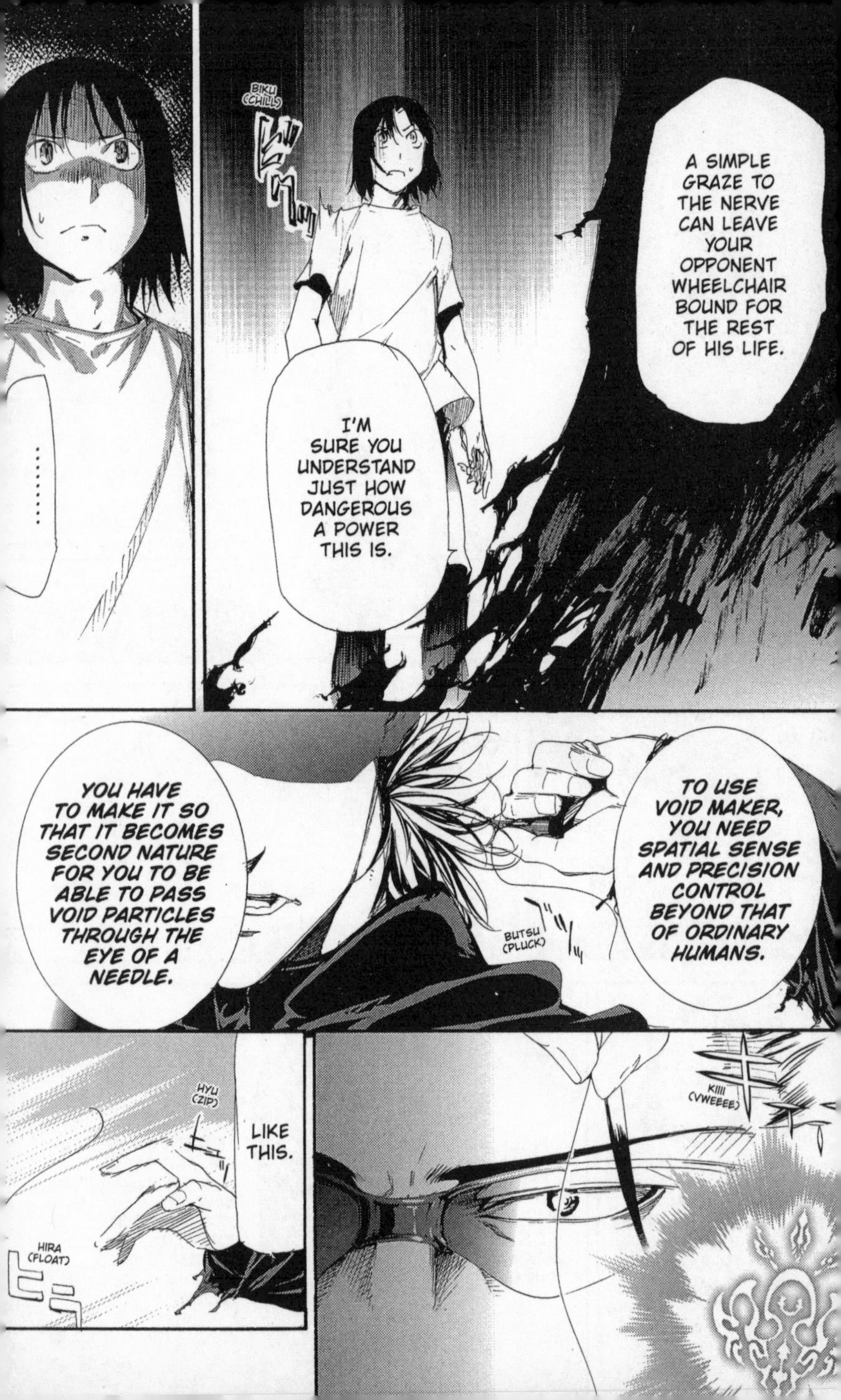
A SIMPLE GRAZE TO THE NERVE CAN LEAVE YOUR OPPONENT WHEELCHAIR BOUND FOR THE REST OF HIS LIFE.
BIKU (CHILL)
I'M SURE YOU UNDERSTAND JUST HOW DANGEROUS A POWER THIS IS.
......
TO USE VOID MAKER, YOU NEED SPATIAL SENSE AND PRECISION CONTROL BEYOND THAT OF ORDINARY HUMANS.
BUTSU (PLUCK)
YOU HAVE TO MAKE IT SO THAT IT BECOMES SECOND NATURE FOR YOU TO BE ABLE TO PASS VOID PARTICLES THROUGH THE EYE OF A NEEDLE.
KIIII (VWEEEE)
LIKE THIS.
HYU (ZIP)
HIRA (FLOAT)

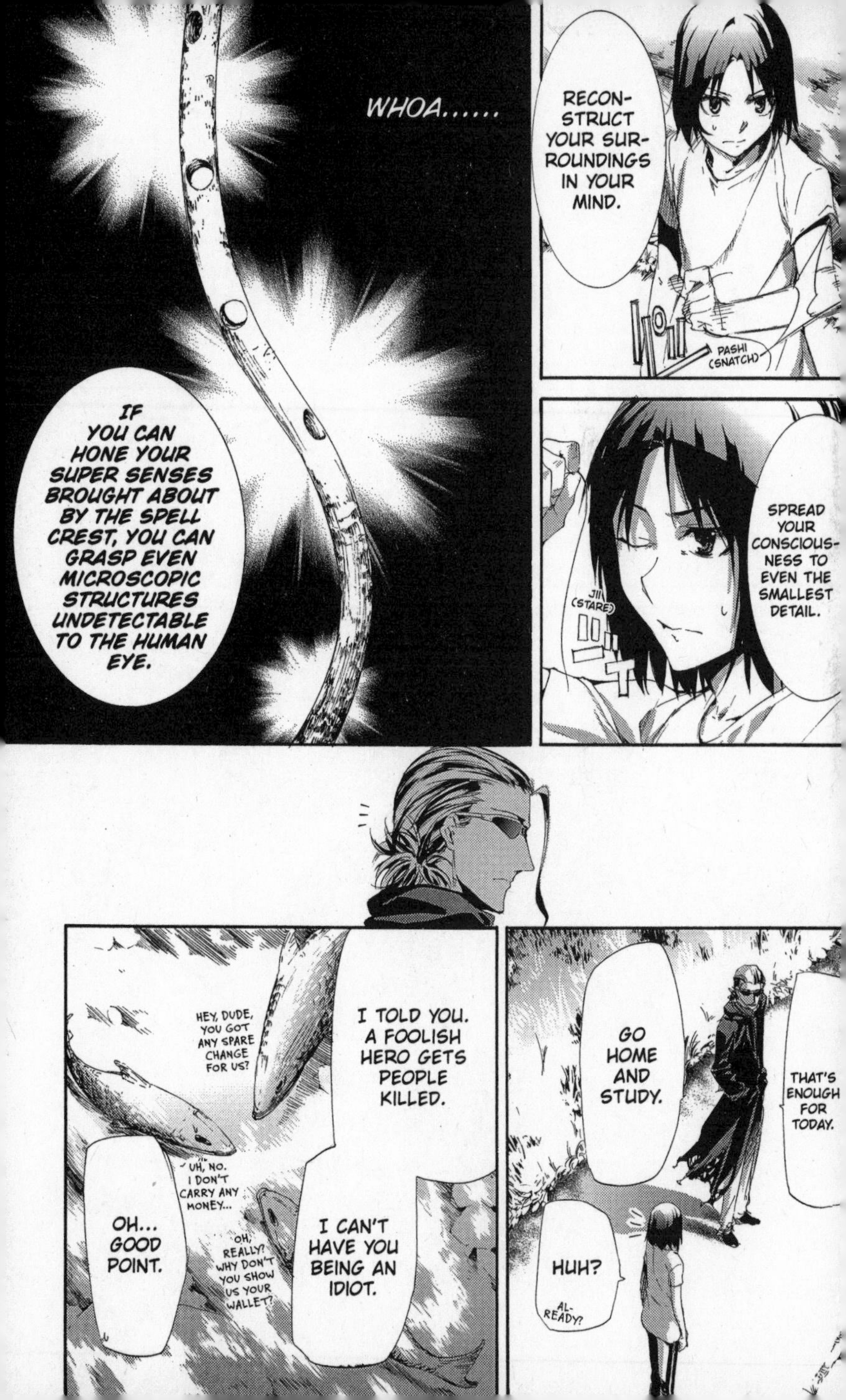
RECON-STRUCT YOUR SUR-ROUNDINGS IN YOUR MIND.
PASHI (SNATCH)
SPREAD YOUR CONSCIOUS-NESS TO EVEN THE SMALLEST DETAIL.
JII (STARE)
WHOA......
IF YOU CAN HONE YOUR SUPER SENSES BROUGHT ABOUT BY THE SPELL CREST, YOU CAN GRASP EVEN MICROSCOPIC STRUCTURES UNDETECTABLE TO THE HUMAN EYE.
THAT'S ENOUGH FOR TODAY.
GO HOME AND STUDY.
HUH?
AL-READY?
I TOLD YOU. A FOOLISH HERO GETS PEOPLE KILLED.
HEY, DUDE, YOU GOT ANY SPARE CHANGE FOR US?
I CAN'T HAVE YOU BEING AN IDIOT.
UH, NO. I DON'T CARRY ANY MONEY...
OH, REALLY? WHY DON'T YOU SHOW US YOUR WALLET?
OH... GOOD POINT.

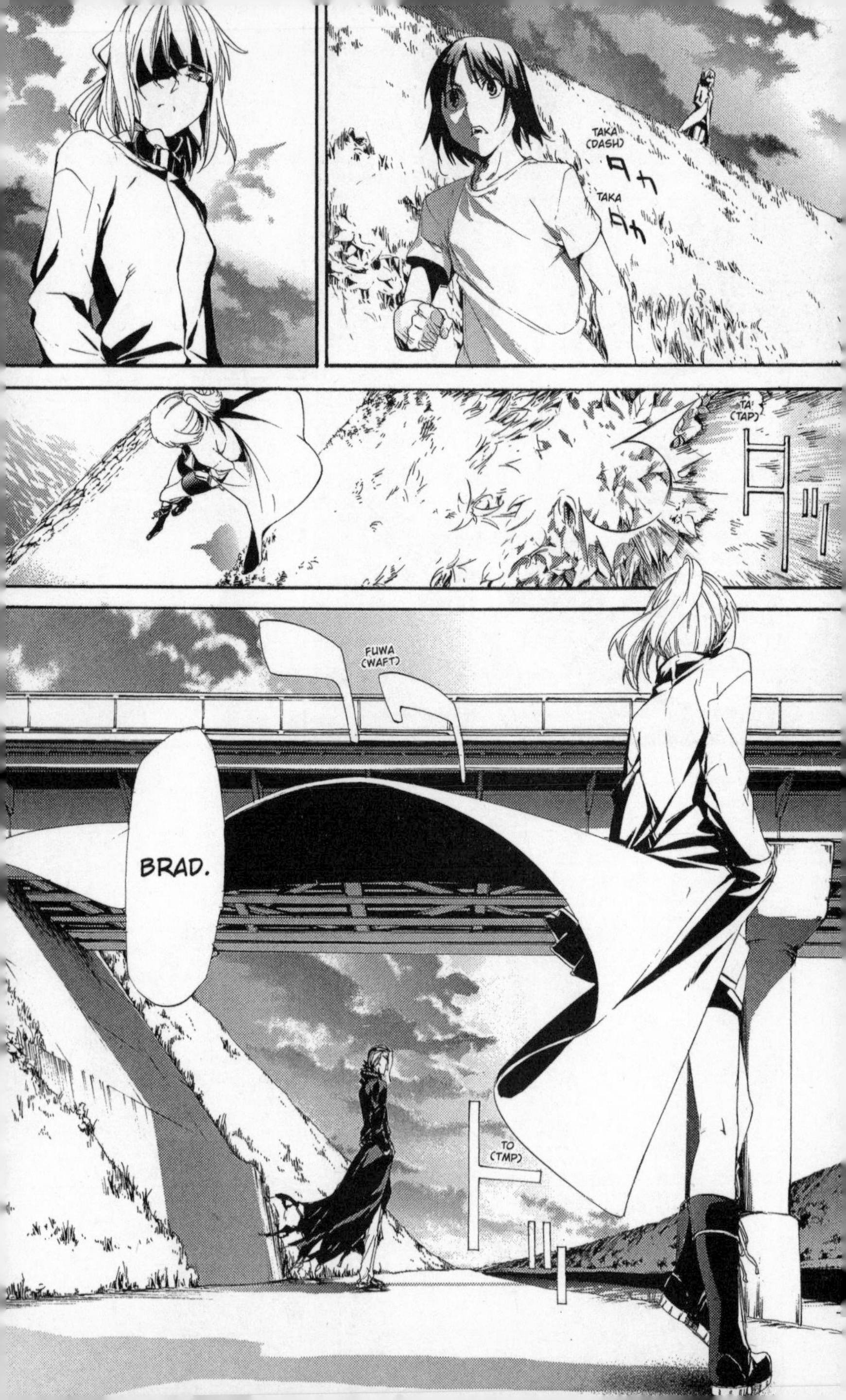
TAKA (DASH)
TAKA
TA! (TAP)
FUWA (WAFT)
BRAD.
TO (TMP)

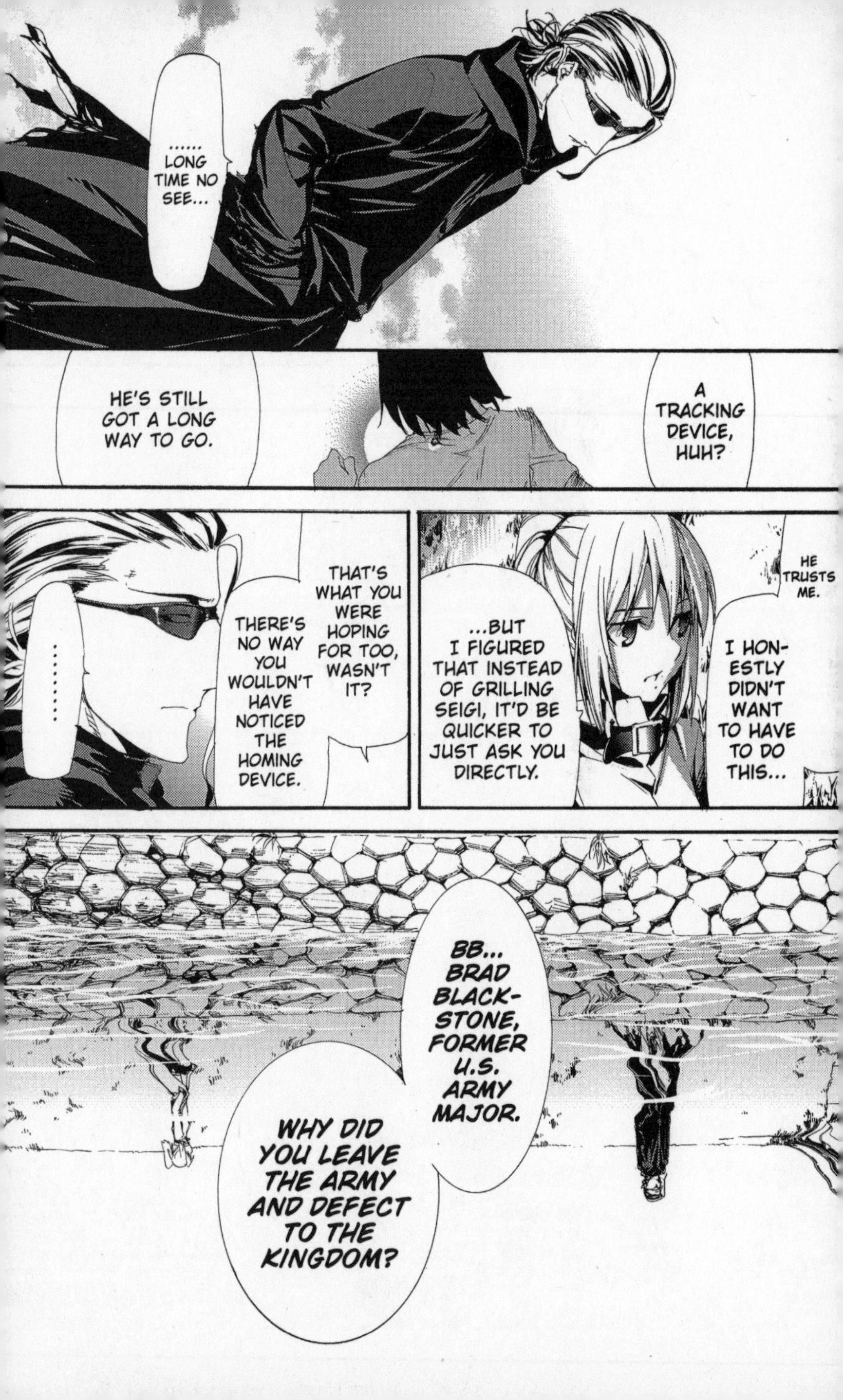

...... LONG TIME NO SEE...
A TRACKING DEVICE, HUH?
HE'S STILL GOT A LONG WAY TO GO.
HE TRUSTS ME.
I HONESTLY DIDN'T WANT TO HAVE TO DO THIS...
...BUT I FIGURED THAT INSTEAD OF GRILLING SEIGI, IT'D BE QUICKER TO JUST ASK YOU DIRECTLY.
THAT'S WHAT YOU WERE HOPING FOR TOO, WASN'T IT?
THERE'S NO WAY YOU WOULDN'T HAVE NOTICED THE HOMING DEVICE.
....
BB... BRAD BLACKSTONE, FORMER U.S. ARMY MAJOR.
WHY DID YOU LEAVE THE ARMY AND DEFECT TO THE KINGDOM?

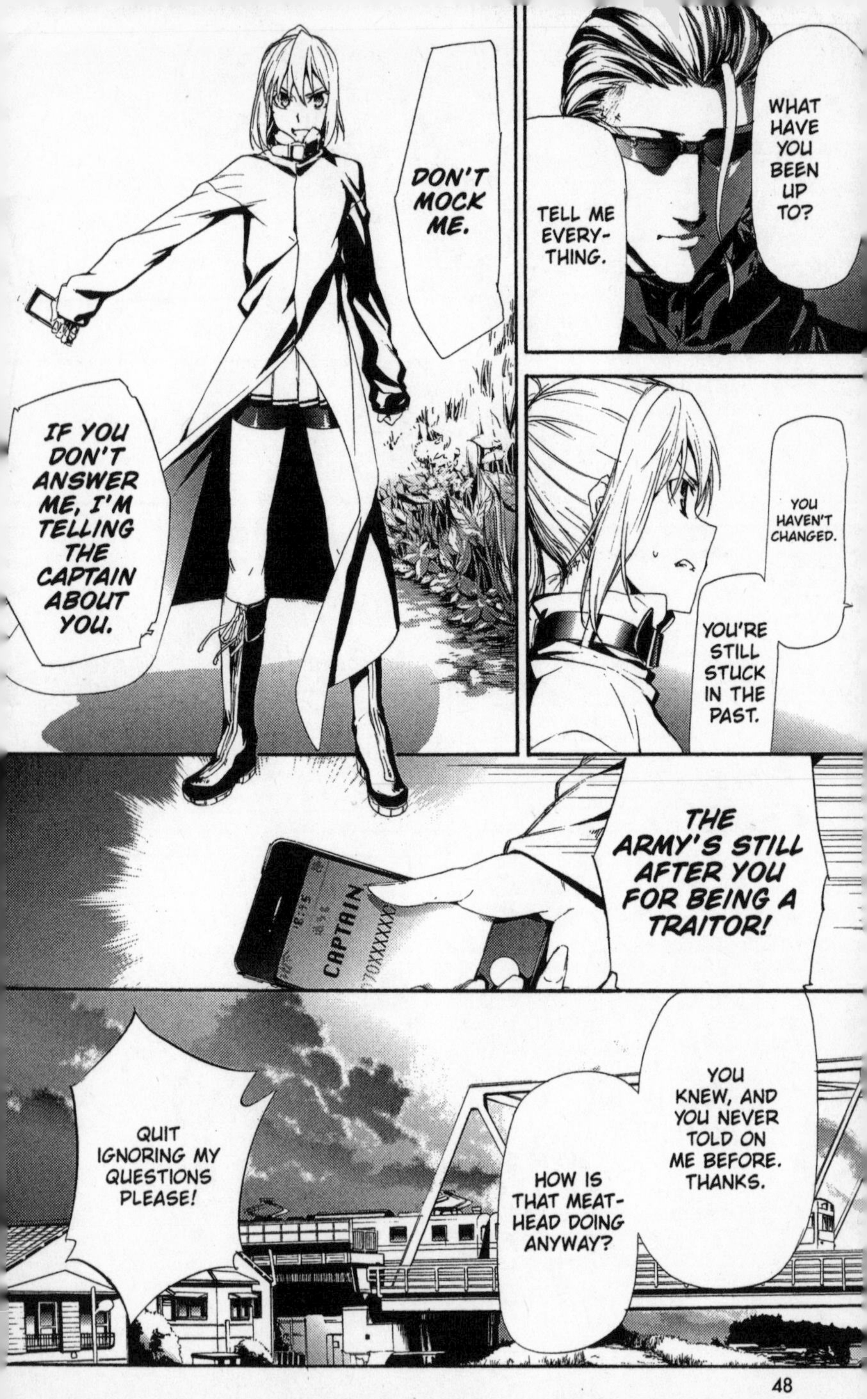
WHAT HAVE YOU BEEN UP TO?
TELL ME EVERY-THING.
YOU HAVEN'T CHANGED.
YOU'RE STILL STUCK IN THE PAST.
DON'T MOCK ME.
IF YOU DON'T ANSWER ME, I'M TELLING THE CAPTAIN ABOUT YOU.
THE ARMY'S STILL AFTER YOU FOR BEING A TRAITOR!
CAPTAIN
YOU KNEW, AND YOU NEVER TOLD ON ME BEFORE. THANKS.
HOW IS THAT MEAT-HEAD DOING ANYWAY?
QUIT IGNORING MY QUESTIONS PLEASE!

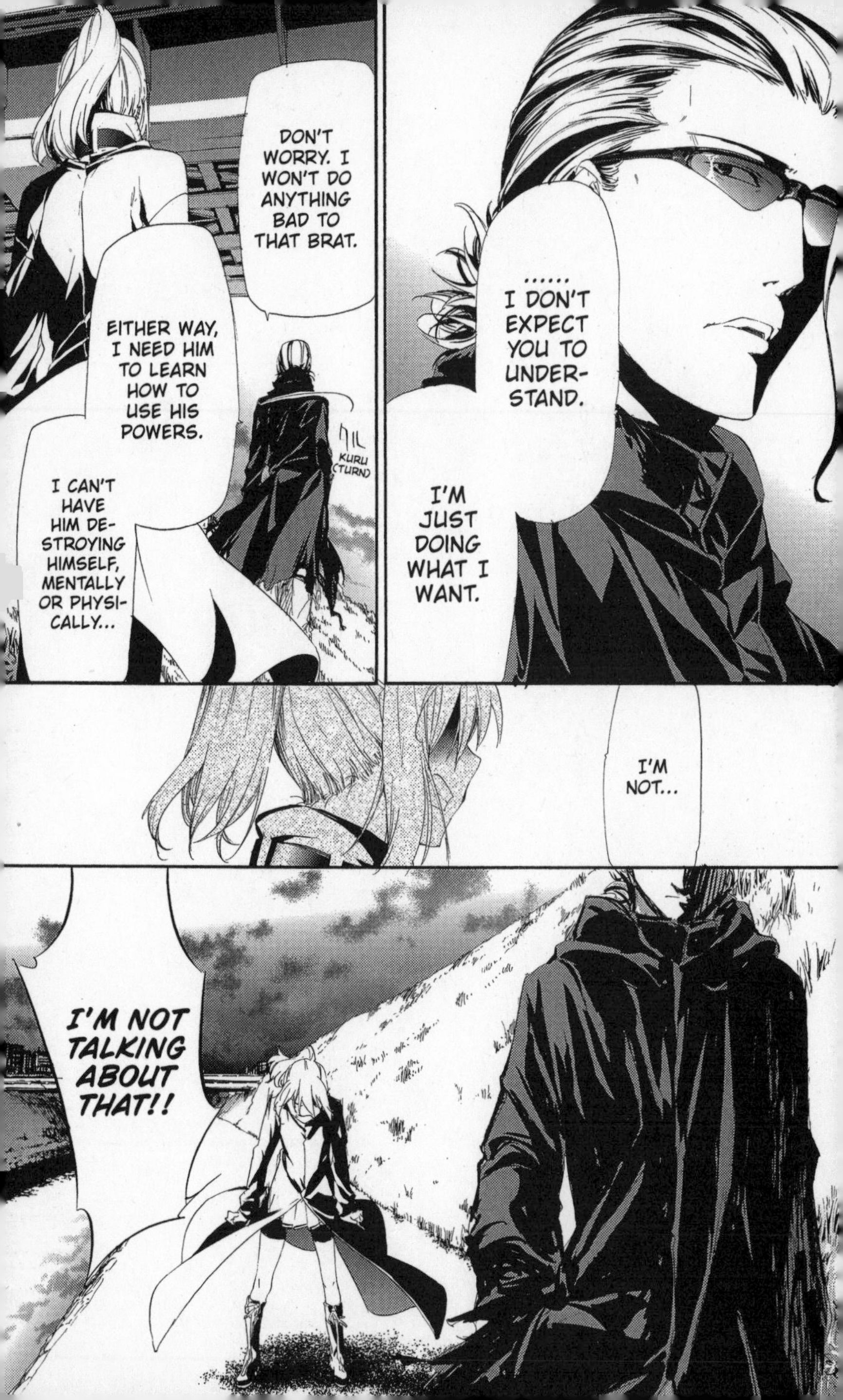

......
I DON'T EXPECT YOU TO UNDER-STAND.
I'M JUST DOING WHAT I WANT.
DON'T WORRY. I WON'T DO ANYTHING BAD TO THAT BRAT.
クル
KURU (TURN)
EITHER WAY, I NEED HIM TO LEARN HOW TO USE HIS POWERS.
I CAN'T HAVE HIM DE-STROYING HIMSELF, MENTALLY OR PHYSI-CALLY...
I'M NOT...
I'M NOT TALKING ABOUT THAT!!

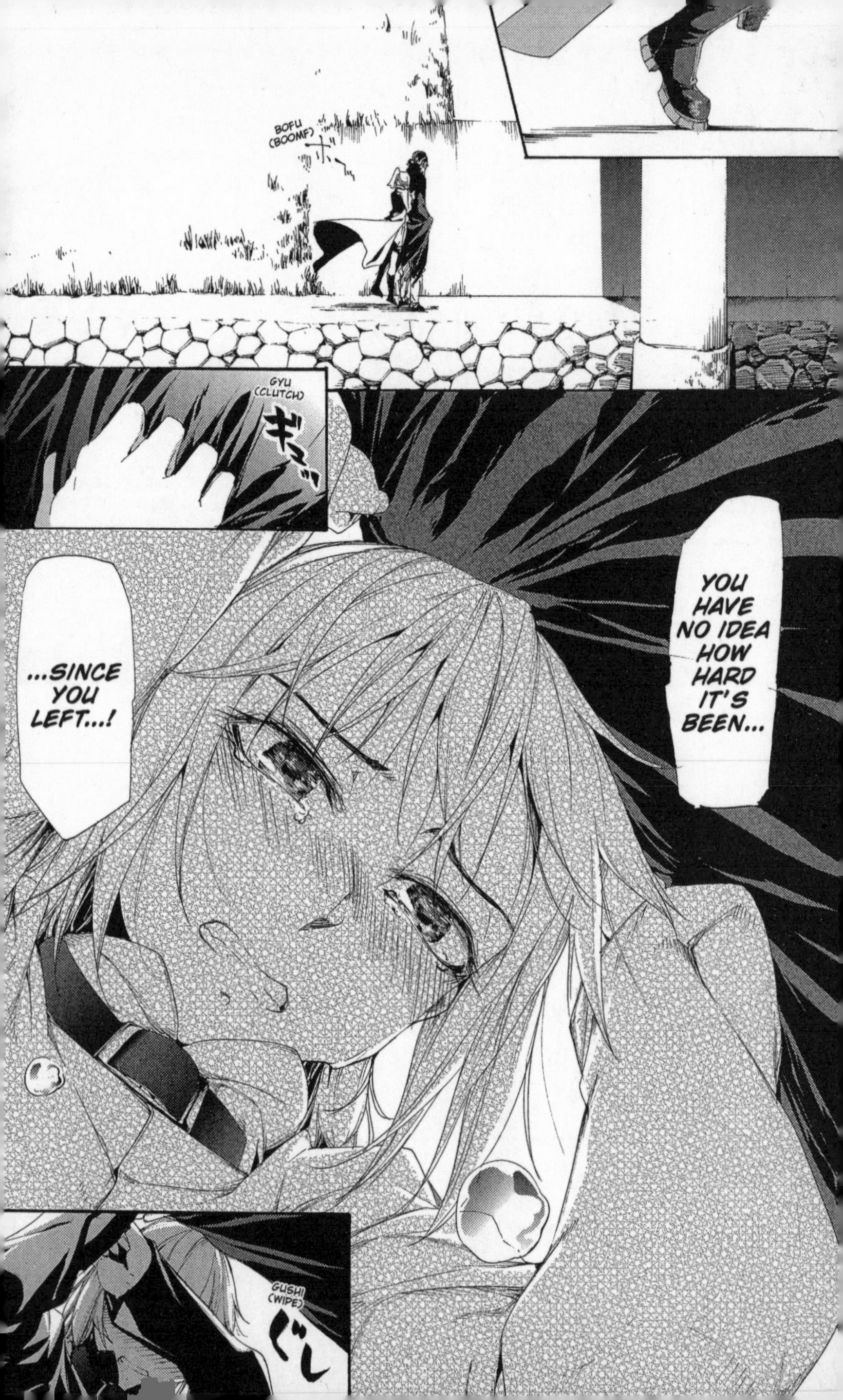
BOFU (BOOMF)
GYU (CLUTCH)
ギュッ
YOU HAVE NO IDEA HOW HARD IT'S BEEN...
...SINCE YOU LEFT...!
GUSHI (WIPE)
ぐし

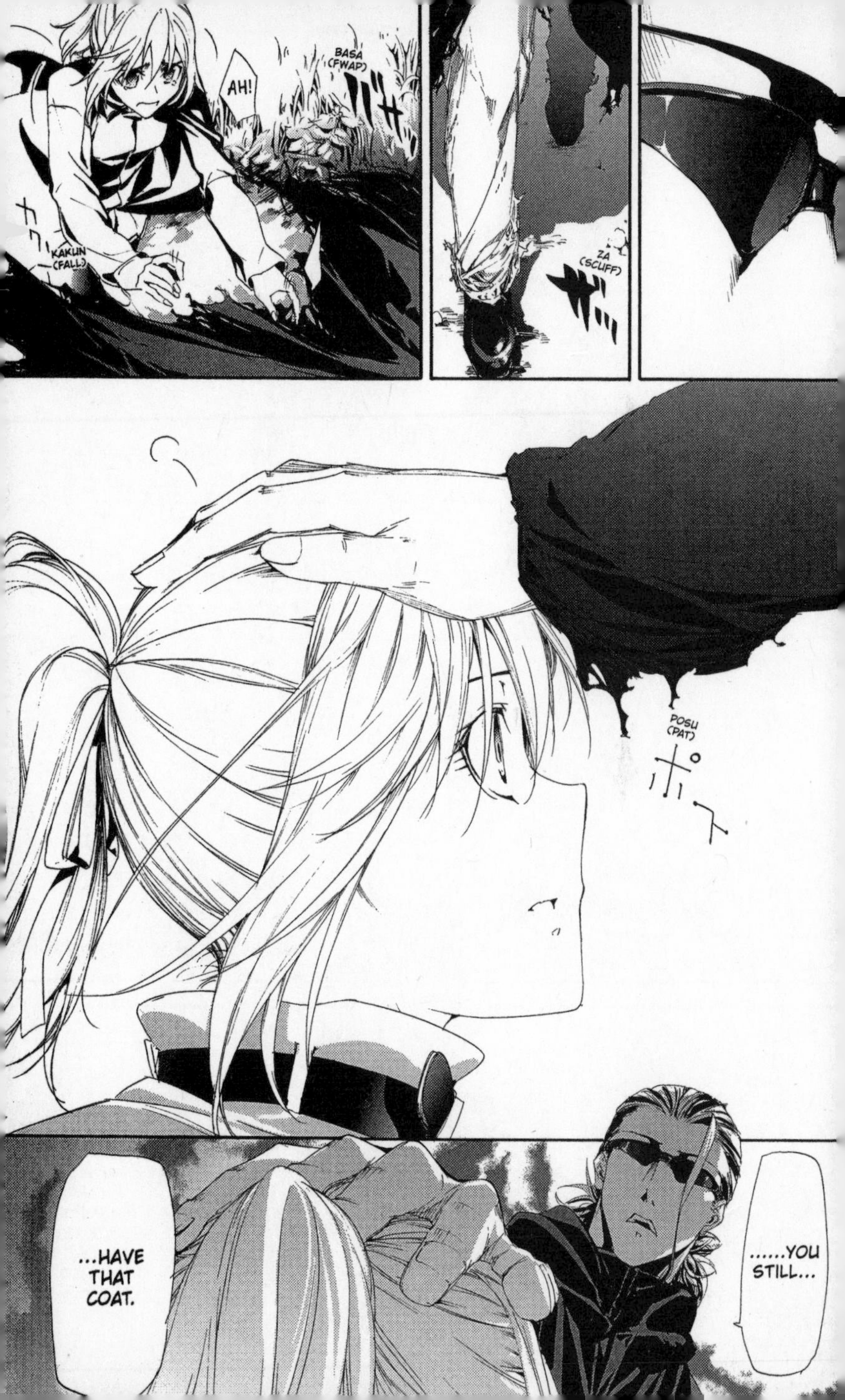
ZA
(SCUFF)
BASA
(FWAP)
AH!
KAKUN
(FALL)
POSU
(PAT)
......YOU STILL...
...HAVE THAT COAT.

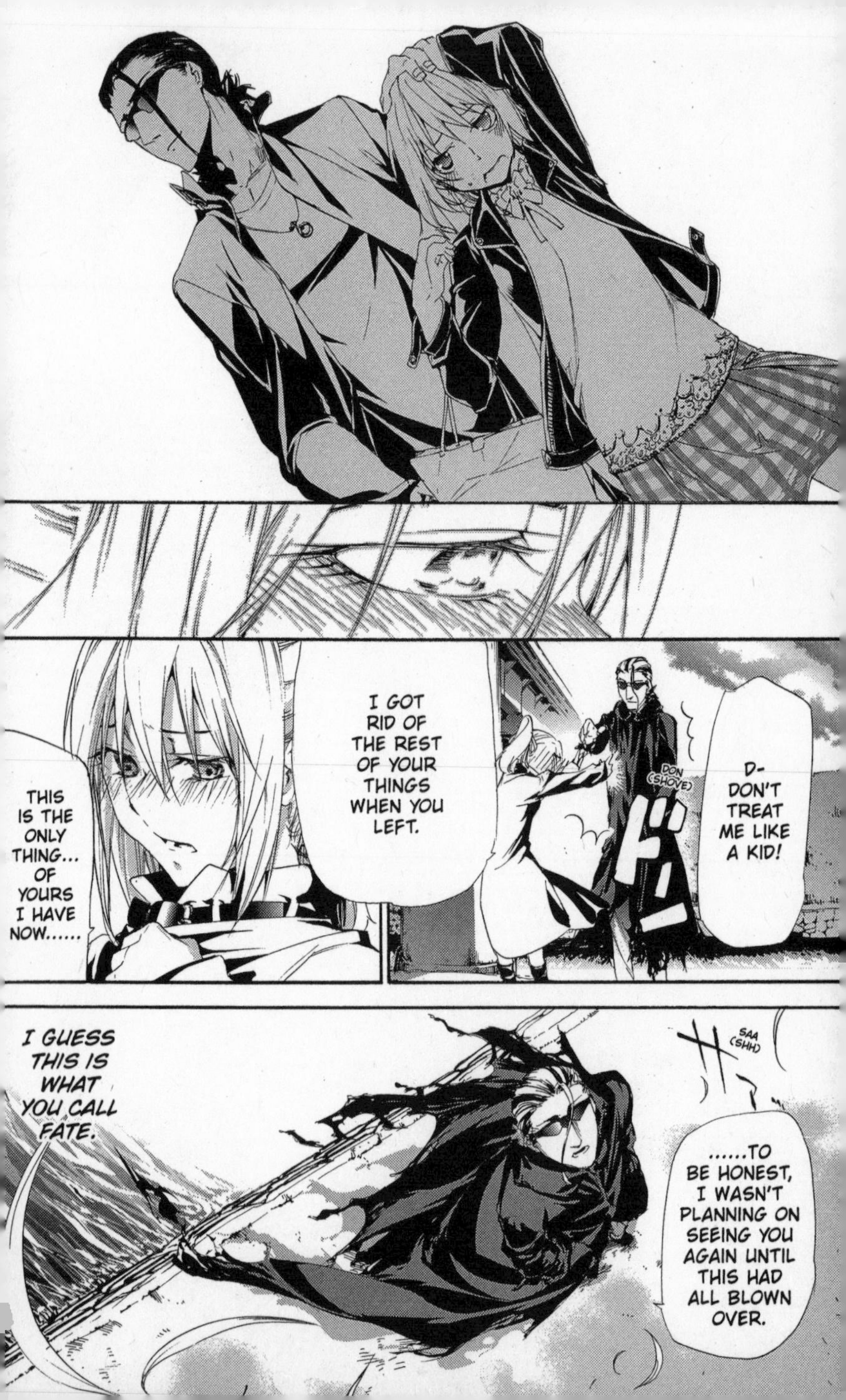
D- DON'T TREAT ME LIKE A KID!
DON (SHOVE)
I GOT RID OF THE REST OF YOUR THINGS WHEN YOU LEFT.
THIS IS THE ONLY THING... OF YOURS I HAVE NOW......
SAA (SHH)
......TO BE HONEST, I WASN'T PLANNING ON SEEING YOU AGAIN UNTIL THIS HAD ALL BLOWN OVER.
I GUESS THIS IS WHAT YOU CALL FATE.

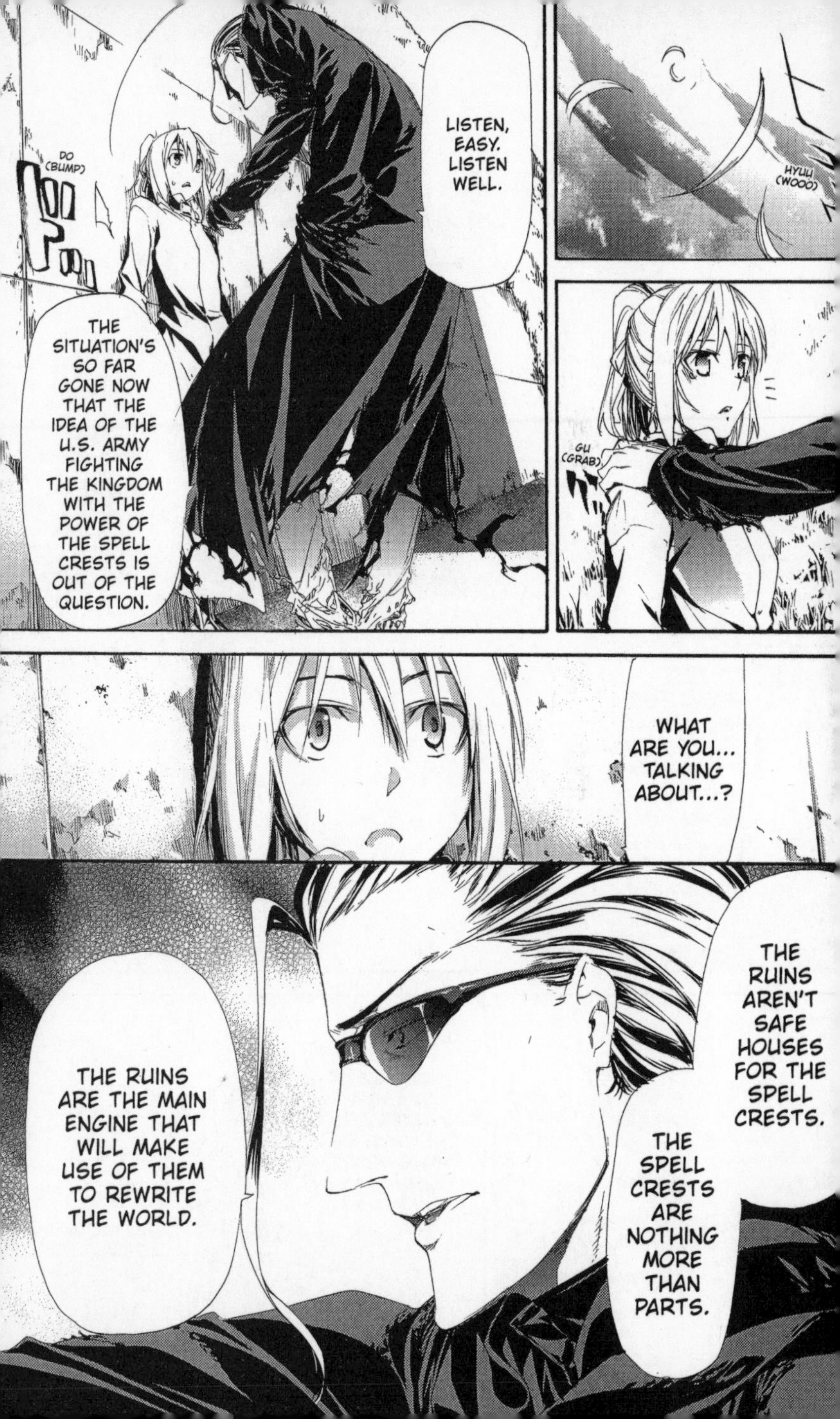
HYUU (WOOO)
GU (GRAB)
LISTEN, EASY. LISTEN WELL.
DO (BUMP)
THE SITUATION'S SO FAR GONE NOW THAT THE IDEA OF THE U.S. ARMY FIGHTING THE KINGDOM WITH THE POWER OF THE SPELL CRESTS IS OUT OF THE QUESTION.
WHAT ARE YOU... TALKING ABOUT...?
THE RUINS AREN'T SAFE HOUSES FOR THE SPELL CRESTS.
THE SPELL CRESTS ARE NOTHING MORE THAN PARTS.
THE RUINS ARE THE MAIN ENGINE THAT WILL MAKE USE OF THEM TO REWRITE THE WORLD.

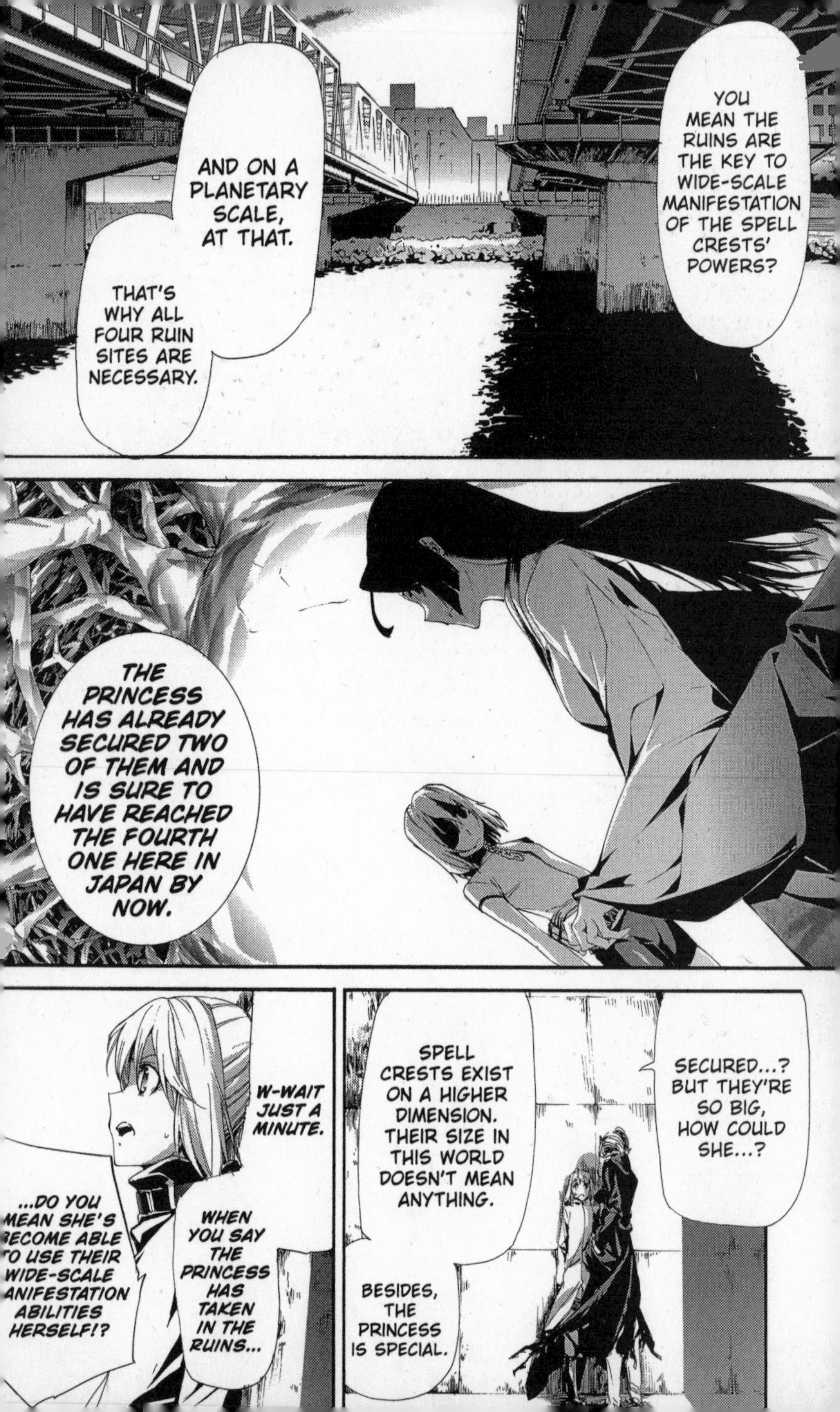
YOU MEAN THE RUINS ARE THE KEY TO WIDE-SCALE MANIFESTATION OF THE SPELL CRESTS' POWERS?
AND ON A PLANETARY SCALE, AT THAT.
THAT'S WHY ALL FOUR RUIN SITES ARE NECESSARY.
THE PRINCESS HAS ALREADY SECURED TWO OF THEM AND IS SURE TO HAVE REACHED THE FOURTH ONE HERE IN JAPAN BY NOW.
SECURED...? BUT THEY'RE SO BIG, HOW COULD SHE...?
SPELL CRESTS EXIST ON A HIGHER DIMENSION. THEIR SIZE IN THIS WORLD DOESN'T MEAN ANYTHING.
BESIDES, THE PRINCESS IS SPECIAL.
W-WAIT JUST A MINUTE.
WHEN YOU SAY THE PRINCESS HAS TAKEN IN THE RUINS...
...DO YOU MEAN SHE'S BECOME ABLE TO USE THEIR WIDE-SCALE MANIFESTATION ABILITIES HERSELF!?

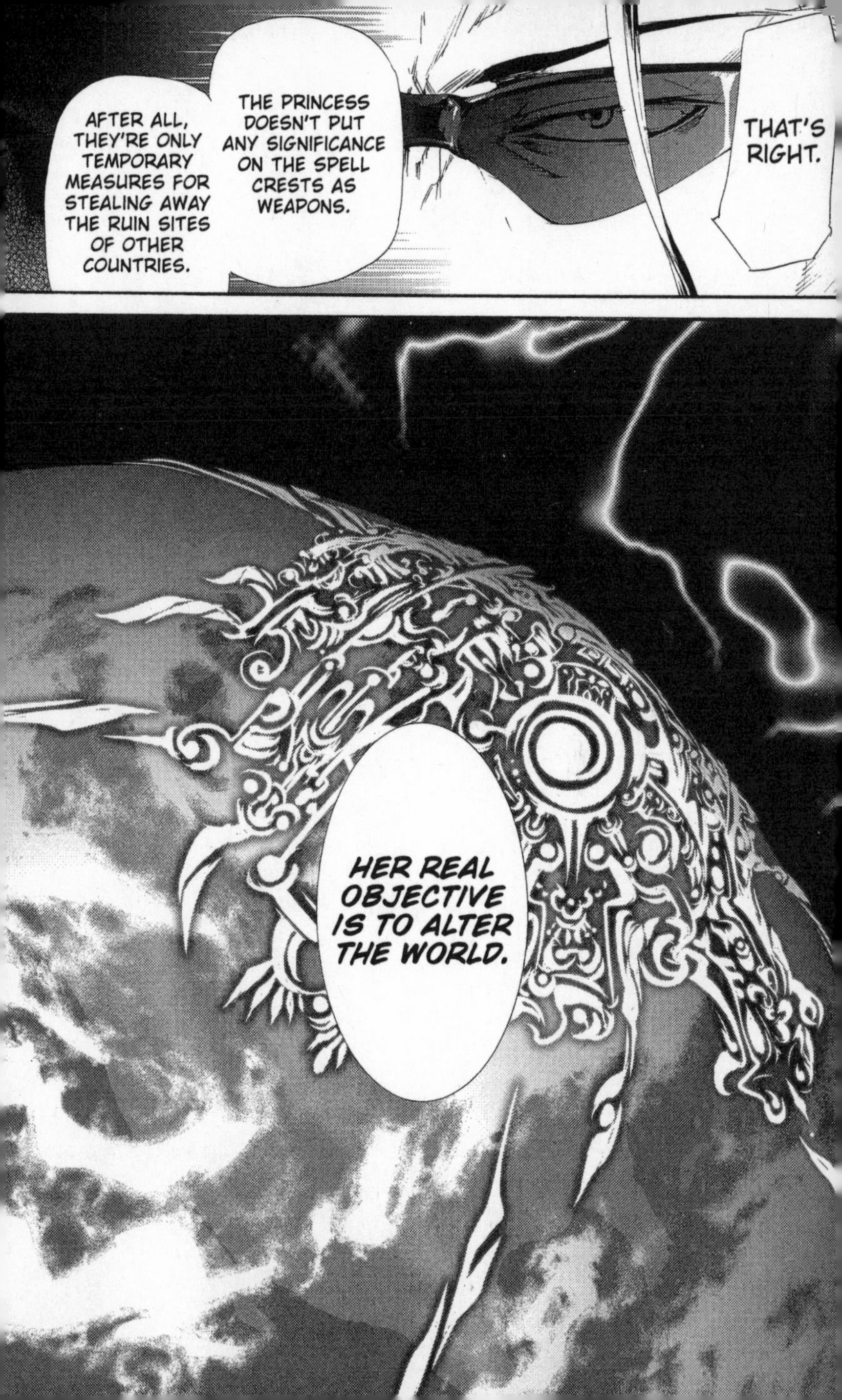
THAT'S RIGHT.
THE PRINCESS DOESN'T PUT ANY SIGNIFICANCE ON THE SPELL CRESTS AS WEAPONS.
AFTER ALL, THEY'RE ONLY TEMPORARY MEASURES FOR STEALING AWAY THE RUIN SITES OF OTHER COUNTRIES.
HER REAL OBJECTIVE IS TO ALTER THE WORLD.

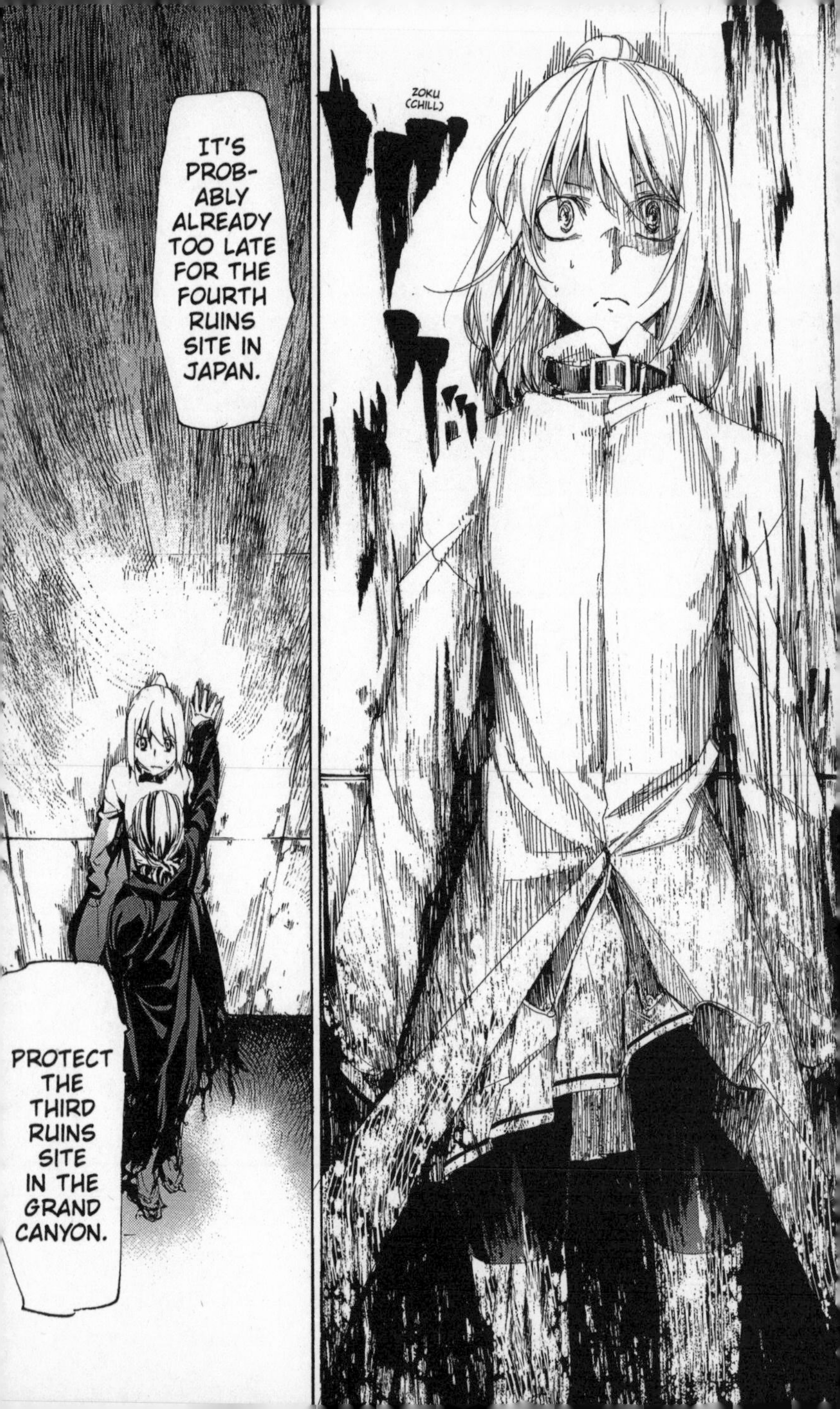
ZOKU (CHILL)
IT'S PROBABLY ALREADY TOO LATE FOR THE FOURTH RUINS SITE IN JAPAN.
PROTECT THE THIRD RUINS SITE IN THE GRAND CANYON.

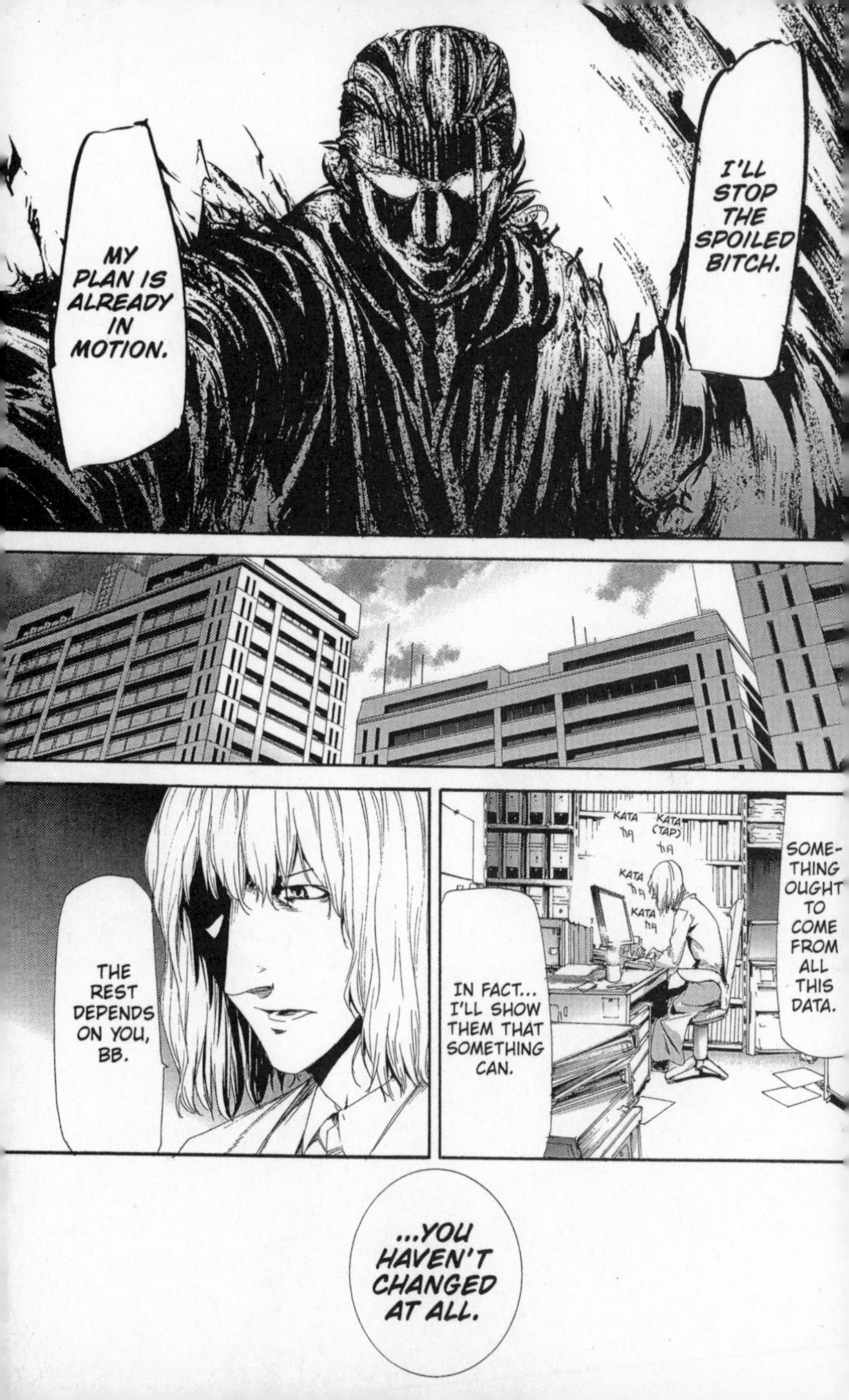
I'LL STOP THE SPOILED BITCH.
MY PLAN IS ALREADY IN MOTION.
SOME-THING OUGHT TO COME FROM ALL THIS DATA.
KATA
KATA (TAP)
KATA
KATA
IN FACT... I'LL SHOW THEM THAT SOMETHING CAN.
THE REST DEPENDS ON YOU, BB.
...YOU HAVEN'T CHANGED AT ALL.

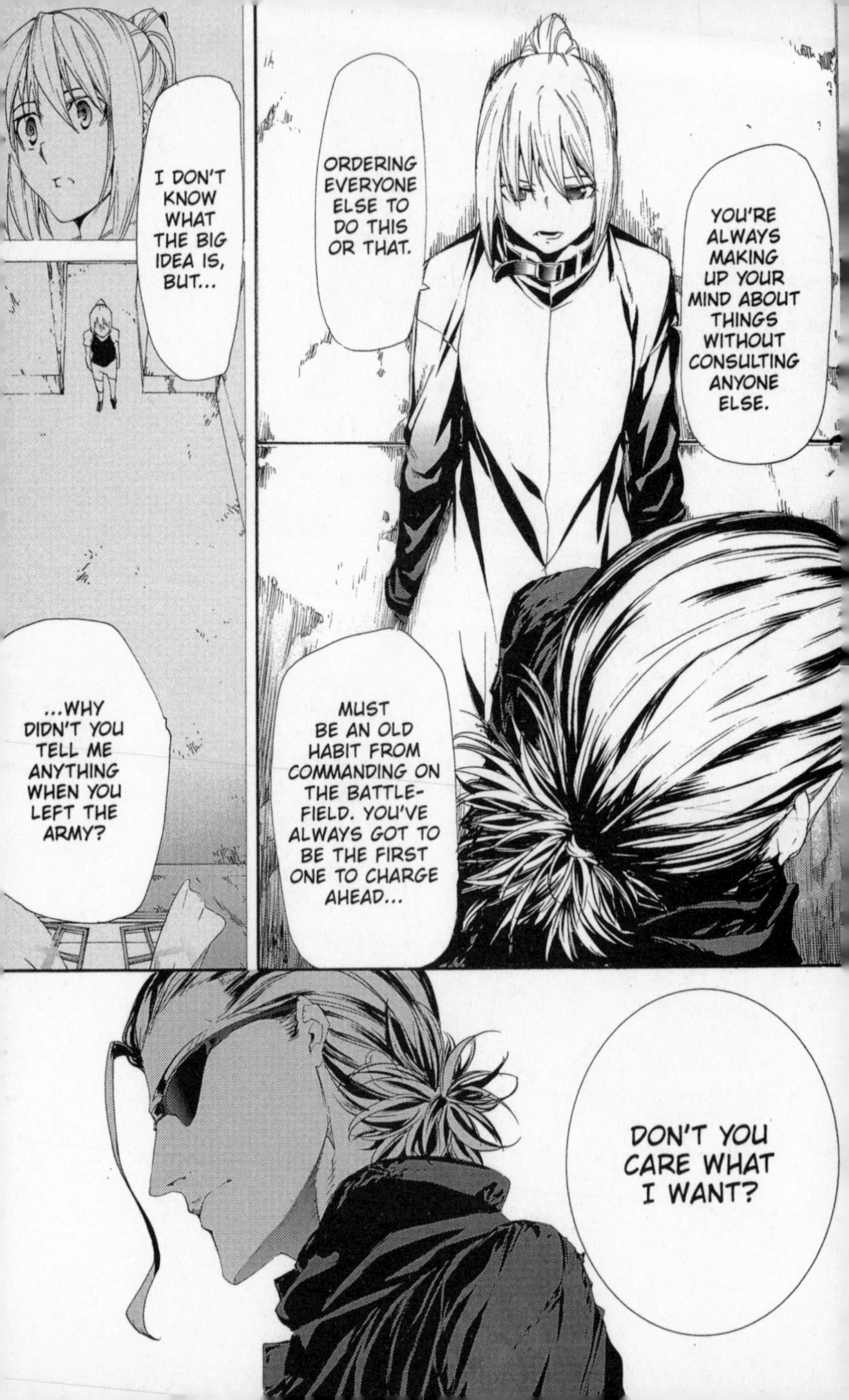
YOU'RE ALWAYS MAKING UP YOUR MIND ABOUT THINGS WITHOUT CONSULTING ANYONE ELSE.
ORDERING EVERYONE ELSE TO DO THIS OR THAT.
MUST BE AN OLD HABIT FROM COMMANDING ON THE BATTLE-FIELD. YOU'VE ALWAYS GOT TO BE THE FIRST ONE TO CHARGE AHEAD...
I DON'T KNOW WHAT THE BIG IDEA IS, BUT...
...WHY DIDN'T YOU TELL ME ANYTHING WHEN YOU LEFT THE ARMY?
DON'T YOU CARE WHAT I WANT?

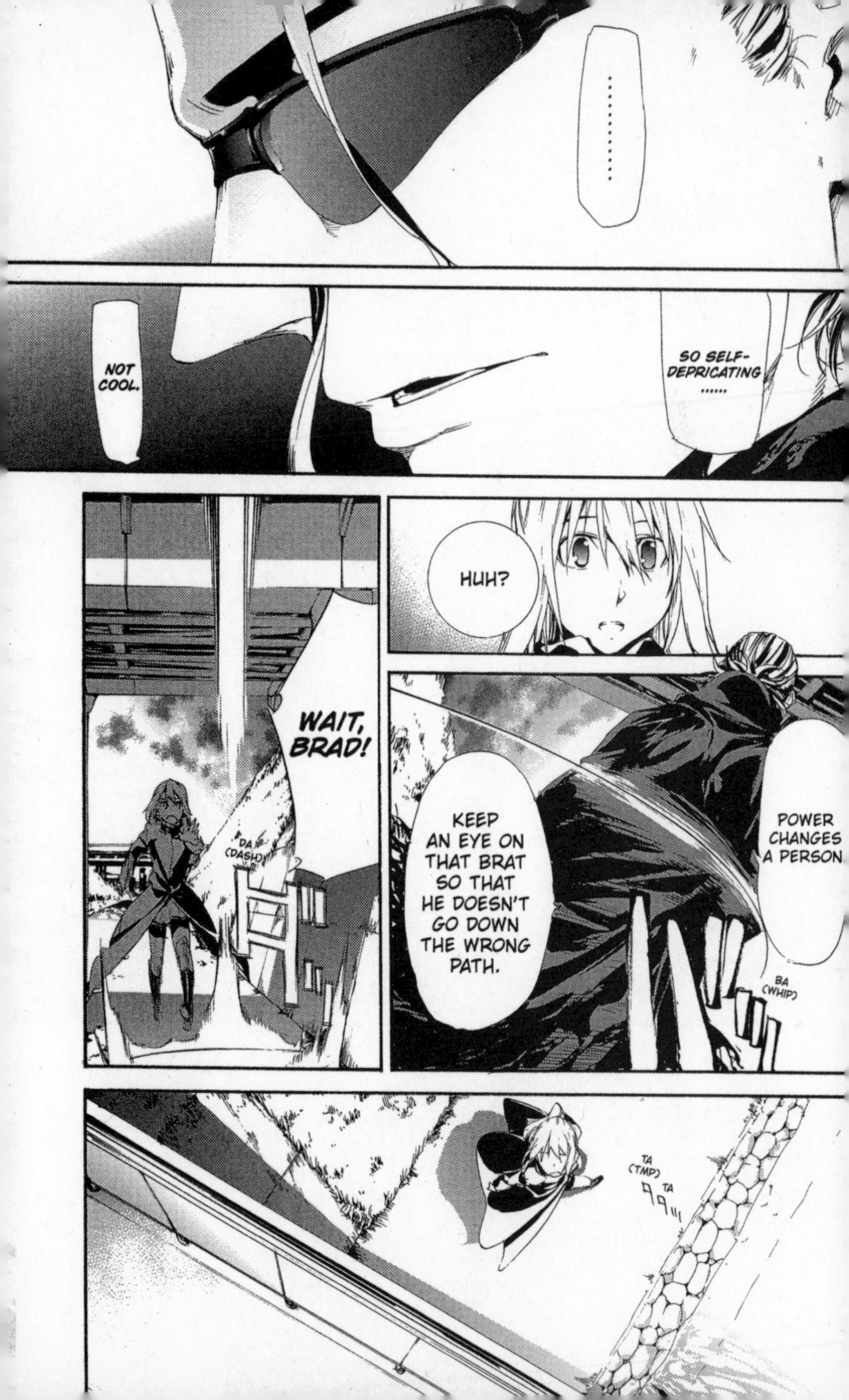
......
SO SELF-DEPRICATING ......
NOT COOL.
HUH?
POWER CHANGES A PERSON.
KEEP AN EYE ON THAT BRAT SO THAT HE DOESN'T GO DOWN THE WRONG PATH.
BA (WHIP)
WAIT, BRAD!
DA (DASH)
TA (TMP) TA

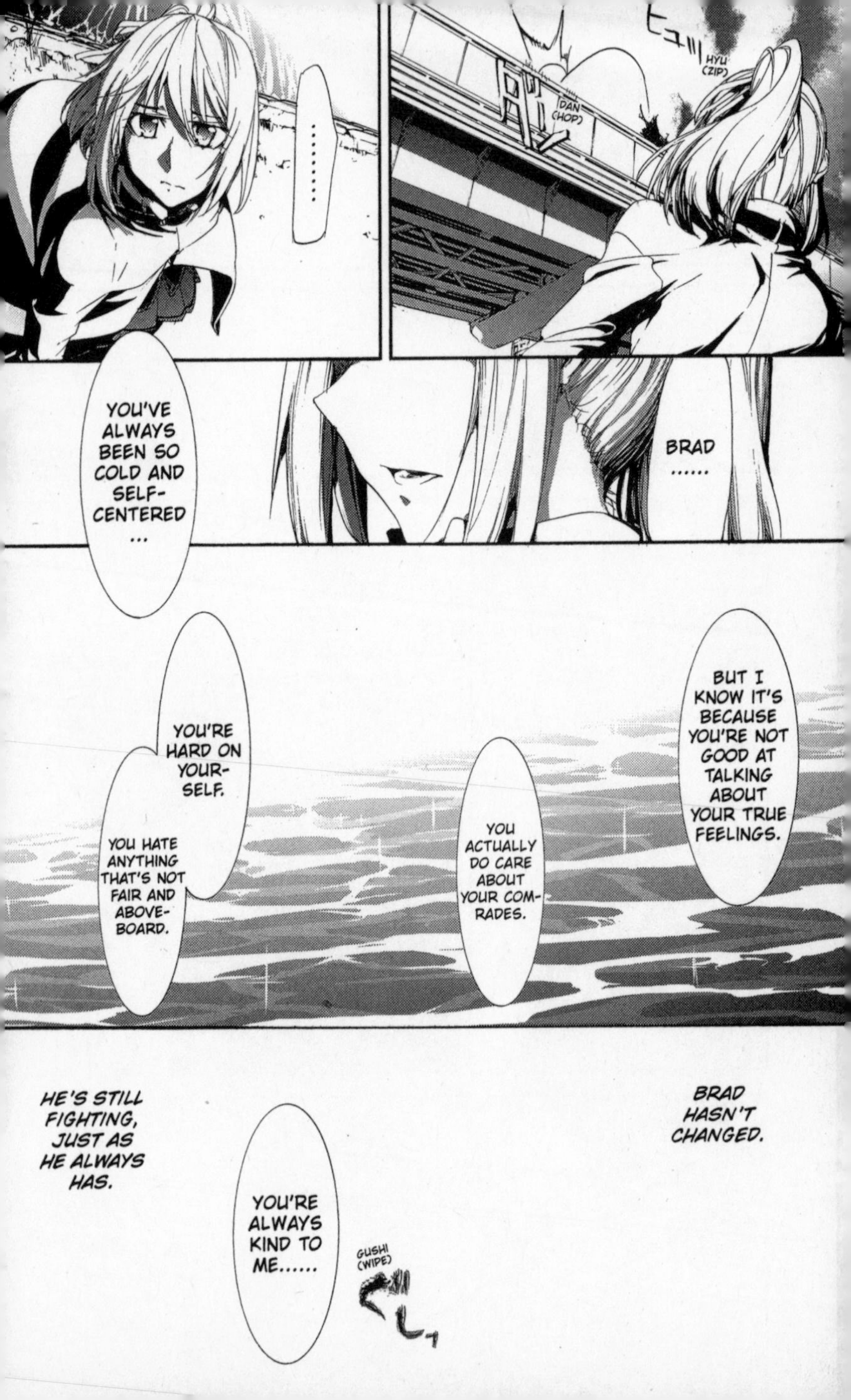

ヒュッ
HYU (ZIP)
DAN (HOP)
......
BRAD ......
YOU'VE ALWAYS BEEN SO COLD AND SELF-CENTERED ...
BUT I KNOW IT'S BECAUSE YOU'RE NOT GOOD AT TALKING ABOUT YOUR TRUE FEELINGS.
YOU ACTUALLY DO CARE ABOUT YOUR COM-RADES.
YOU'RE HARD ON YOUR-SELF.
YOU HATE ANYTHING THAT'S NOT FAIR AND ABOVE-BOARD.
BRAD HASN'T CHANGED.
HE'S STILL FIGHTING, JUST AS HE ALWAYS HAS.
YOU'RE ALWAYS KIND TO ME......
GUSHI (WIPE)

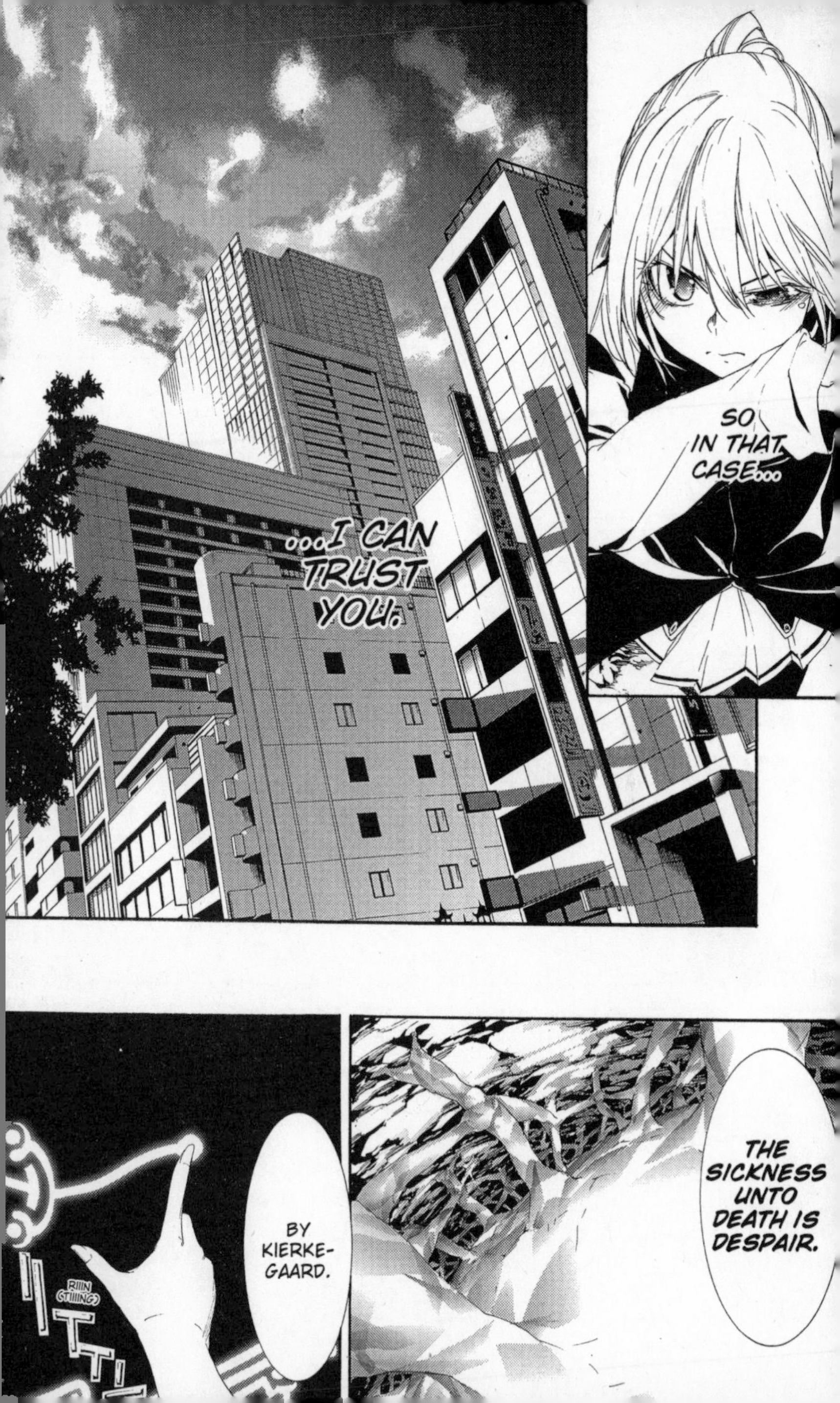
SO IN THAT CASE...
...I CAN TRUST YOU.
THE SICKNESS UNTO DEATH IS DESPAIR.
BY KIERKE-GAARD.
RIIN (TIIIING)

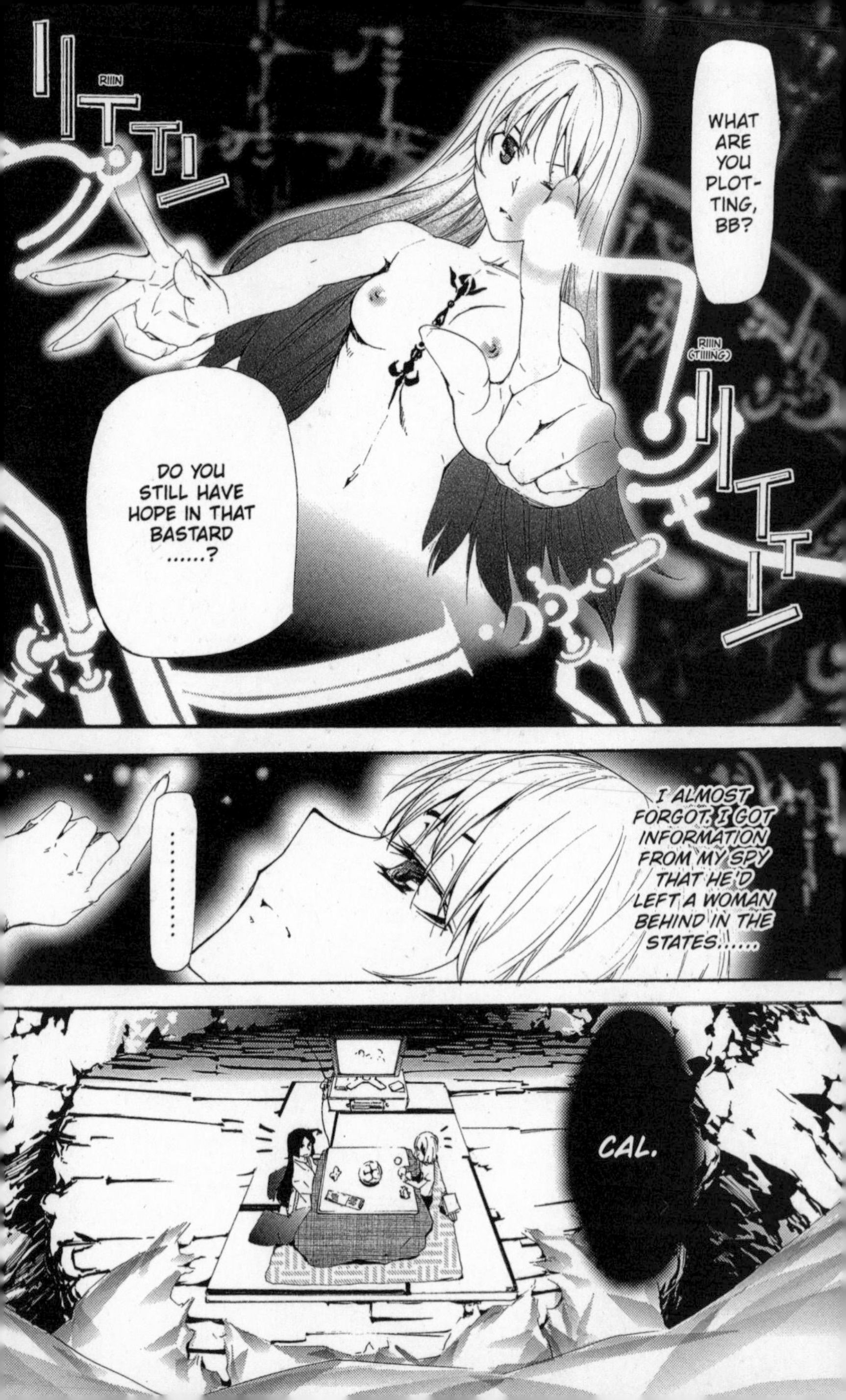
WHAT ARE YOU PLOTTING, BB?
RIIIN (TIIIING)
RIIIN
DO YOU STILL HAVE HOPE IN THAT BASTARD ......?
I ALMOST FORGOT. I GOT INFORMATION FROM MY SPY THAT HE'D LEFT A WOMAN BEHIND IN THE STATES......
......
CAL.

TABOO TATTOO

TABOO TATTOO

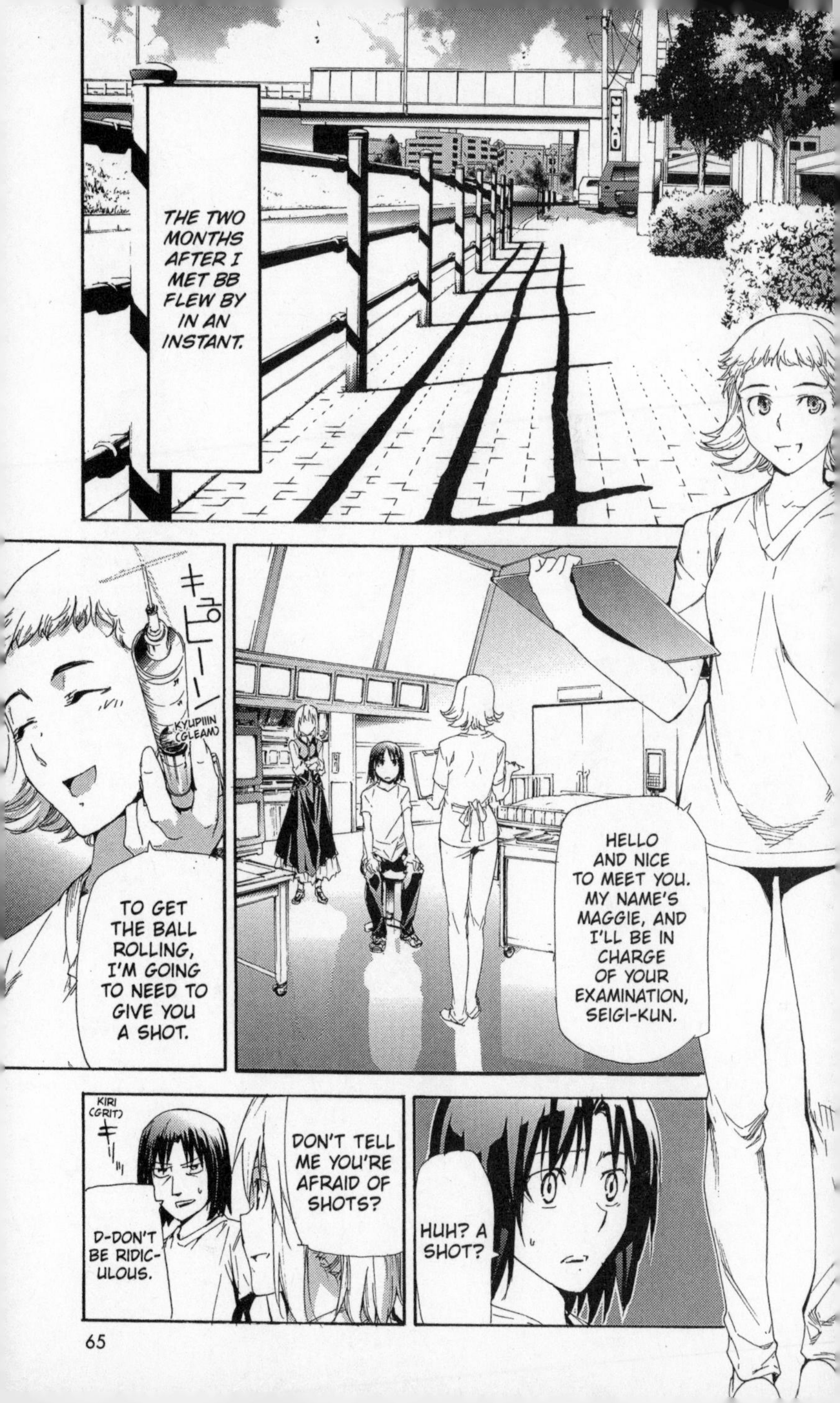
THE TWO MONTHS AFTER I MET BB FLEW BY IN AN INSTANT.
HELLO AND NICE TO MEET YOU. MY NAME'S MAGGIE, AND I'LL BE IN CHARGE OF YOUR EXAMINATION, SEIGI-KUN.
KYUPIIIN (GLEAM)
TO GET THE BALL ROLLING, I'M GOING TO NEED TO GIVE YOU A SHOT.
HUH? A SHOT?
DON'T TELL ME YOU'RE AFRAID OF SHOTS?
KIRI (GRIT)
D-DON'T BE RIDIC-ULOUS.

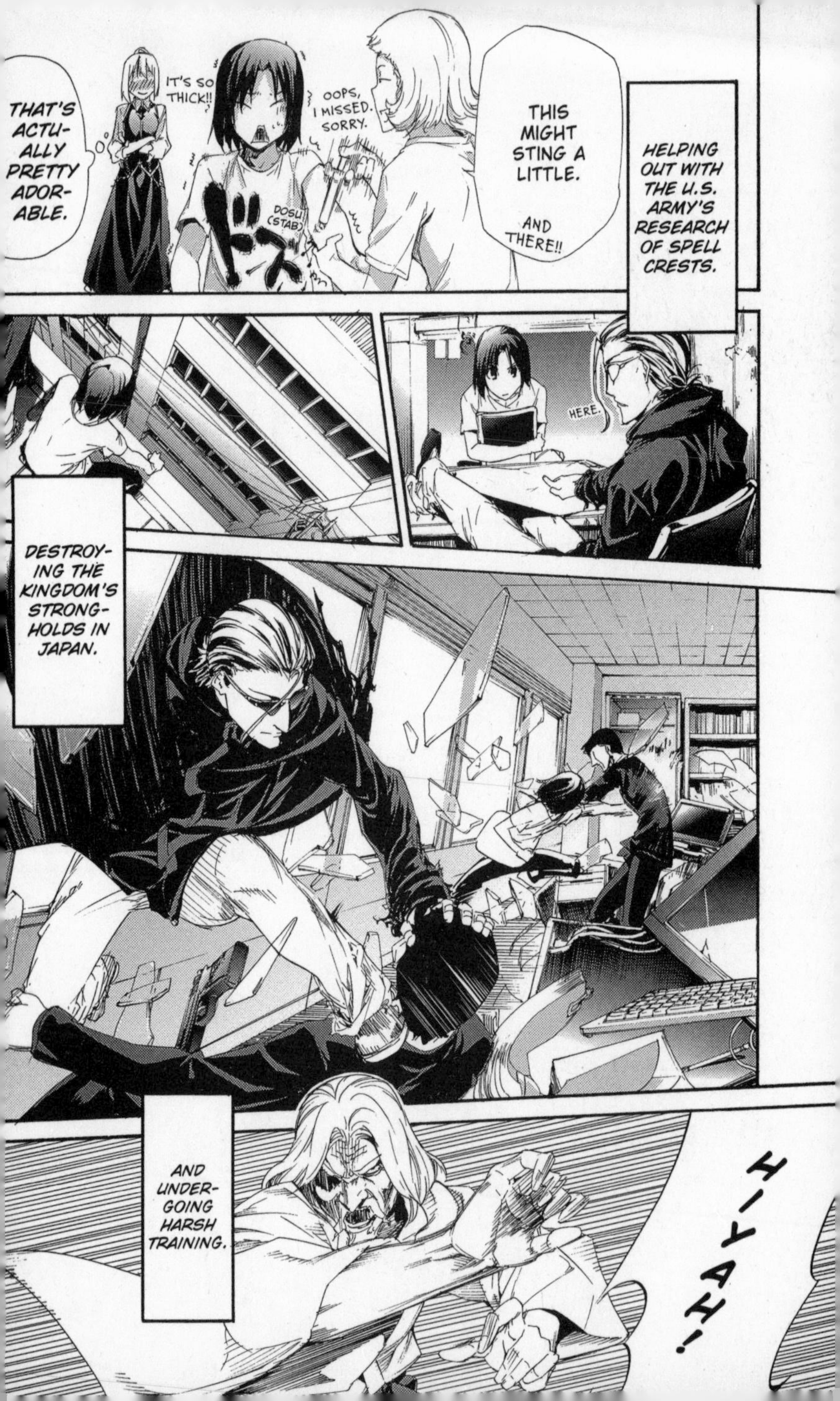
HELPING OUT WITH THE U.S. ARMY'S RESEARCH OF SPELL CRESTS.
THIS MIGHT STING A LITTLE.
AND THERE!!
OOPS, I MISSED. SORRY.
DOSU (STAB)
IT'S SO THICK!!
THAT'S ACTUALLY PRETTY ADORABLE.
HERE.
DESTROYING THE KINGDOM'S STRONGHOLDS IN JAPAN.
HI-YAH!
AND UNDERGOING HARSH TRAINING.

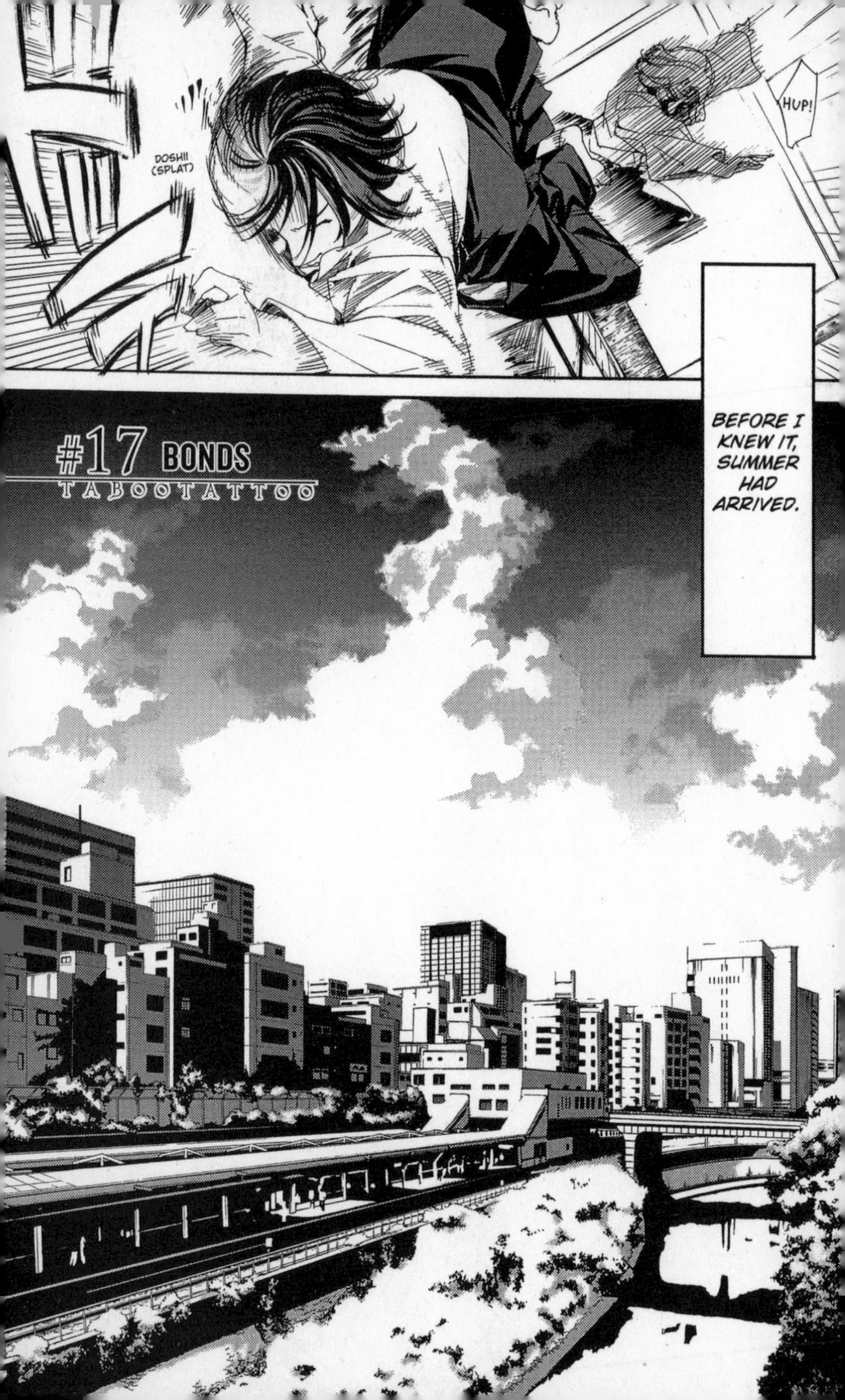
HUP!
DOSHII (SPLAT)
BEFORE I KNEW IT, SUMMER HAD ARRIVED.
#17 BONDS
TABOOTATTOO

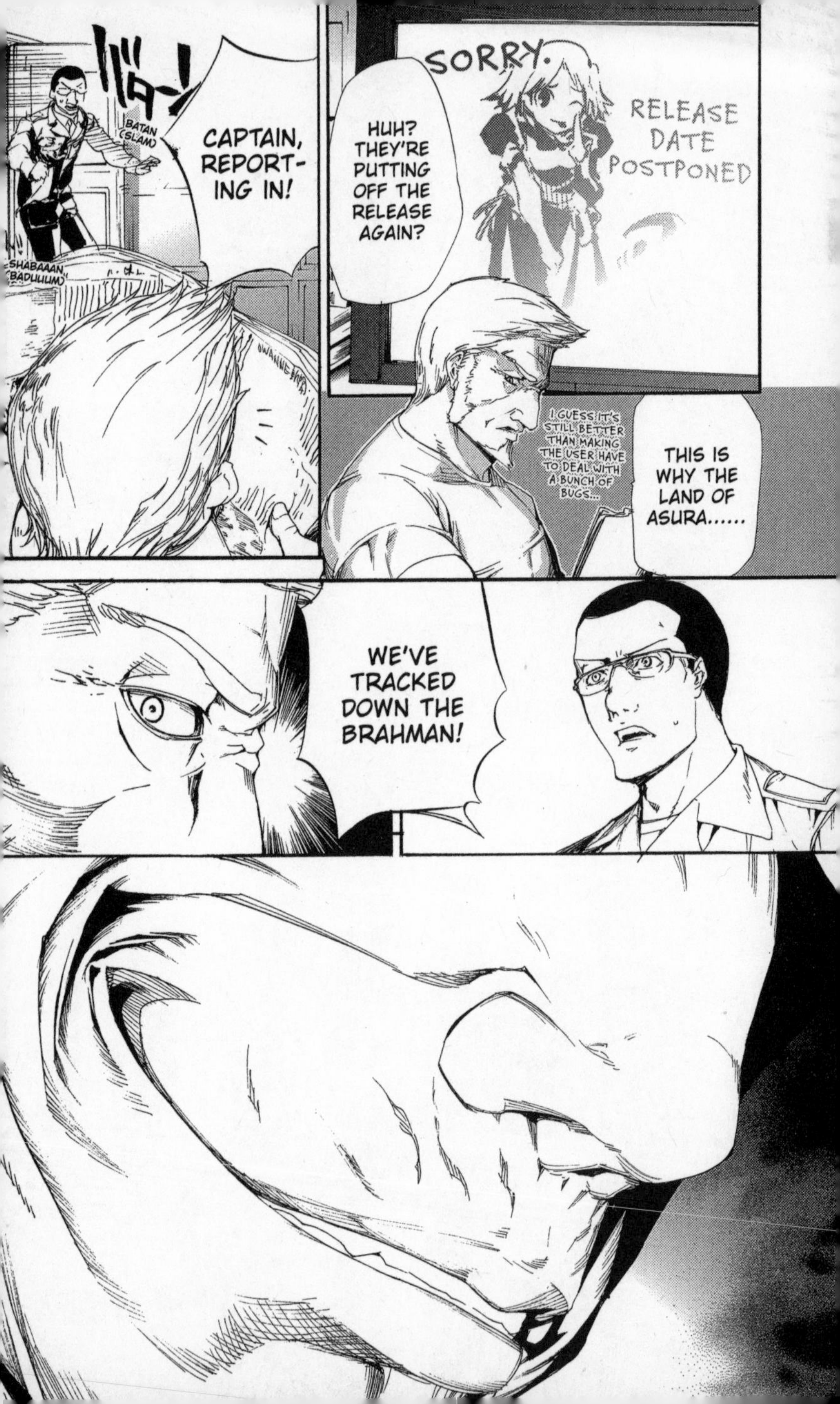
SORRY.
RELEASE DATE POSTPONED
HUH? THEY'RE PUTTING OFF THE RELEASE AGAIN?
I GUESS IT'S STILL BETTER THAN MAKING THE USER HAVE TO DEAL WITH A BUNCH OF BUGS...
THIS IS WHY THE LAND OF ASURA......
BATAN (SLAM)
CAPTAIN, REPORTING IN!
SHABAAAN (BADUUUM)
WE'VE TRACKED DOWN THE BRAHMAN!

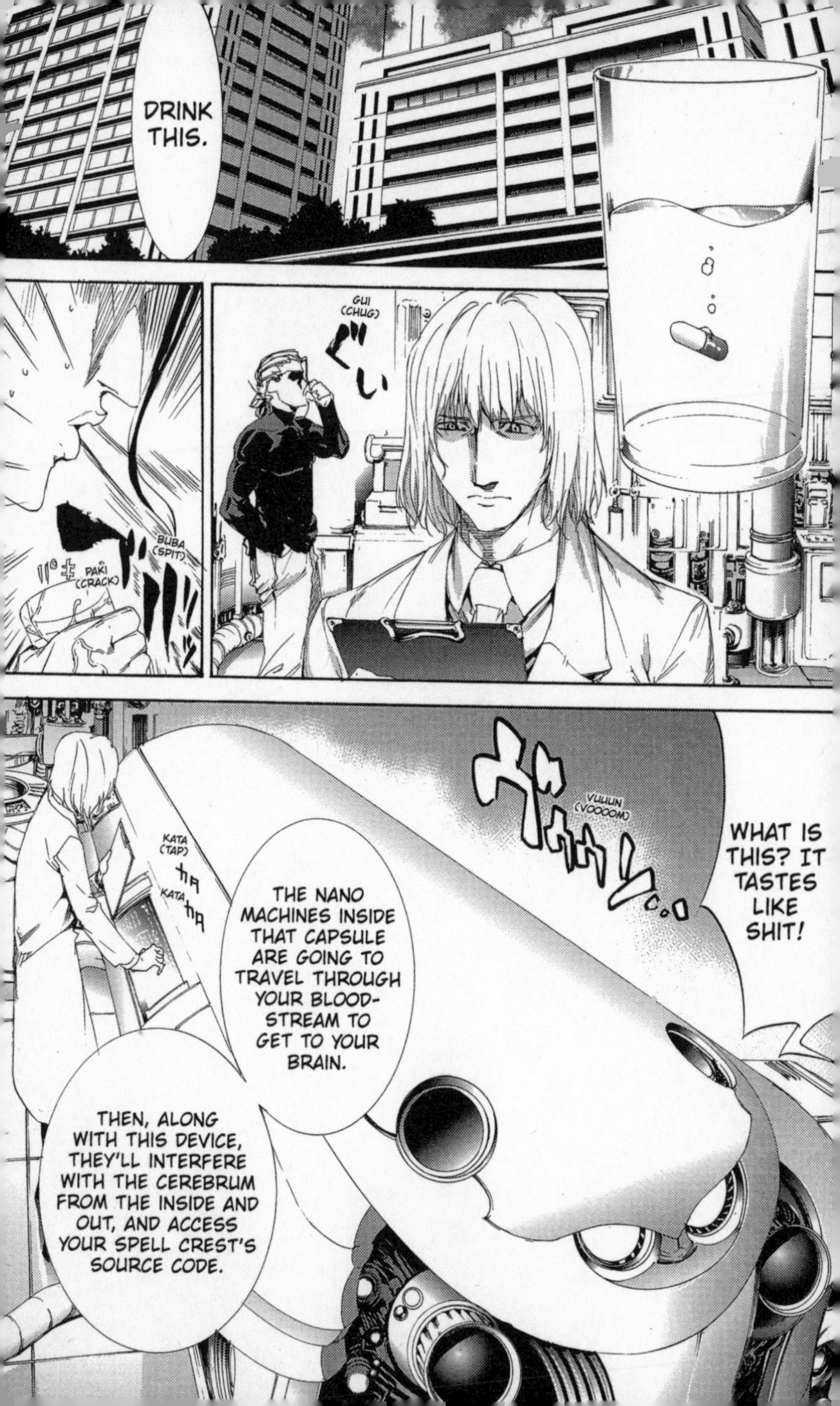
DRINK THIS.
GUI (CHUG)
ぐい
BUBA (SPIT)
PAKI (CRACK)
WHAT IS THIS? IT TASTES LIKE SHIT!
VUUUN (VOOOOM)
THE NANO MACHINES INSIDE THAT CAPSULE ARE GOING TO TRAVEL THROUGH YOUR BLOOD-STREAM TO GET TO YOUR BRAIN.
KATA (TAP)
KATA
THEN, ALONG WITH THIS DEVICE, THEY'LL INTERFERE WITH THE CEREBRUM FROM THE INSIDE AND OUT, AND ACCESS YOUR SPELL CREST'S SOURCE CODE.

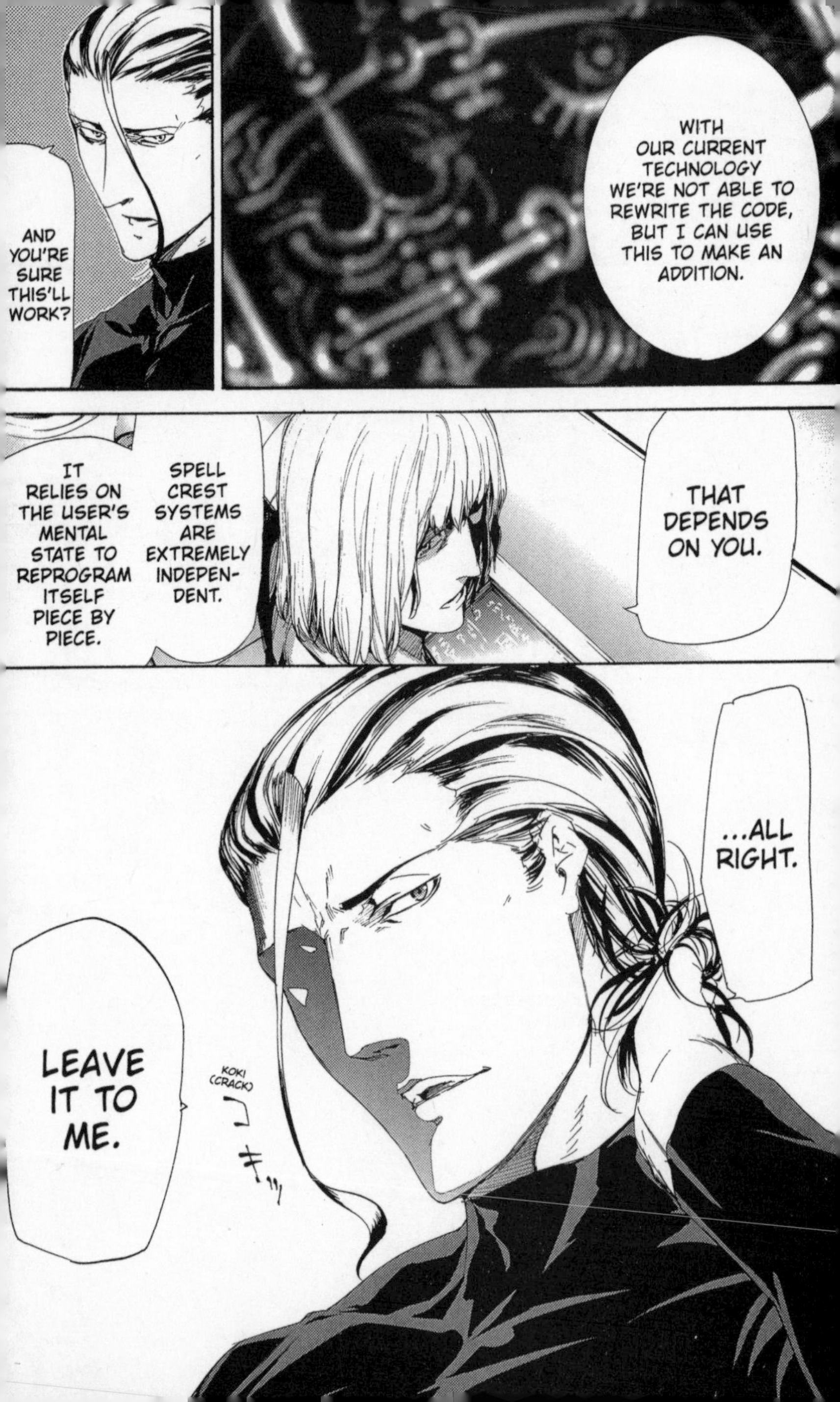
WITH OUR CURRENT TECHNOLOGY WE'RE NOT ABLE TO REWRITE THE CODE, BUT I CAN USE THIS TO MAKE AN ADDITION.
AND YOU'RE SURE THIS'LL WORK?
THAT DEPENDS ON YOU.
SPELL CREST SYSTEMS ARE EXTREMELY INDEPEN-DENT.
IT RELIES ON THE USER'S MENTAL STATE TO REPROGRAM ITSELF PIECE BY PIECE.
...ALL RIGHT.
KOKI (CRACK)
LEAVE IT TO ME.

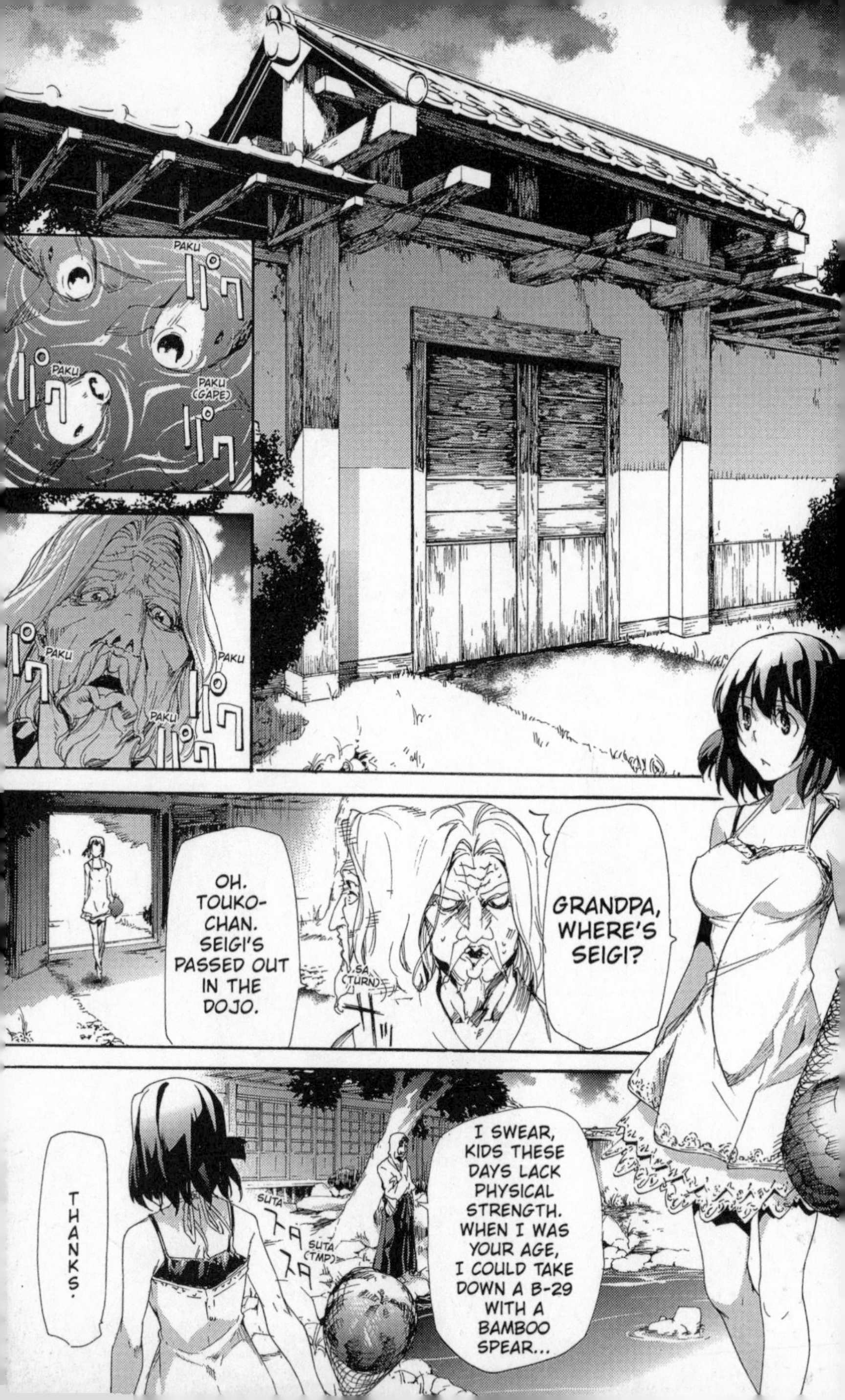
PAKU
PAKU (GAPE)
PAKU
PAKU
PAKU
PAKU
GRANDPA, WHERE'S SEIGI?
SA (TURN)
OH. TOUKO-CHAN. SEIGI'S PASSED OUT IN THE DOJO.
I SWEAR, KIDS THESE DAYS LACK PHYSICAL STRENGTH. WHEN I WAS YOUR AGE, I COULD TAKE DOWN A B-29 WITH A BAMBOO SPEAR...
SUTA
SUTA (TMP)
THANKS.

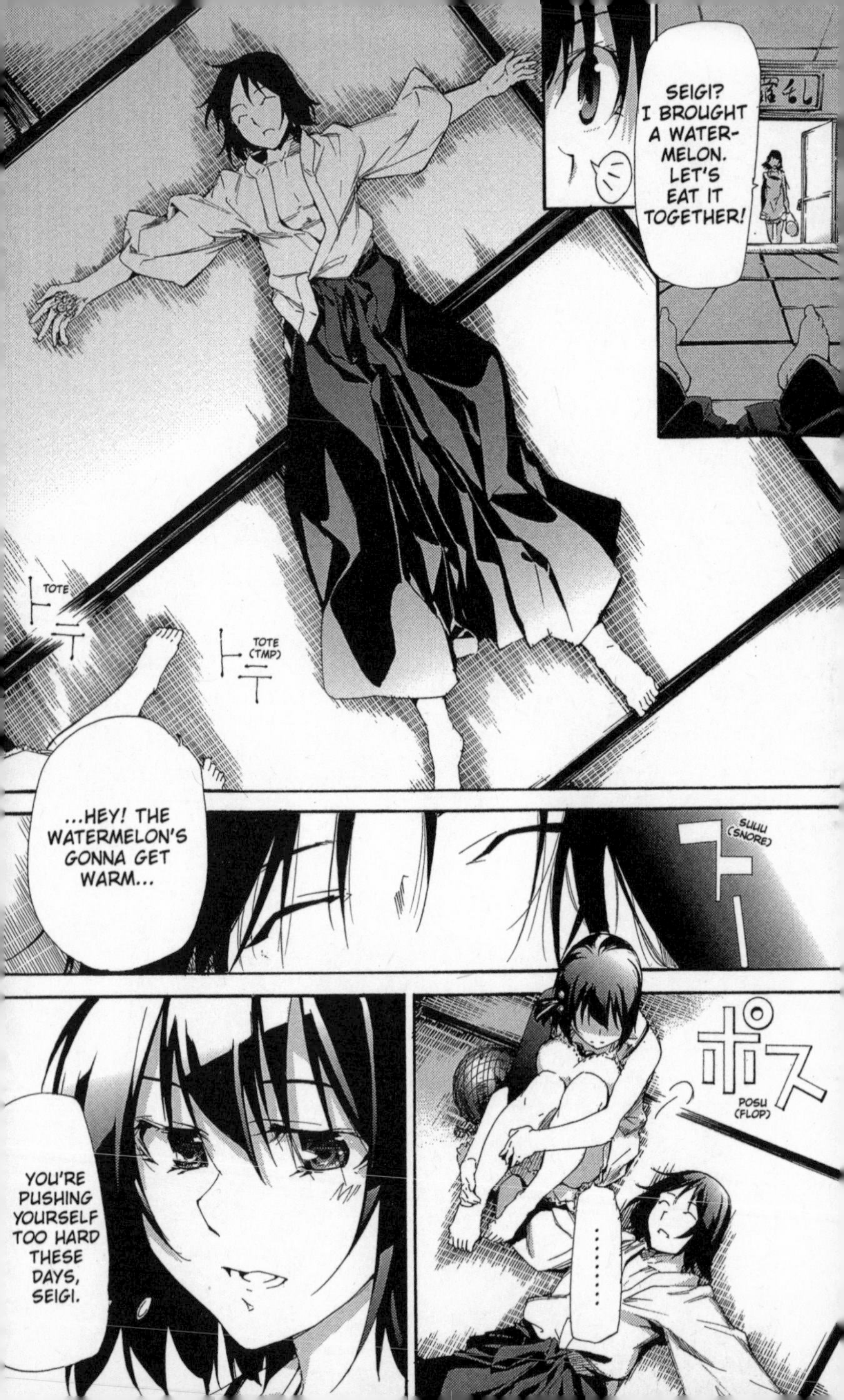
SEIGI? I BROUGHT A WATER-MELON. LET'S EAT IT TOGETHER!
TOTE
TOTE (TMP)
...HEY! THE WATERMELON'S GONNA GET WARM...
SUUU (SNORE)
ポス
POSU (FLOP)
......
YOU'RE PUSHING YOURSELF TOO HARD THESE DAYS, SEIGI.

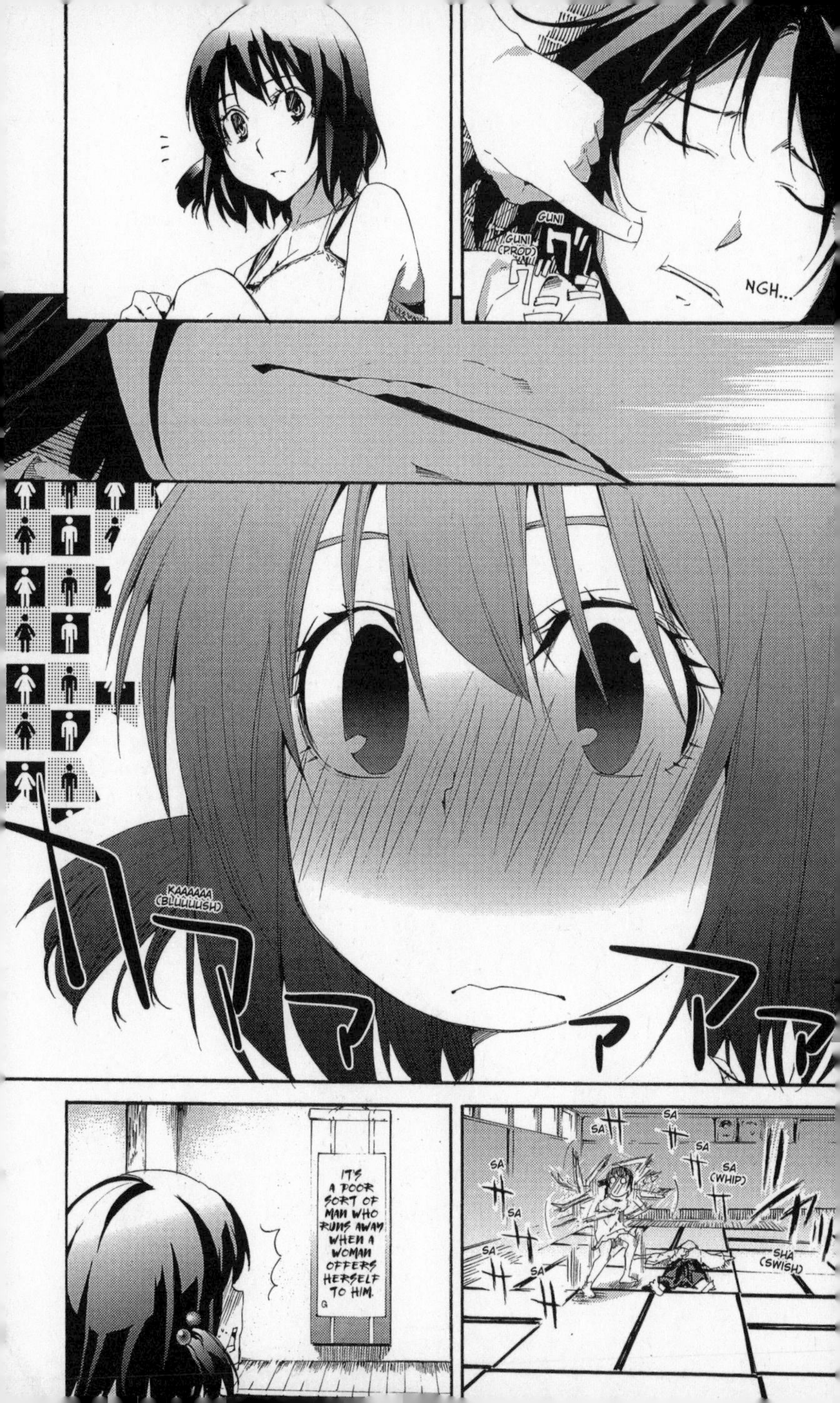
GUNI
GUNI
(PROD)
NGH...
KAAAAAA
(BLUUUUSH)
SA
SA
SA
SA (WHIP)
SA
SA
SA
SA
SHA (SWISH)
IT'S A POOR SORT OF MAN WHO RUNS AWAY WHEN A WOMAN OFFERS HERSELF TO HIM.

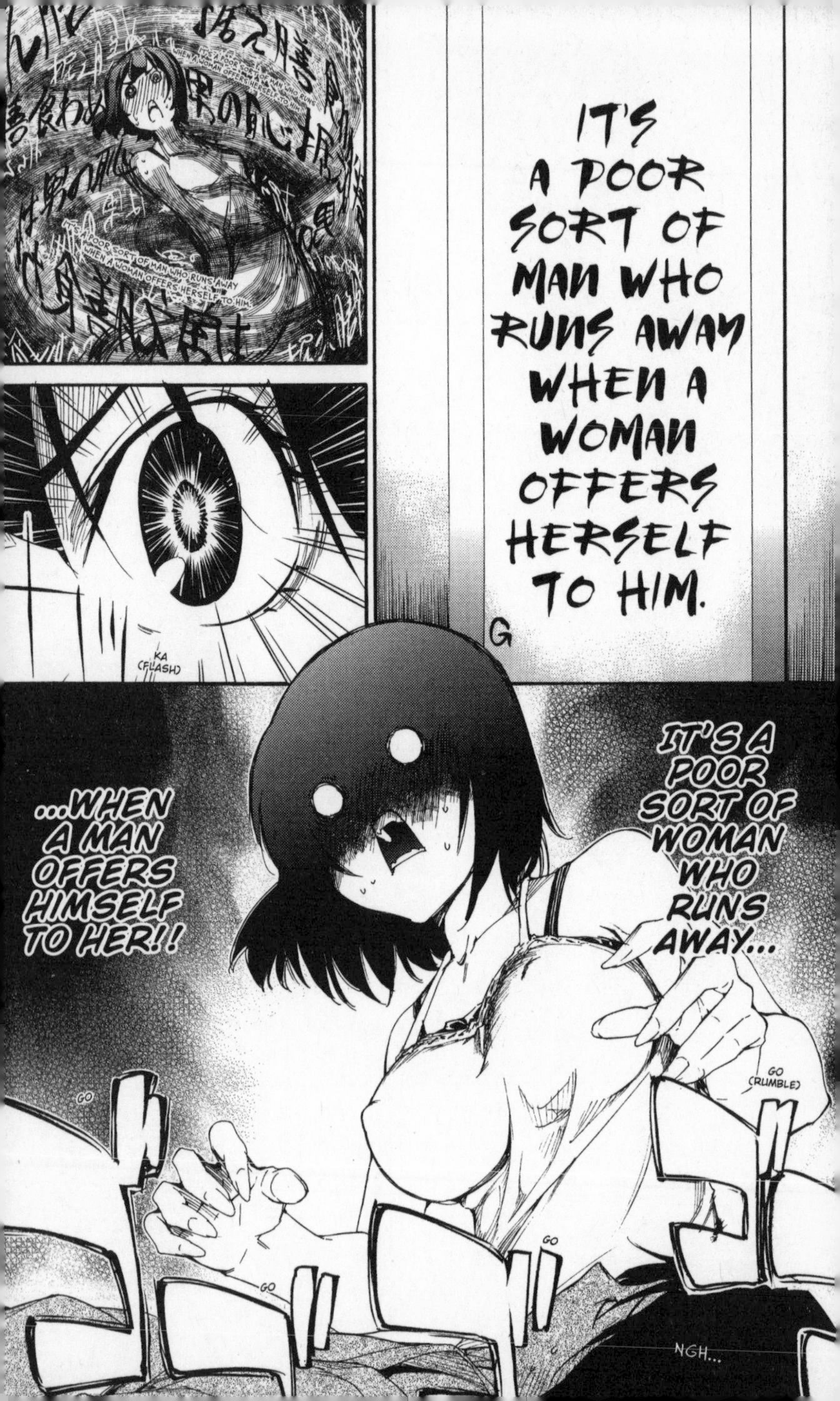
IT'S A POOR SORT OF MAN WHO RUNS AWAY WHEN A WOMAN OFFERS HERSELF TO HIM.
G
IT'S A POOR SORT OF MAN WHO RUNS WHEN A WOMAN OFFERS HERSELF TO HIM
IT'S A POOR SORT OF MAN WHO RUNS AWAY WHEN A WOMAN OFFERS HERSELF TO HIM.
KA (FLASH)
IT'S A POOR SORT OF WOMAN WHO RUNS AWAY...
...WHEN A MAN OFFERS HIMSELF TO HER!!
GO (RUMBLE)
GO
GO
GO
NGH...

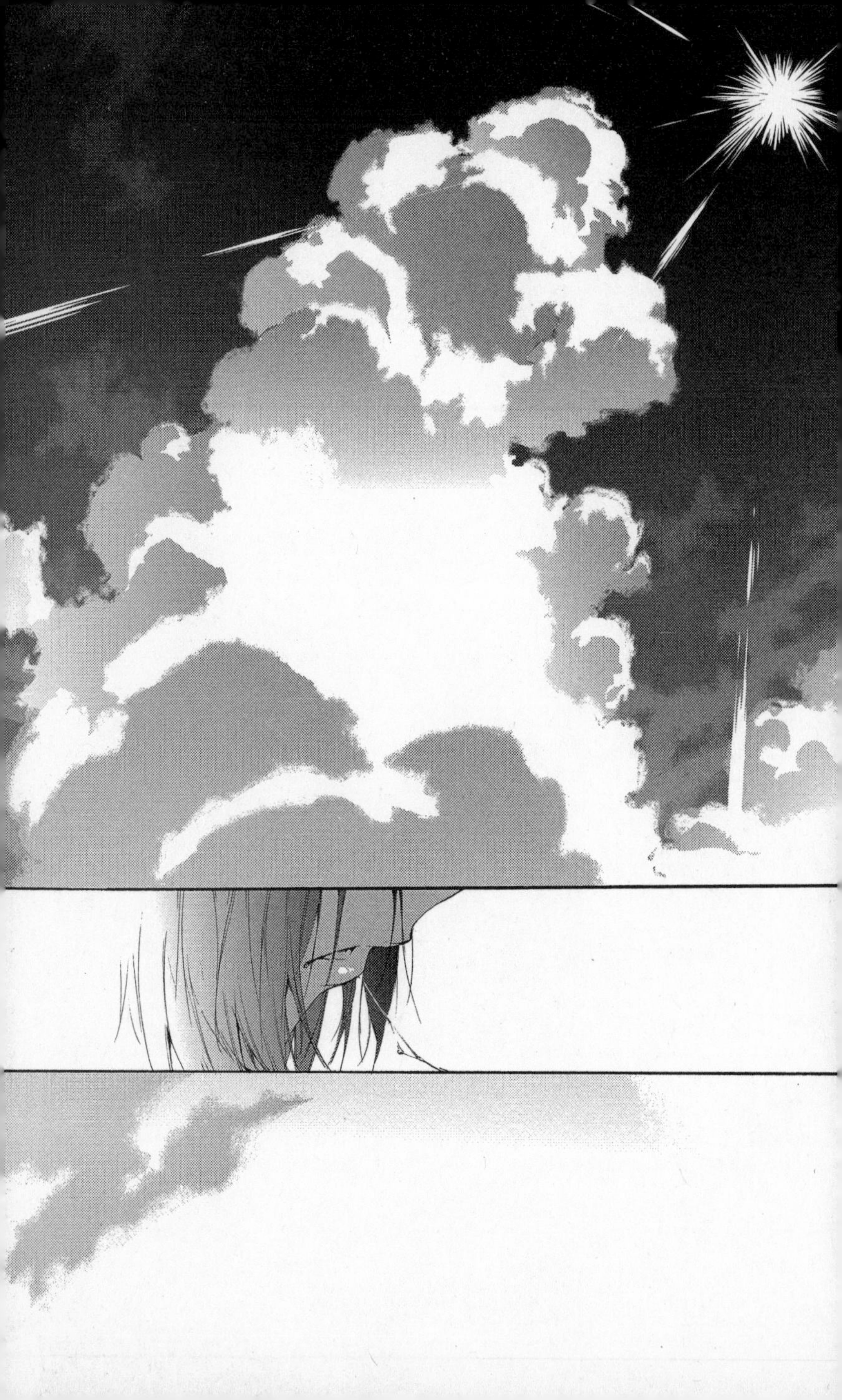

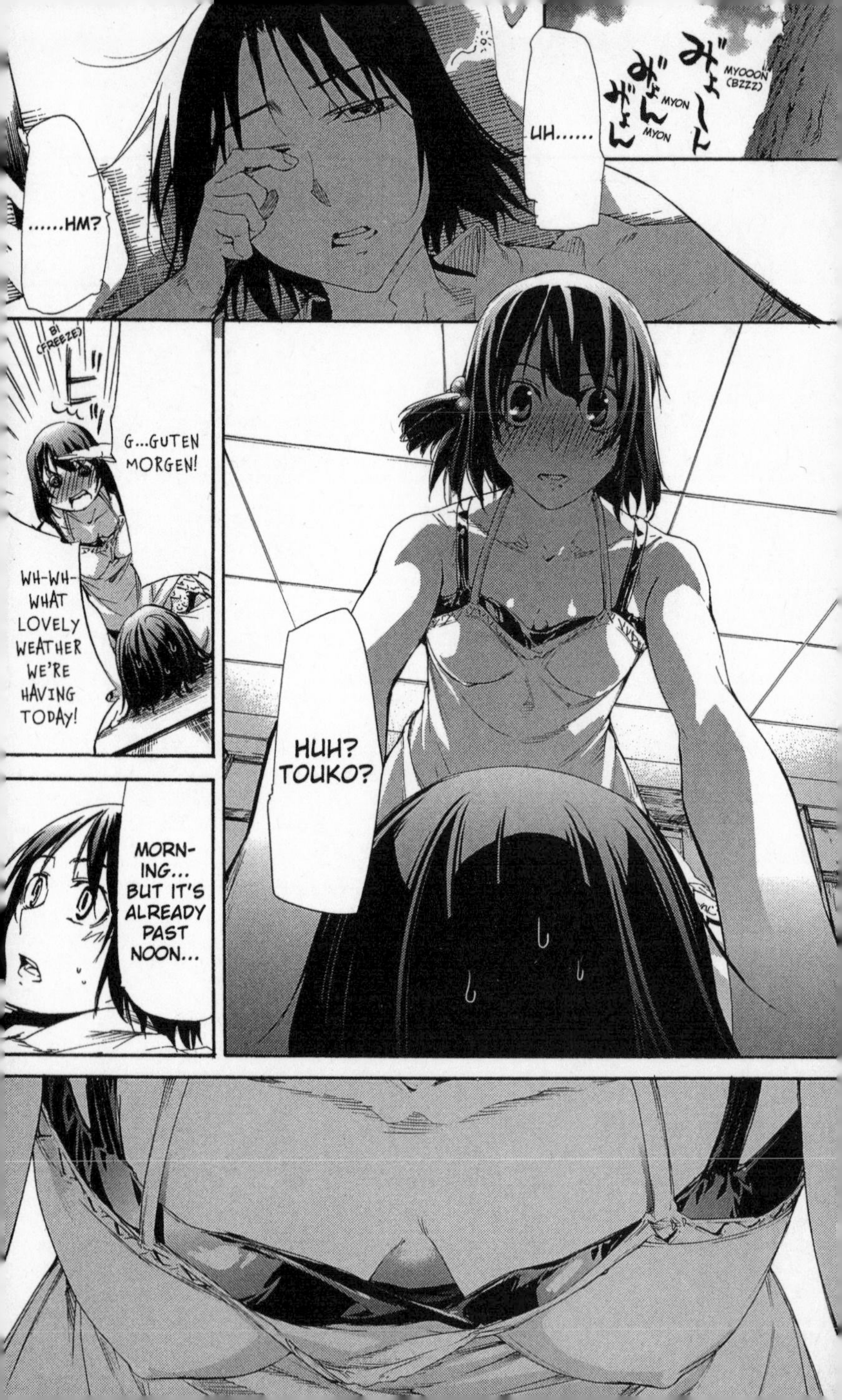

みょーん
MYOOON (BZZZ)
みょん
MYON
みょん
MYON
UH......
......HM?
HUH? TOUKO?
ビ
BI (FREEZE)
G...GUTEN MORGEN!
WH-WH-WHAT LOVELY WEATHER WE'RE HAVING TODAY!
MORNING... BUT IT'S ALREADY PAST NOON...

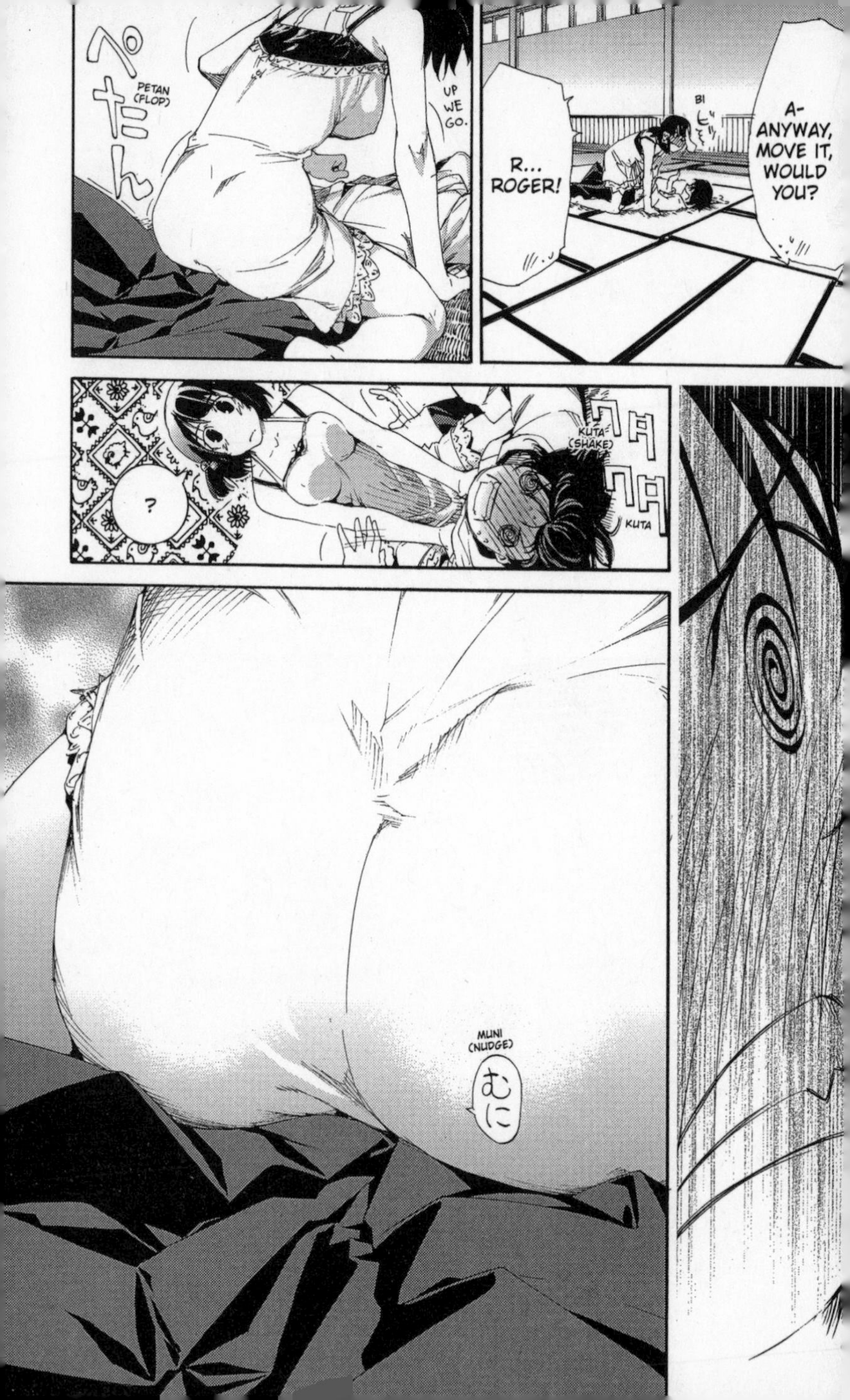
A- ANYWAY, MOVE IT, WOULD YOU?
BI
ビ
R... ROGER!
UP WE GO.
PETAN (FLOP)
ぺたん
KUTA (SHAKE)
クタ
KUTA
クタ
?
MUNI (NUDGE)
むに

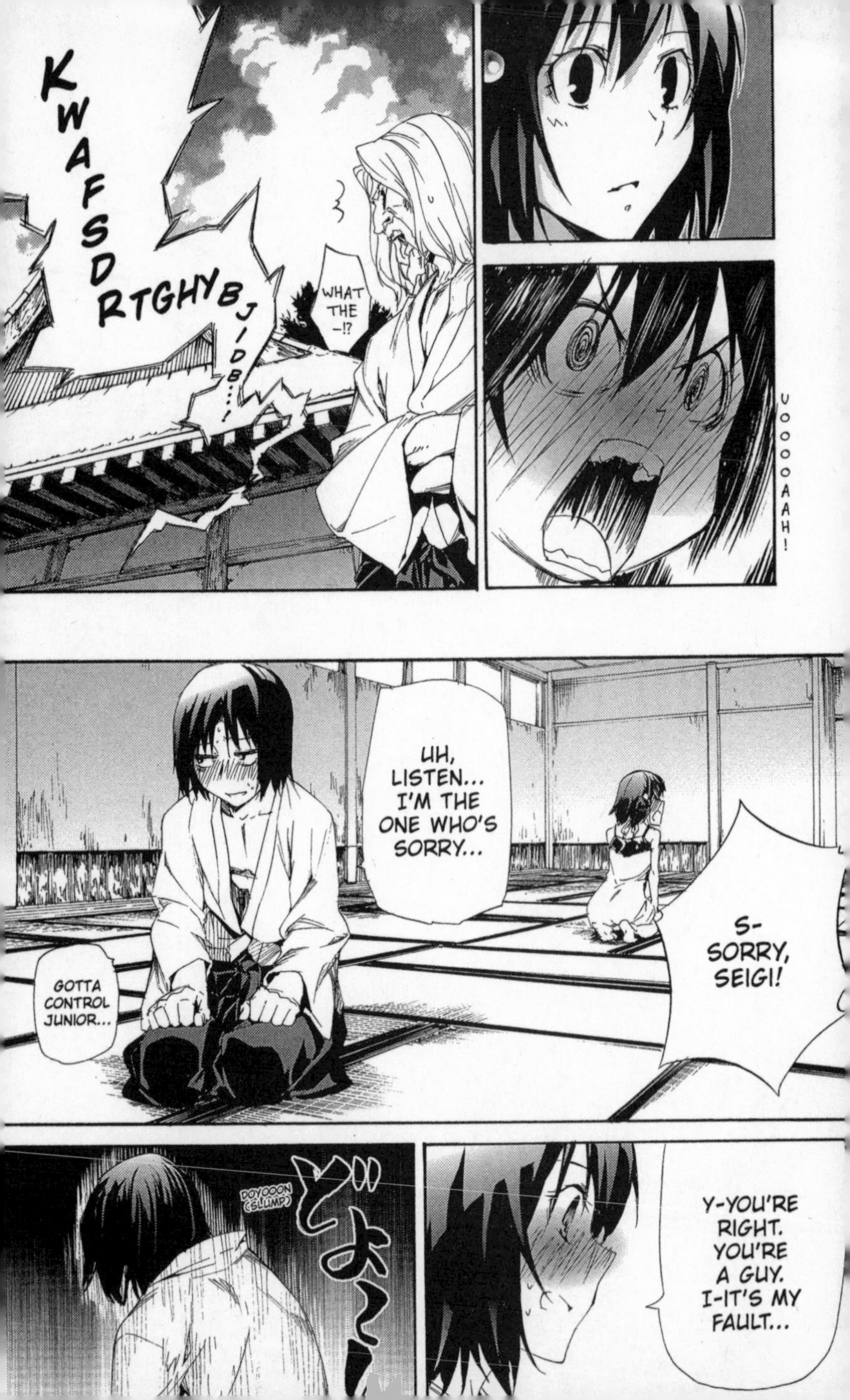
UOOOOAAH!
KWAFSDRTGHYBJIDB...!
WHAT THE —!?
S-SORRY, SEIGI!
UH, LISTEN... I'M THE ONE WHO'S SORRY...
GOTTA CONTROL JUNIOR...
Y-YOU'RE RIGHT. YOU'RE A GUY. I-IT'S MY FAULT...
DOYOOON (SLUMP)

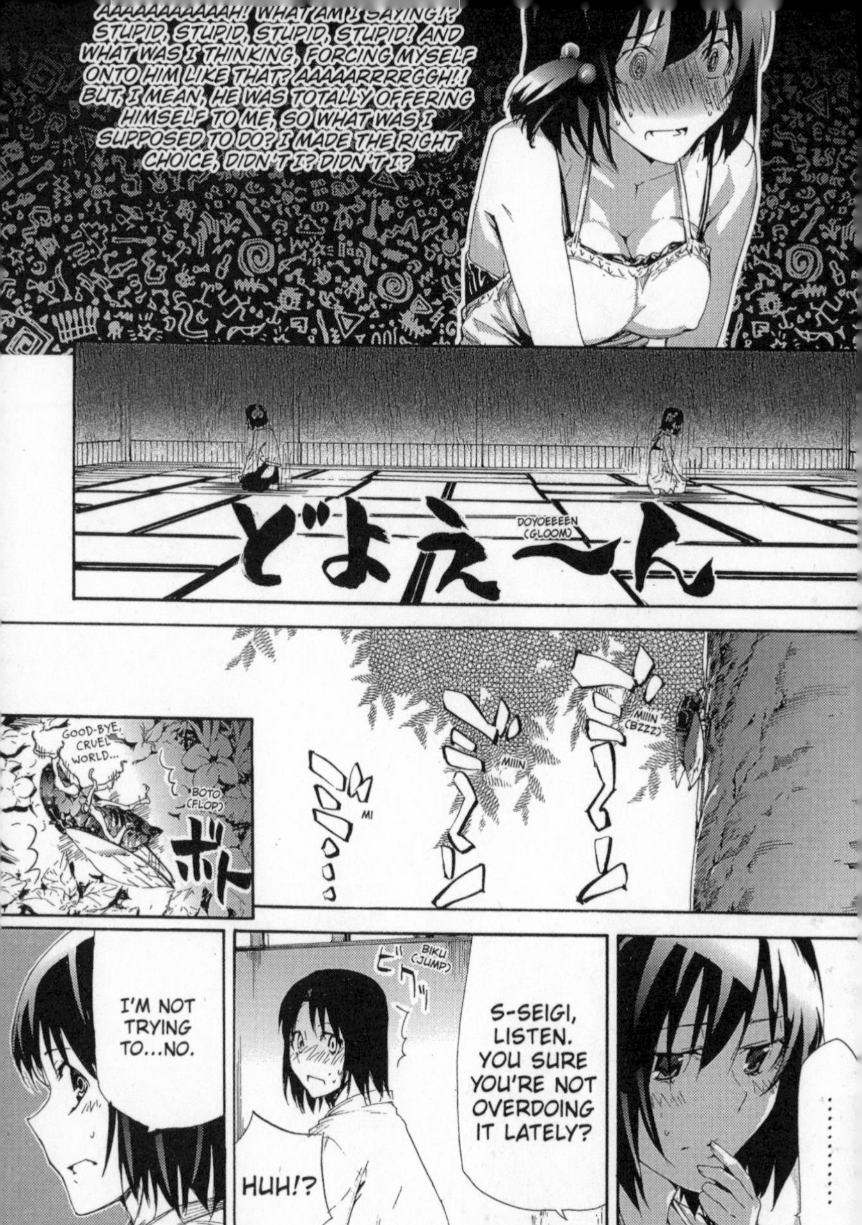
AAAAAAAAAAAAH! WHAT AM I SAYING!? STUPID, STUPID, STUPID, STUPID! AND WHAT WAS I THINKING, FORCING MYSELF ONTO HIM LIKE THAT? AAAAARRRRGGH!! BUT, I MEAN, HE WAS TOTALLY OFFERING HIMSELF TO ME, SO WHAT WAS I SUPPOSED TO DO? I MADE THE RIGHT CHOICE, DIDN'T I? DIDN'T I?
どよえ〜ん
DOYOEEEEN (GLOOM)
MIIIN (BZZZ)
MIIIN
MI
GOOD-BYE, CRUEL WORLD...
ボト
BOTO (FLOP)
......
S-SEIGI, LISTEN. YOU SURE YOU'RE NOT OVERDOING IT LATELY?
BIKU (JUMP)
HUH!?
I'M NOT TRYING TO...NO.

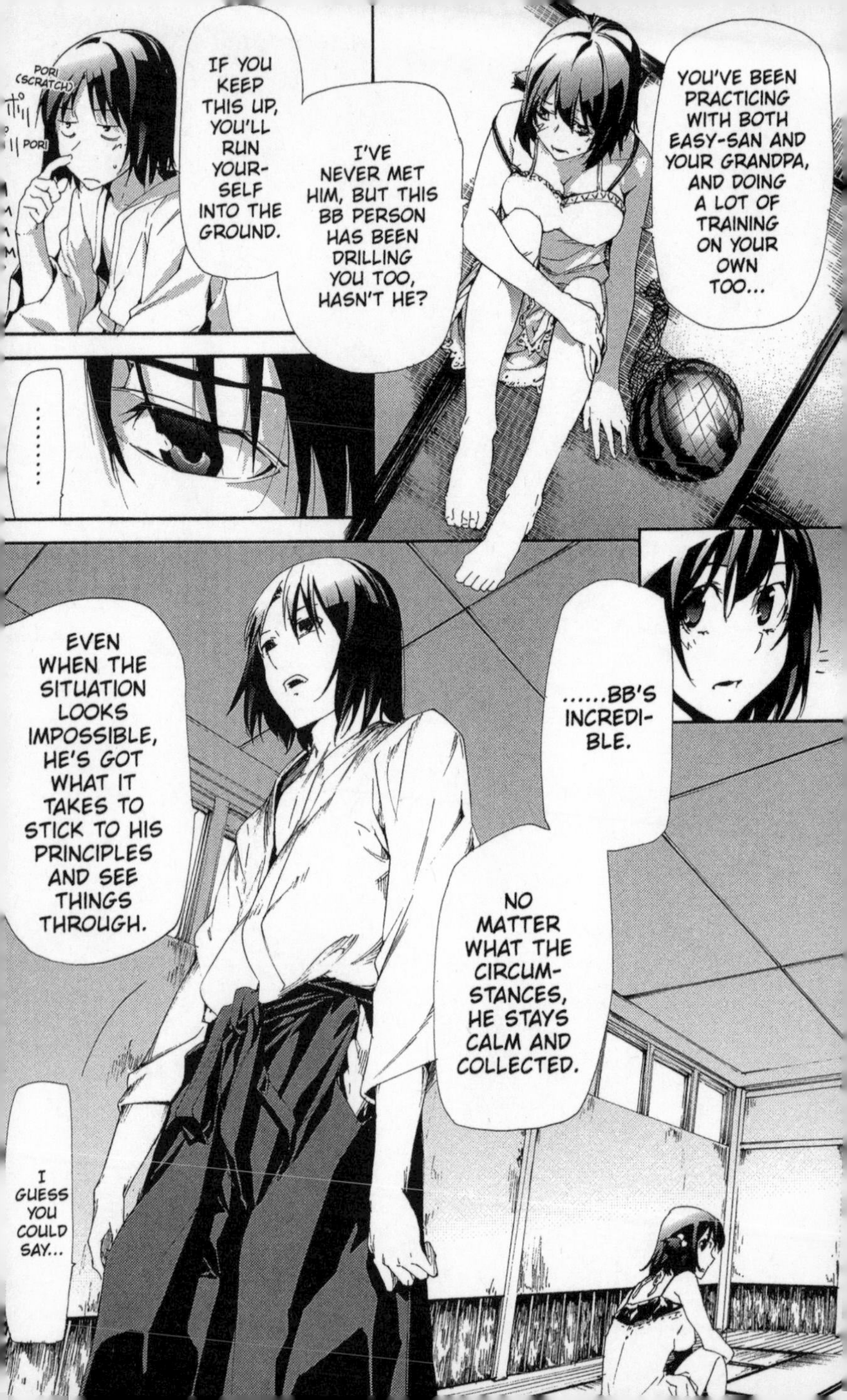

YOU'VE BEEN PRACTICING WITH BOTH EASY-SAN AND YOUR GRANDPA, AND DOING A LOT OF TRAINING ON YOUR OWN TOO...
I'VE NEVER MET HIM, BUT THIS BB PERSON HAS BEEN DRILLING YOU TOO, HASN'T HE?
IF YOU KEEP THIS UP, YOU'LL RUN YOUR-SELF INTO THE GROUND.
PORI (SCRATCH)
PORI
......
......BB'S INCREDI-BLE.
NO MATTER WHAT THE CIRCUM-STANCES, HE STAYS CALM AND COLLECTED.
EVEN WHEN THE SITUATION LOOKS IMPOSSIBLE, HE'S GOT WHAT IT TAKES TO STICK TO HIS PRINCIPLES AND SEE THINGS THROUGH.
I GUESS YOU COULD SAY...

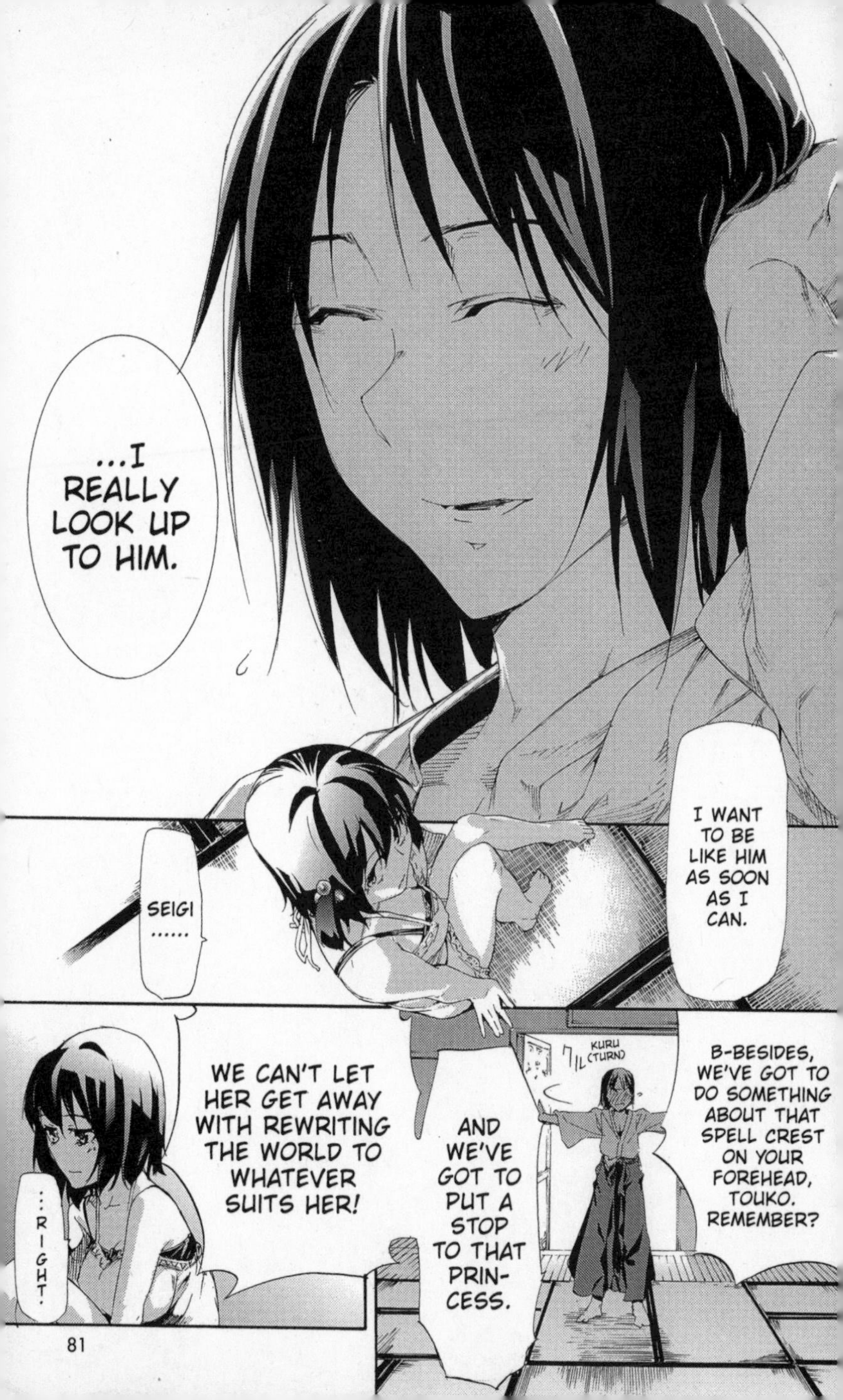
...I REALLY LOOK UP TO HIM.
I WANT TO BE LIKE HIM AS SOON AS I CAN.
SEIGI ......
KURU (TURN)
B-BESIDES, WE'VE GOT TO DO SOMETHING ABOUT THAT SPELL CREST ON YOUR FOREHEAD, TOUKO. REMEMBER?
AND WE'VE GOT TO PUT A STOP TO THAT PRIN-CESS.
WE CAN'T LET HER GET AWAY WITH REWRITING THE WORLD TO WHATEVER SUITS HER!
...RIGHT.

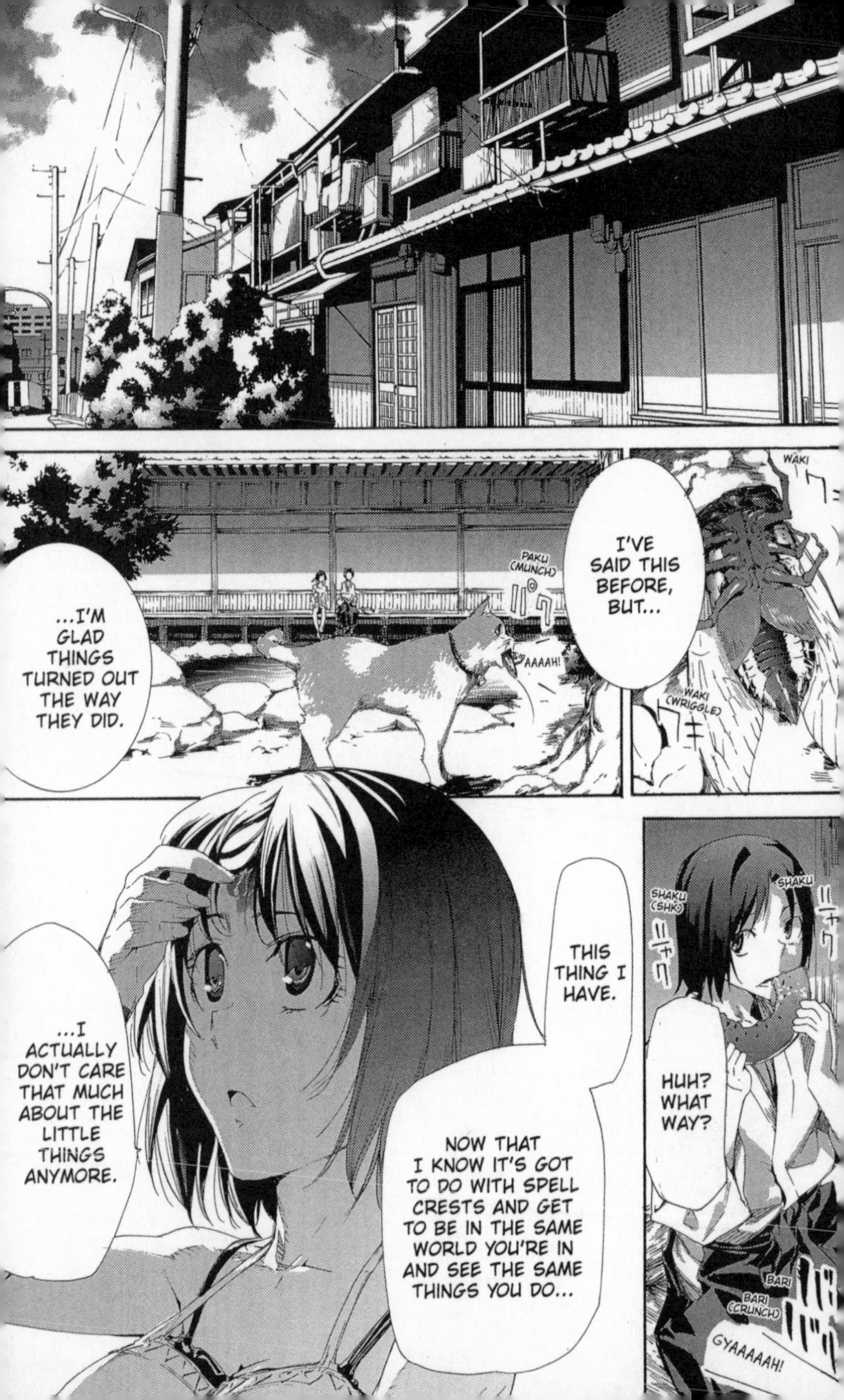
WAKI
I'VE SAID THIS BEFORE, BUT...
WAKI (WRIGGLE)
PAKU (MUNCH)
AAAAH!
...I'M GLAD THINGS TURNED OUT THE WAY THEY DID.
SHAKU
SHAKU (SHK)
HUH? WHAT WAY?
BARI
BARI (CRUNCH)
GYAAAAAH!
THIS THING I HAVE.
NOW THAT I KNOW IT'S GOT TO DO WITH SPELL CRESTS AND GET TO BE IN THE SAME WORLD YOU'RE IN AND SEE THE SAME THINGS YOU DO...
...I ACTUALLY DON'T CARE THAT MUCH ABOUT THE LITTLE THINGS ANYMORE.

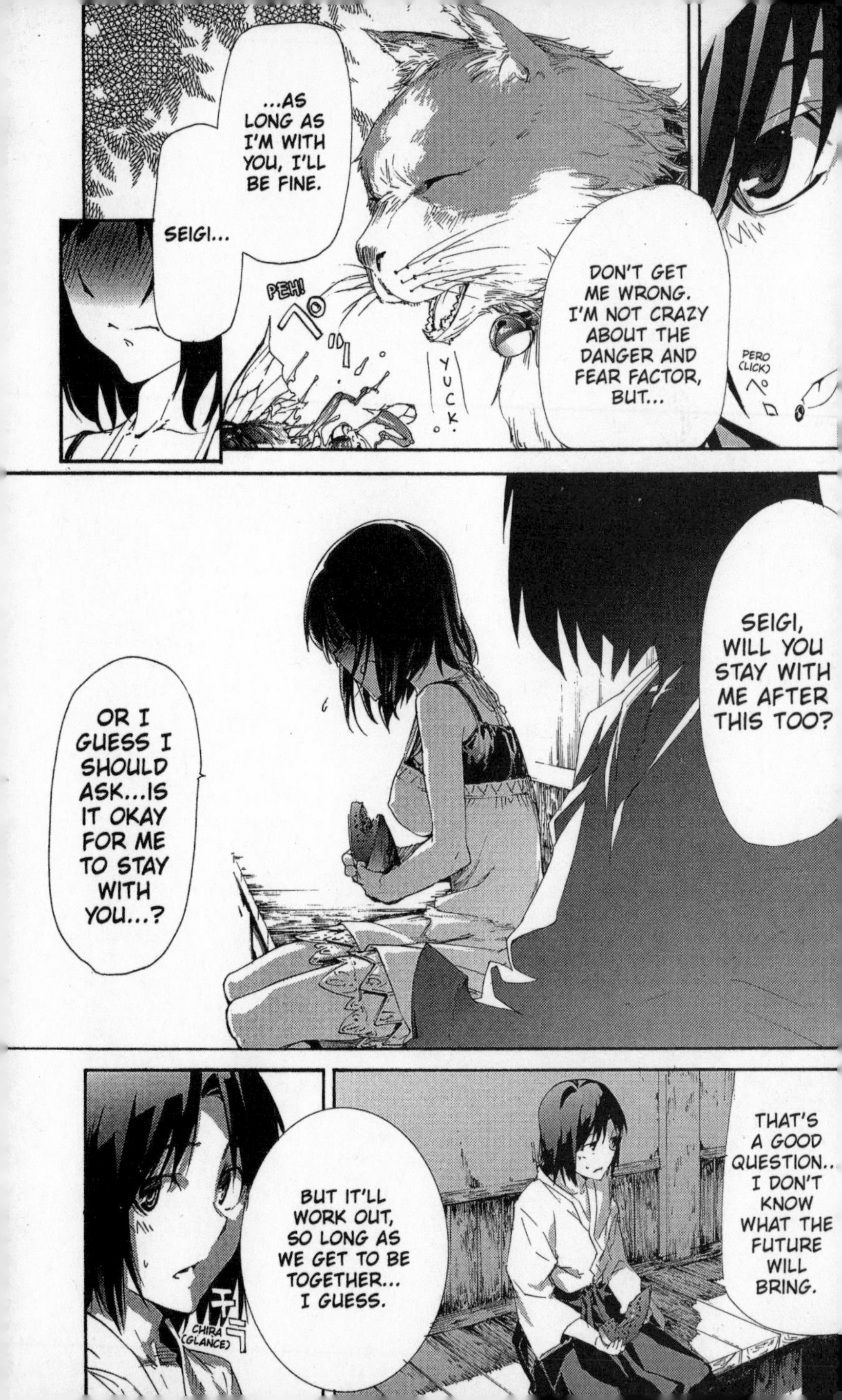
PERO (LICK)
DON'T GET ME WRONG. I'M NOT CRAZY ABOUT THE DANGER AND FEAR FACTOR, BUT...
...AS LONG AS I'M WITH YOU, I'LL BE FINE.
YUCK.
PEH!
SEIGI...
SEIGI, WILL YOU STAY WITH ME AFTER THIS TOO?
OR I GUESS I SHOULD ASK...IS IT OKAY FOR ME TO STAY WITH YOU...?
THAT'S A GOOD QUESTION... I DON'T KNOW WHAT THE FUTURE WILL BRING.
BUT IT'LL WORK OUT, SO LONG AS WE GET TO BE TOGETHER... I GUESS.
CHIRA (GLANCE)

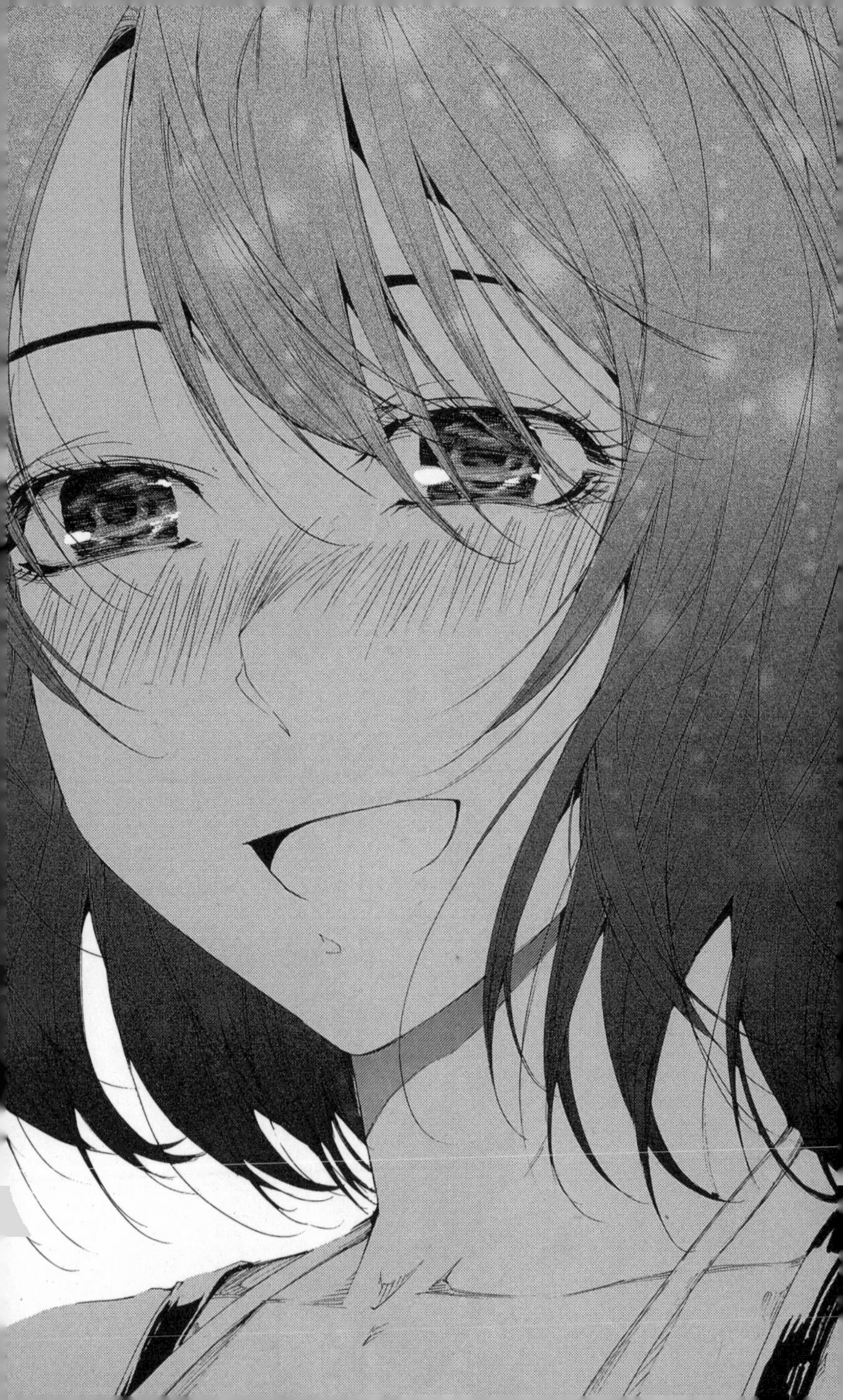

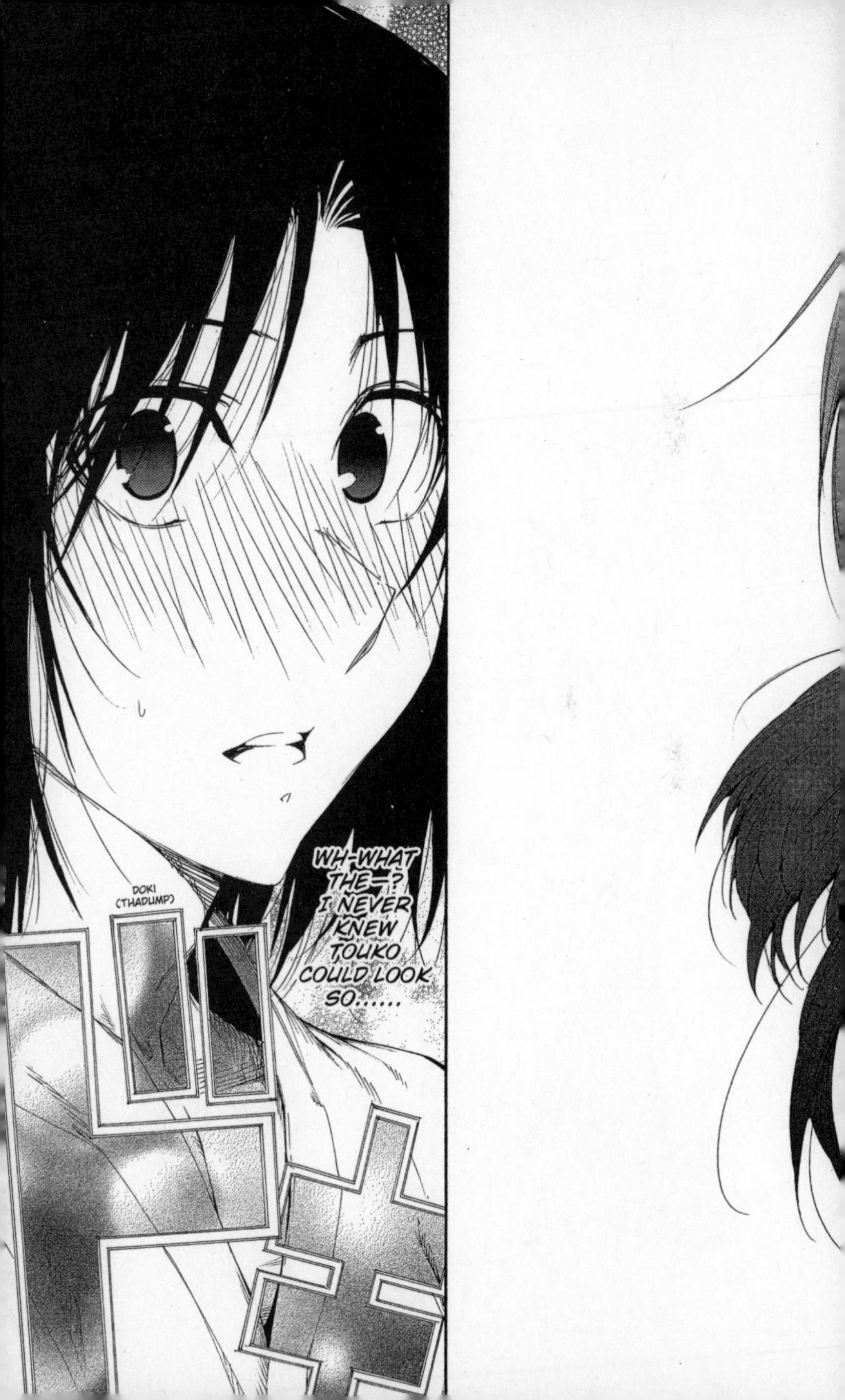
WH-WHAT THE—? I NEVER KNEW TOUKO COULD LOOK SO......
DOKI (THADUMP)

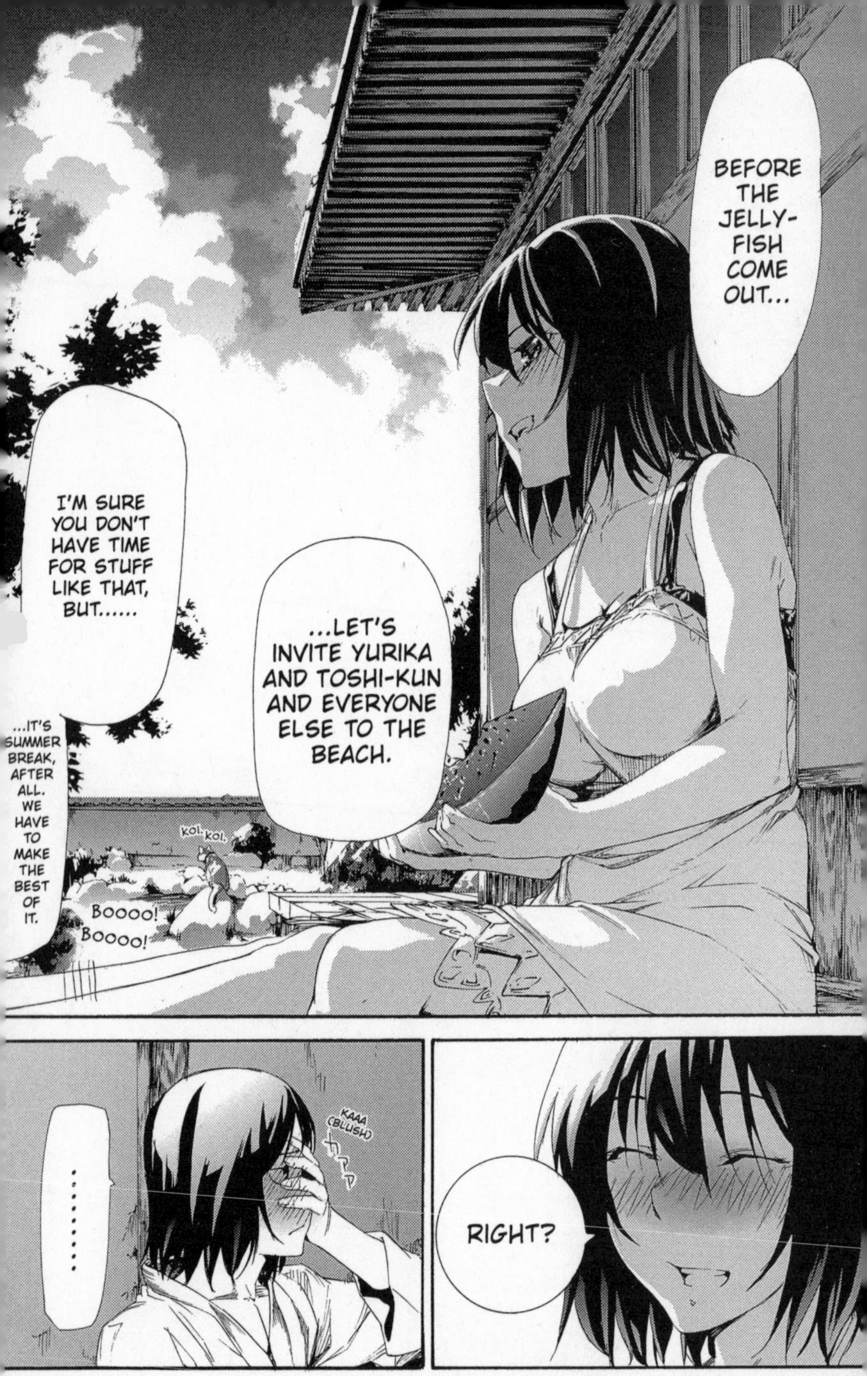
BEFORE THE JELLY-FISH COME OUT...
...LET'S INVITE YURIKA AND TOSHI-KUN AND EVERYONE ELSE TO THE BEACH.
I'M SURE YOU DON'T HAVE TIME FOR STUFF LIKE THAT, BUT......
...IT'S SUMMER BREAK, AFTER ALL. WE HAVE TO MAKE THE BEST OF IT.
KOI. KOI.
BOOOO! BOOOO!
RIGHT?
KAAA (BLUSH)
....

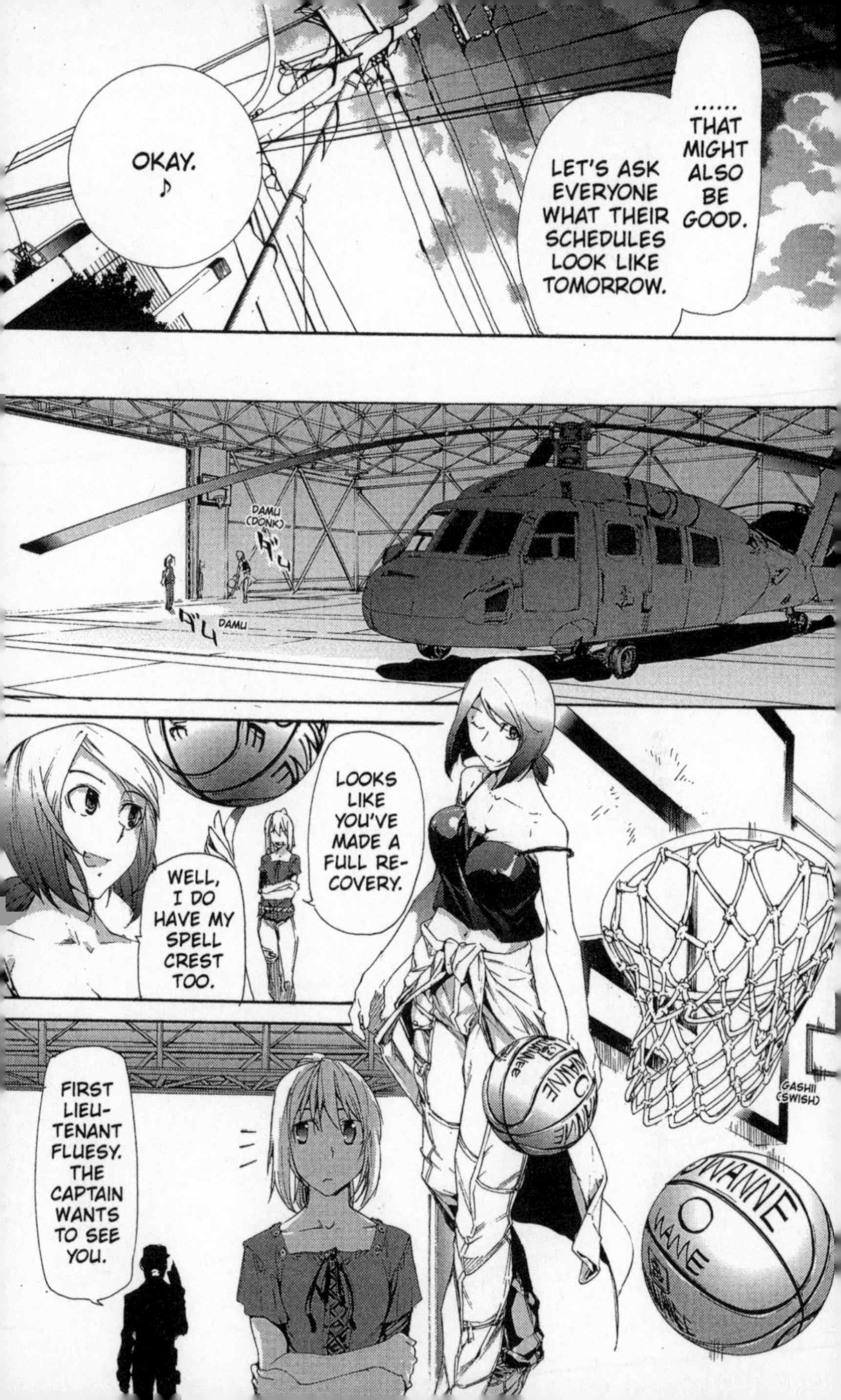
...... THAT MIGHT ALSO BE GOOD.
LET'S ASK EVERYONE WHAT THEIR SCHEDULES LOOK LIKE TOMORROW.
OKAY. ♪
DAMU (DONK)
DAMU
GASHII (SWISH)
LOOKS LIKE YOU'VE MADE A FULL RE-COVERY.
WELL, I DO HAVE MY SPELL CREST TOO.
FIRST LIEU-TENANT FLUESY. THE CAPTAIN WANTS TO SEE YOU.

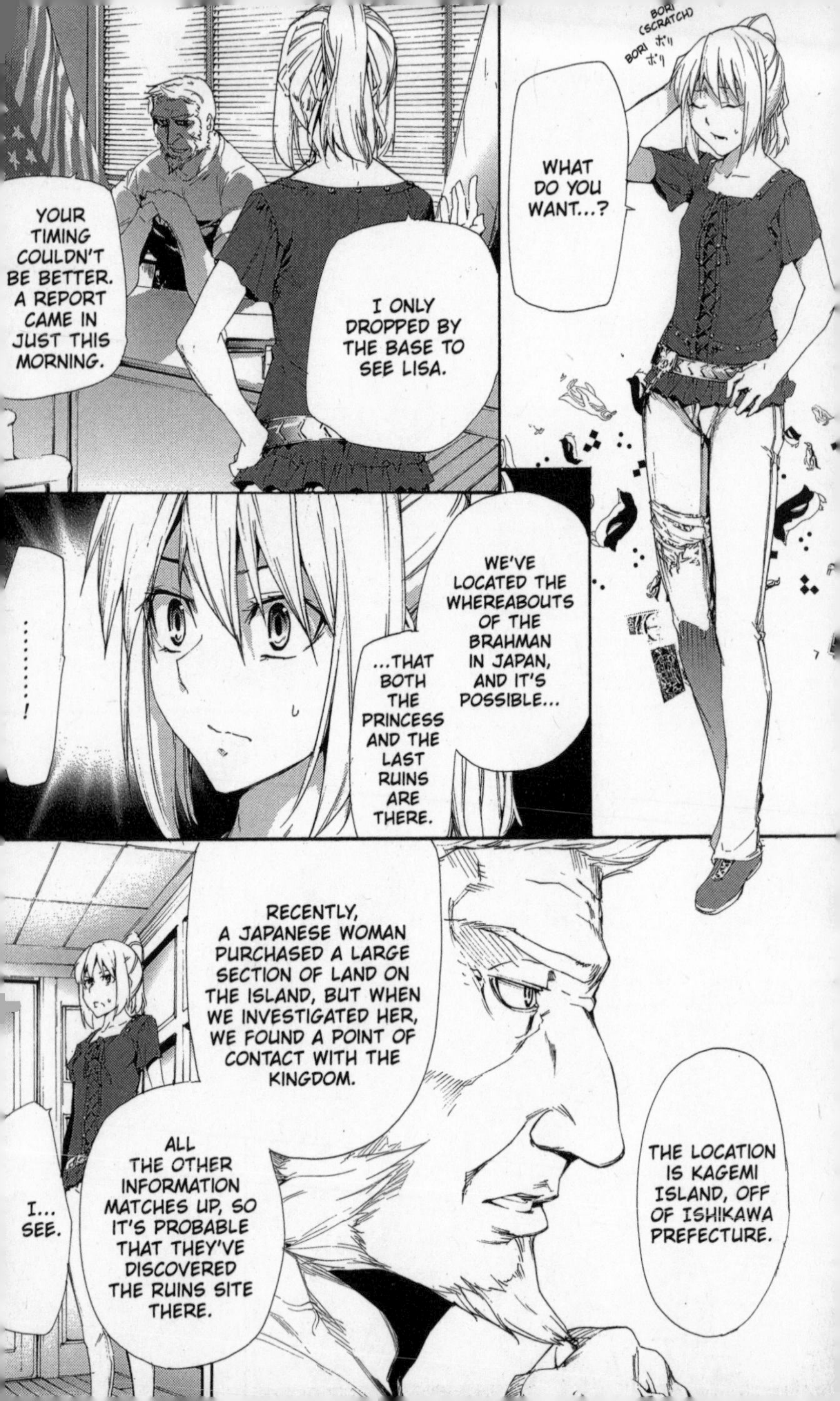

BORI BORI (SCRATCH)
ボリ ボリ
WHAT DO YOU WANT...?
I ONLY DROPPED BY THE BASE TO SEE LISA.
YOUR TIMING COULDN'T BE BETTER. A REPORT CAME IN JUST THIS MORNING.
WE'VE LOCATED THE WHEREABOUTS OF THE BRAHMAN IN JAPAN, AND IT'S POSSIBLE...
...THAT BOTH THE PRINCESS AND THE LAST RUINS ARE THERE.
......!
RECENTLY, A JAPANESE WOMAN PURCHASED A LARGE SECTION OF LAND ON THE ISLAND, BUT WHEN WE INVESTIGATED HER, WE FOUND A POINT OF CONTACT WITH THE KINGDOM.
THE LOCATION IS KAGEMI ISLAND, OFF OF ISHIKAWA PREFECTURE.
ALL THE OTHER INFORMATION MATCHES UP, SO IT'S PROBABLE THAT THEY'VE DISCOVERED THE RUINS SITE THERE.
I... SEE.

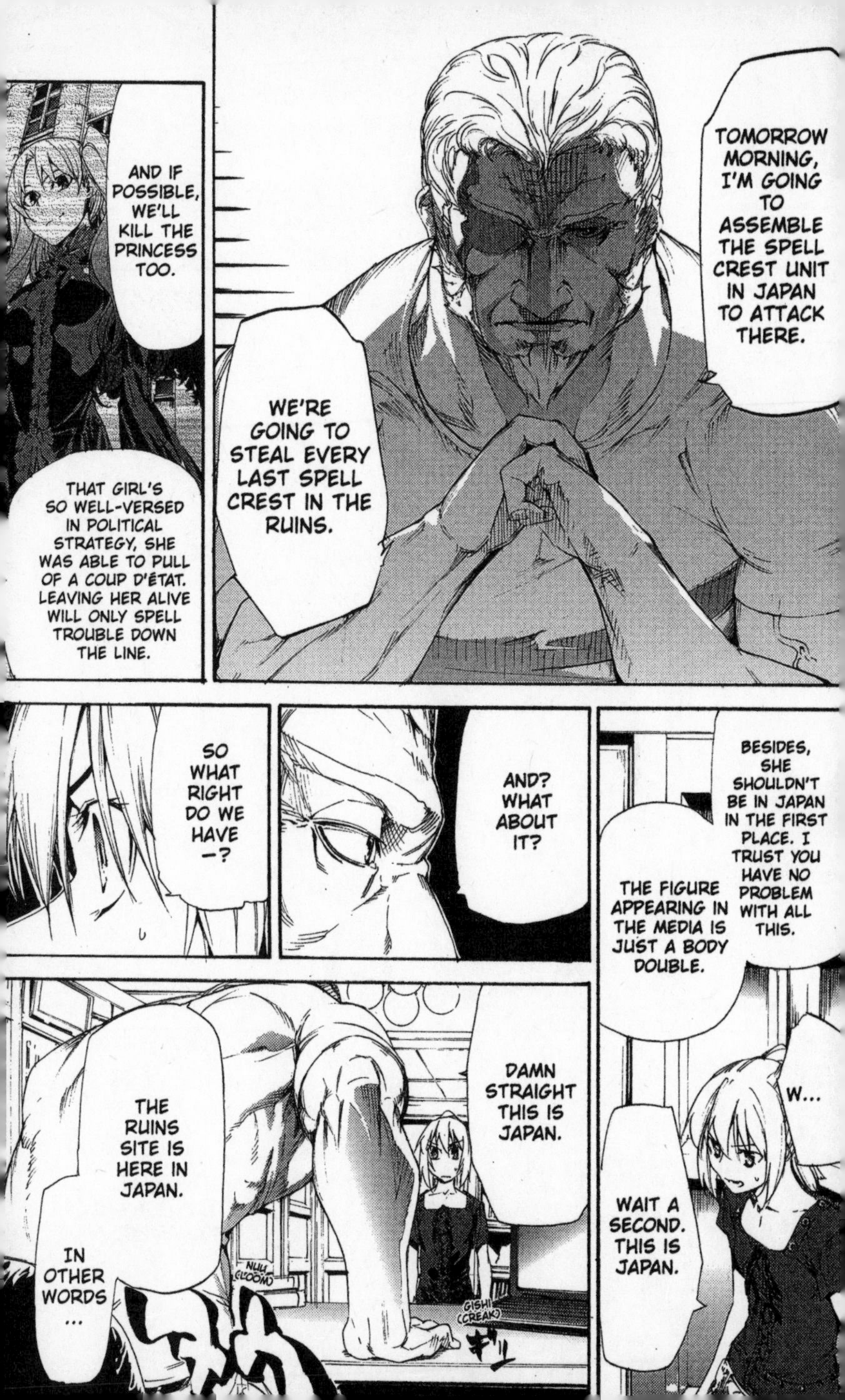
TOMORROW MORNING, I'M GOING TO ASSEMBLE THE SPELL CREST UNIT IN JAPAN TO ATTACK THERE.
WE'RE GOING TO STEAL EVERY LAST SPELL CREST IN THE RUINS.
AND IF POSSIBLE, WE'LL KILL THE PRINCESS TOO.
THAT GIRL'S SO WELL-VERSED IN POLITICAL STRATEGY, SHE WAS ABLE TO PULL OF A COUP D'ÉTAT. LEAVING HER ALIVE WILL ONLY SPELL TROUBLE DOWN THE LINE.
BESIDES, SHE SHOULDN'T BE IN JAPAN IN THE FIRST PLACE. I TRUST YOU HAVE NO PROBLEM WITH ALL THIS.
THE FIGURE APPEARING IN THE MEDIA IS JUST A BODY DOUBLE.
AND? WHAT ABOUT IT?
SO WHAT RIGHT DO WE HAVE —?
W...
WAIT A SECOND. THIS IS JAPAN.
DAMN STRAIGHT THIS IS JAPAN.
GISHI (CREAK)
THE RUINS SITE IS HERE IN JAPAN.
NUU (LOOM)
IN OTHER WORDS ...

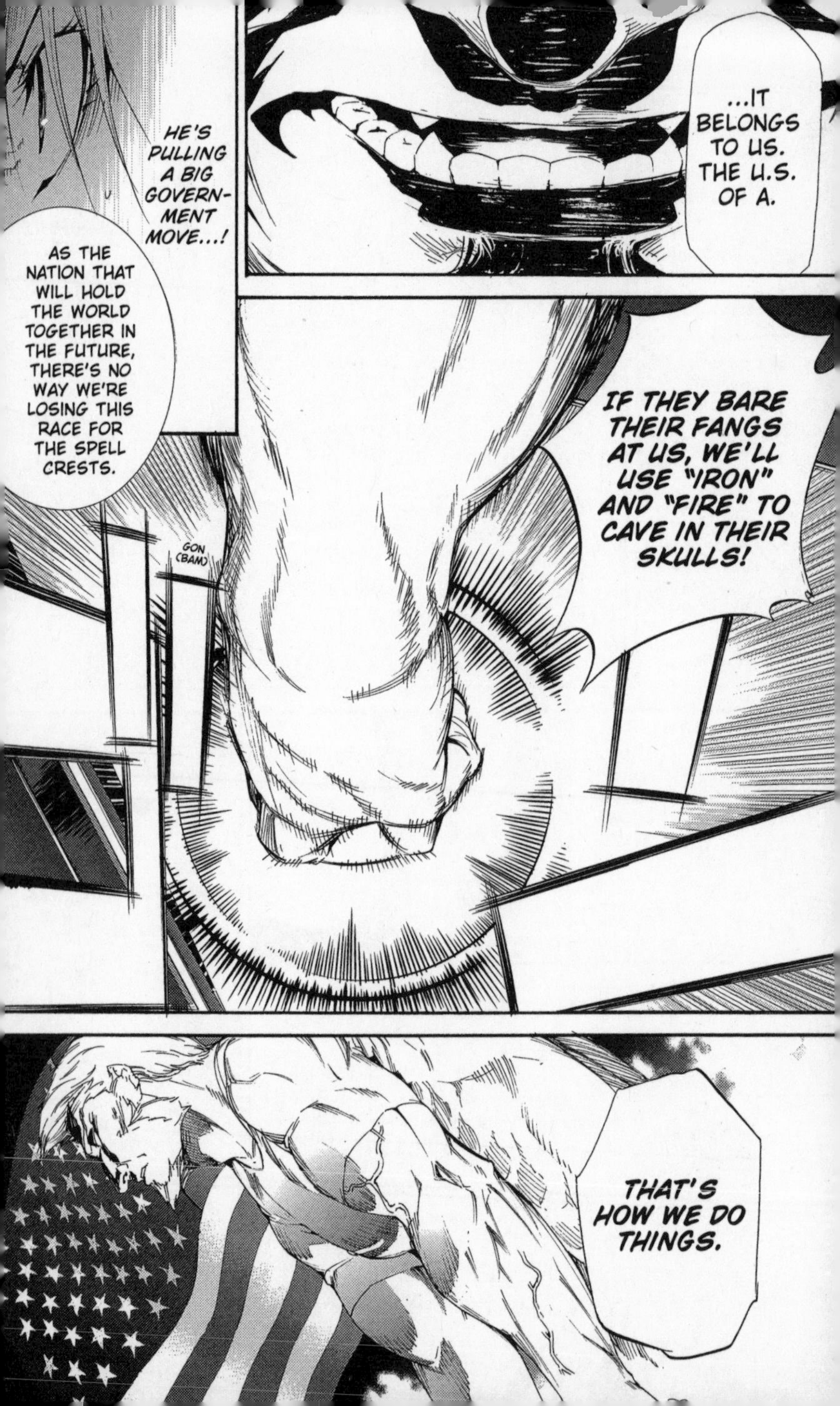

...IT BELONGS TO US. THE U.S. OF A.
HE'S PULLING A BIG GOVERNMENT MOVE...!
AS THE NATION THAT WILL HOLD THE WORLD TOGETHER IN THE FUTURE, THERE'S NO WAY WE'RE LOSING THIS RACE FOR THE SPELL CRESTS.
IF THEY BARE THEIR FANGS AT US, WE'LL USE "IRON" AND "FIRE" TO CAVE IN THEIR SKULLS!
GON (BAM)
THAT'S HOW WE DO THINGS.

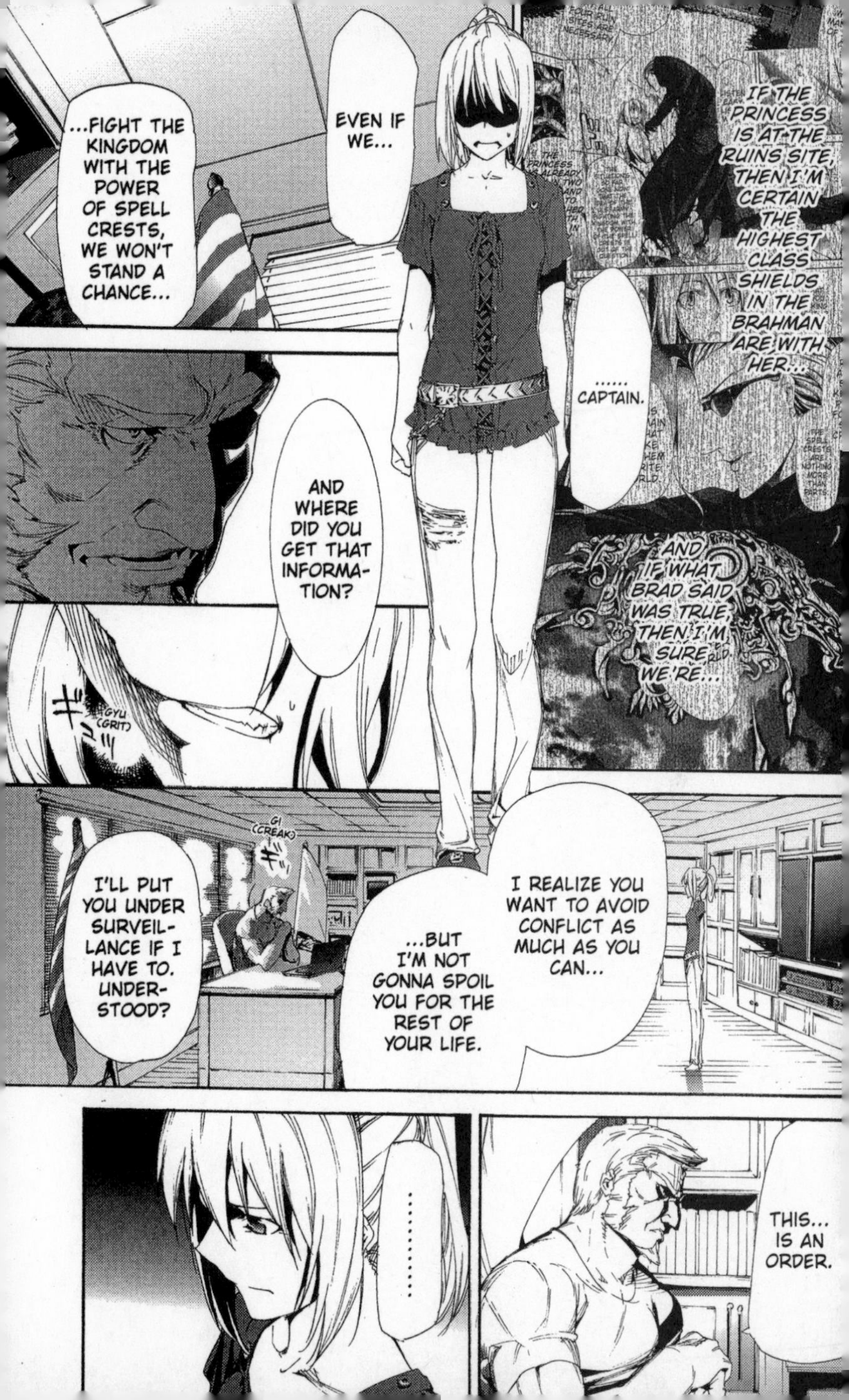
ALL FOUR RUIN SITES ARE NECESSARY
IF THE PRINCESS IS AT THE RUINS SITE, THEN I'M CERTAIN THE HIGHEST CLASS SHIELDS IN THE BRAHMAN ARE WITH HER...
THE SPELL CRESTS ARE NOTHING MORE THAN PARTS.
AND IF WHAT BRAD SAID WAS TRUE, THEN I'M SURE WE'RE...
EVEN IF WE...
...FIGHT THE KINGDOM WITH THE POWER OF SPELL CRESTS, WE WON'T STAND A CHANCE...
...... CAPTAIN.
AND WHERE DID YOU GET THAT INFORMATION?
GYU (GRIT)
I REALIZE YOU WANT TO AVOID CONFLICT AS MUCH AS YOU CAN...
...BUT I'M NOT GONNA SPOIL YOU FOR THE REST OF YOUR LIFE.
GI (CREAK)
I'LL PUT YOU UNDER SURVEIL-LANCE IF I HAVE TO. UNDER-STOOD?
THIS... IS AN ORDER.
......

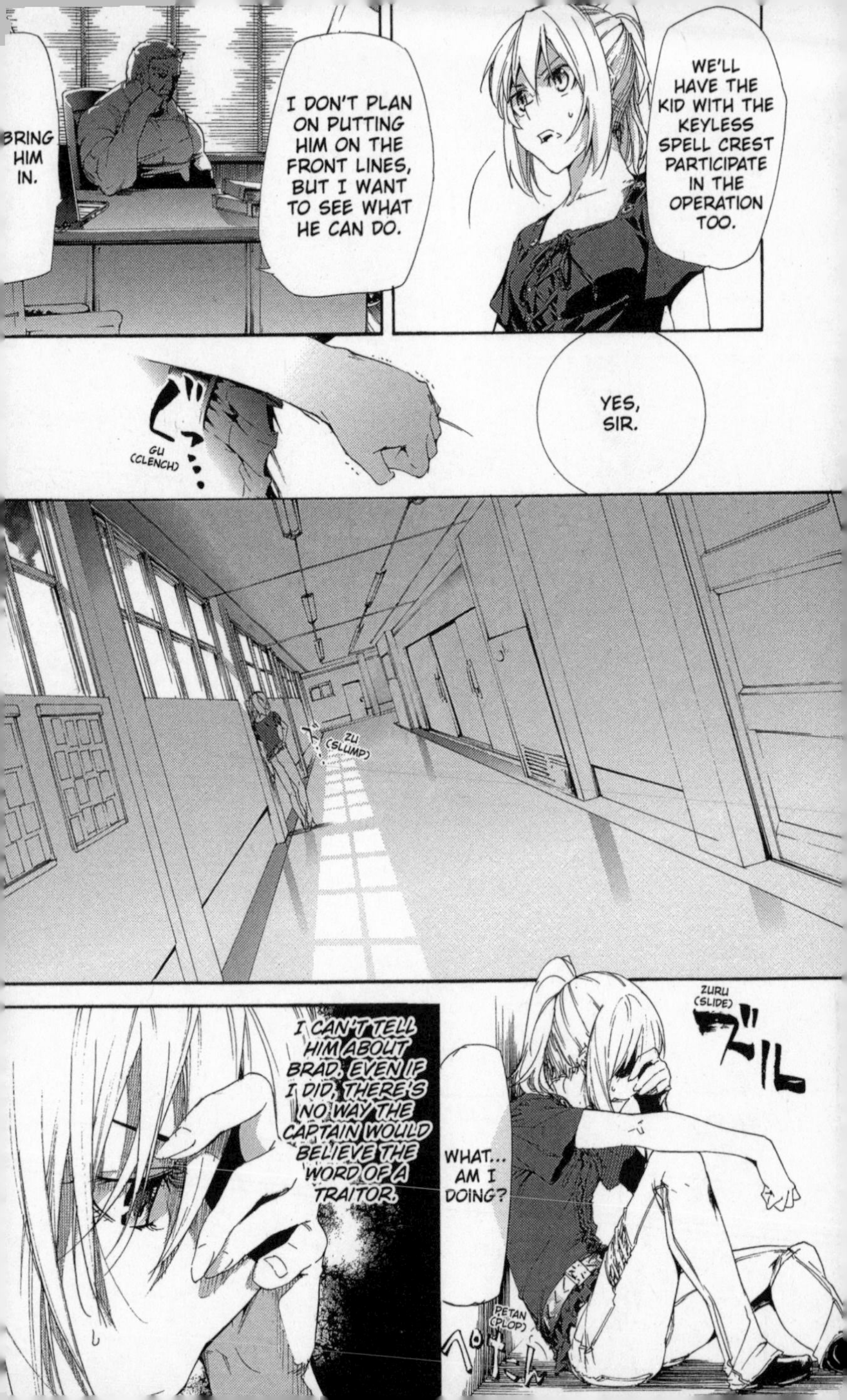
WE'LL HAVE THE KID WITH THE KEYLESS SPELL CREST PARTICIPATE IN THE OPERATION TOO.
I DON'T PLAN ON PUTTING HIM ON THE FRONT LINES, BUT I WANT TO SEE WHAT HE CAN DO.
BRING HIM IN.
YES, SIR.
GU (CLENCH)
ZU (SLUMP)
ZURU (SLIDE)
WHAT... AM I DOING?
PETAN (PLOP)
I CAN'T TELL HIM ABOUT BRAD. EVEN IF I DID, THERE'S NO WAY THE CAPTAIN WOULD BELIEVE THE WORD OF A TRAITOR.

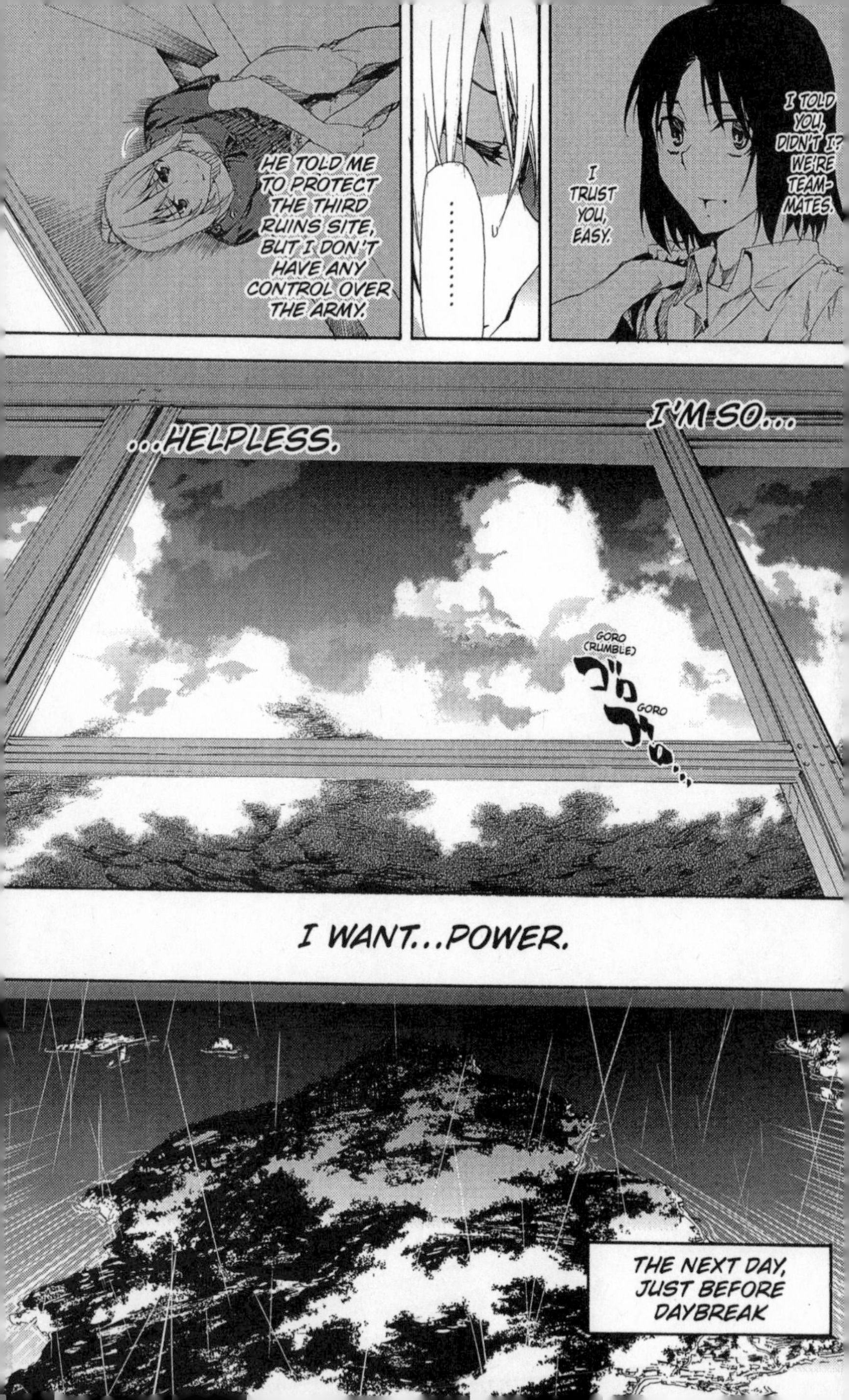
I TOLD YOU, DIDN'T I? WE'RE TEAM-MATES.
I TRUST YOU, EASY.
HE TOLD ME TO PROTECT THE THIRD RUINS SITE, BUT I DON'T HAVE ANY CONTROL OVER THE ARMY.
I'M SO...
...HELPLESS.
GORO (RUMBLE)
GORO
I WANT...POWER.
THE NEXT DAY, JUST BEFORE DAYBREAK

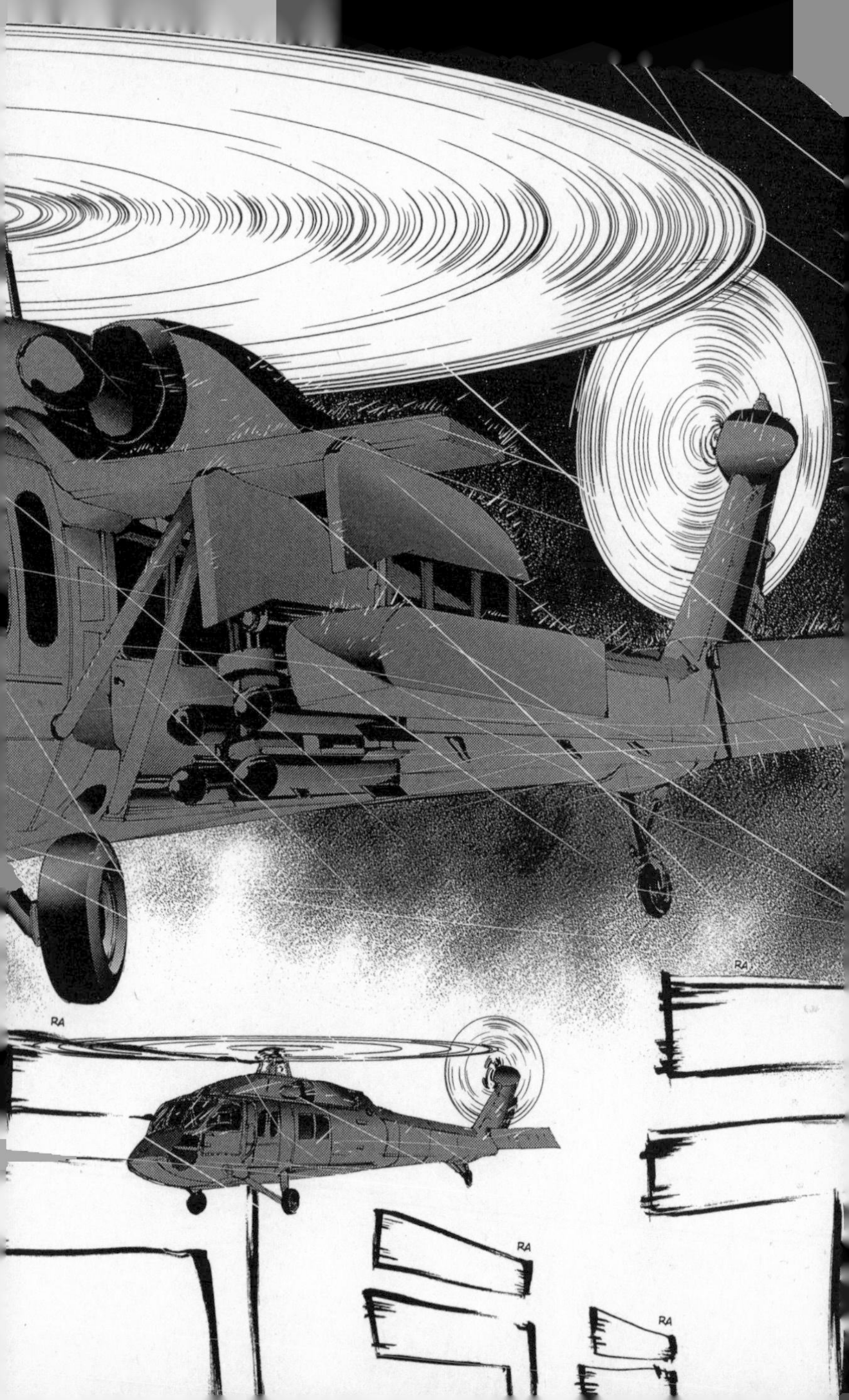
RA
RA
RA
RA

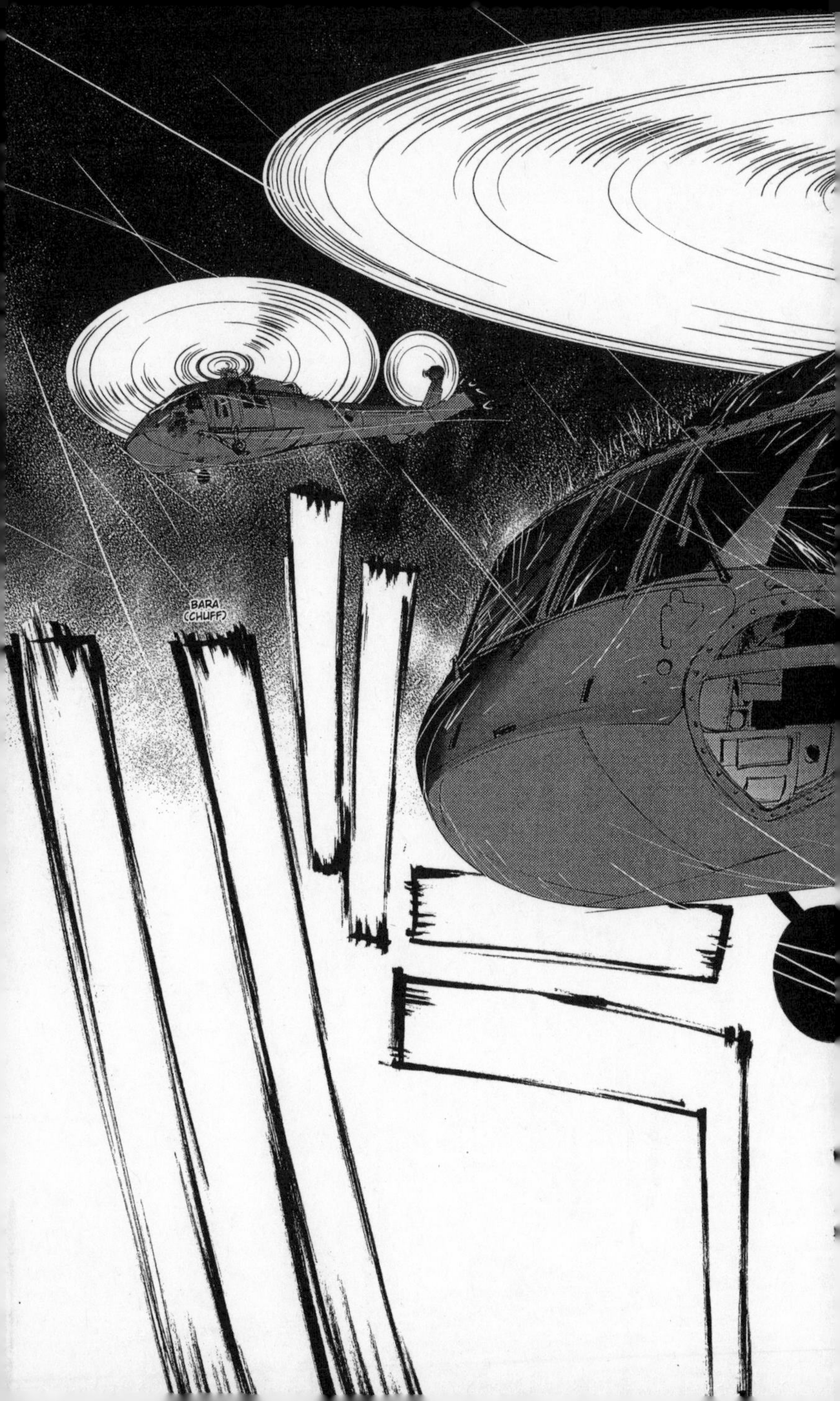
BARA (CHUFF)

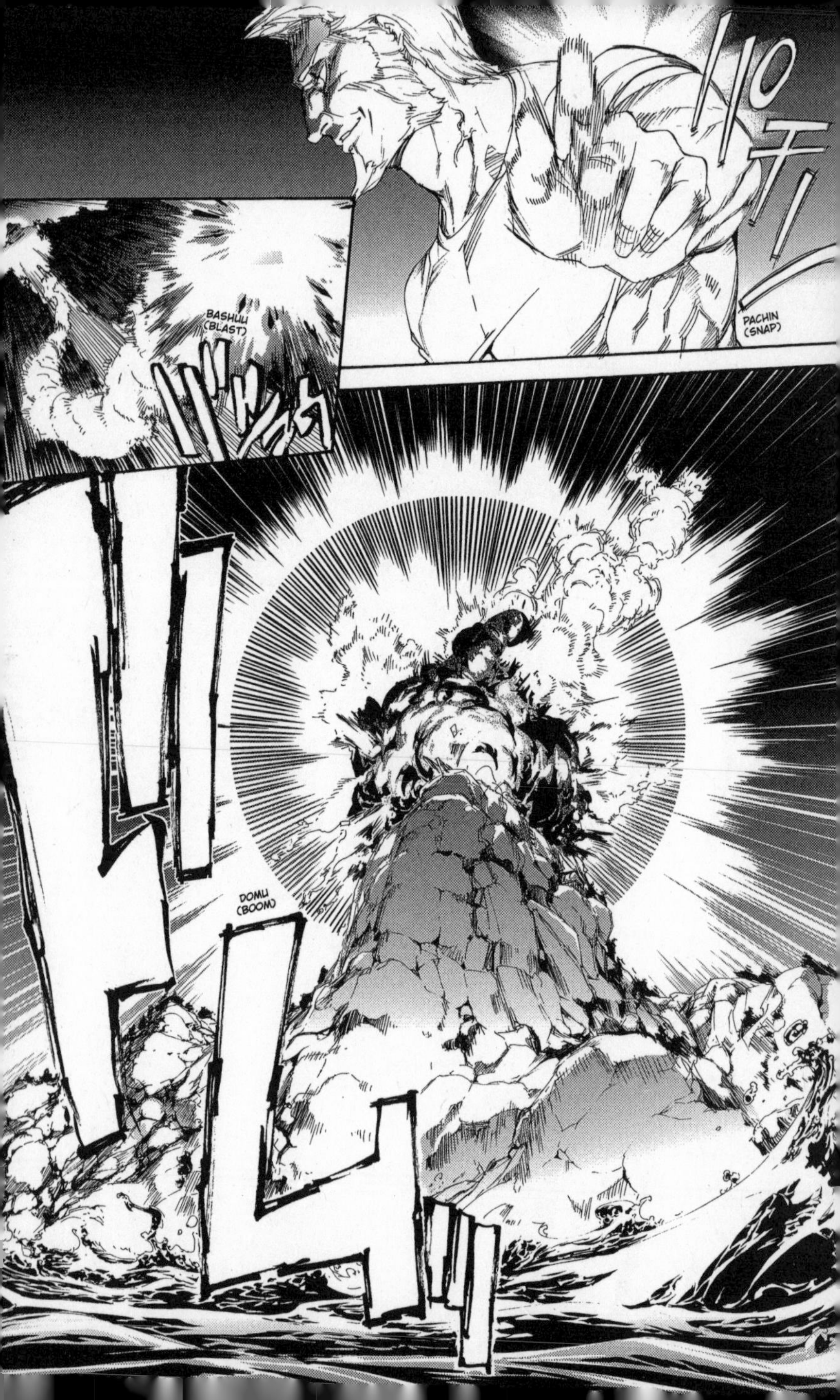
PACHIN
(SNAP)
BASHUU
(BLAST)
DOMU
(BOOM)

TABOO TATTOO

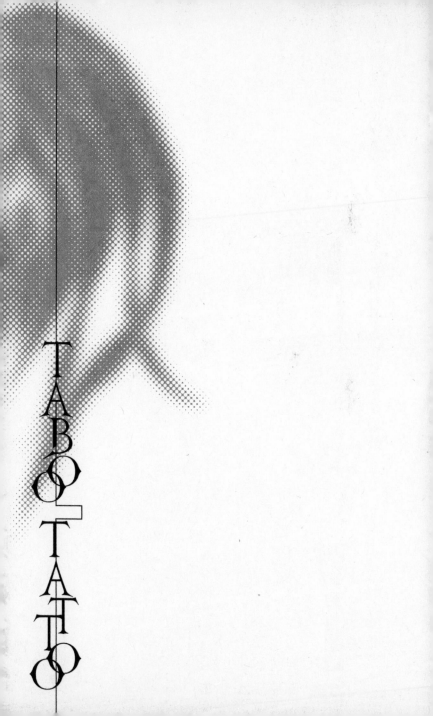

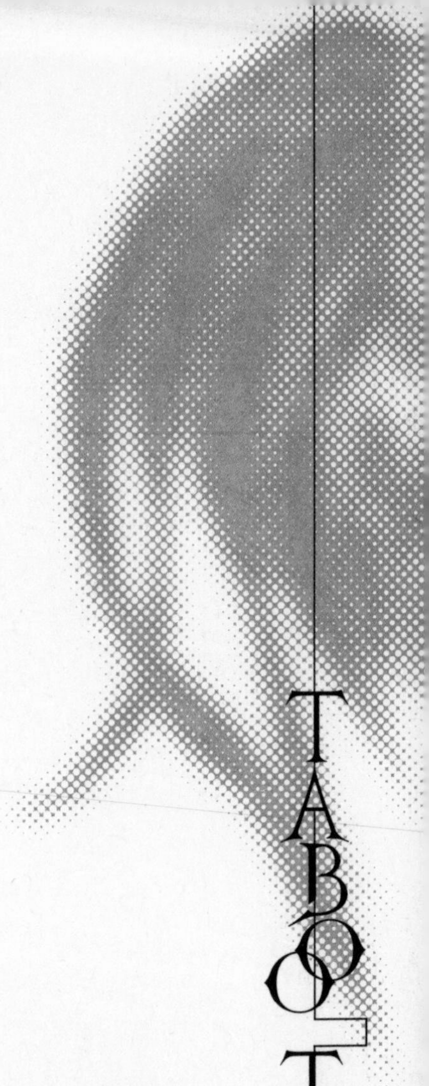

TABOO TATTOO

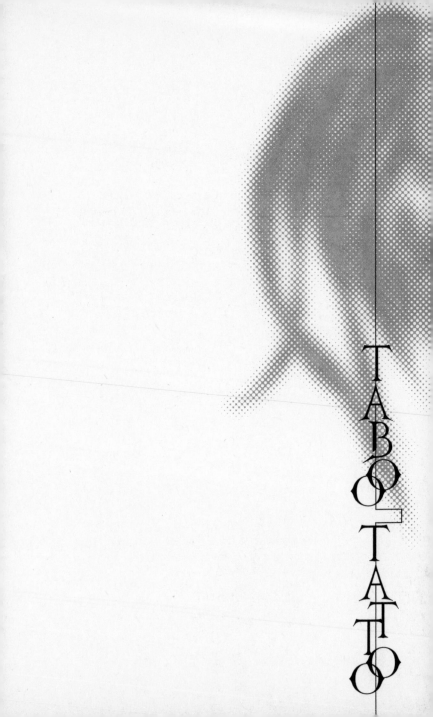

#18 STORM

TABOOTATTOO

A FEW HOURS EARLIER...

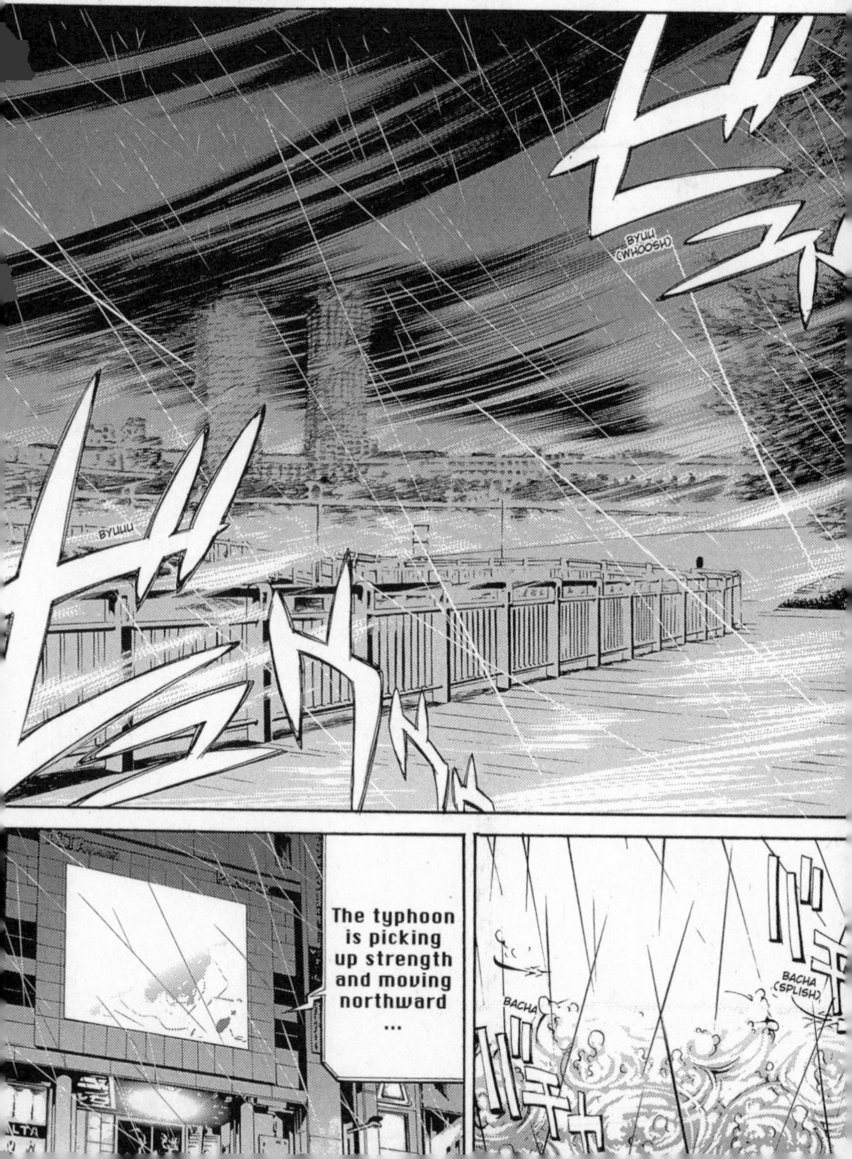
BYUU (WHOOSH)
BYUUU
BACHA (SPLISH)
BACHA
The typhoon is picking up strength and moving northward ...

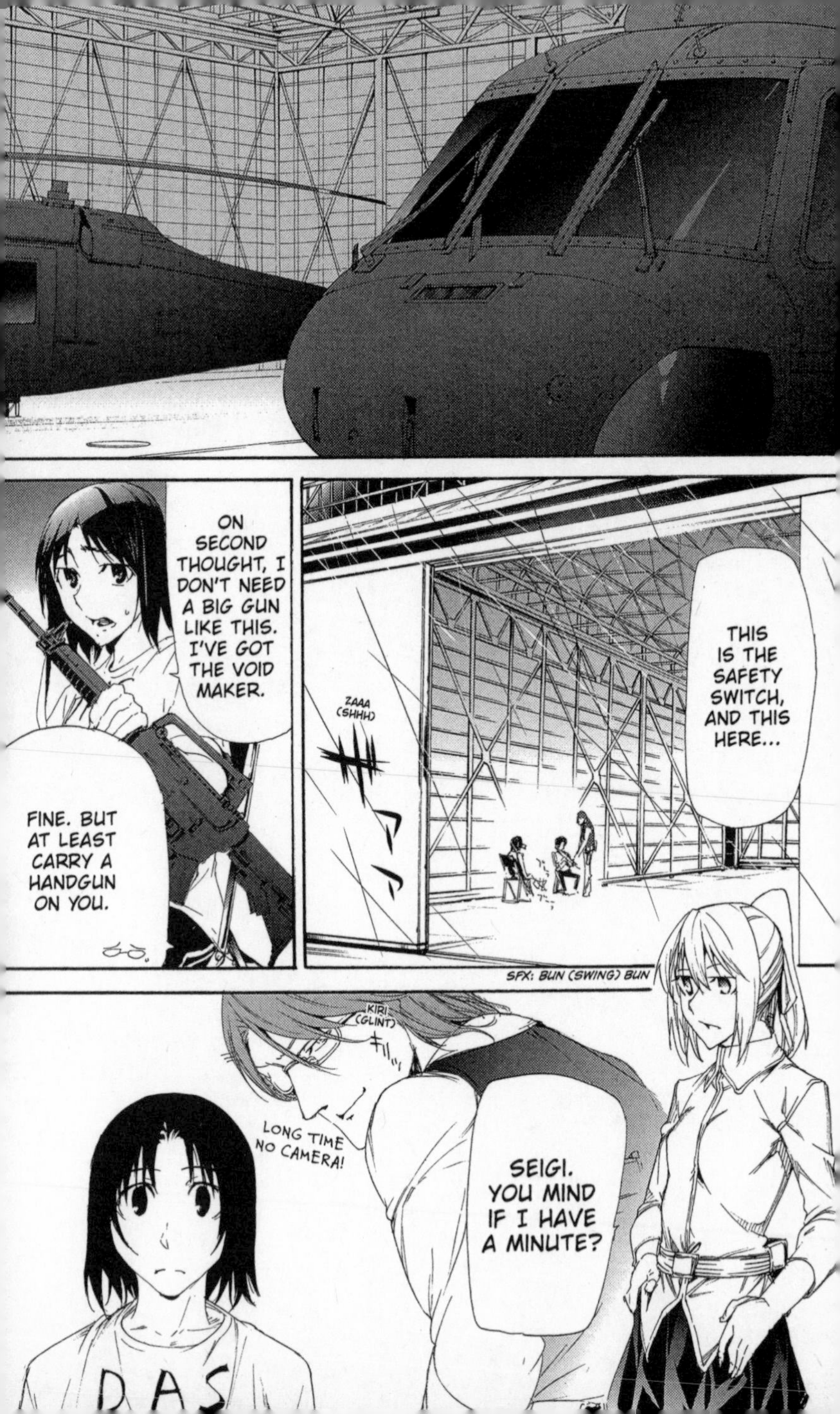
THIS IS THE SAFETY SWITCH, AND THIS HERE...
ZAAA (SHHH)
SFX: BUN (SWING) BUN
ON SECOND THOUGHT, I DON'T NEED A BIG GUN LIKE THIS. I'VE GOT THE VOID MAKER.
FINE. BUT AT LEAST CARRY A HANDGUN ON YOU.
KIRI (GLINT)
SEIGI. YOU MIND IF I HAVE A MINUTE?
LONG TIME NO CAMERA!
DAS

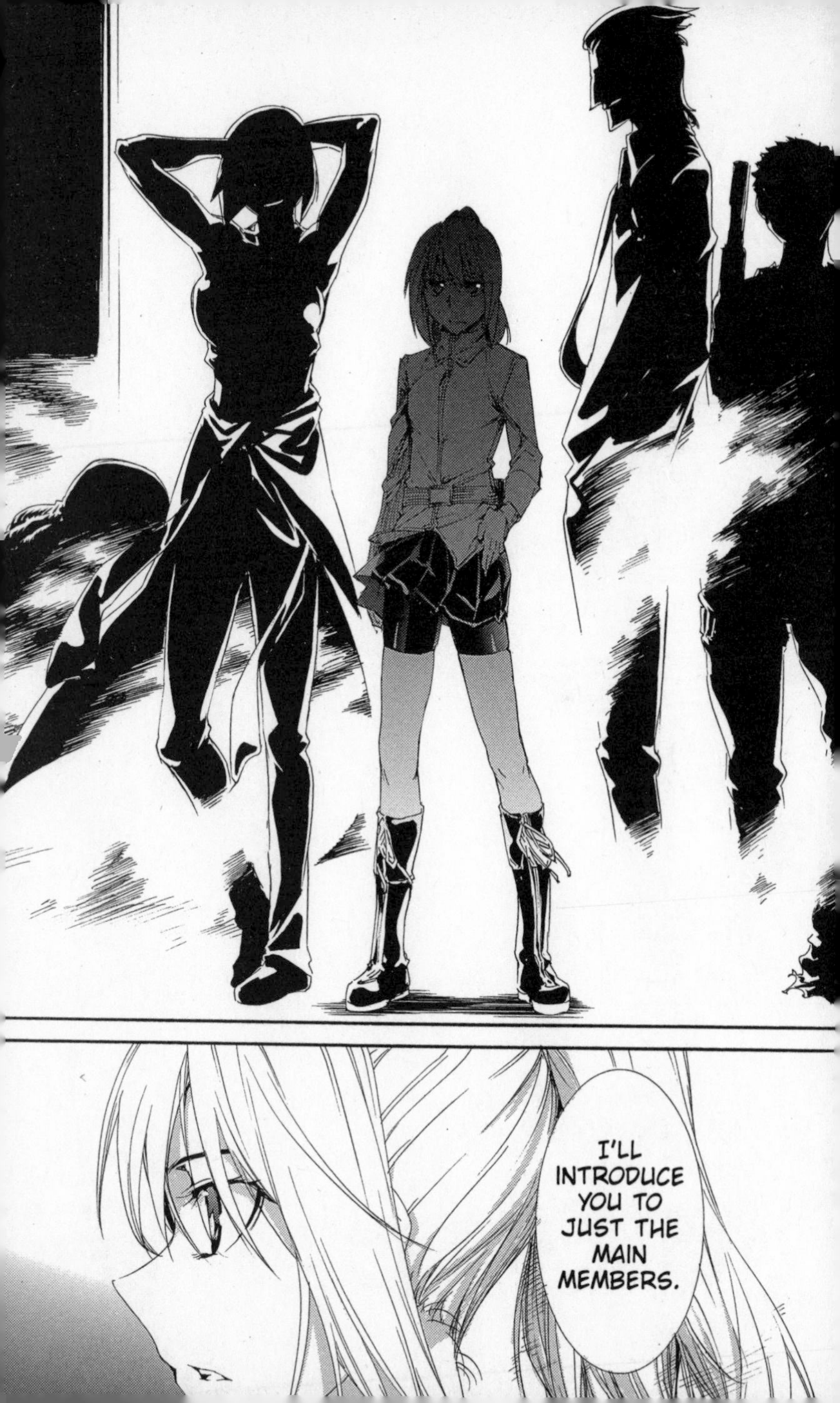
I'LL INTRODUCE YOU TO JUST THE MAIN MEMBERS.

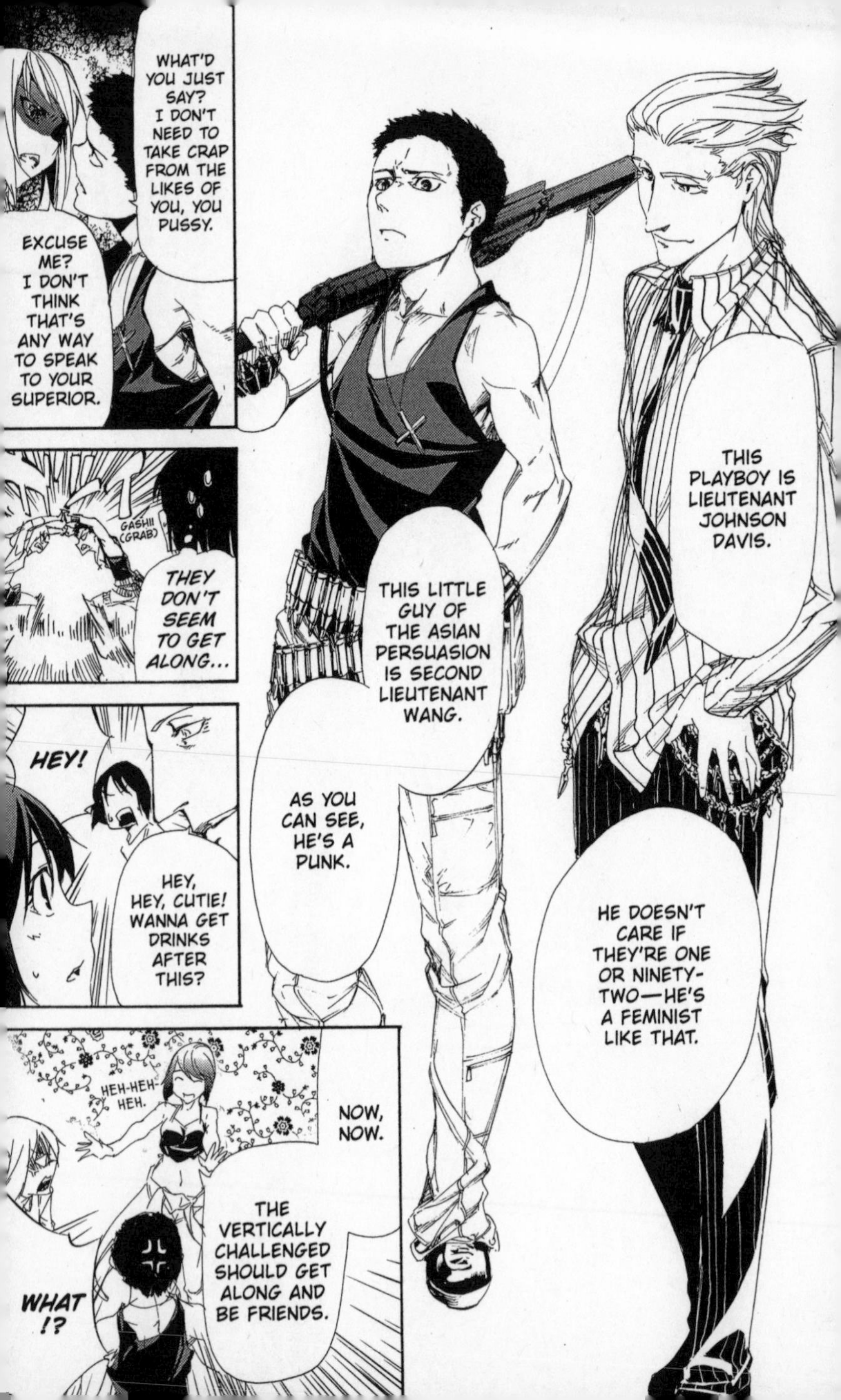
THIS PLAYBOY IS LIEUTENANT JOHNSON DAVIS.
HE DOESN'T CARE IF THEY'RE ONE OR NINETY-TWO—HE'S A FEMINIST LIKE THAT.
THIS LITTLE GUY OF THE ASIAN PERSUASION IS SECOND LIEUTENANT WANG.
AS YOU CAN SEE, HE'S A PUNK.
WHAT'D YOU JUST SAY? I DON'T NEED TO TAKE CRAP FROM THE LIKES OF YOU, YOU PUSSY.
EXCUSE ME? I DON'T THINK THAT'S ANY WAY TO SPEAK TO YOUR SUPERIOR.
GASHII (GRAB)
THEY DON'T SEEM TO GET ALONG...
HEY!
HEY, HEY, CUTIE! WANNA GET DRINKS AFTER THIS?
HEH-HEH-HEH.
NOW, NOW.
THE VERTICALLY CHALLENGED SHOULD GET ALONG AND BE FRIENDS.
WHAT !?

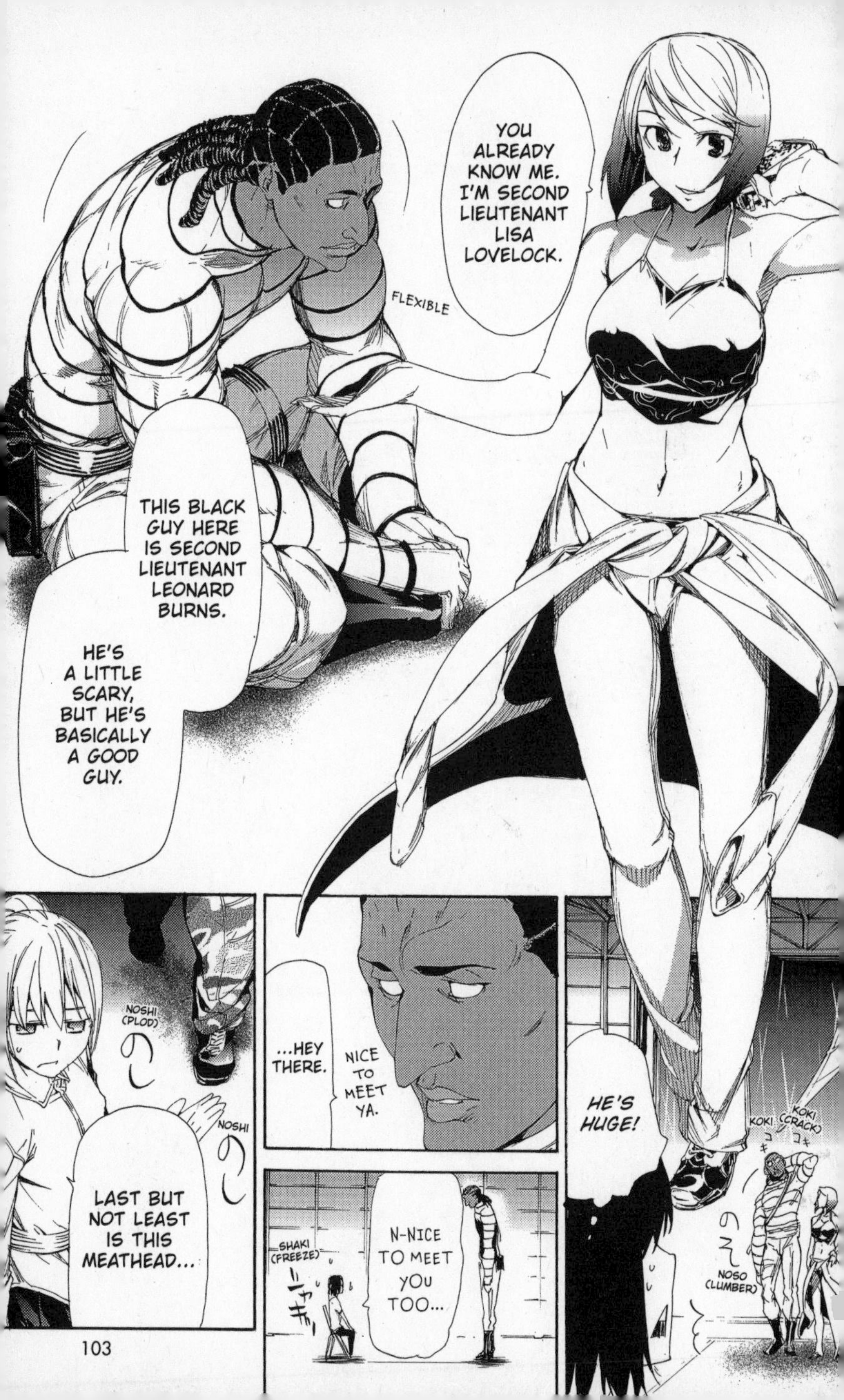
YOU ALREADY KNOW ME. I'M SECOND LIEUTENANT LISA LOVELOCK.
FLEXIBLE
THIS BLACK GUY HERE IS SECOND LIEUTENANT LEONARD BURNS.
HE'S A LITTLE SCARY, BUT HE'S BASICALLY A GOOD GUY.
KOKI (CRACK)
KOKI
HE'S HUGE!
NOSO (LUMBER)
...HEY THERE.
NICE TO MEET YA.
SHAKI (FREEZE)
N-NICE TO MEET YOU TOO...
NOSHI (PLOD)
NOSHI
LAST BUT NOT LEAST IS THIS MEATHEAD...

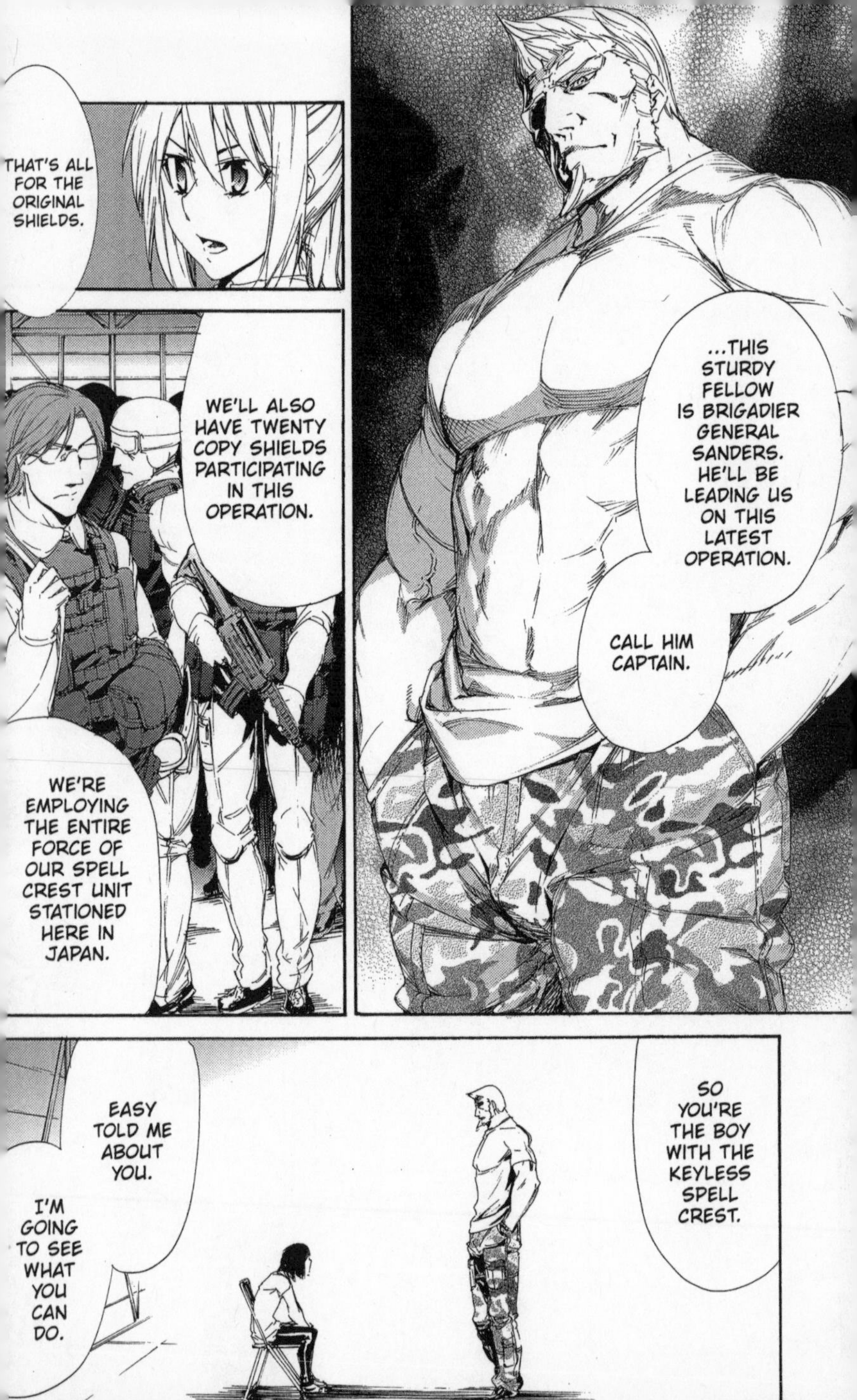
...THIS STURDY FELLOW IS BRIGADIER GENERAL SANDERS. HE'LL BE LEADING US ON THIS LATEST OPERATION.
CALL HIM CAPTAIN.
THAT'S ALL FOR THE ORIGINAL SHIELDS.
WE'LL ALSO HAVE TWENTY COPY SHIELDS PARTICIPATING IN THIS OPERATION.
WE'RE EMPLOYING THE ENTIRE FORCE OF OUR SPELL CREST UNIT STATIONED HERE IN JAPAN.
SO YOU'RE THE BOY WITH THE KEYLESS SPELL CREST.
EASY TOLD ME ABOUT YOU.
I'M GOING TO SEE WHAT YOU CAN DO.

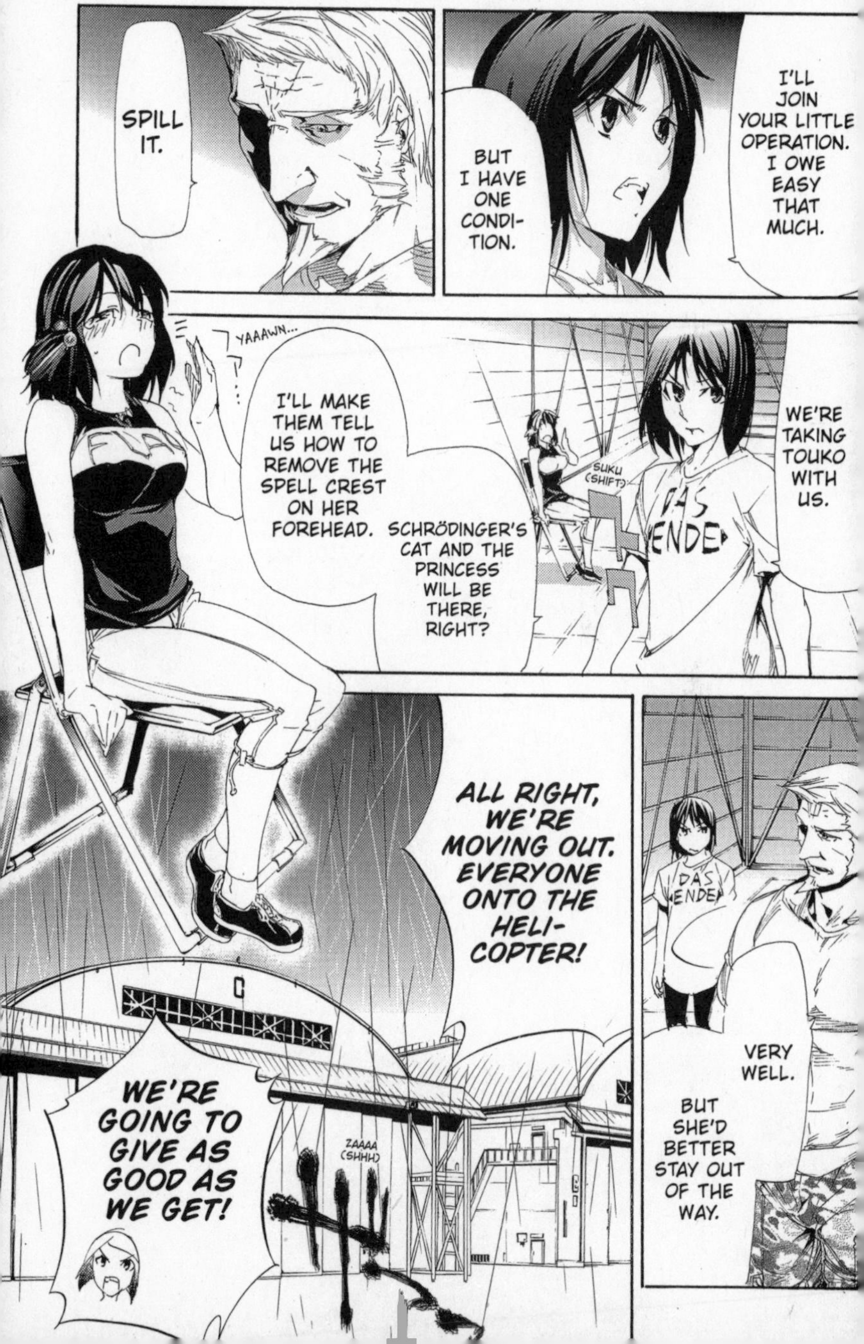
I'LL JOIN YOUR LITTLE OPERATION. I OWE EASY THAT MUCH.
BUT I HAVE ONE CONDITION.
SPILL IT.
WE'RE TAKING TOUKO WITH US.
SUKU (SHIFT)
I'LL MAKE THEM TELL US HOW TO REMOVE THE SPELL CREST ON HER FOREHEAD.
SCHRÖDINGER'S CAT AND THE PRINCESS WILL BE THERE, RIGHT?
YAAAWN...
VERY WELL.
BUT SHE'D BETTER STAY OUT OF THE WAY.
ALL RIGHT, WE'RE MOVING OUT. EVERYONE ONTO THE HELICOPTER!
ZAAAA (SHHH)
WE'RE GOING TO GIVE AS GOOD AS WE GET!

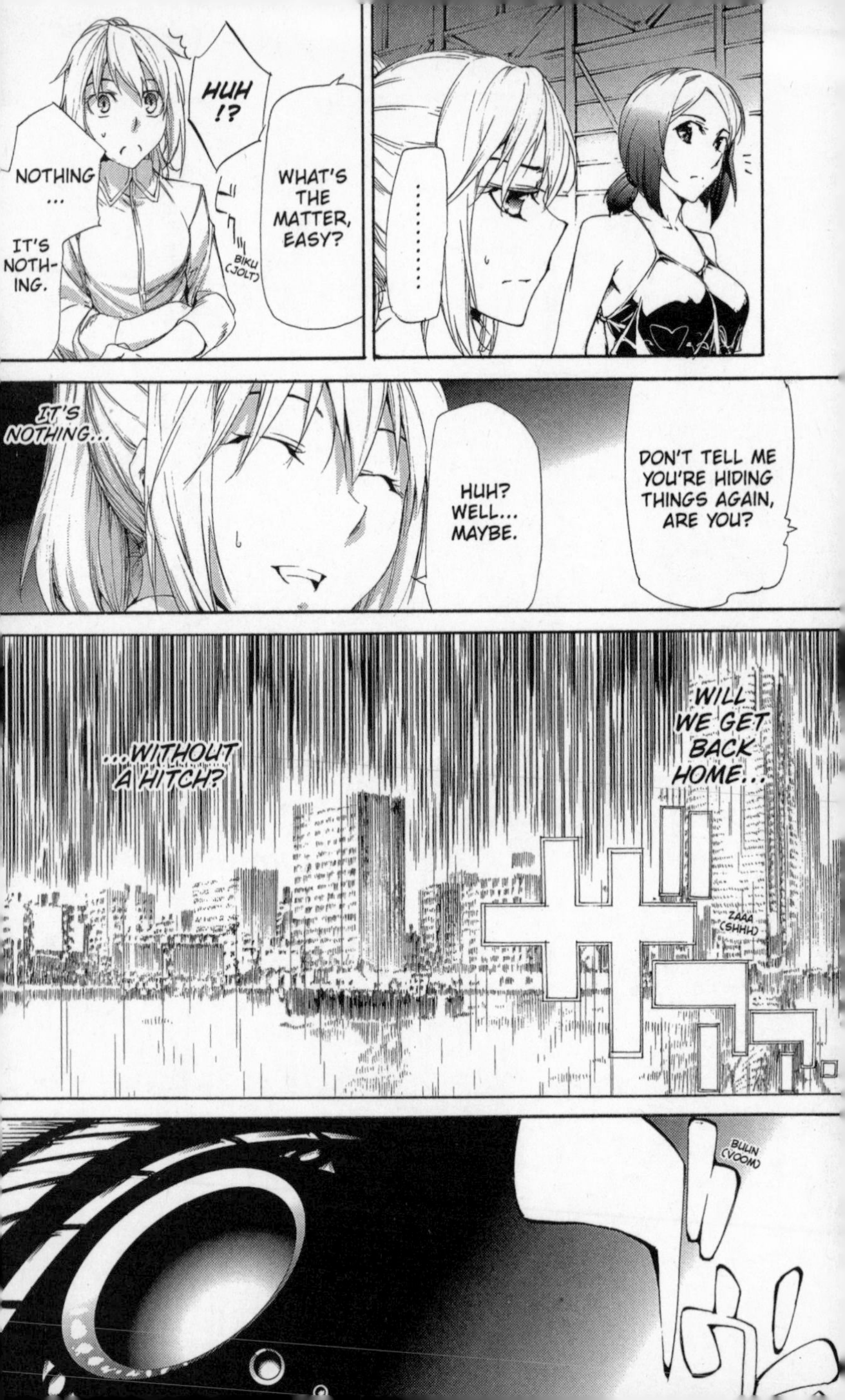
……
WHAT'S THE MATTER, EASY?
HUH !?
BIKU (JOLT)
NOTHING ...
IT'S NOTHING.
DON'T TELL ME YOU'RE HIDING THINGS AGAIN, ARE YOU?
HUH? WELL... MAYBE.
IT'S NOTHING...
WILL WE GET BACK HOME...
ZAAA (SHHH)
...WITHOUT A HITCH?
BULUN (VOOM)

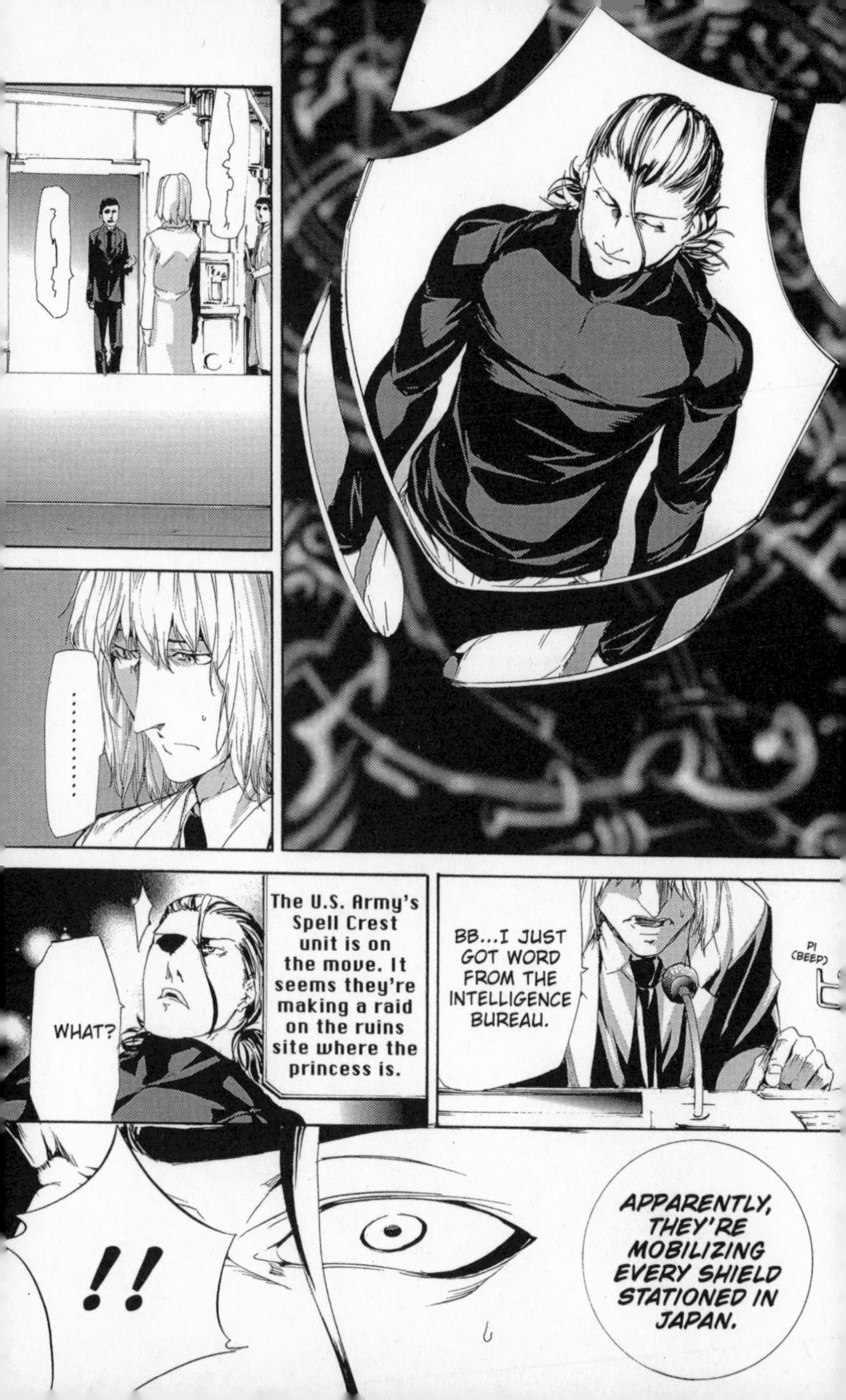
......
PI (BEEP)
BB...I JUST GOT WORD FROM THE INTELLIGENCE BUREAU.
The U.S. Army's Spell Crest unit is on the move. It seems they're making a raid on the ruins site where the princess is.
WHAT?
APPARENTLY, THEY'RE MOBILIZING EVERY SHIELD STATIONED IN JAPAN.
!!

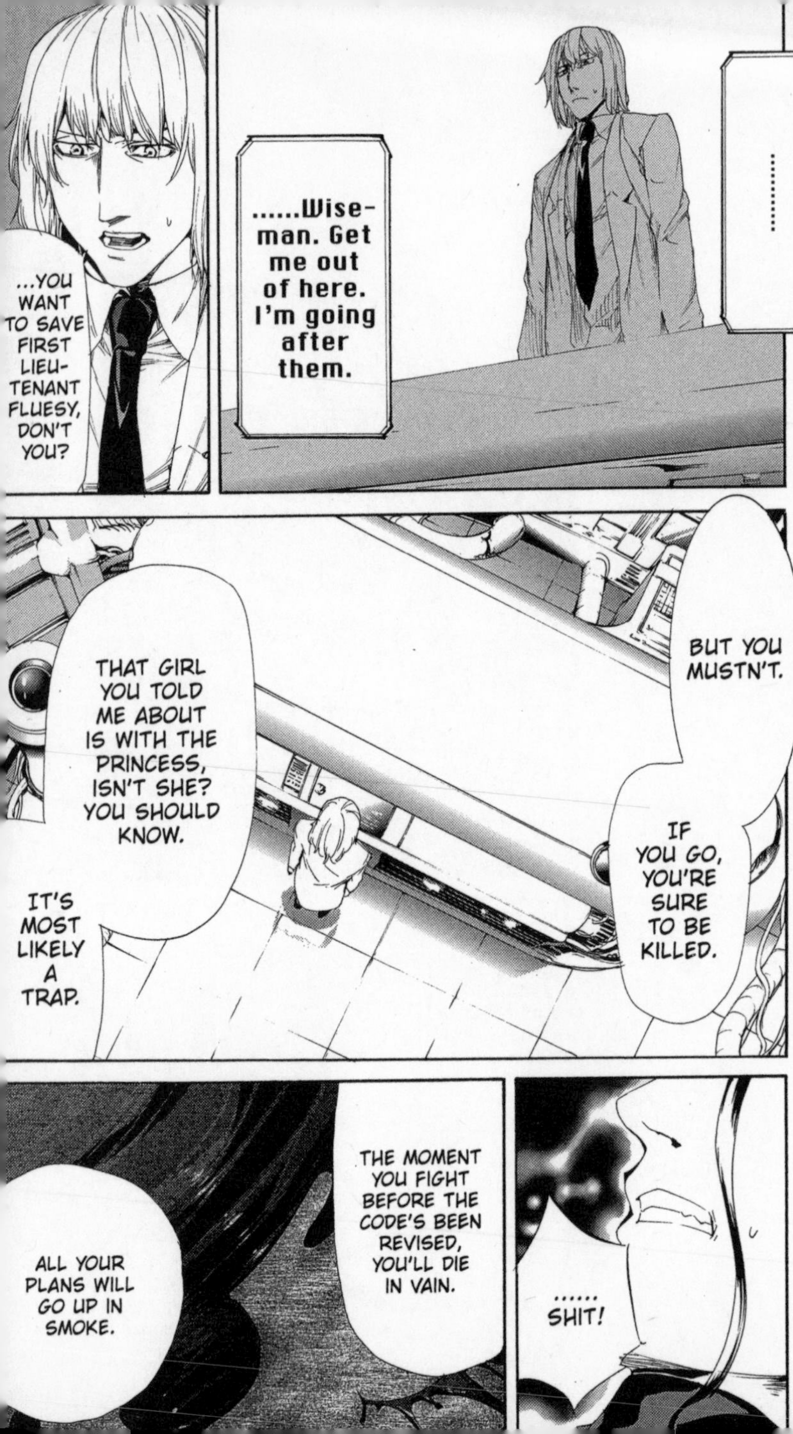
......
......Wise-man. Get me out of here. I'm going after them.
...YOU WANT TO SAVE FIRST LIEU-TENANT FLUESY, DON'T YOU?
BUT YOU MUSTN'T.
IF YOU GO, YOU'RE SURE TO BE KILLED.
THAT GIRL YOU TOLD ME ABOUT IS WITH THE PRINCESS, ISN'T SHE? YOU SHOULD KNOW.
IT'S MOST LIKELY A TRAP.
...... SHIT!
THE MOMENT YOU FIGHT BEFORE THE CODE'S BEEN REVISED, YOU'LL DIE IN VAIN.
ALL YOUR PLANS WILL GO UP IN SMOKE.

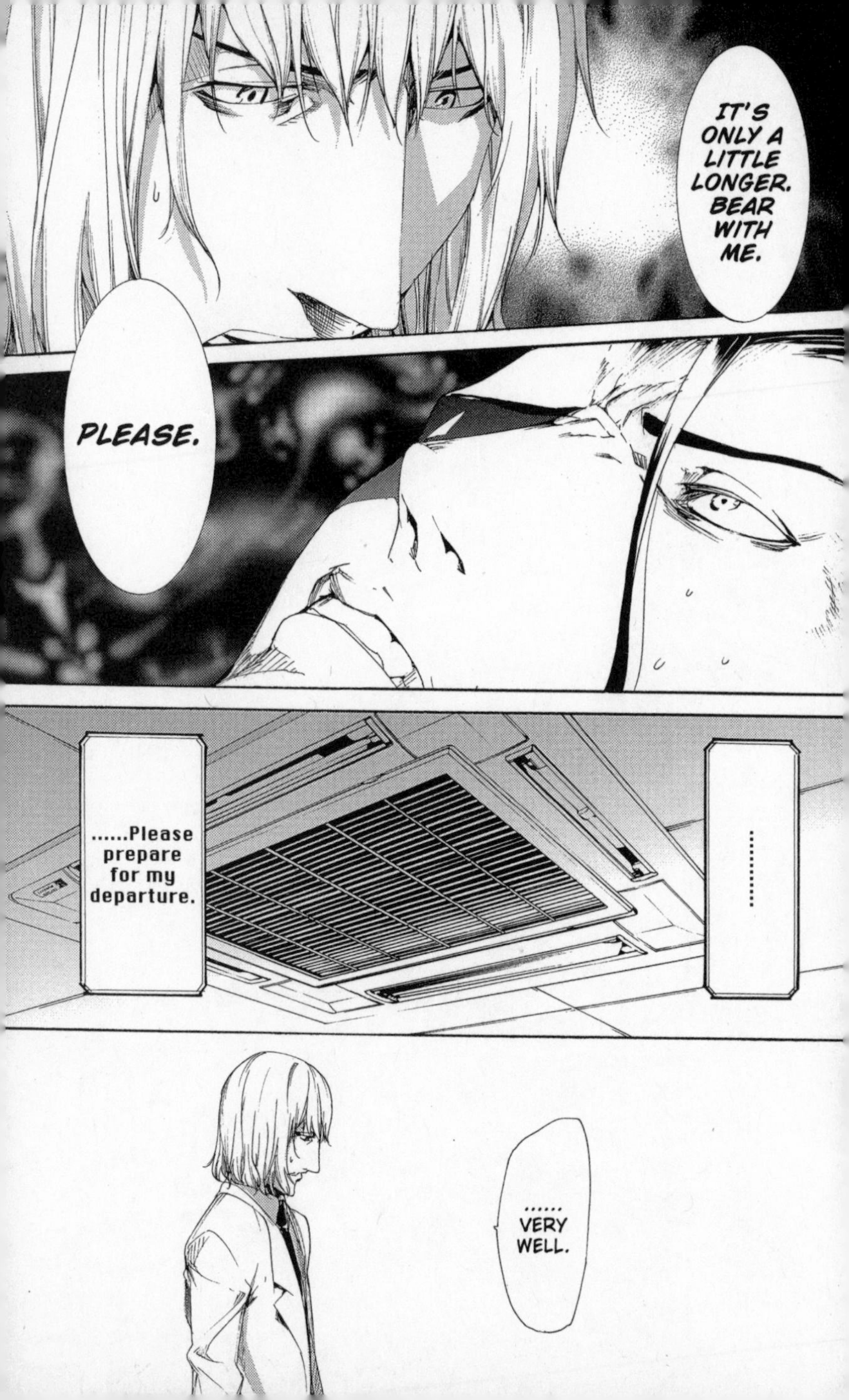
IT'S ONLY A LITTLE LONGER. BEAR WITH ME.
PLEASE.
......
......Please prepare for my departure.
...... VERY WELL.

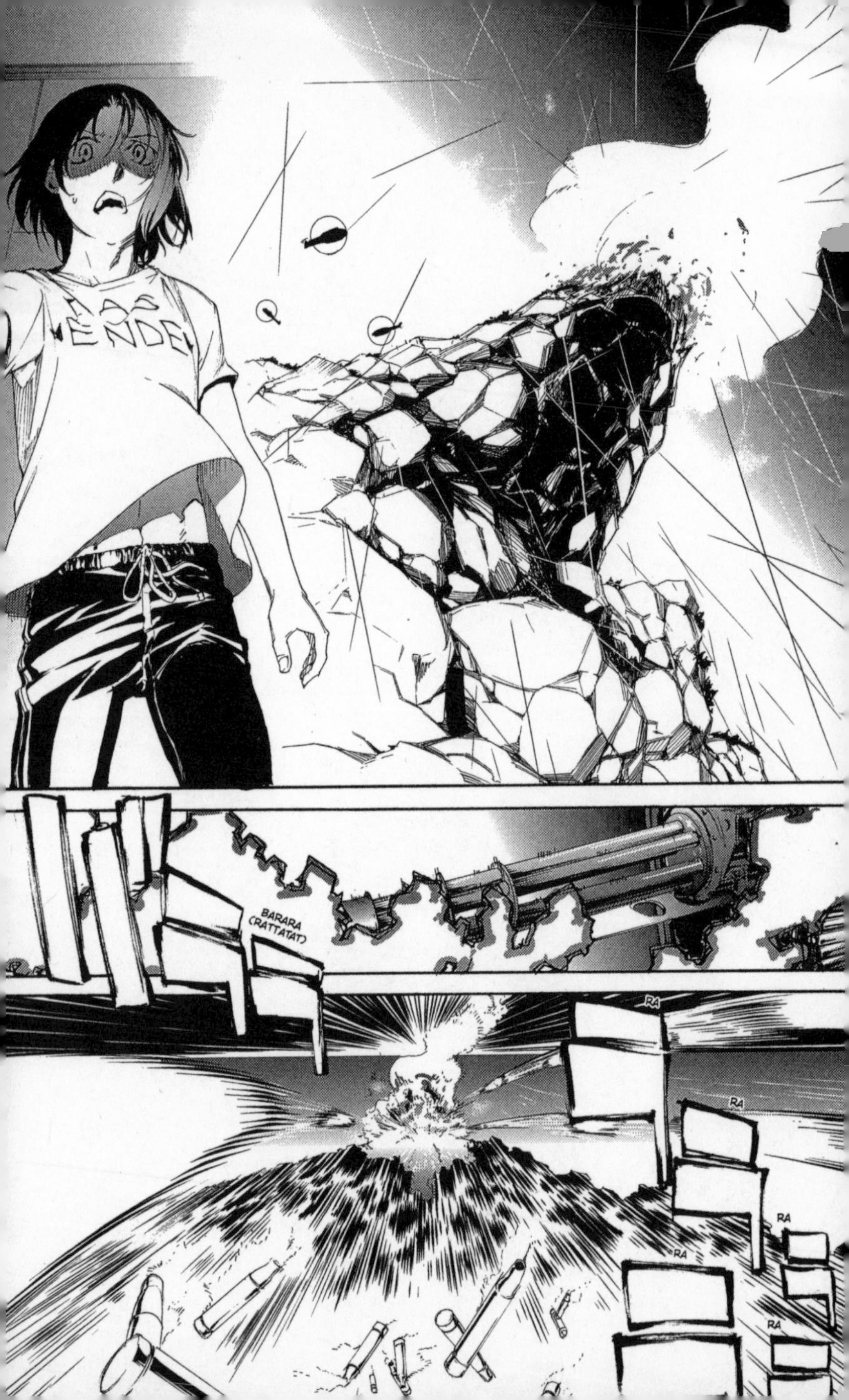
BARARA
(RATTATAT)
RA
RA
RA
RA
RA

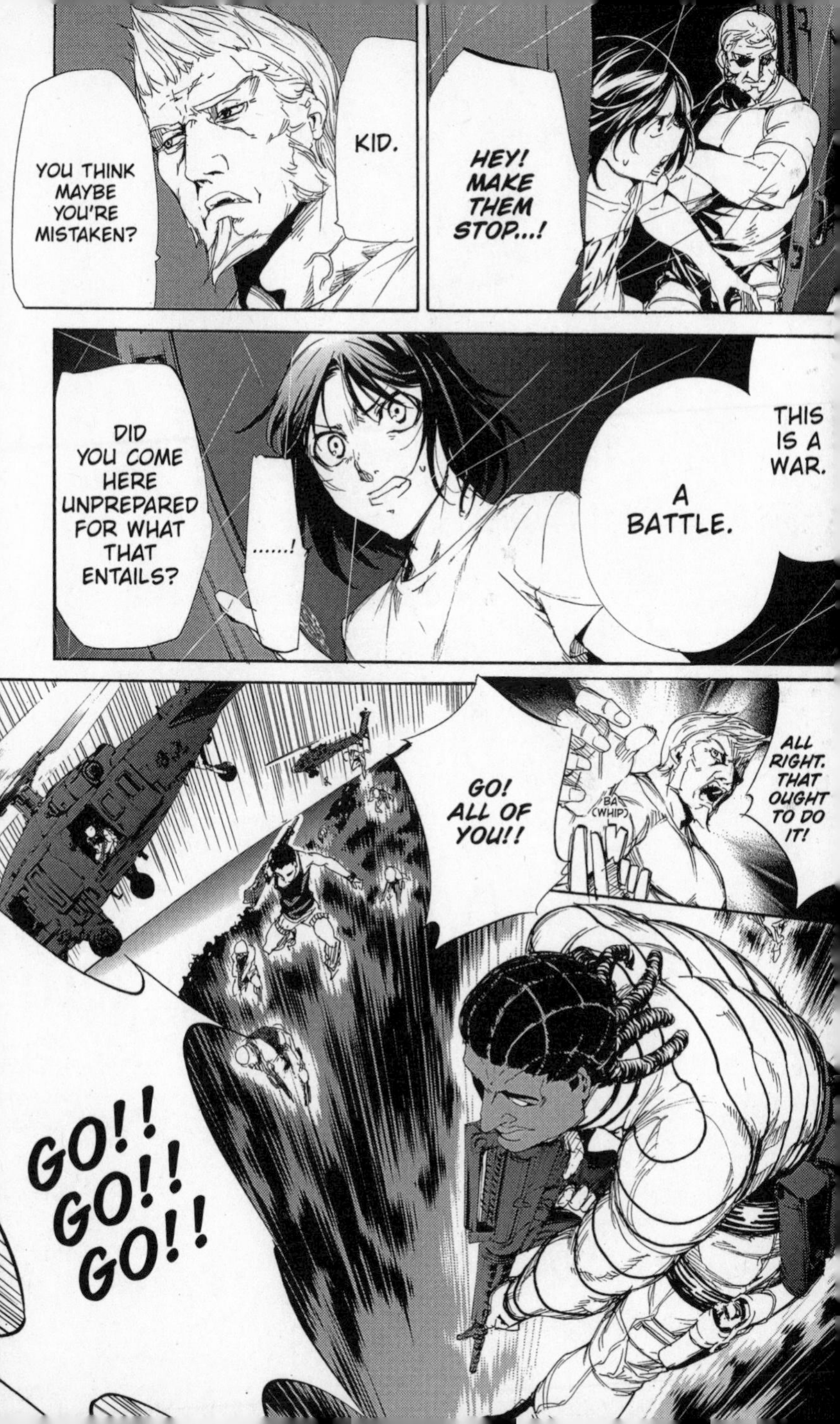
HEY! MAKE THEM STOP...!
KID.
YOU THINK MAYBE YOU'RE MISTAKEN?
THIS IS A WAR.
A BATTLE.
......!
DID YOU COME HERE UNPREPARED FOR WHAT THAT ENTAILS?
ALL RIGHT. THAT OUGHT TO DO IT!
BA (WHIP)
GO! ALL OF YOU!!
GO!! GO!! GO!!

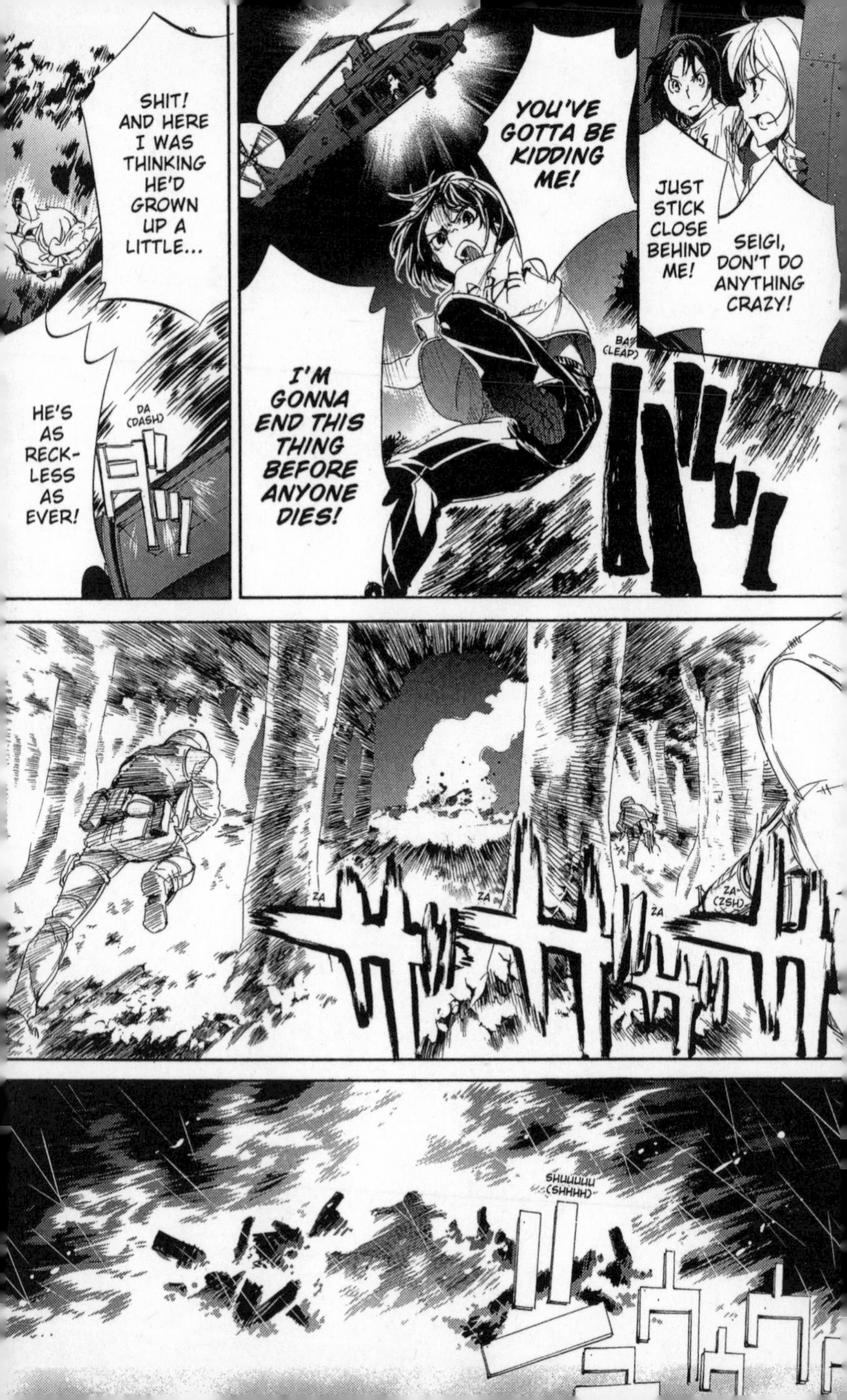
JUST STICK CLOSE BEHIND ME!
SEIGI, DON'T DO ANYTHING CRAZY!
BA (LEAP)
YOU'VE GOTTA BE KIDDING ME!
I'M GONNA END THIS THING BEFORE ANYONE DIES!
SHIT! AND HERE I WAS THINKING HE'D GROWN UP A LITTLE...
HE'S AS RECK-LESS AS EVER!
DA (DASH)
ZA (ZSH)
ZA
ZA
ZA
SHUUUUUU (SHHHH)

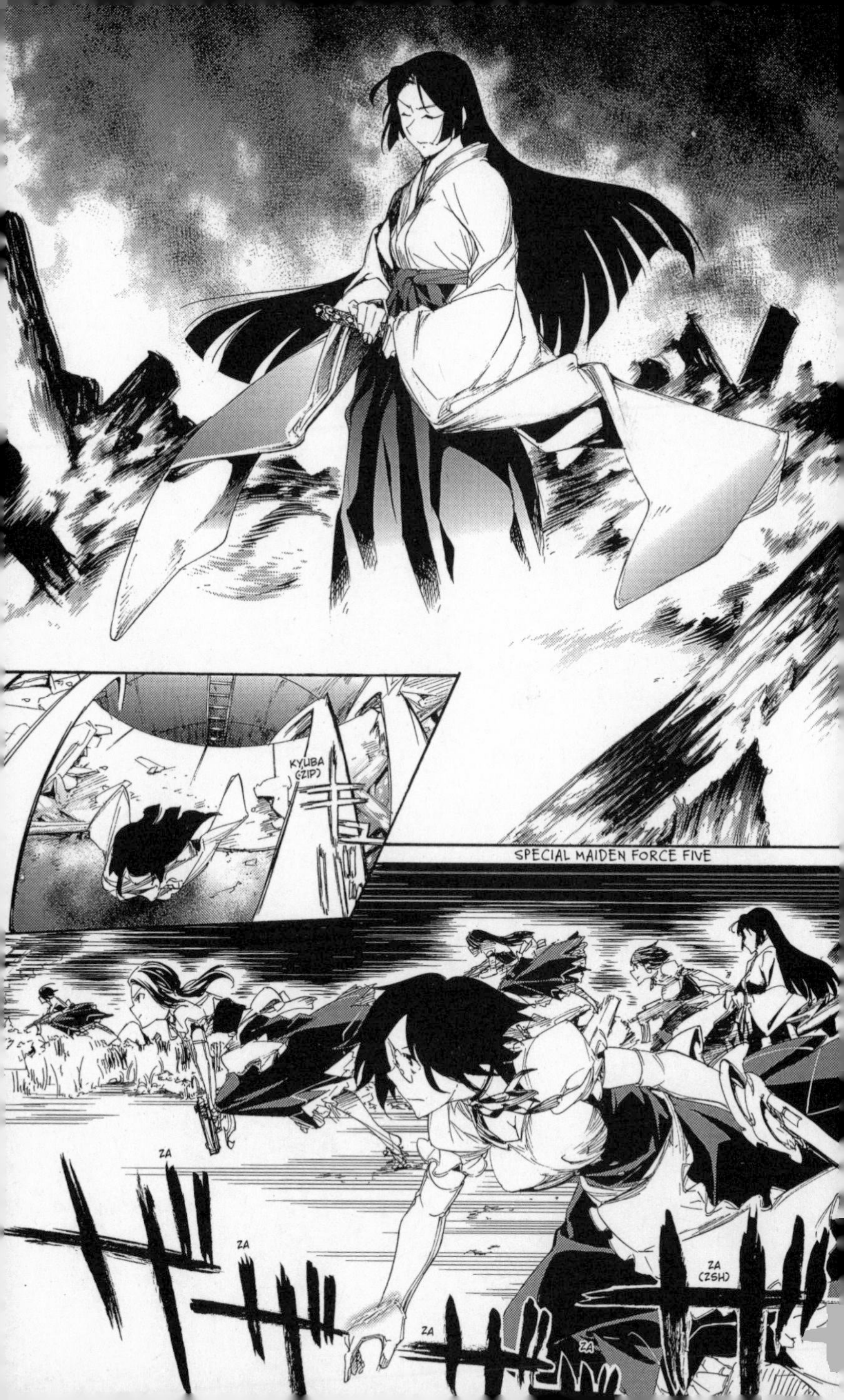
KYUBA (ZIP)
SPECIAL MAIDEN FORCE FIVE
ZA (ZSH)
ZA
ZA
ZA
ZA

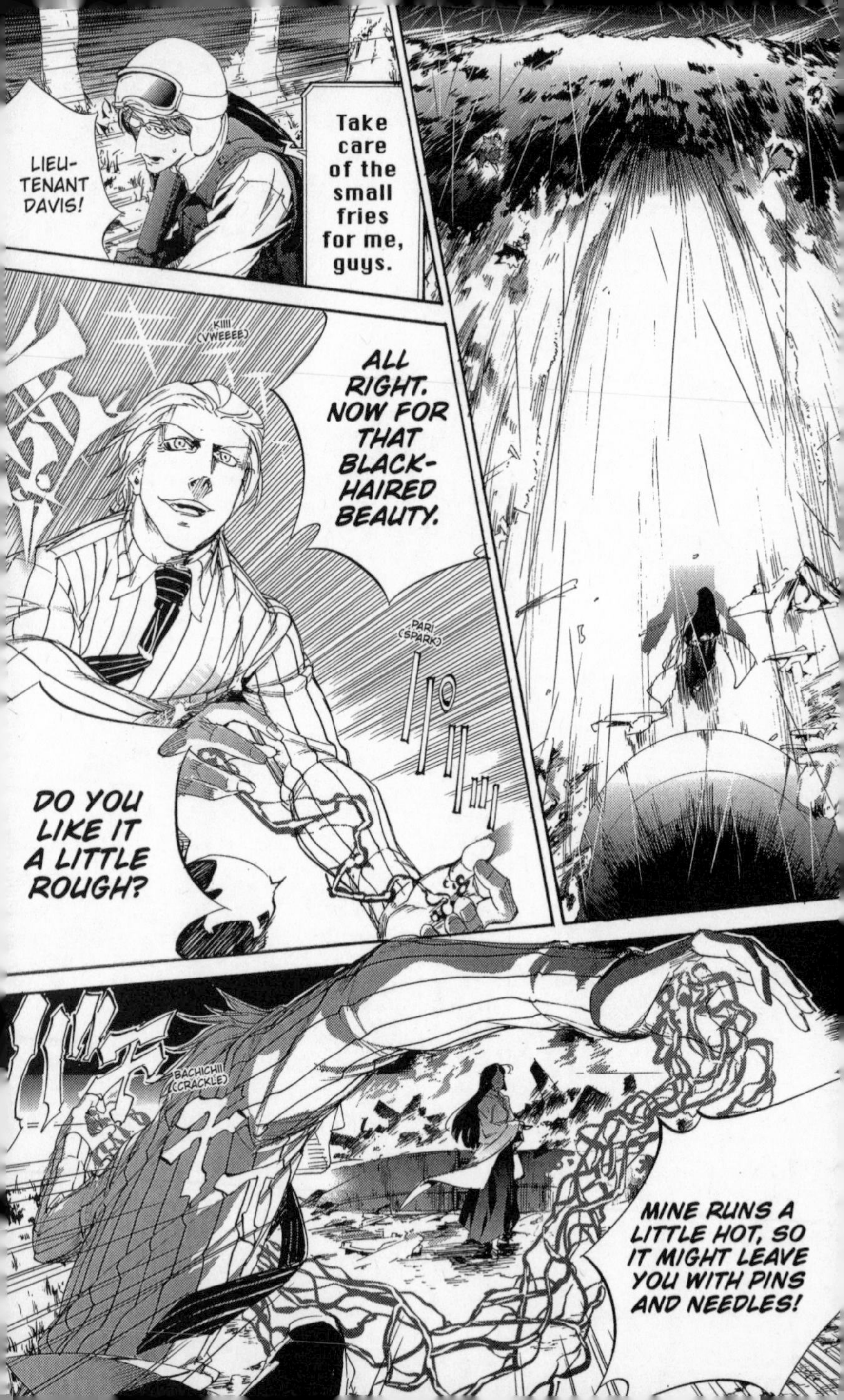
Take care of the small fries for me, guys.
LIEU-TENANT DAVIS!
KIIII (VWEEEE)
ALL RIGHT. NOW FOR THAT BLACK-HAIRED BEAUTY.
PARI (SPARK)
DO YOU LIKE IT A LITTLE ROUGH?
BACHICHII (CRACKLE)
MINE RUNS A LITTLE HOT, SO IT MIGHT LEAVE YOU WITH PINS AND NEEDLES!

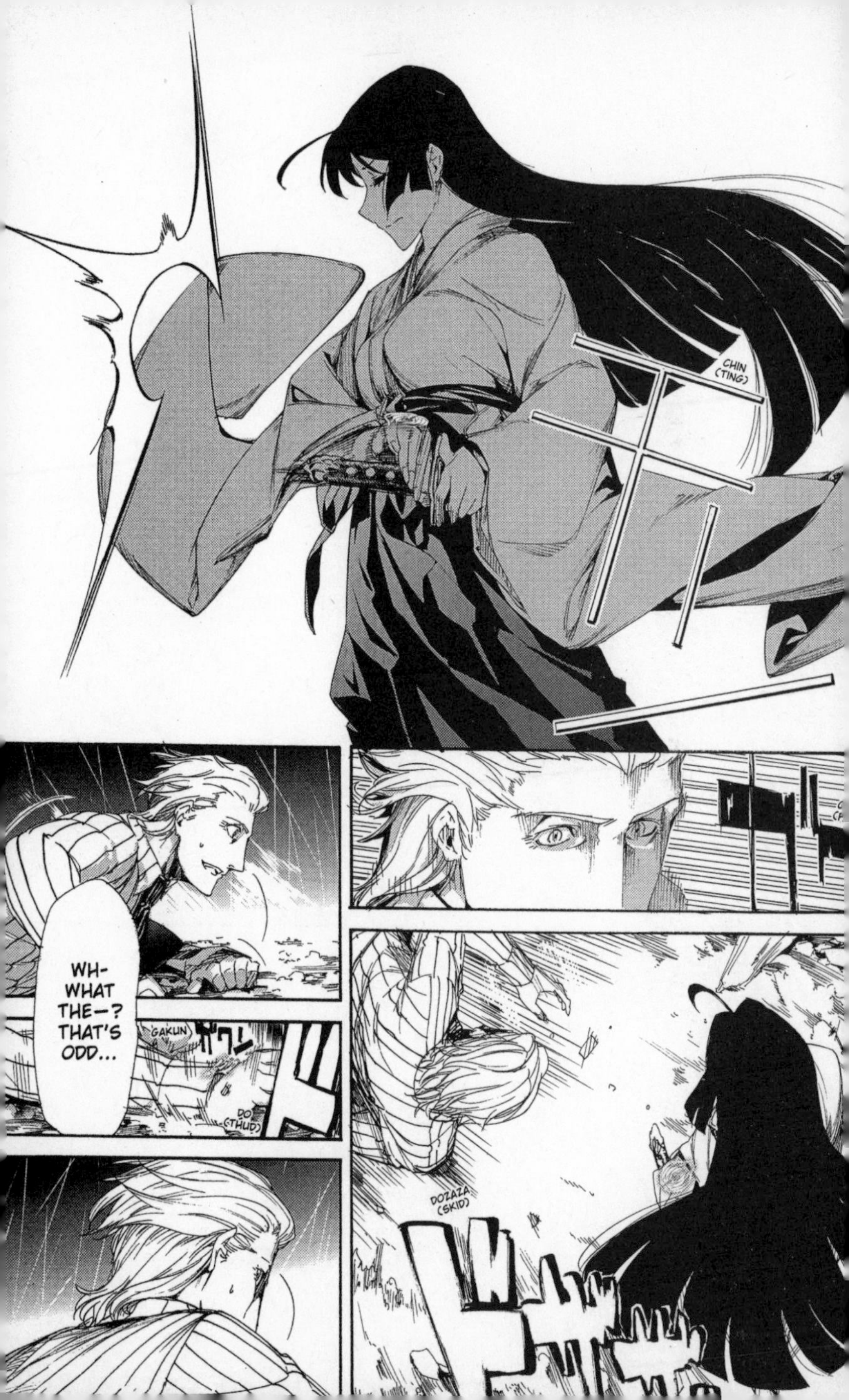
CHIN
(TING)
WH-
WHAT
THE—?
THAT'S
ODD...
DOZAZA
(SKID)
GAKUN
DO
(THUD)

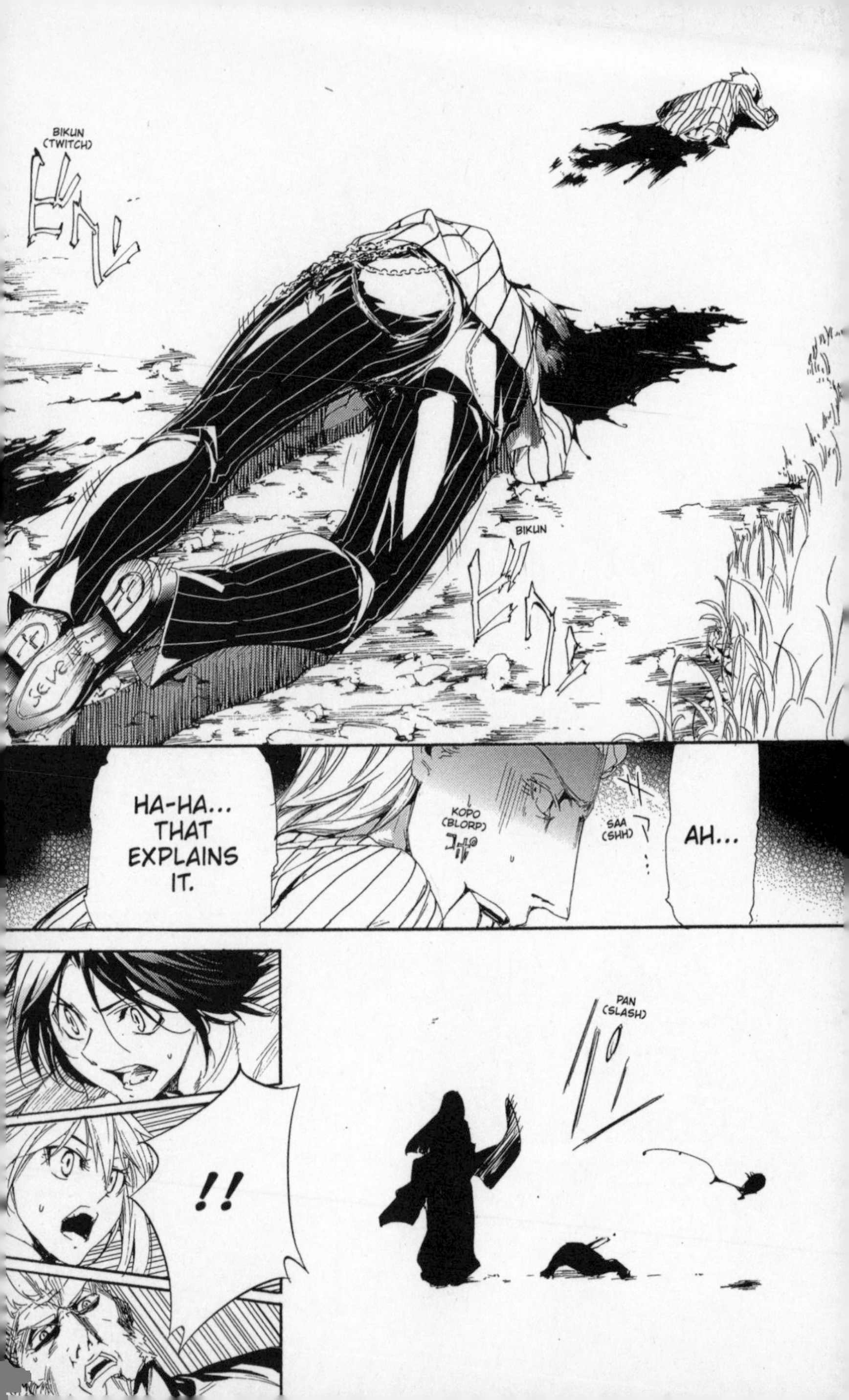
BIKUN (TWITCH)
BIKUN
AH...
SAA (SHH)
KOPO (BLORP)
HA-HA... THAT EXPLAINS IT.
PAN (SLASH)
!!

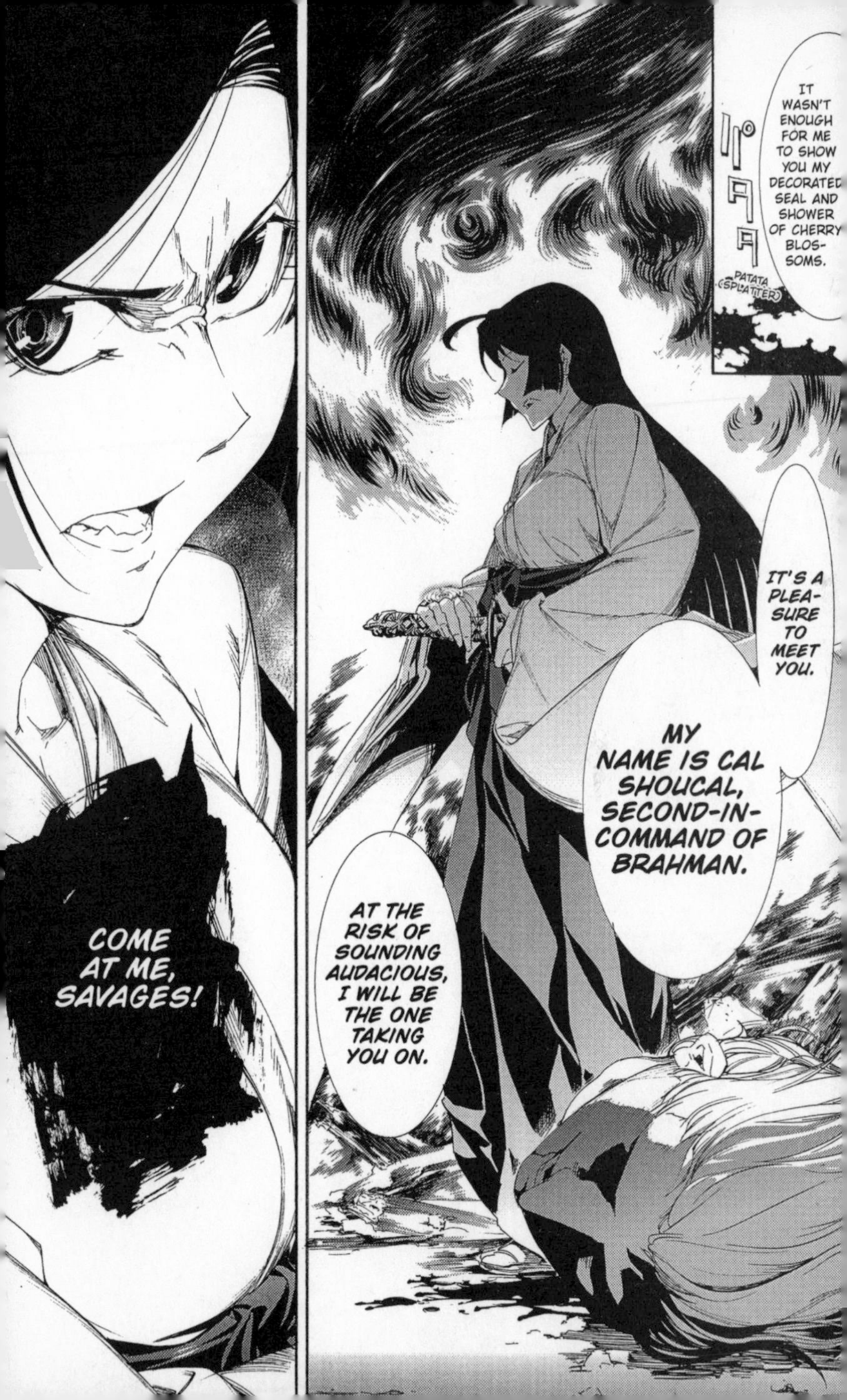
IT WASN'T ENOUGH FOR ME TO SHOW YOU MY DECORATED SEAL AND SHOWER OF CHERRY BLOS-SOMS.
PATATA (SPLATTER)
IT'S A PLEA-SURE TO MEET YOU.
MY NAME IS CAL SHOUCAL, SECOND-IN-COMMAND OF BRAHMAN.
AT THE RISK OF SOUNDING AUDACIOUS, I WILL BE THE ONE TAKING YOU ON.
COME AT ME, SAVAGES!

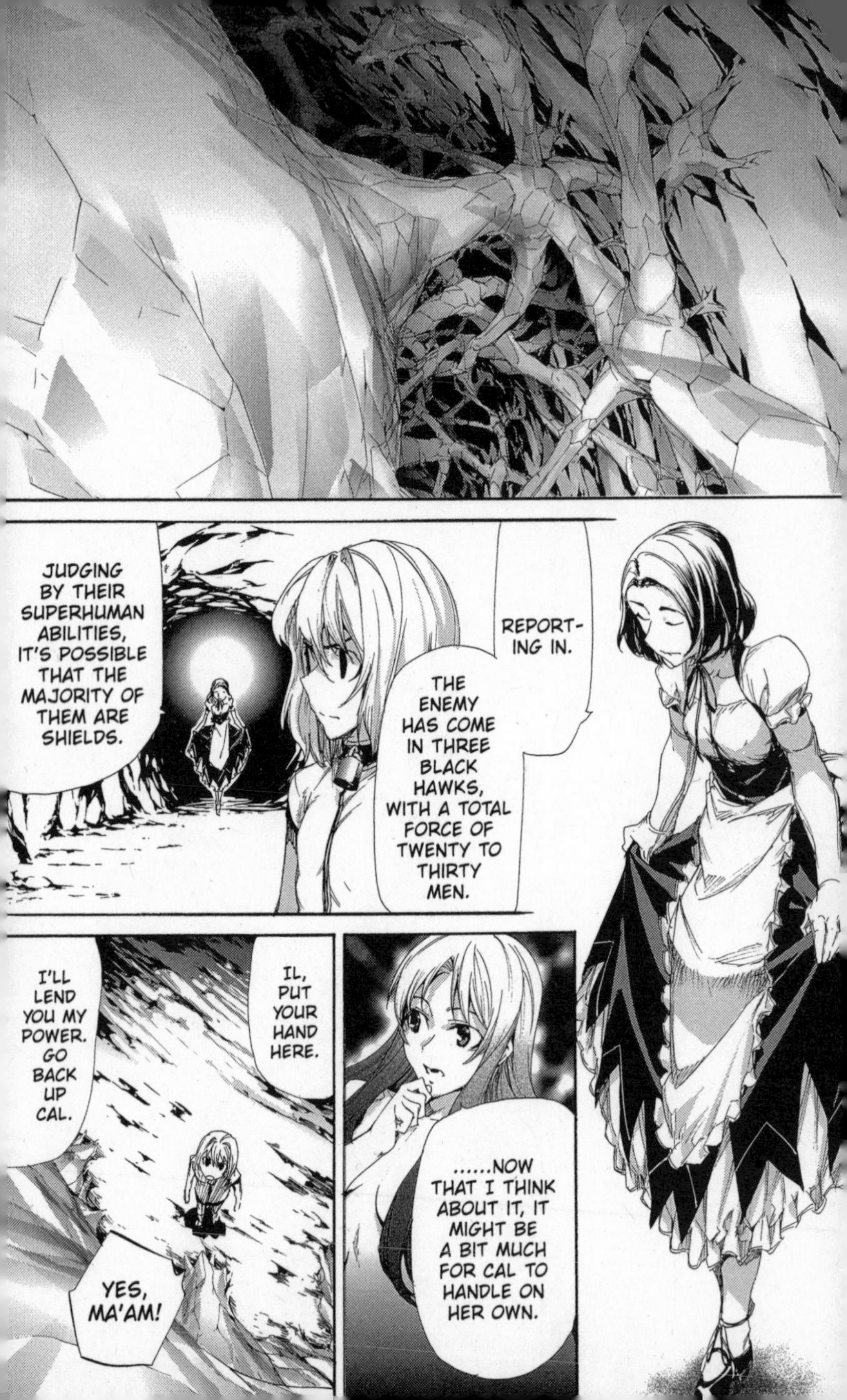
REPORT-ING IN.
THE ENEMY HAS COME IN THREE BLACK HAWKS, WITH A TOTAL FORCE OF TWENTY TO THIRTY MEN.
JUDGING BY THEIR SUPERHUMAN ABILITIES, IT'S POSSIBLE THAT THE MAJORITY OF THEM ARE SHIELDS.
......NOW THAT I THINK ABOUT IT, IT MIGHT BE A BIT MUCH FOR CAL TO HANDLE ON HER OWN.
IL, PUT YOUR HAND HERE.
I'LL LEND YOU MY POWER. GO BACK UP CAL.
YES, MA'AM!

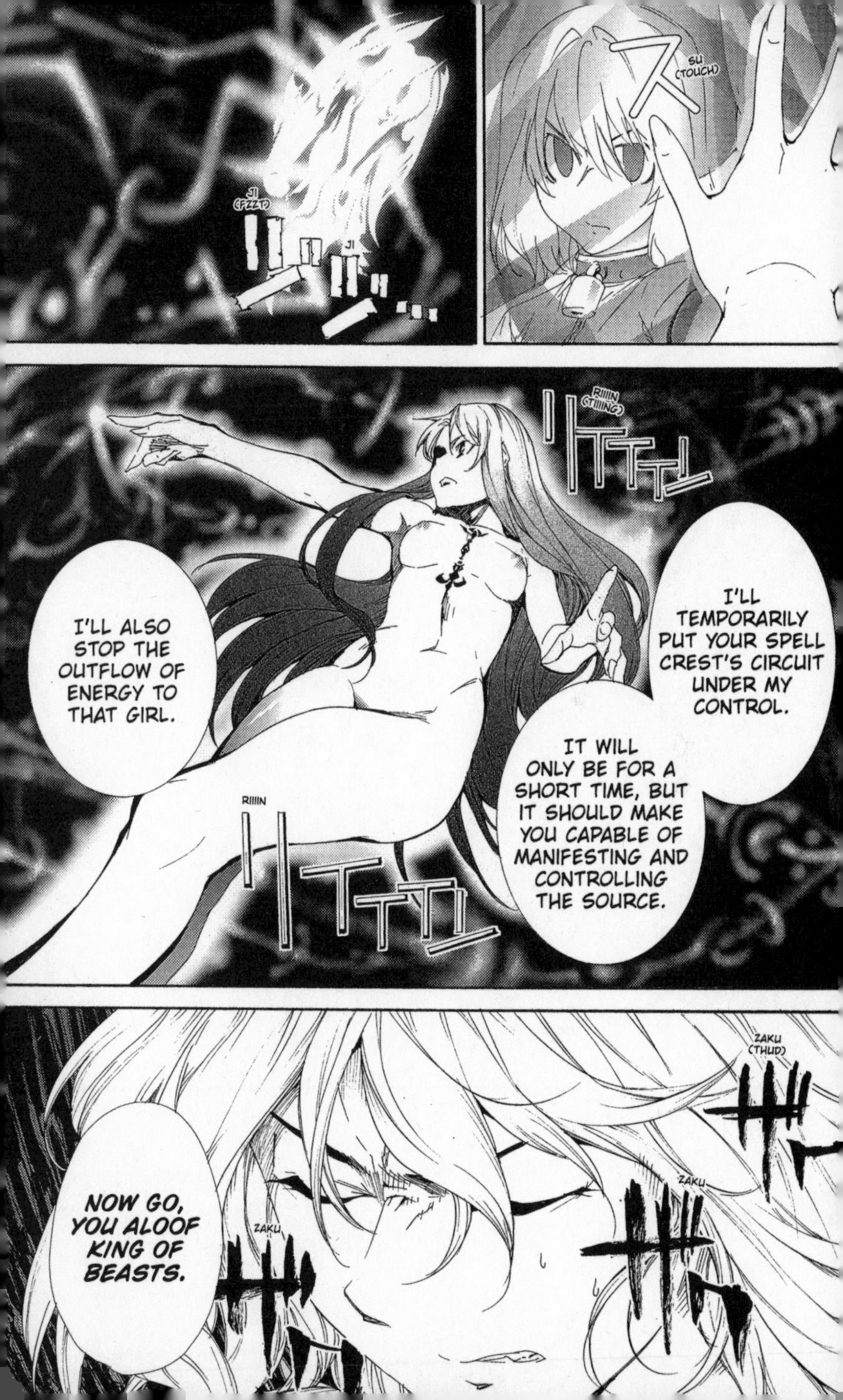
SU (TOUCH)
JI (FZZT)
JI
RIIIN (TIIIING)
I'LL TEMPORARILY PUT YOUR SPELL CREST'S CIRCUIT UNDER MY CONTROL.
IT WILL ONLY BE FOR A SHORT TIME, BUT IT SHOULD MAKE YOU CAPABLE OF MANIFESTING AND CONTROLLING THE SOURCE.
I'LL ALSO STOP THE OUTFLOW OF ENERGY TO THAT GIRL.
RIIIN
ZAKU (THUD)
ZAKU
NOW GO, YOU ALOOF KING OF BEASTS.
ZAKU

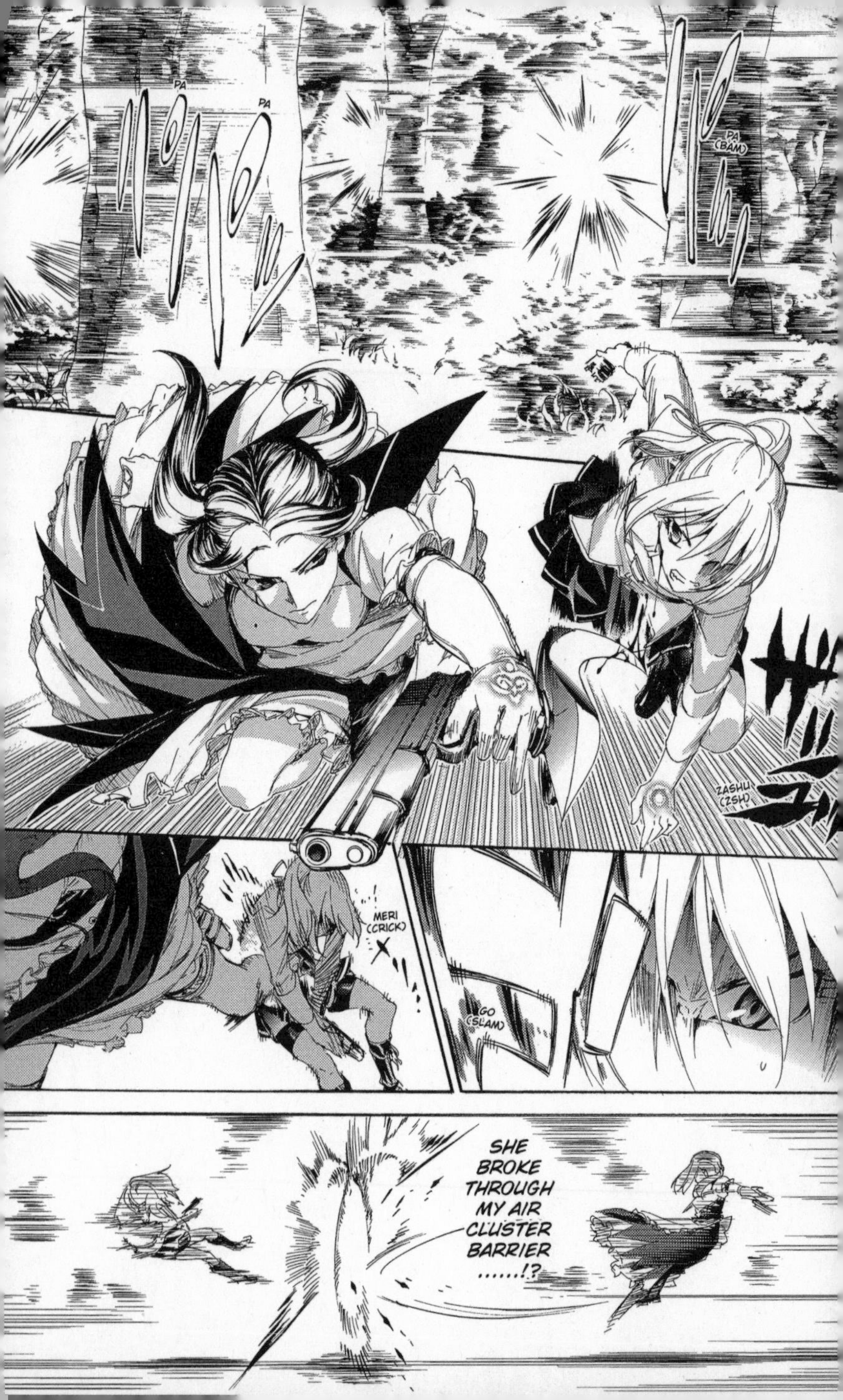
PA (BAM)
PA
PA
ZASHU (ZSH)
GO (SLAM)
MERI (CRICK)
SHE BROKE THROUGH MY AIR CLUSTER BARRIER ......!?

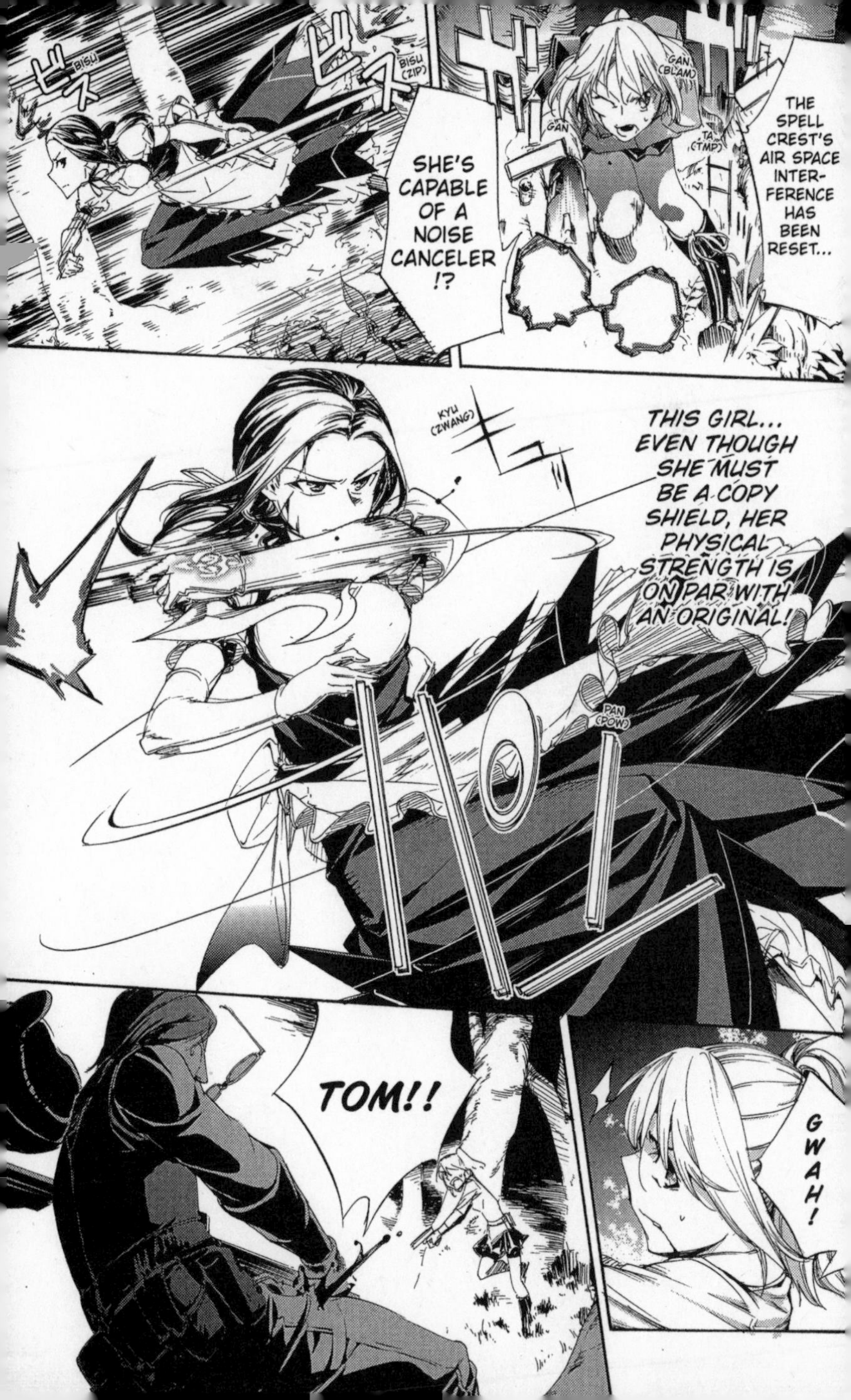

GAN (BLAM)
GAN
TA (TMP)
THE SPELL CREST'S AIR SPACE INTERFERENCE HAS BEEN RESET...
SHE'S CAPABLE OF A NOISE CANCELER !?
BISU (ZIP)
BISU
KYU (ZWANG)
THIS GIRL... EVEN THOUGH SHE MUST BE A COPY SHIELD, HER PHYSICAL STRENGTH IS ON PAR WITH AN ORIGINAL!
PAN (POW)
GWAH!
TOM!!

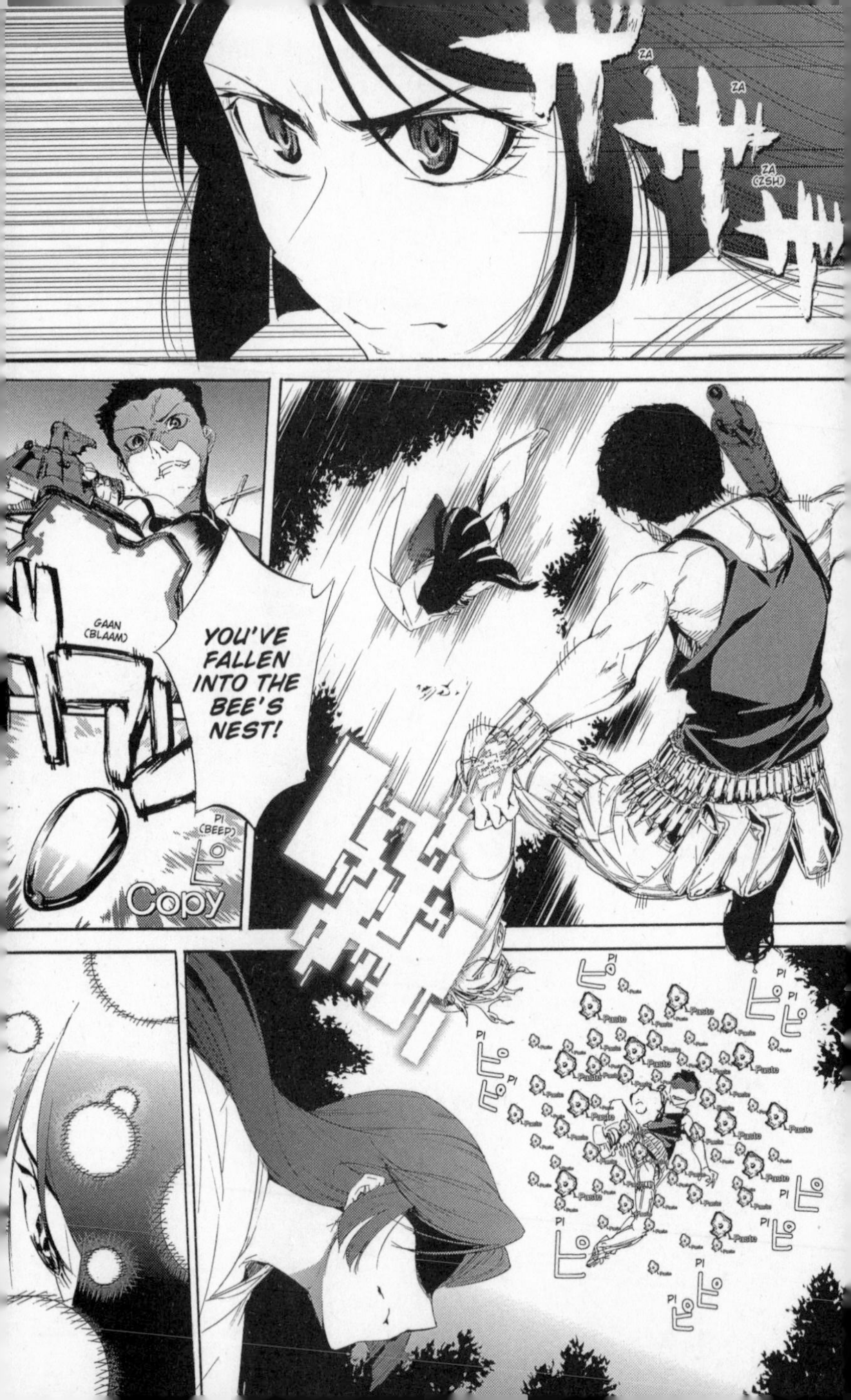
ZA
ZA
ZA (ZSH)
YOU'VE FALLEN INTO THE BEE'S NEST!
GAAN (BLAAM)
PI (BEEP)
Copy
PI
PI
PI
PI
PI
Paste
PI
PI
PI
PI

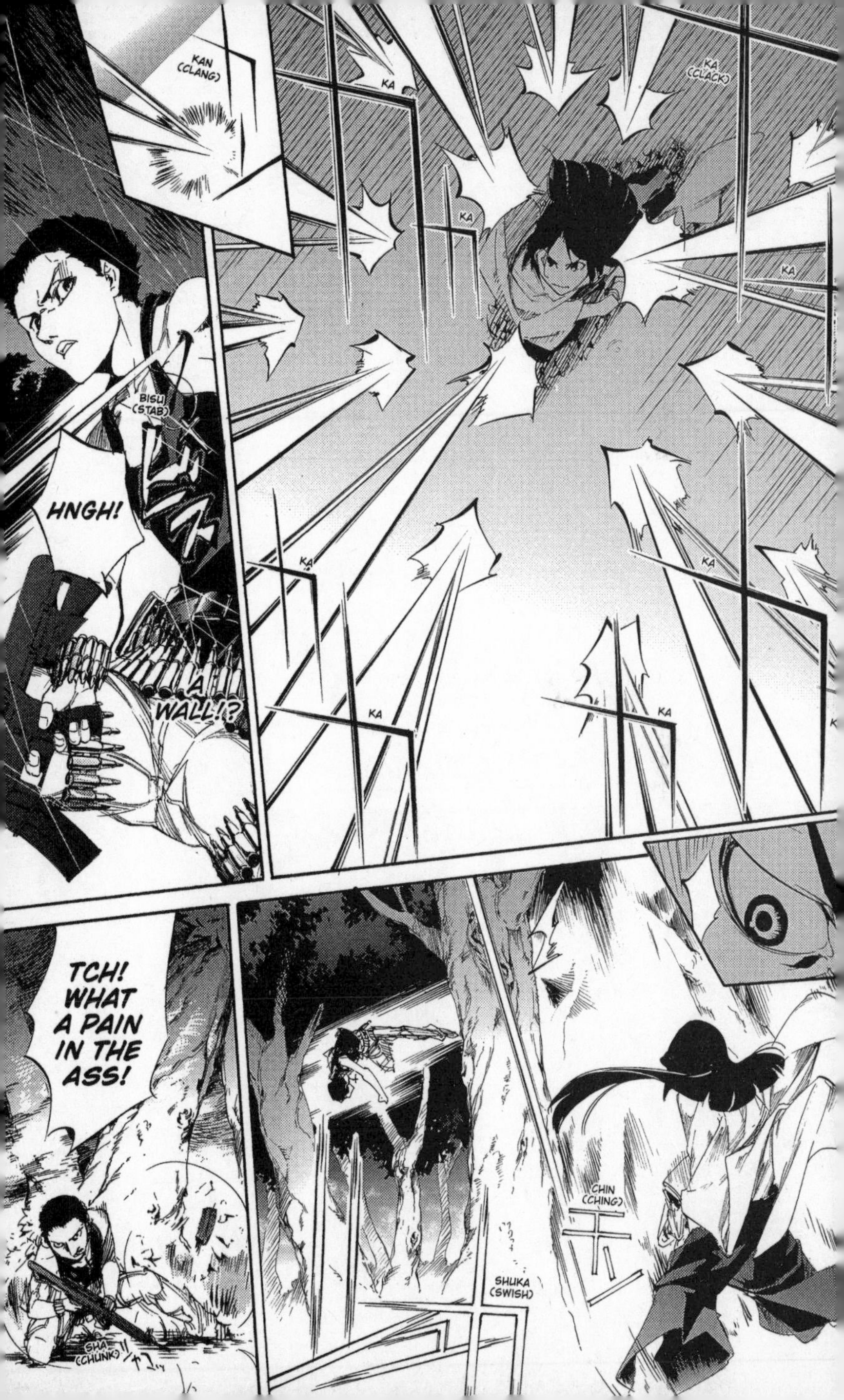

KA (CLACK)
KA
KA
KA
KA
KA
KA
KAN (CLANG)
BISU (STAB)
HNGH!
A WALL!?
CHIN (CHING)
SHUKA (SWISH)
TCH! WHAT A PAIN IN THE ASS!
SHA (CHUNK)

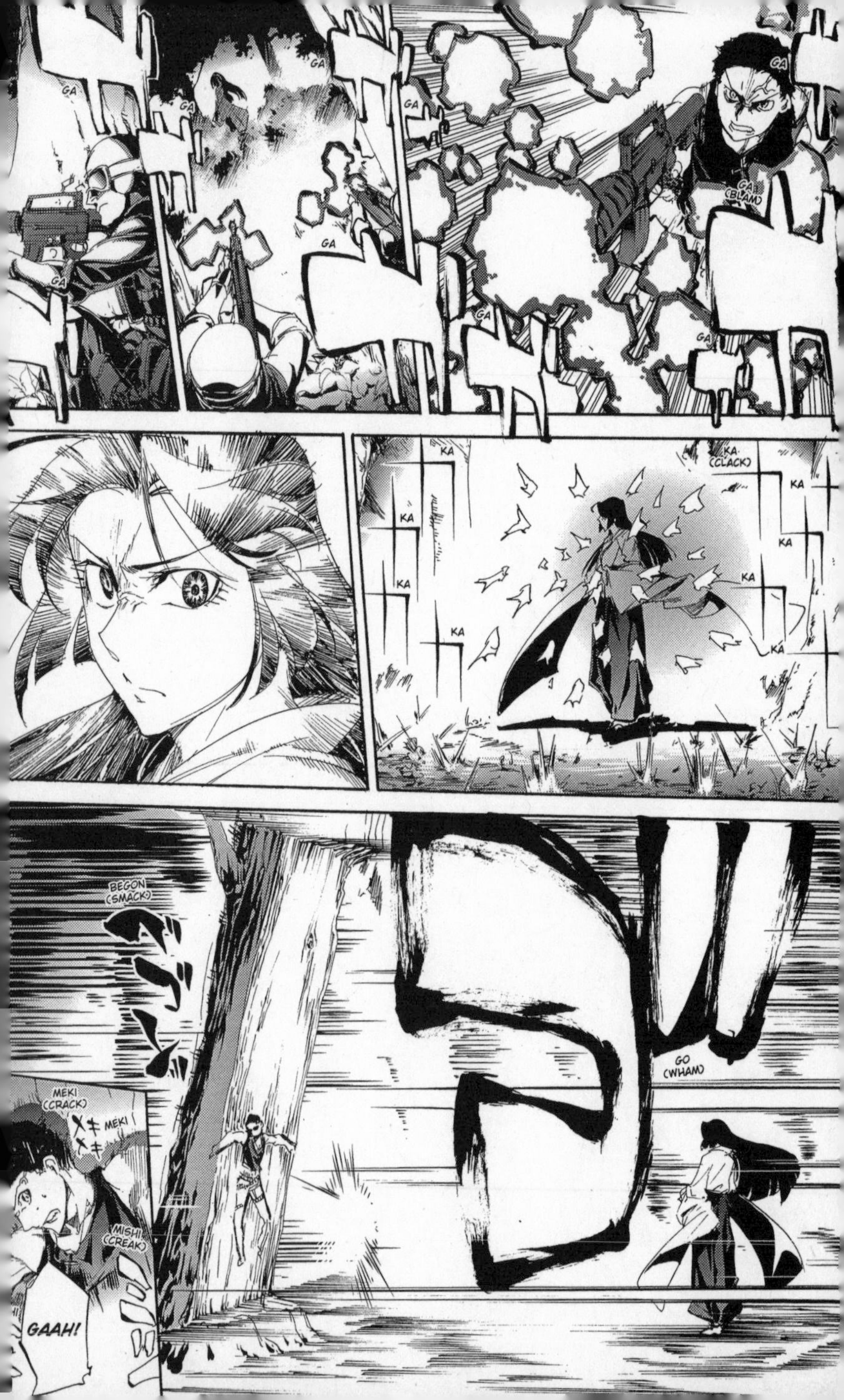
GA
GA
(BLAM)
GA
GA
GA
GA
GA
GA
GA
GA
KA
(CLACK)
KA
KA
KA
KA
KA
KA
KA
KA
GO
(WHAM)
BEGON
(SMACK)
MEKI
(CRACK)
メキ
メキ
MEKI
MISHI
(CREAK)
GAAH!

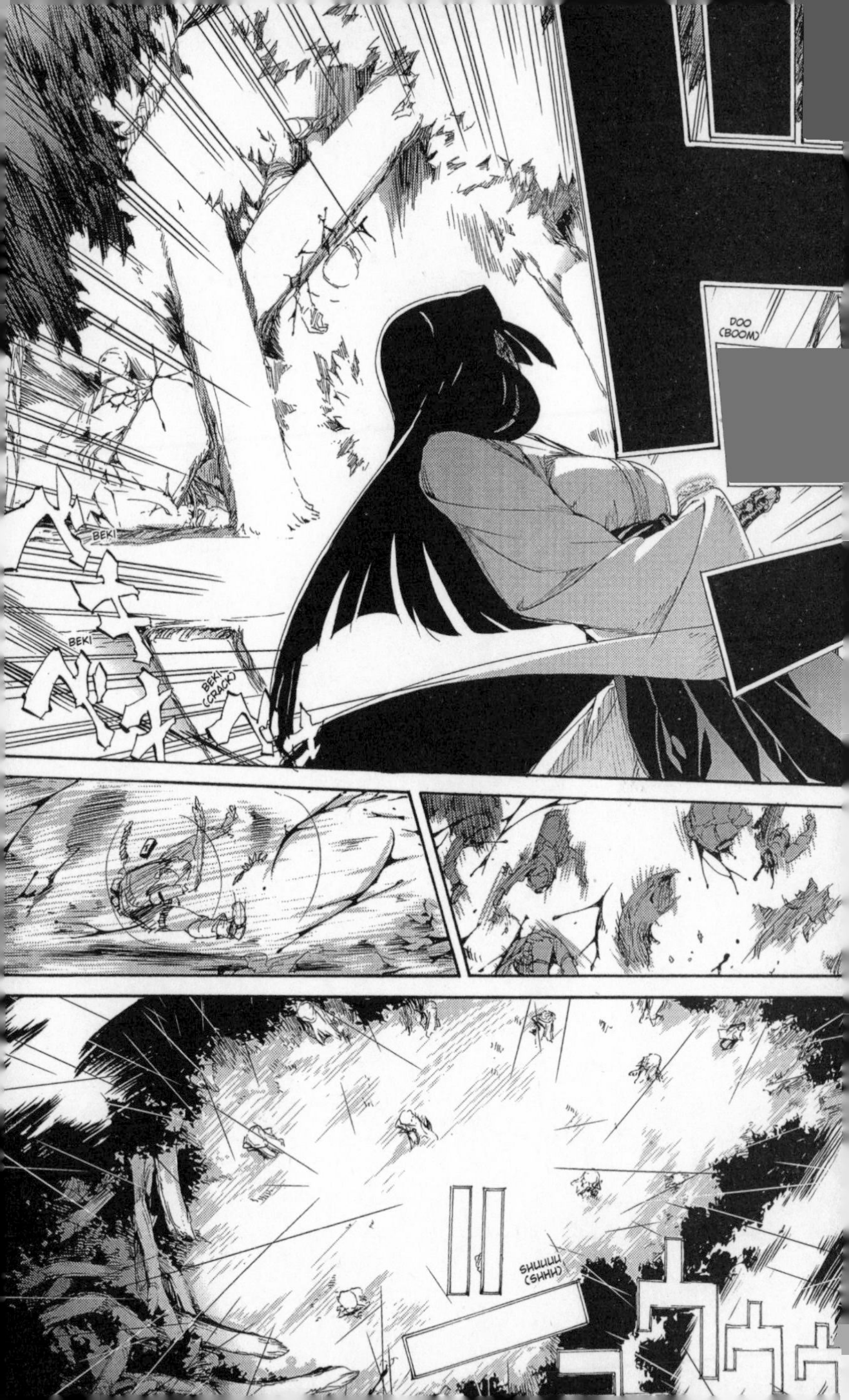
DOO
(BOOM)
BEKI
BEKI
BEKI
(CRACK)
SHUUUU
(SHHH)

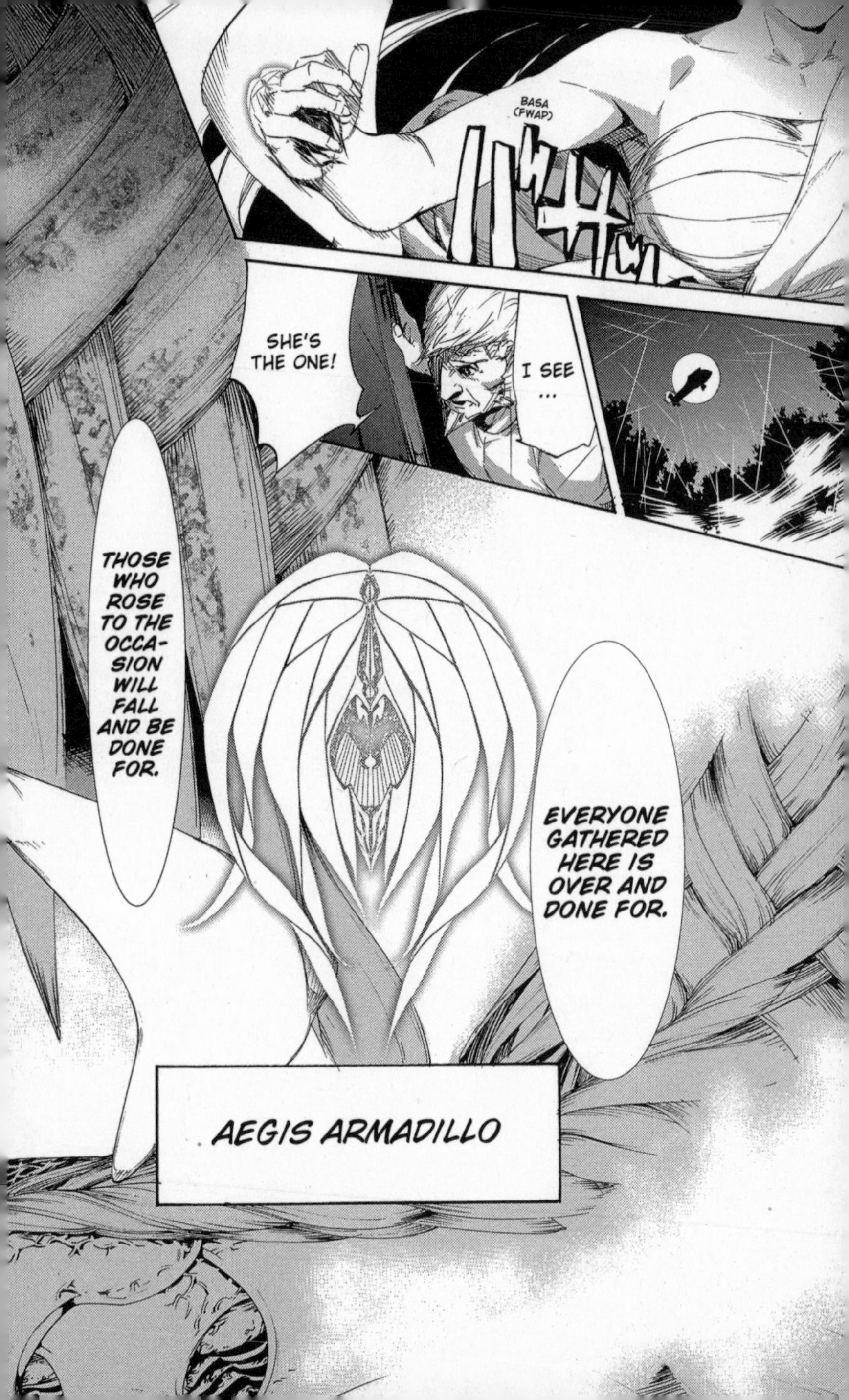
BASA (FWAP)
SHE'S THE ONE!
I SEE ...
EVERYONE GATHERED HERE IS OVER AND DONE FOR.
THOSE WHO ROSE TO THE OCCASION WILL FALL AND BE DONE FOR.
AEGIS ARMADILLO

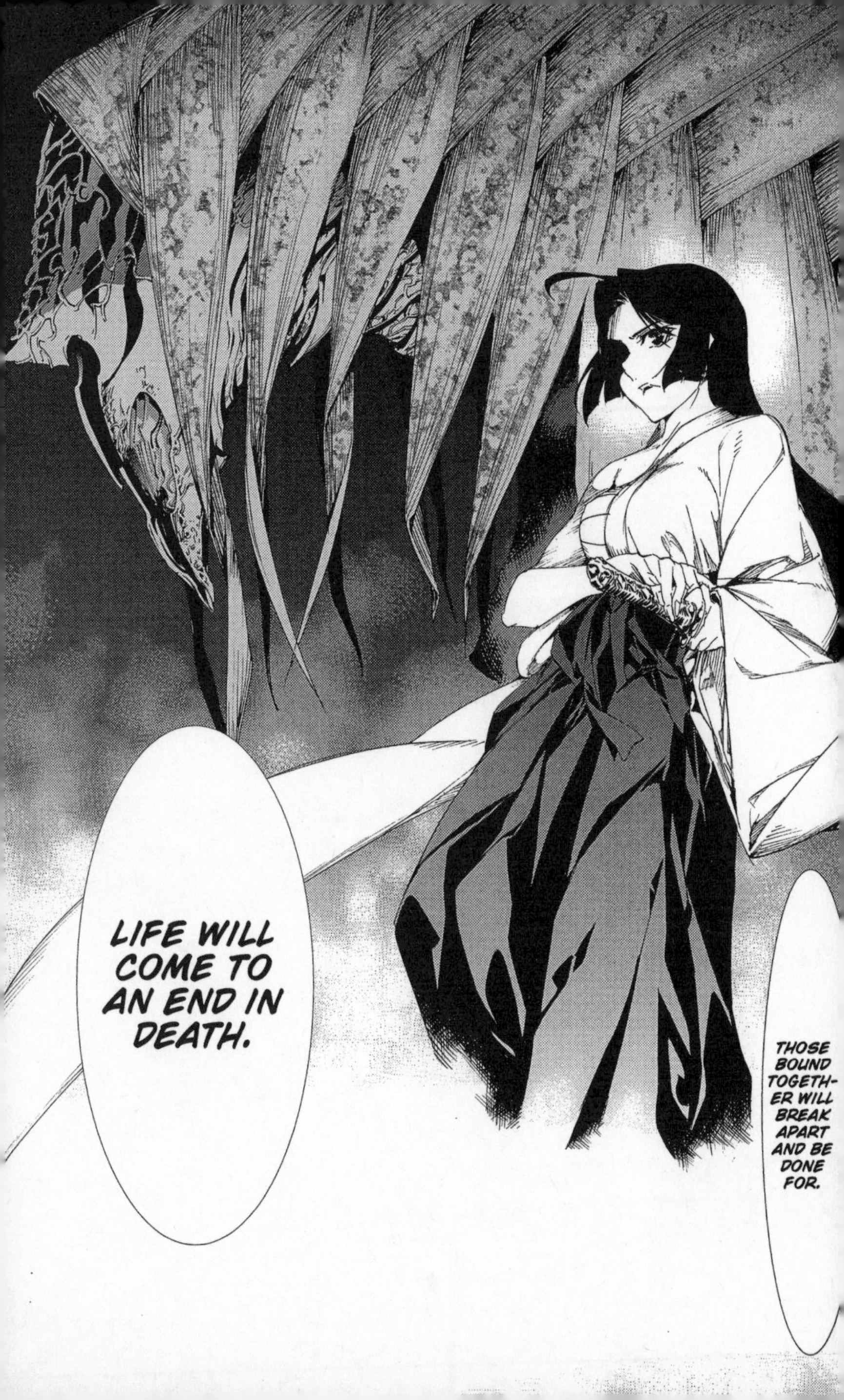
THOSE BOUND TOGETH-ER WILL BREAK APART AND BE DONE FOR.
LIFE WILL COME TO AN END IN DEATH.

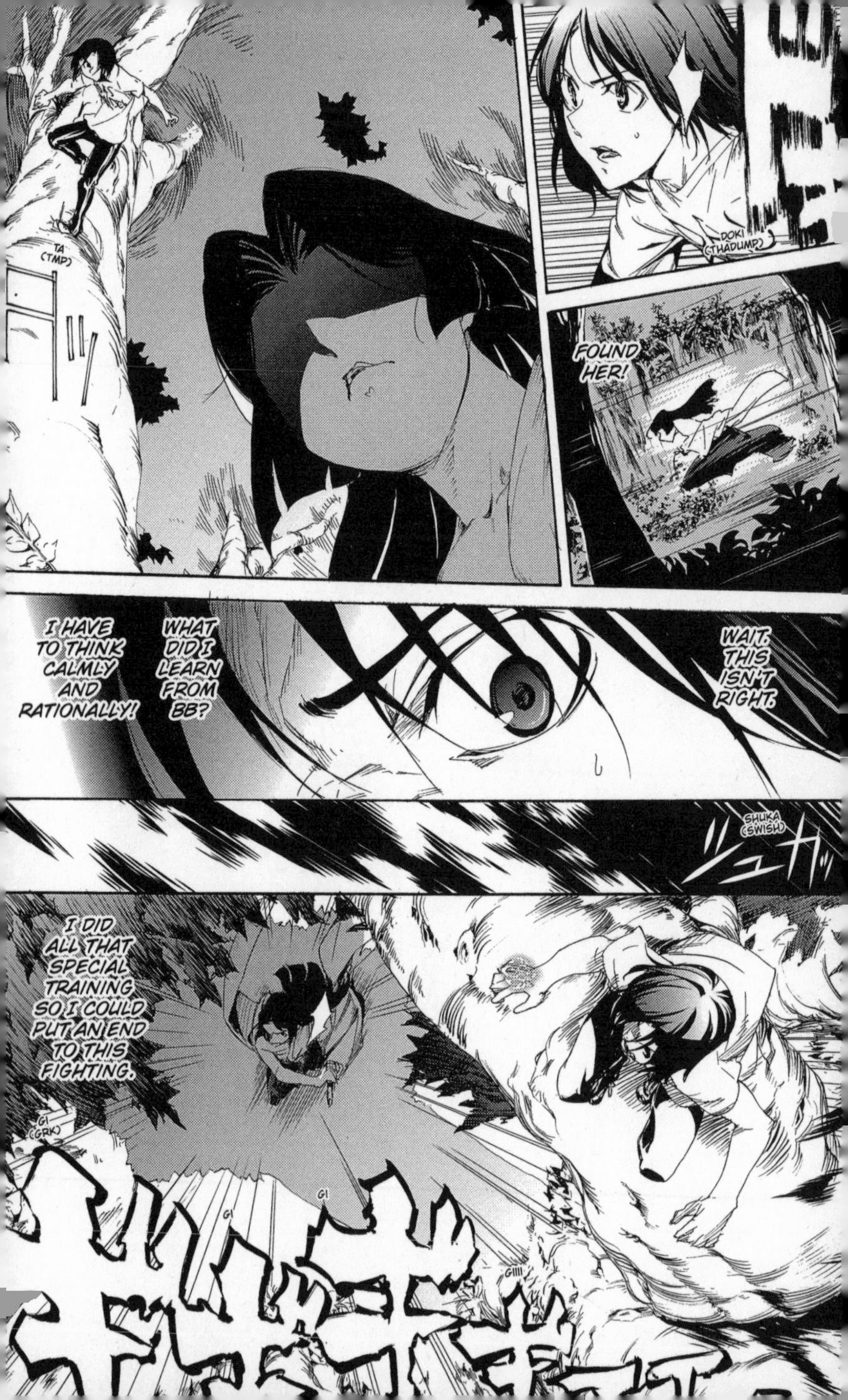
DOKI (THADUMP)
FOUND HER!
TA (TMP)
WAIT. THIS ISN'T RIGHT.
WHAT DID I LEARN FROM BB?
I HAVE TO THINK CALMLY AND RATIONALLY!
SHUKA (SWISH)
I DID ALL THAT SPECIAL TRAINING SO I COULD PUT AN END TO THIS FIGHTING.
GI (GRK)
GI
GI
GIII

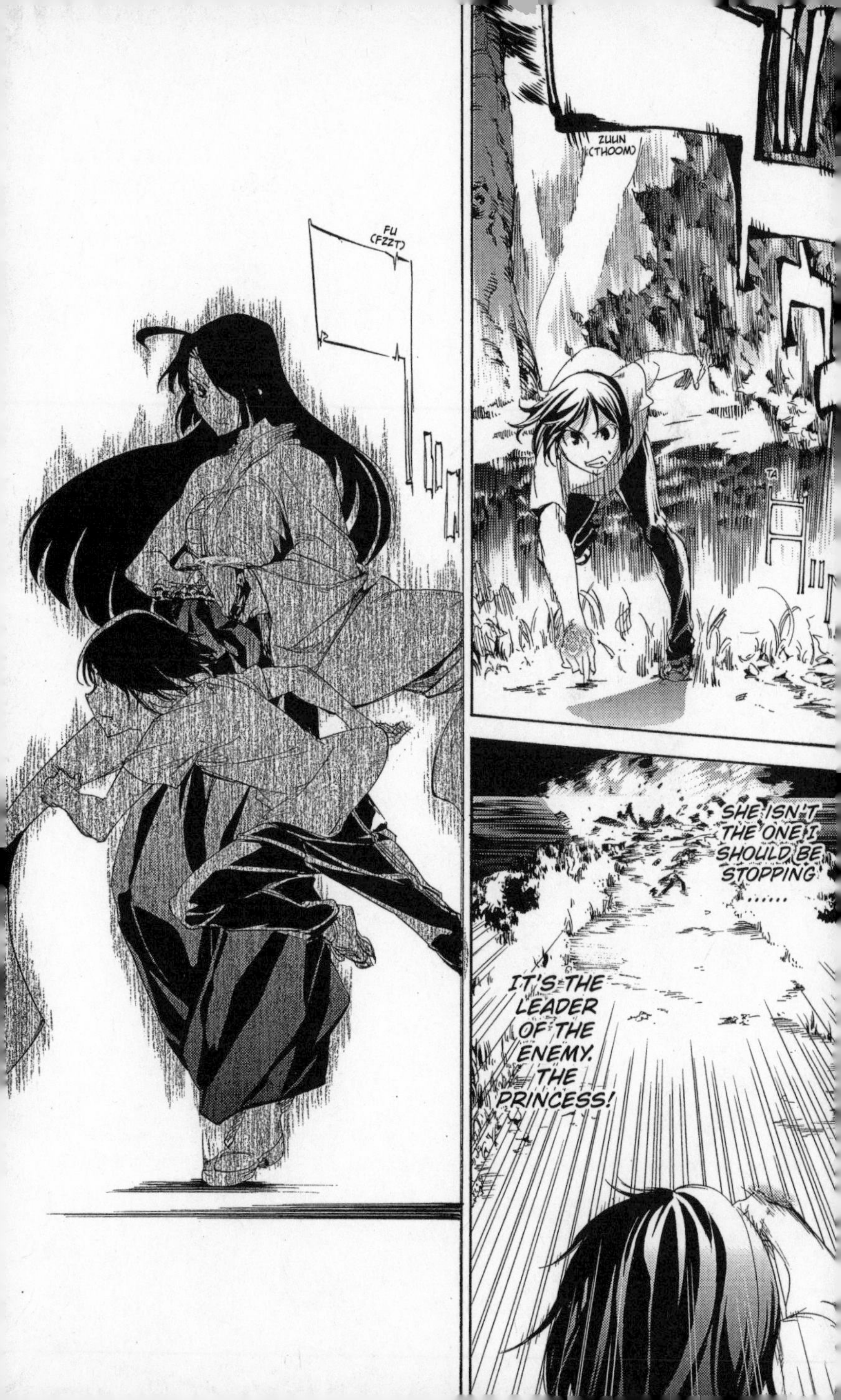
ZUUN (THOOM)
TA
SHE ISN'T THE ONE I SHOULD BE STOPPING ......
IT'S THE LEADER OF THE ENEMY. THE PRINCESS!
FU (FZZT)

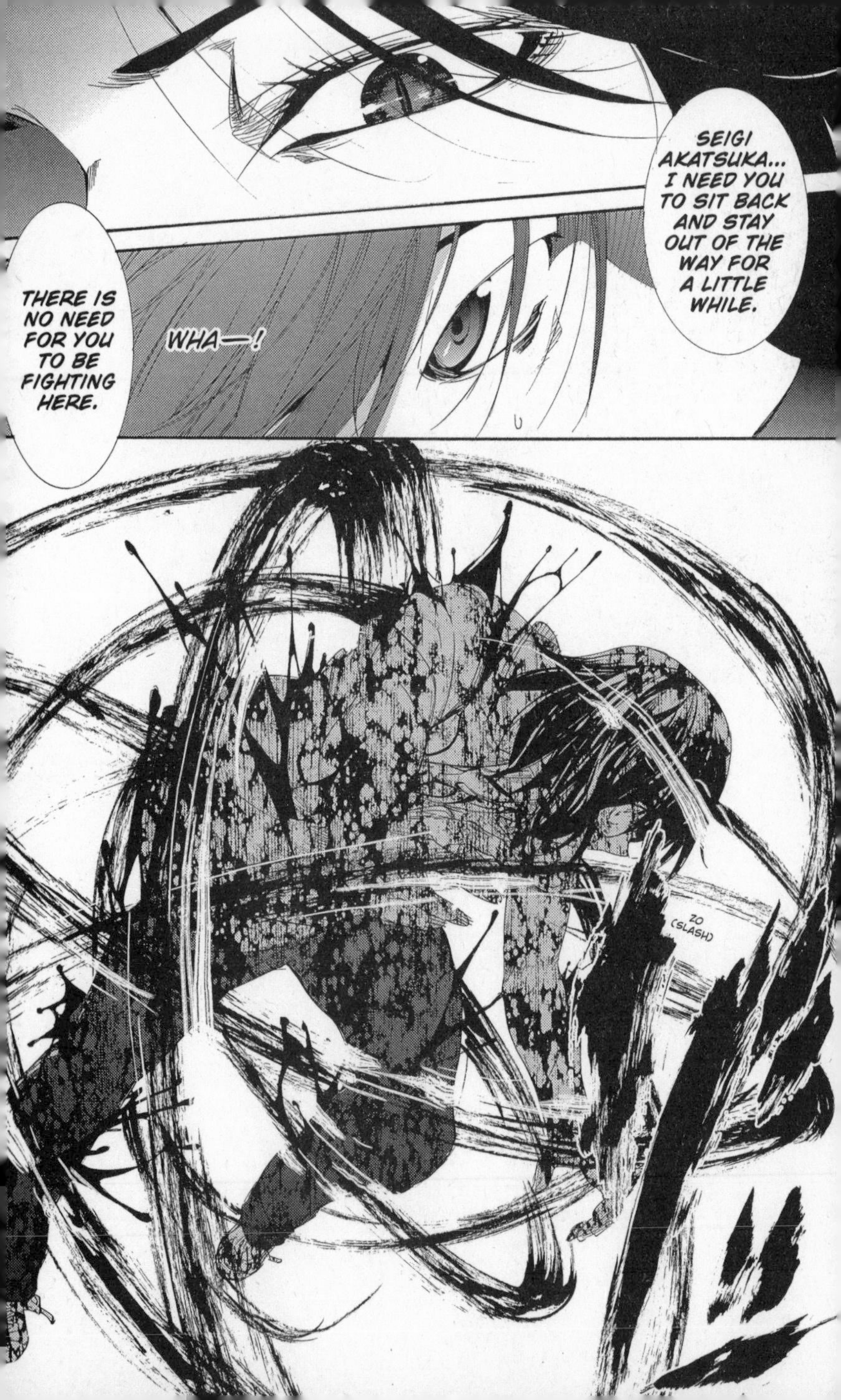
SEIGI AKATSUKA... I NEED YOU TO SIT BACK AND STAY OUT OF THE WAY FOR A LITTLE WHILE.
WHA—!
THERE IS NO NEED FOR YOU TO BE FIGHTING HERE.
ZO (SLASH)

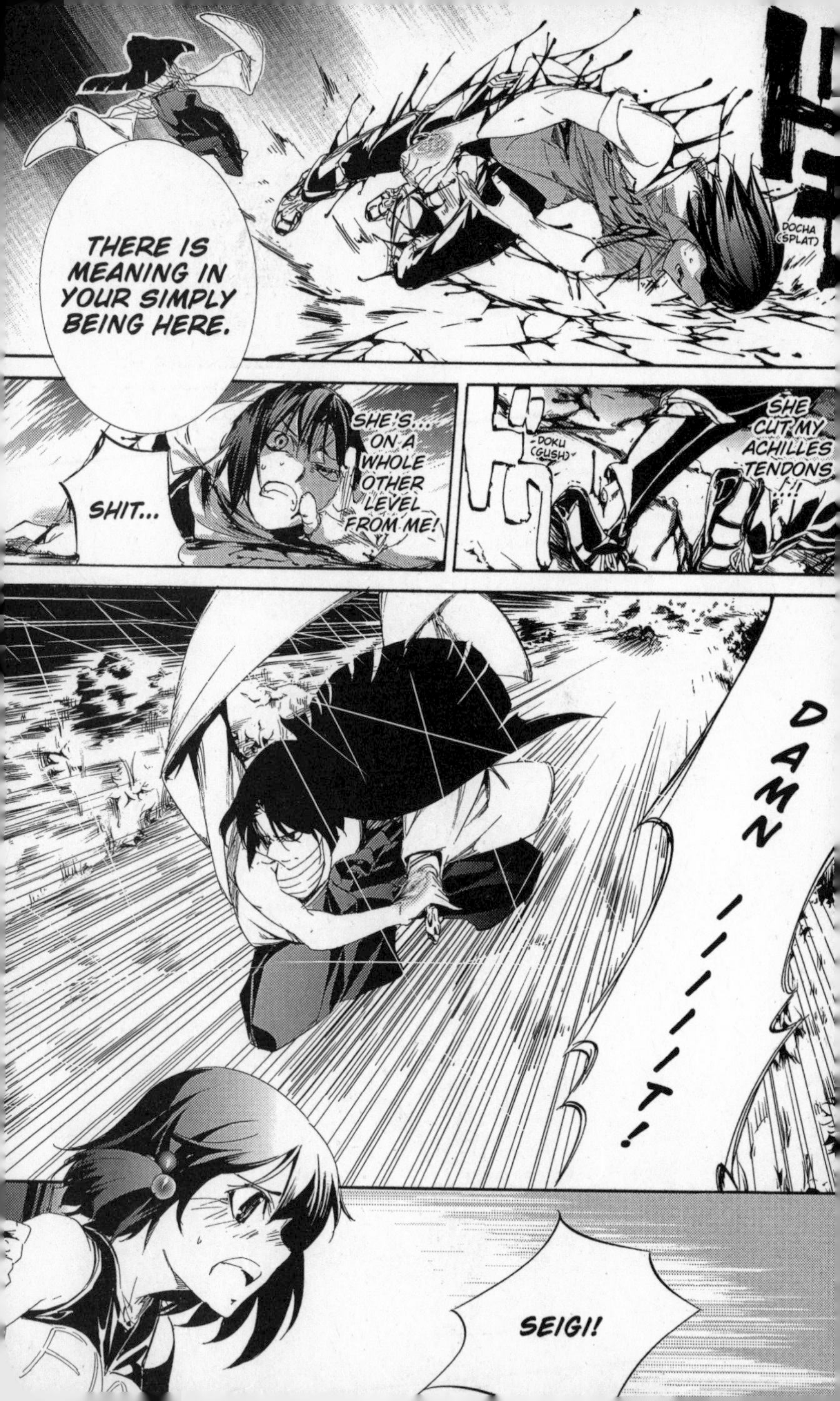
DOCHA (SPLAT)
THERE IS MEANING IN YOUR SIMPLY BEING HERE.
SHE CUT MY ACHILLES TENDONS...!!
DOKU (GUSH)
SHE'S... ON A WHOLE OTHER LEVEL FROM ME!
SHIT...
DAMN IIIIT!
SEIGI!

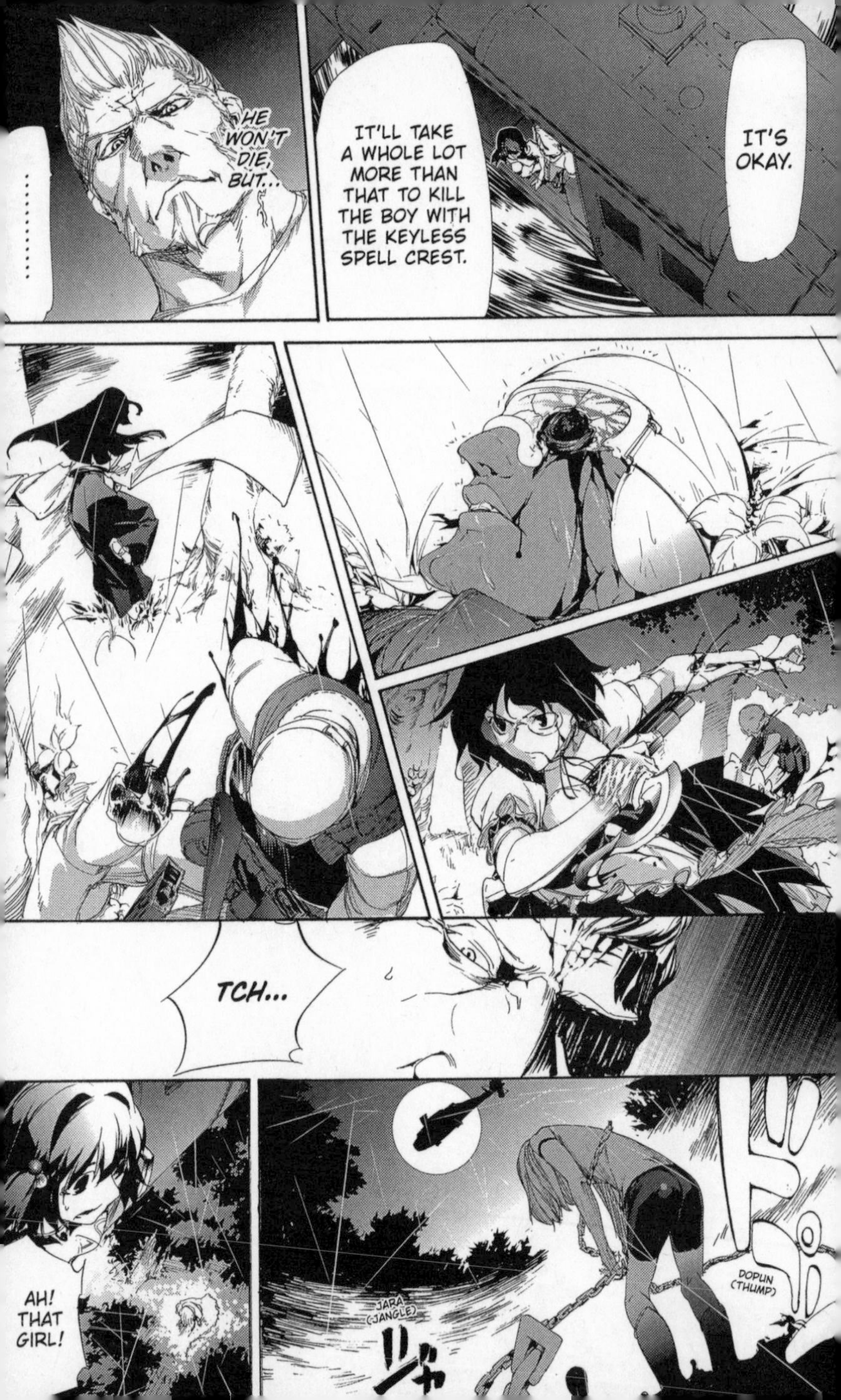
IT'S OKAY.
IT'LL TAKE A WHOLE LOT MORE THAN THAT TO KILL THE BOY WITH THE KEYLESS SPELL CREST.
HE WON'T DIE, BUT...
......
TCH...
DOPUN (THUMP)
JARA (JANGLE)
AH! THAT GIRL!

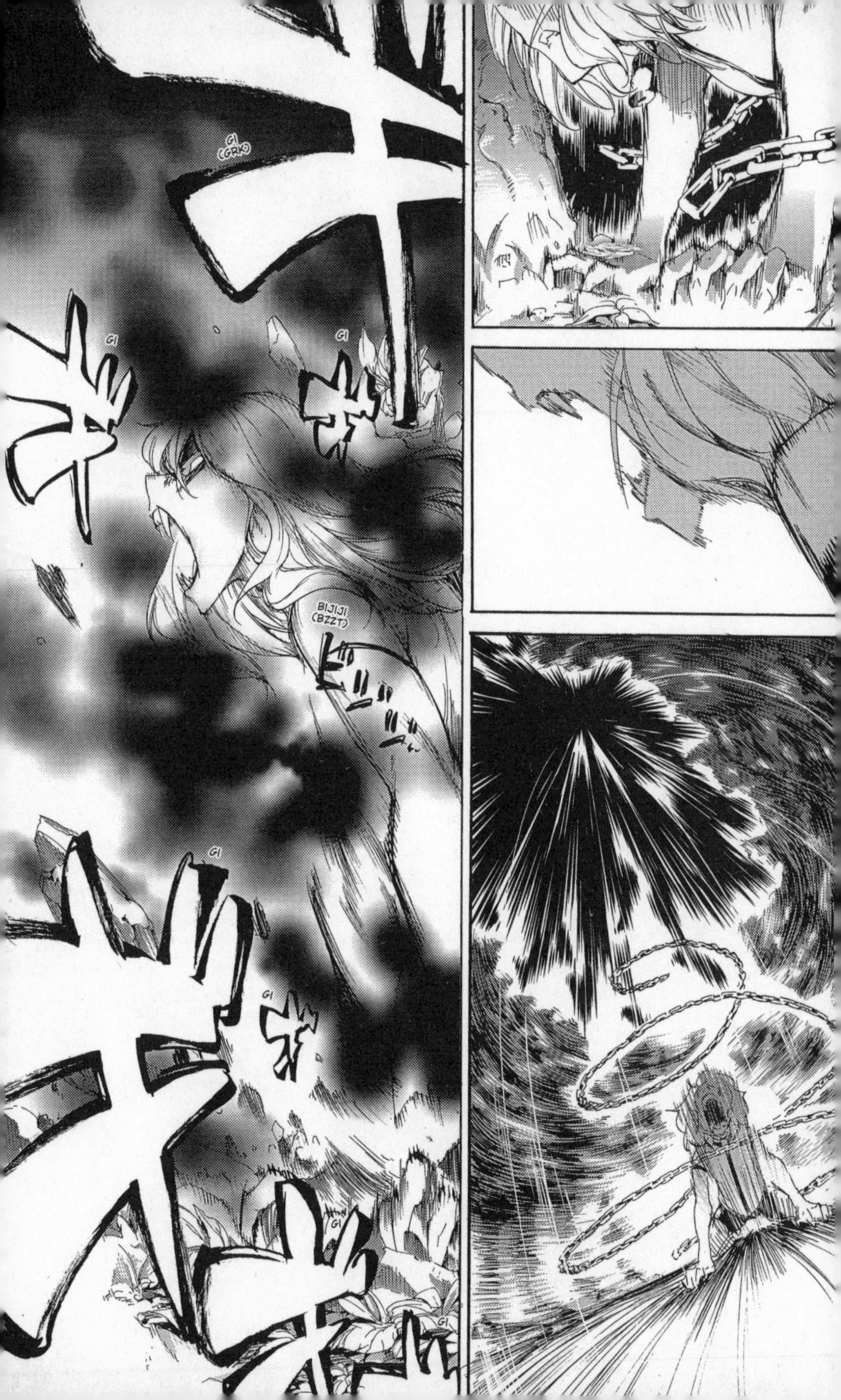
GI (GRK)
GI
GI
BIJIJI (BZZT)
GI
GI
GI
GI

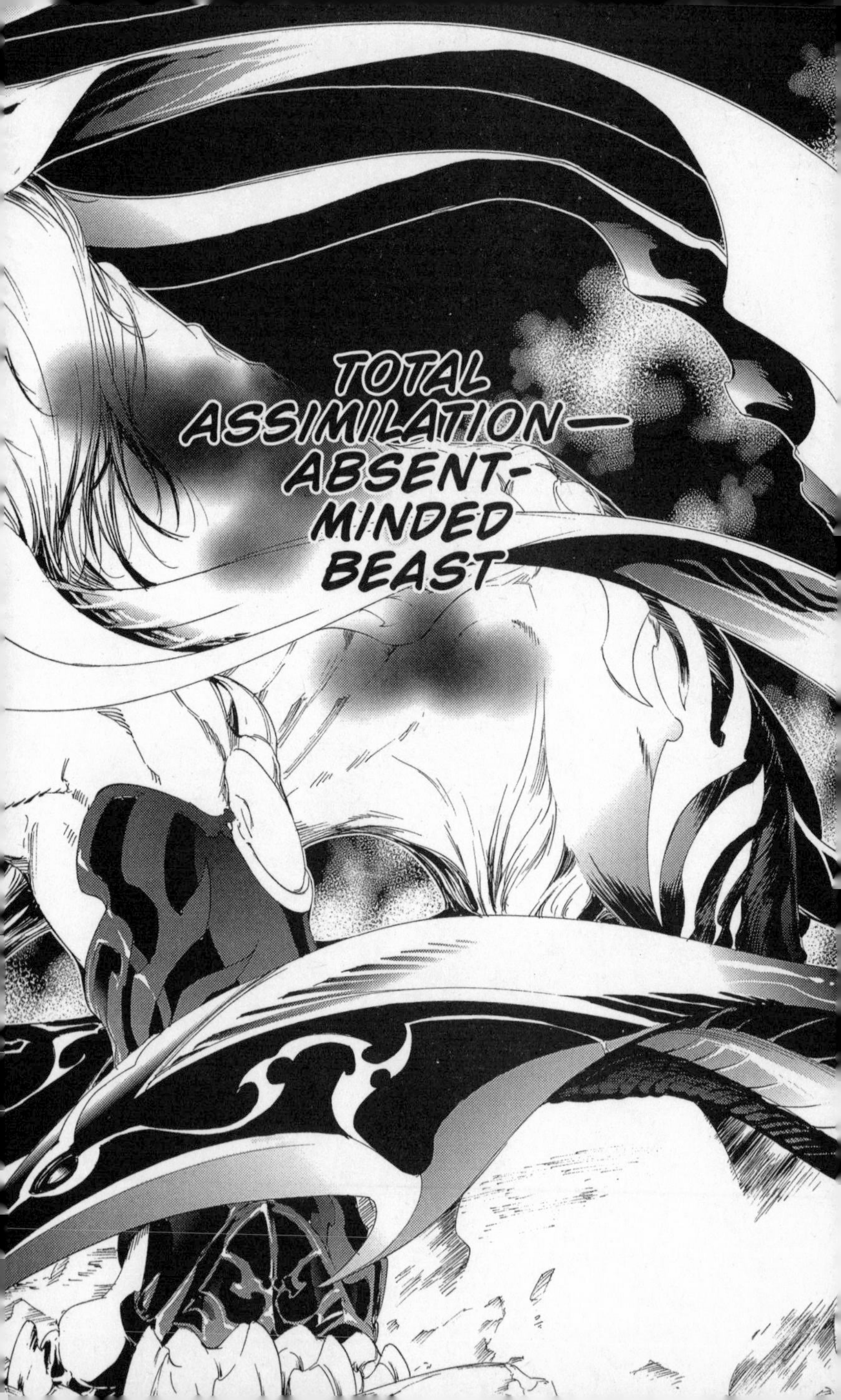
TOTAL ASSIMILATION— ABSENT-MINDED BEAST

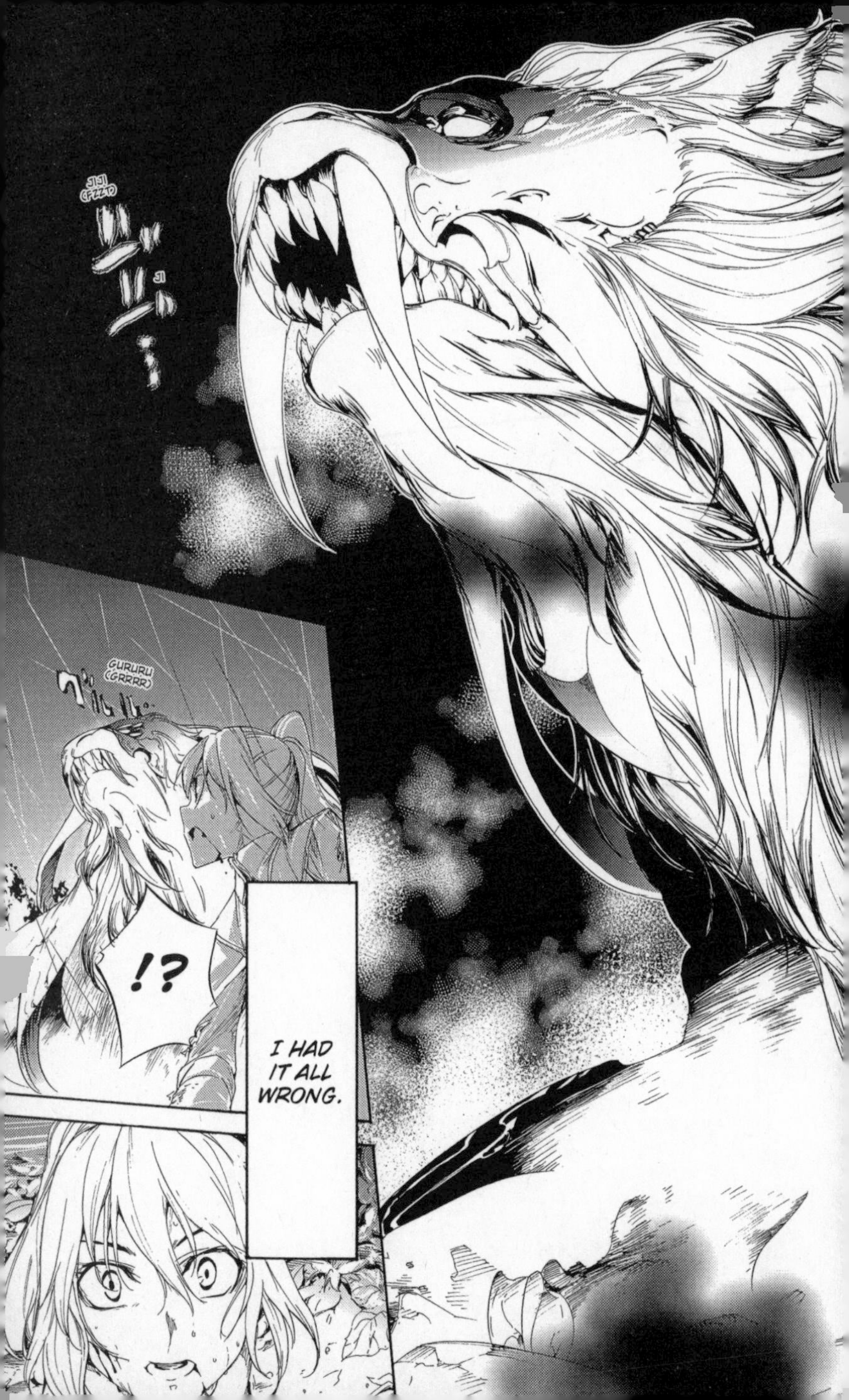
JIJI (FZZT)
JI
GURURU (GRRRR)
!?
I HAD IT ALL WRONG.

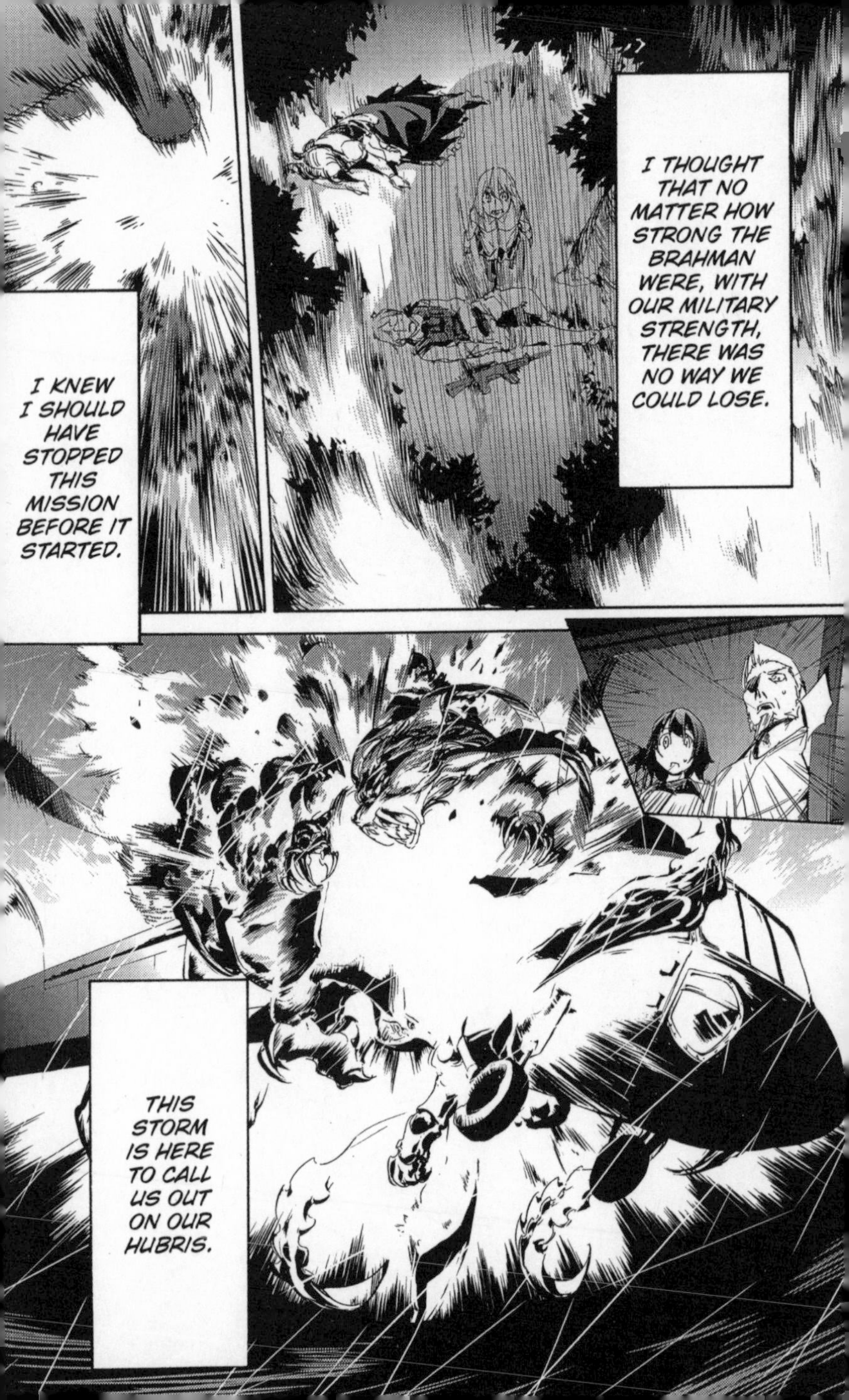
I THOUGHT THAT NO MATTER HOW STRONG THE BRAHMAN WERE, WITH OUR MILITARY STRENGTH, THERE WAS NO WAY WE COULD LOSE.
I KNEW I SHOULD HAVE STOPPED THIS MISSION BEFORE IT STARTED.
THIS STORM IS HERE TO CALL US OUT ON OUR HUBRIS.

TABOO TATTOO

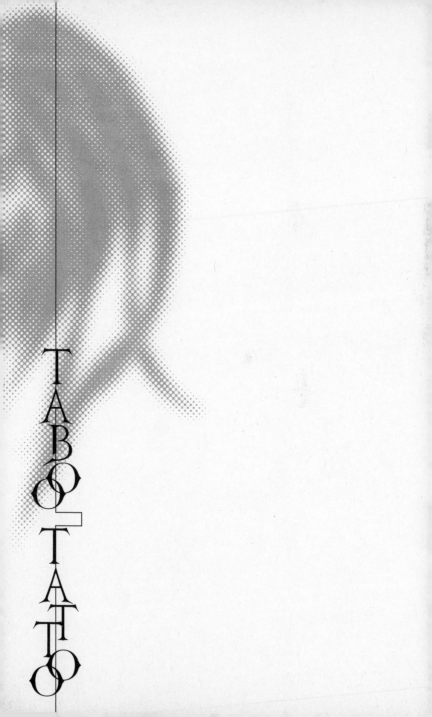

TABOO TATTOO

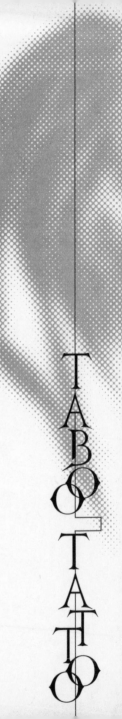

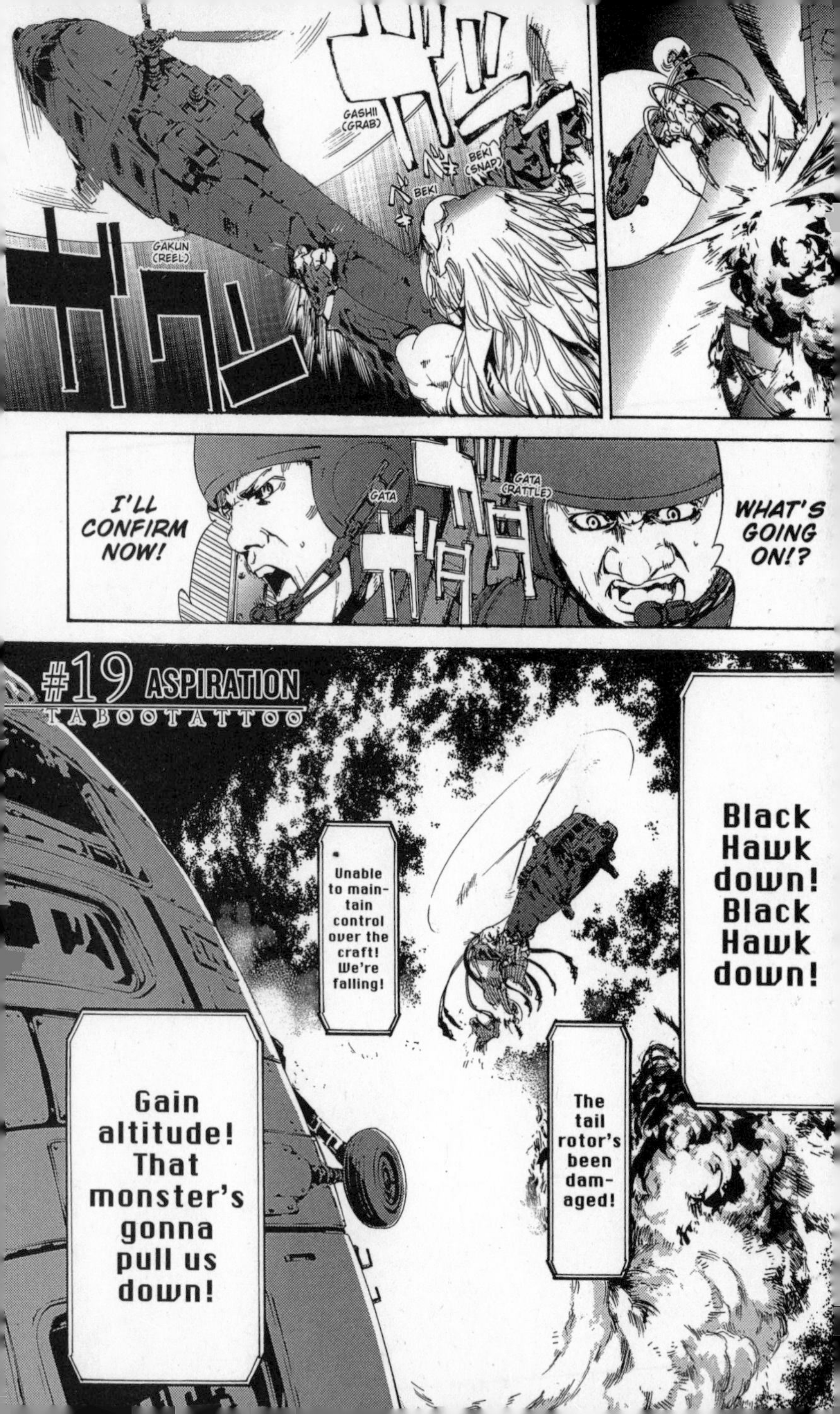
GASHII (GRAB)
BEKI (SNAP)
BEKI
GAKUN (REEL)
WHAT'S GOING ON!?
GATA (RATTLE)
GATA
I'LL CONFIRM NOW!
#19 ASPIRATION
TABOOTATTOO
Black Hawk down! Black Hawk down!
The tail rotor's been dam-aged!
Unable to main-tain control over the craft! We're falling!
Gain altitude! That monster's gonna pull us down!

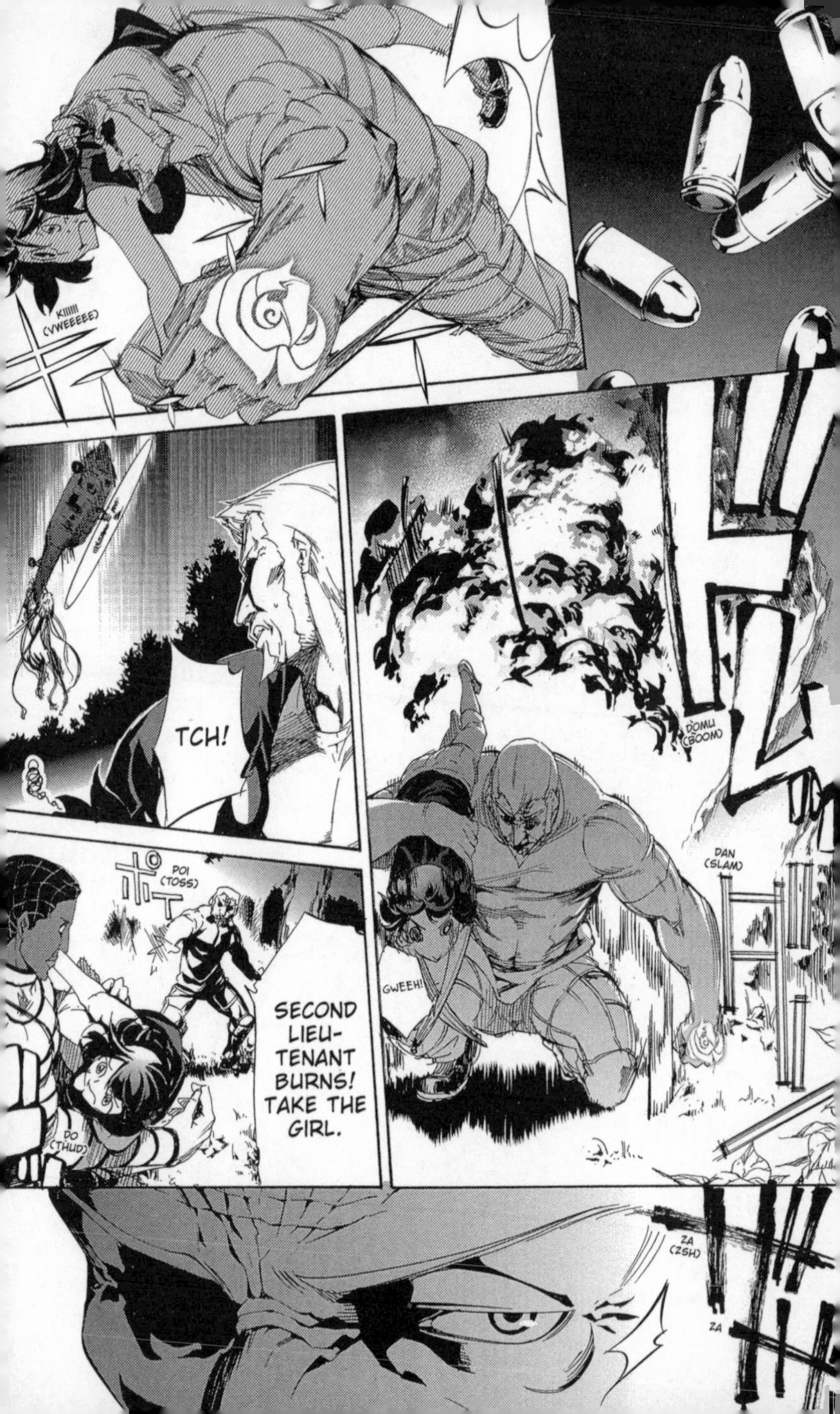
KIIIII (VWEEEEE)
DOMU (BOOM)
DAN (SLAM)
GWEEH!
TCH!
POI (TOSS)
SECOND LIEU-TENANT BURNS! TAKE THE GIRL.
DO (THUD)
ZA (ZSH)
ZA

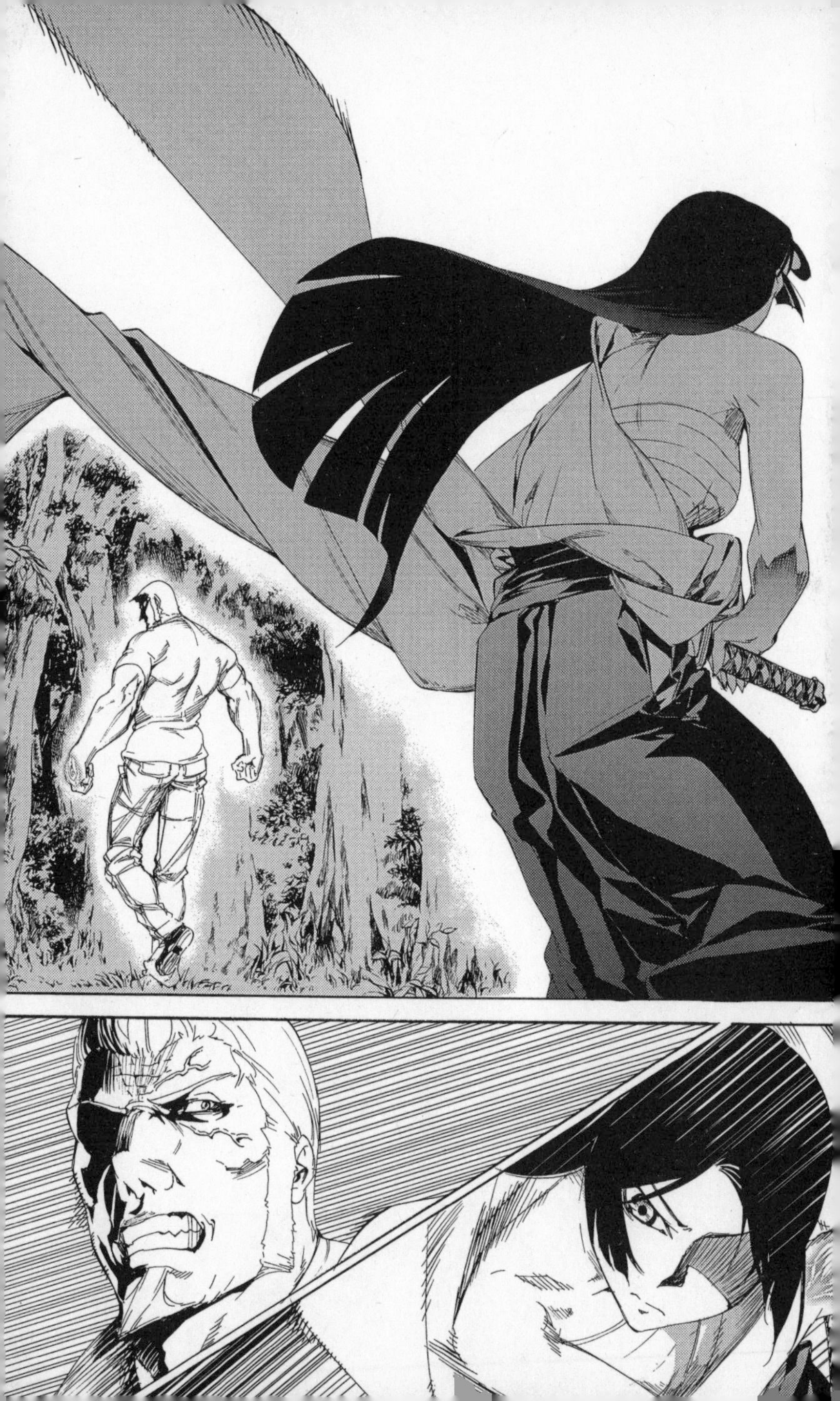

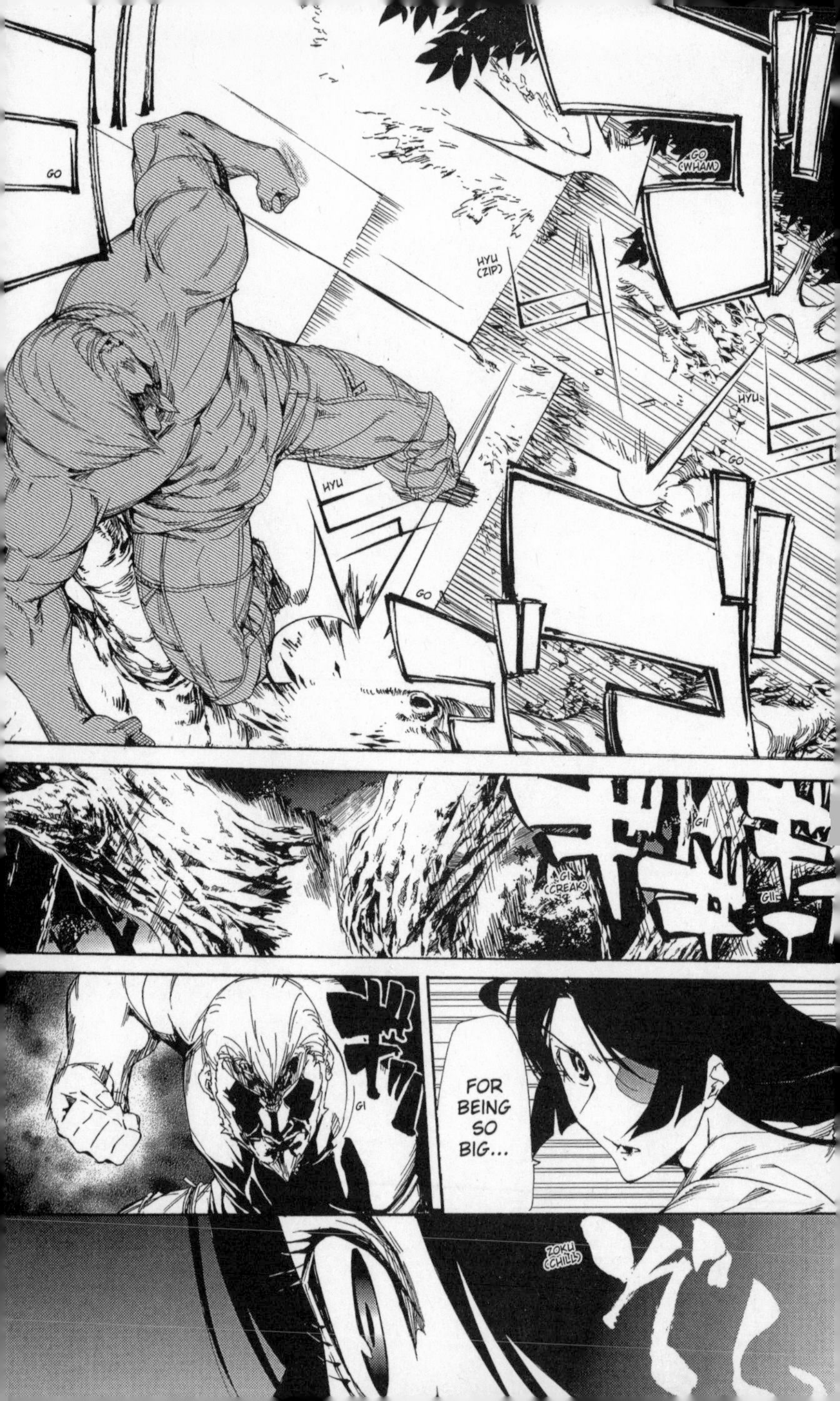

GO (WHAM)
HYU
GO
HYU (ZIP)
HYU
GO
GO
GII
GI (CREAK)
GII
FOR BEING SO BIG...
GI
ZOKU (CHILL)

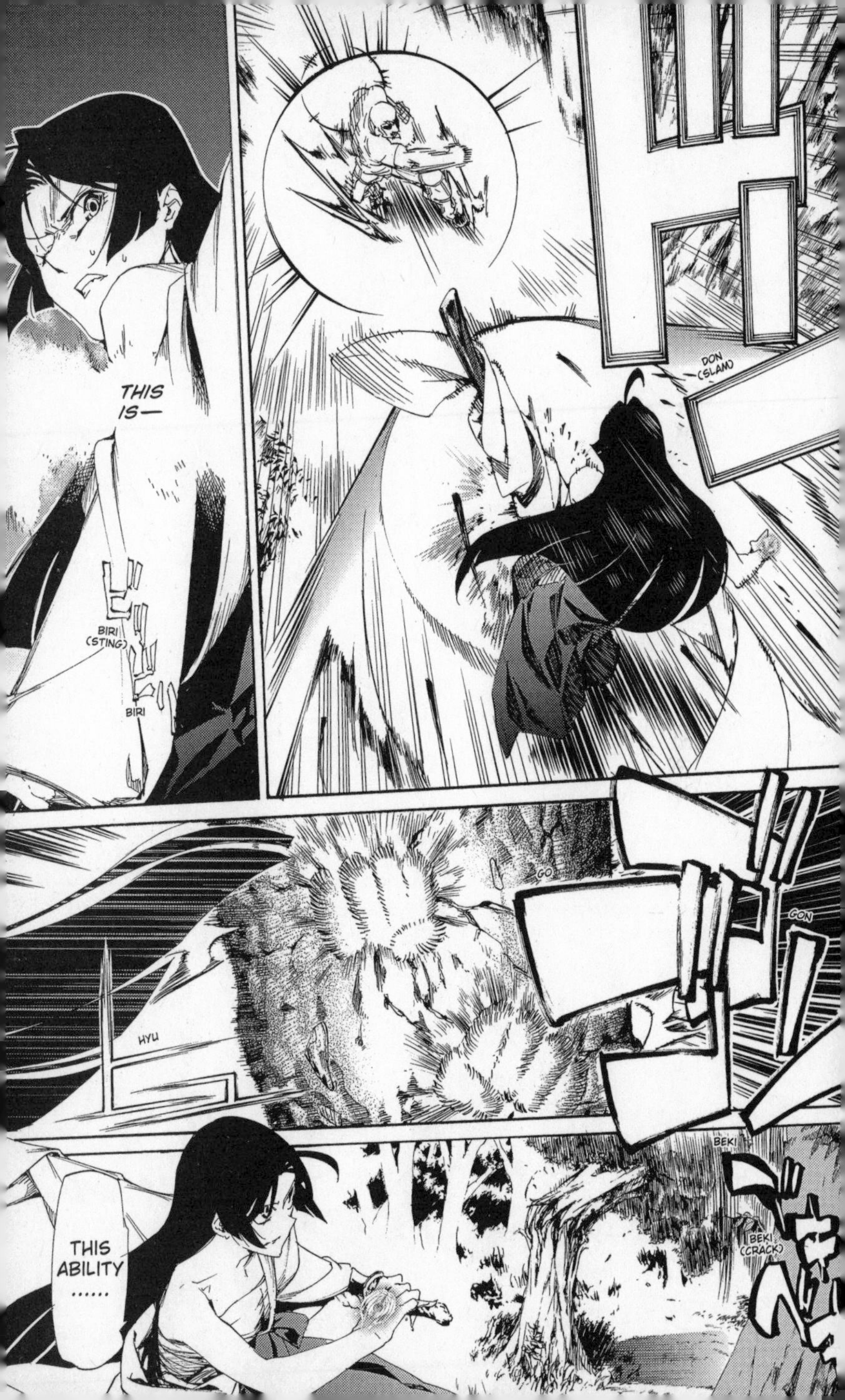
DON (SLAM)
THIS IS—
BIRI (STING)
BIRI
GO
GON
HYU
BEKI
BEKI (CRACK)
THIS ABILITY ......

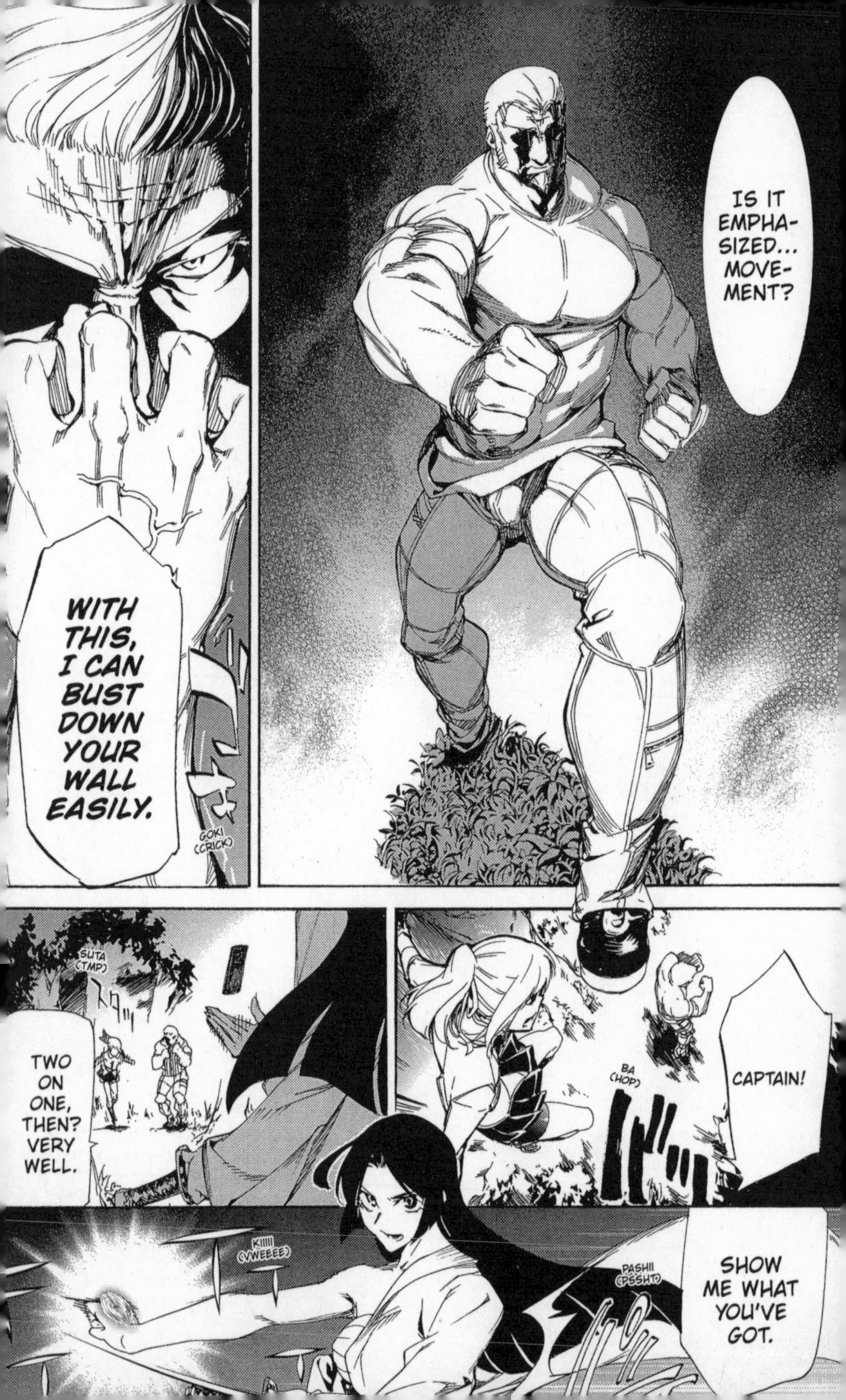
IS IT EMPHASIZED... MOVEMENT?
WITH THIS, I CAN BUST DOWN YOUR WALL EASILY.
GOKI (CRICK)
CAPTAIN!
BA (HOP)
SUTA (TMP)
TWO ON ONE, THEN? VERY WELL.
SHOW ME WHAT YOU'VE GOT.
PASHII (PSSHT)
KIIIII (VWEEEE)

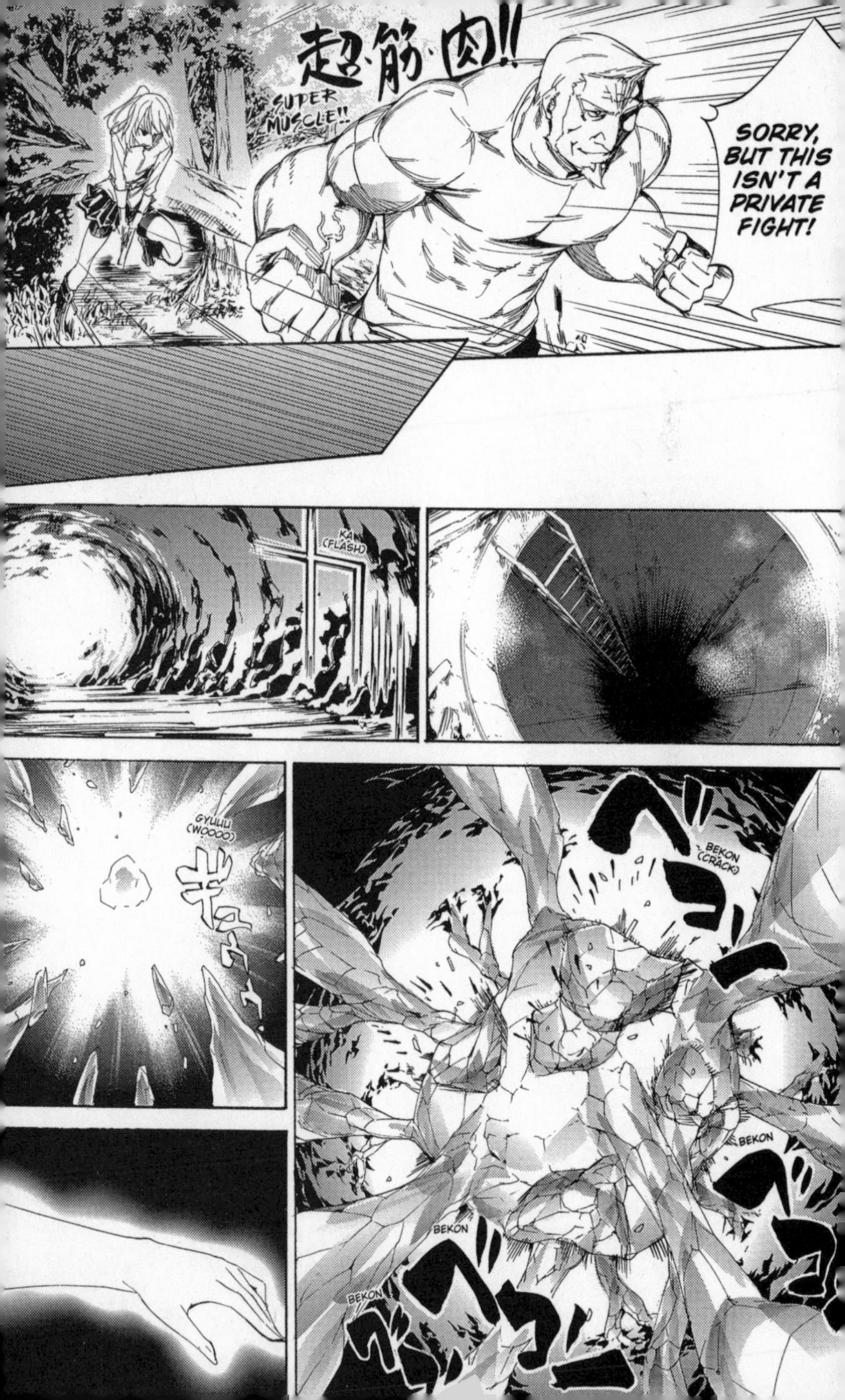
SORRY, BUT THIS ISN'T A PRIVATE FIGHT!
超筋肉!!
SUPER MUSCLE!!
KA (FLASH)
BEKON (CRACK)
BEKON
BEKON
BEKON
GYUUU (WOOOO)

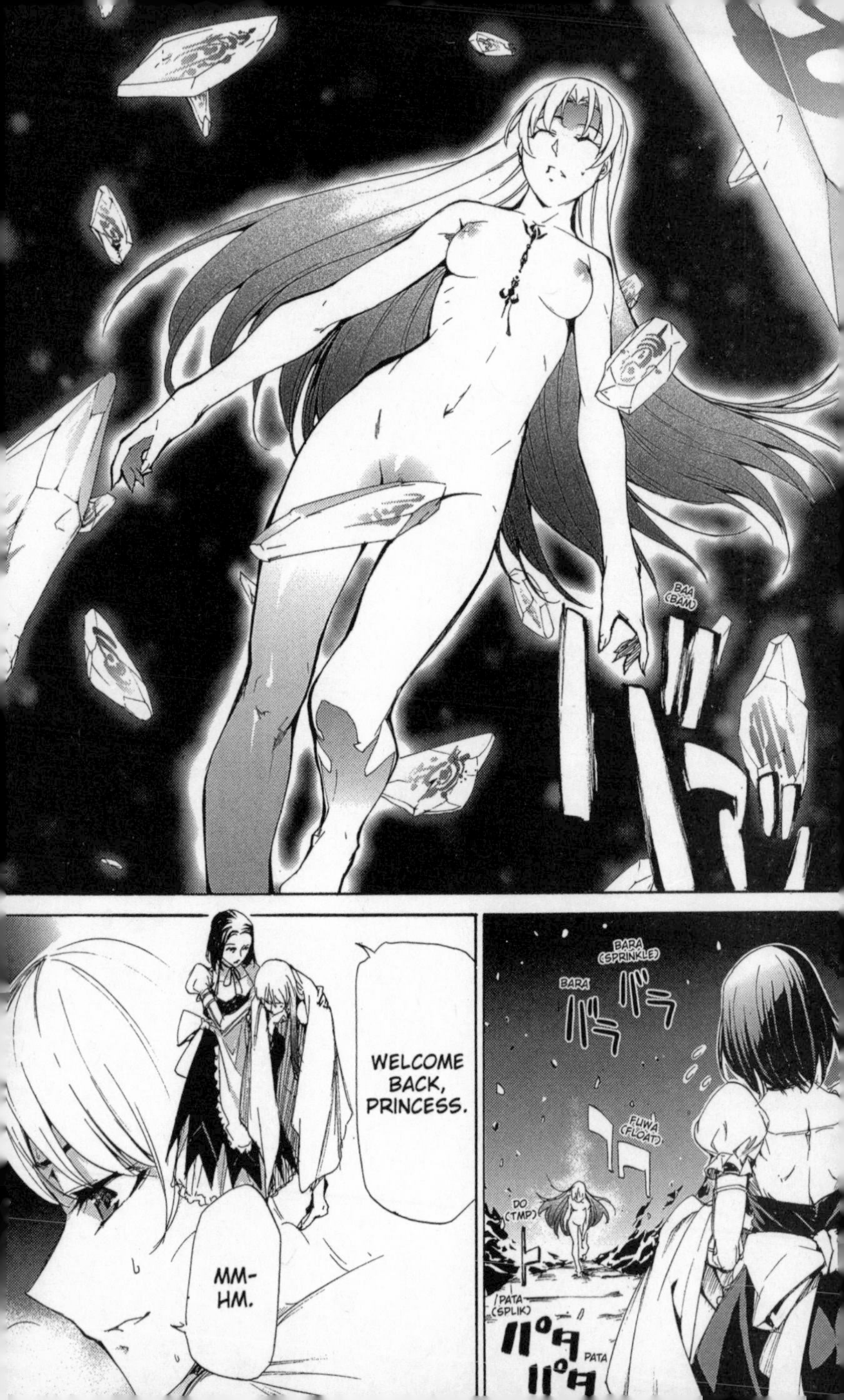

BAA (BAM)
BARA (SPRINKLE)
バラ
BARA
バラ
FUWA (FLOAT)
DO (TMP)
PATA (SPLIK)
パタ
PATA
パタ
WELCOME BACK, PRINCESS.
MM-HM.

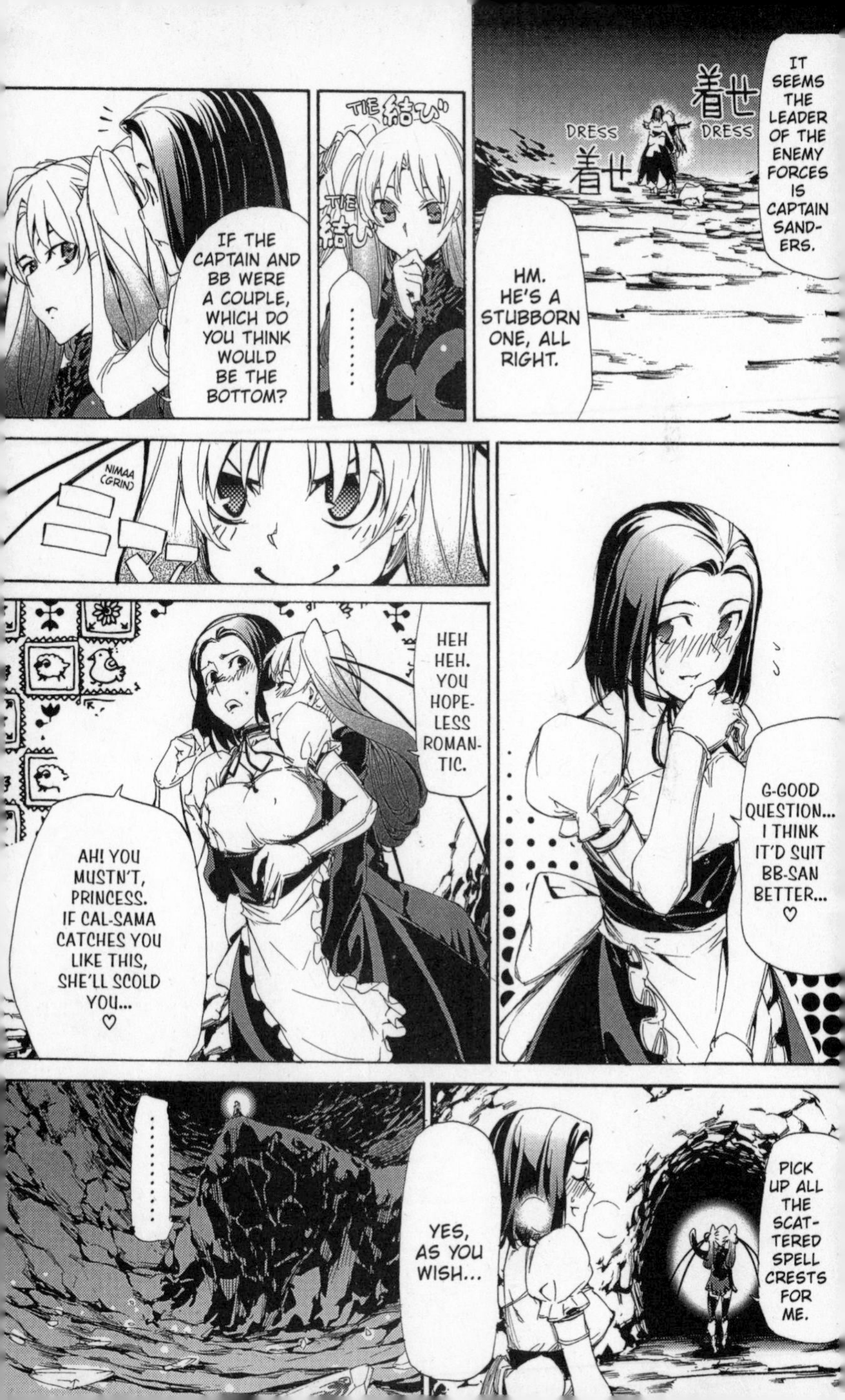

IT SEEMS THE LEADER OF THE ENEMY FORCES IS CAPTAIN SANDERS.
着せ DRESS
着せ DRESS
HM. HE'S A STUBBORN ONE, ALL RIGHT.
結び TIE
結び TIE
......
IF THE CAPTAIN AND BB WERE A COUPLE, WHICH DO YOU THINK WOULD BE THE BOTTOM?
G-GOOD QUESTION... I THINK IT'D SUIT BB-SAN BETTER... ♡
NIMAA (GRIN)
HEH HEH. YOU HOPELESS ROMANTIC.
AH! YOU MUSTN'T, PRINCESS. IF CAL-SAMA CATCHES YOU LIKE THIS, SHE'LL SCOLD YOU... ♡
PICK UP ALL THE SCATTERED SPELL CRESTS FOR ME.
YES, AS YOU WISH...
......

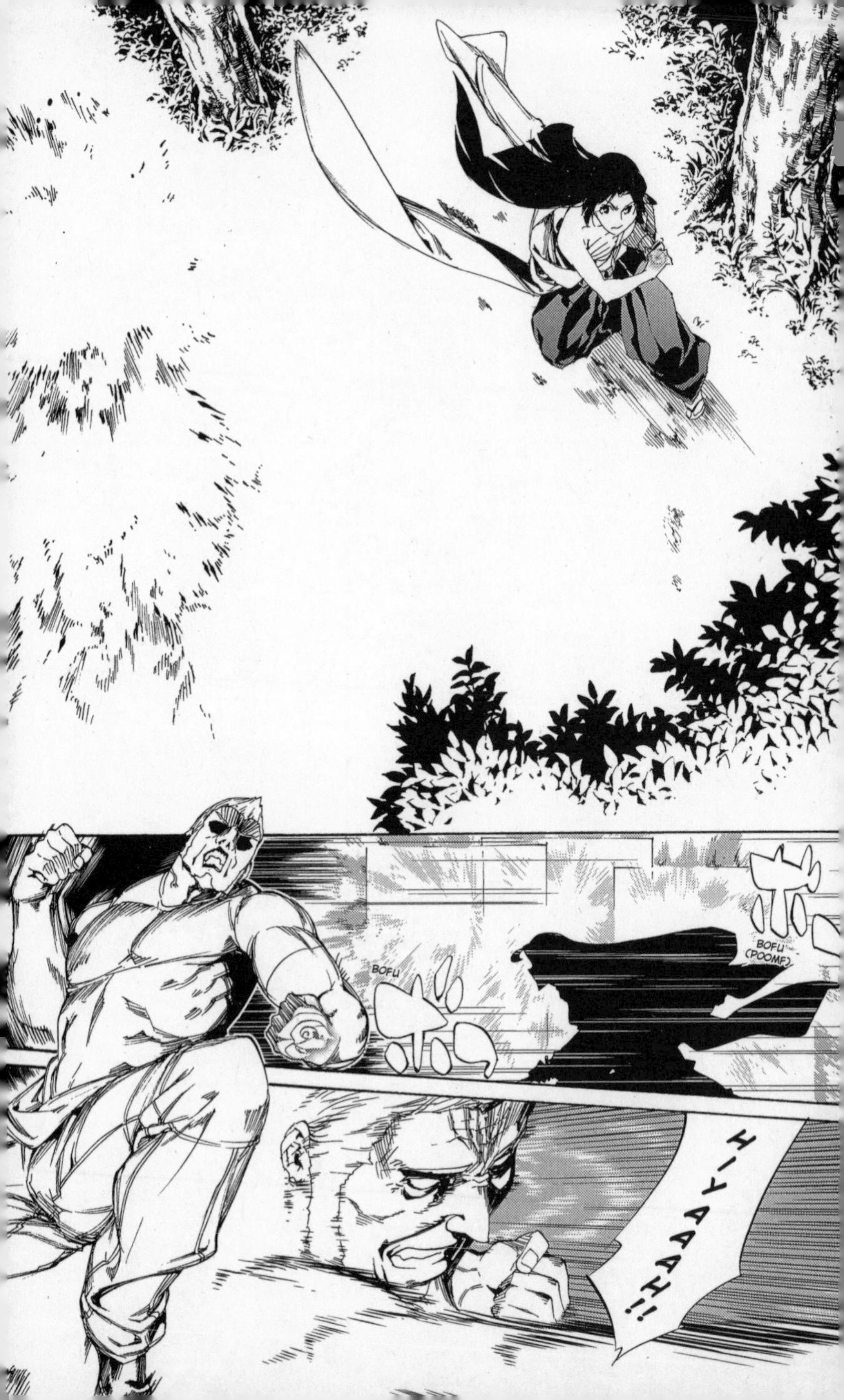
BOFU
(POOMF)
BOFU
HIYAAAH!!

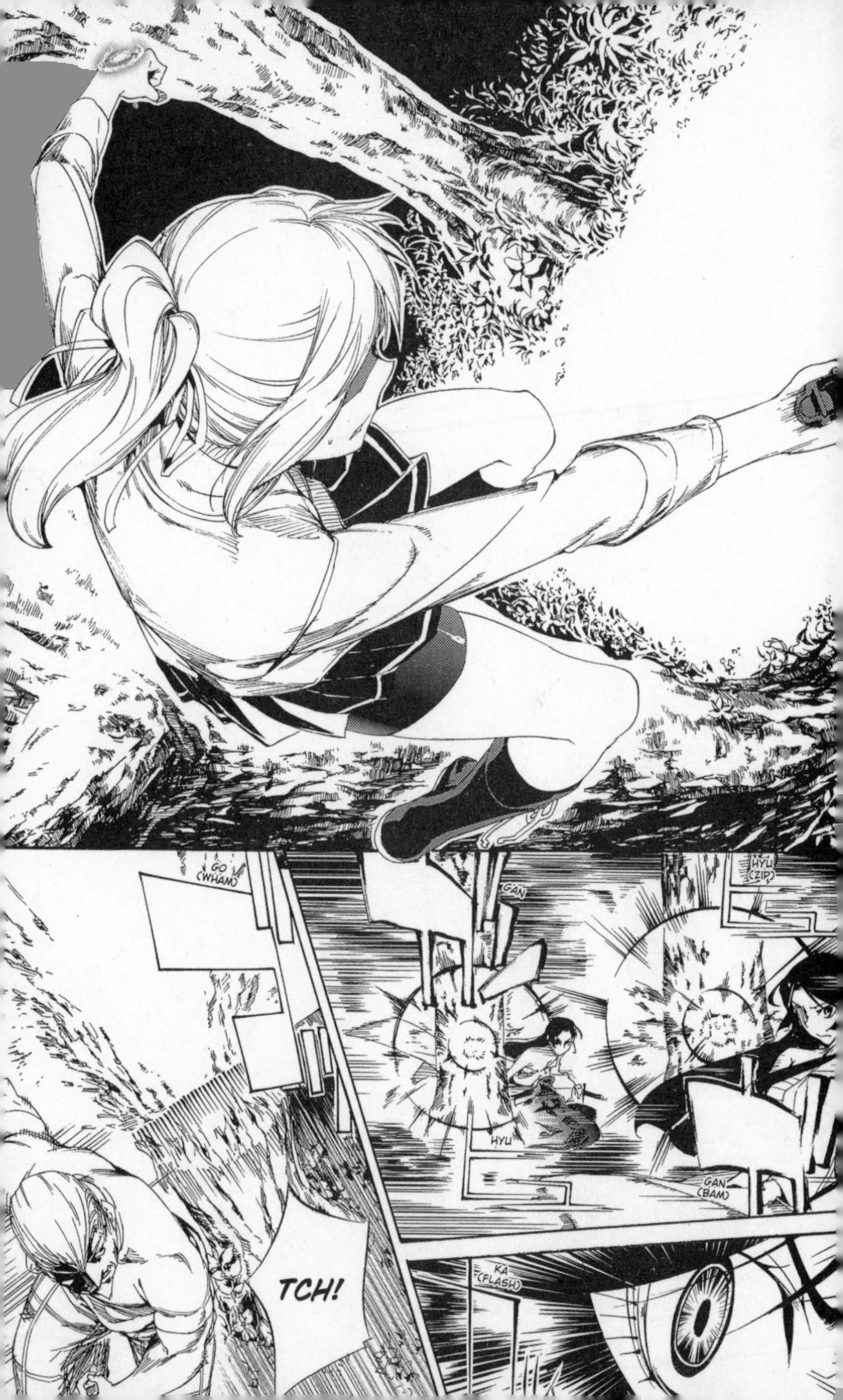
HYU (ZIP)
GAN
GO (WHAM)
GAN (BAM)
HYU
KA (FLASH)
TCH!

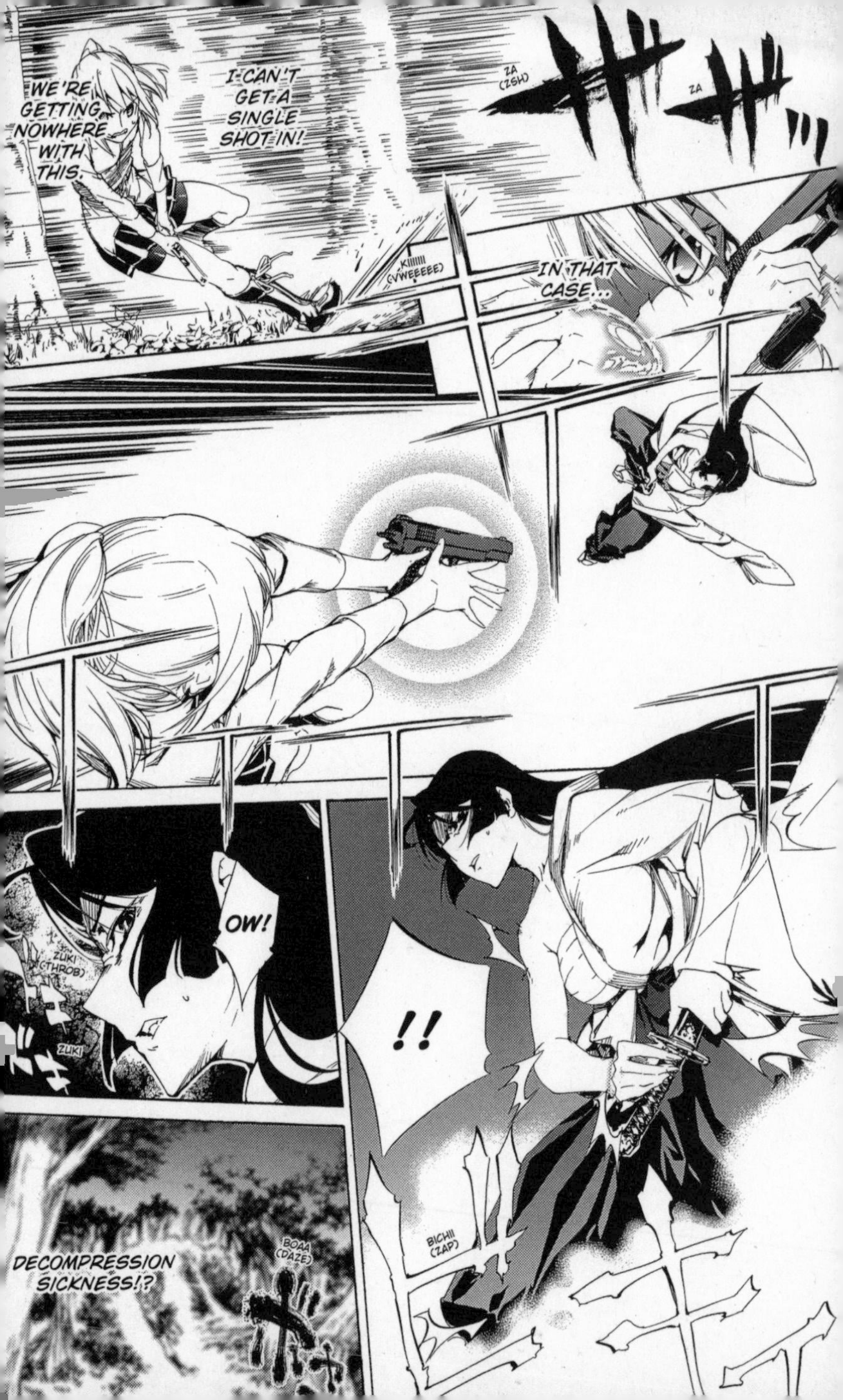
ZA (ZSH)
ZA
I CAN'T GET A SINGLE SHOT IN!
WE'RE GETTING NOWHERE WITH THIS.
KIIIIIII (VWEEEEE)
IN THAT CASE...
!!
BICHII (ZAP)
OW!
ZUKI (THROB)
ZUKI
BOAA (DAZE)
DECOMPRESSION SICKNESS!?

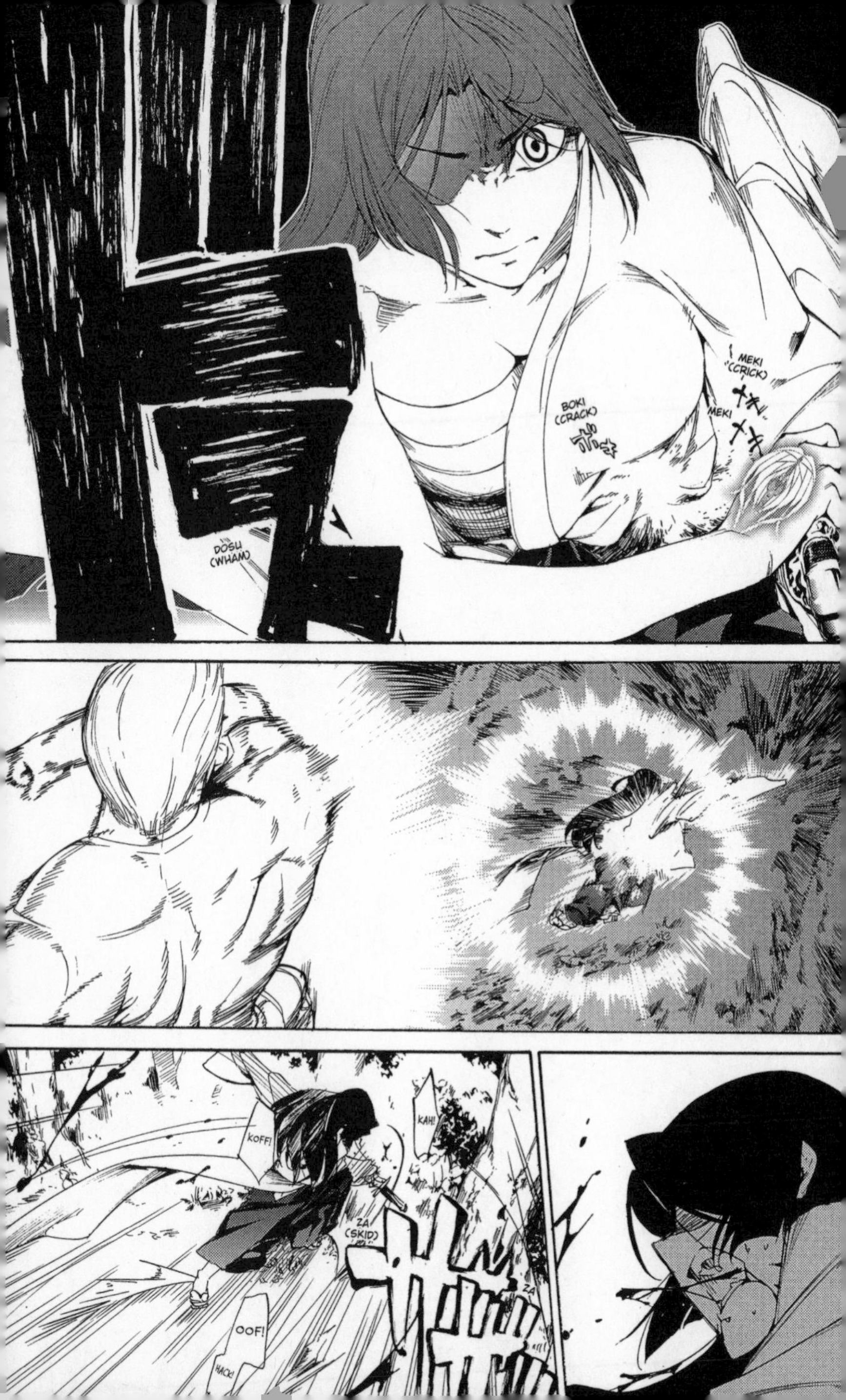
MEKI (CRICK)
MEKI
BOKI (CRACK)
DOSU (WHAM)
KAH!
KOFF!
ZA (SKID)
ZA
OOF!
HACK!

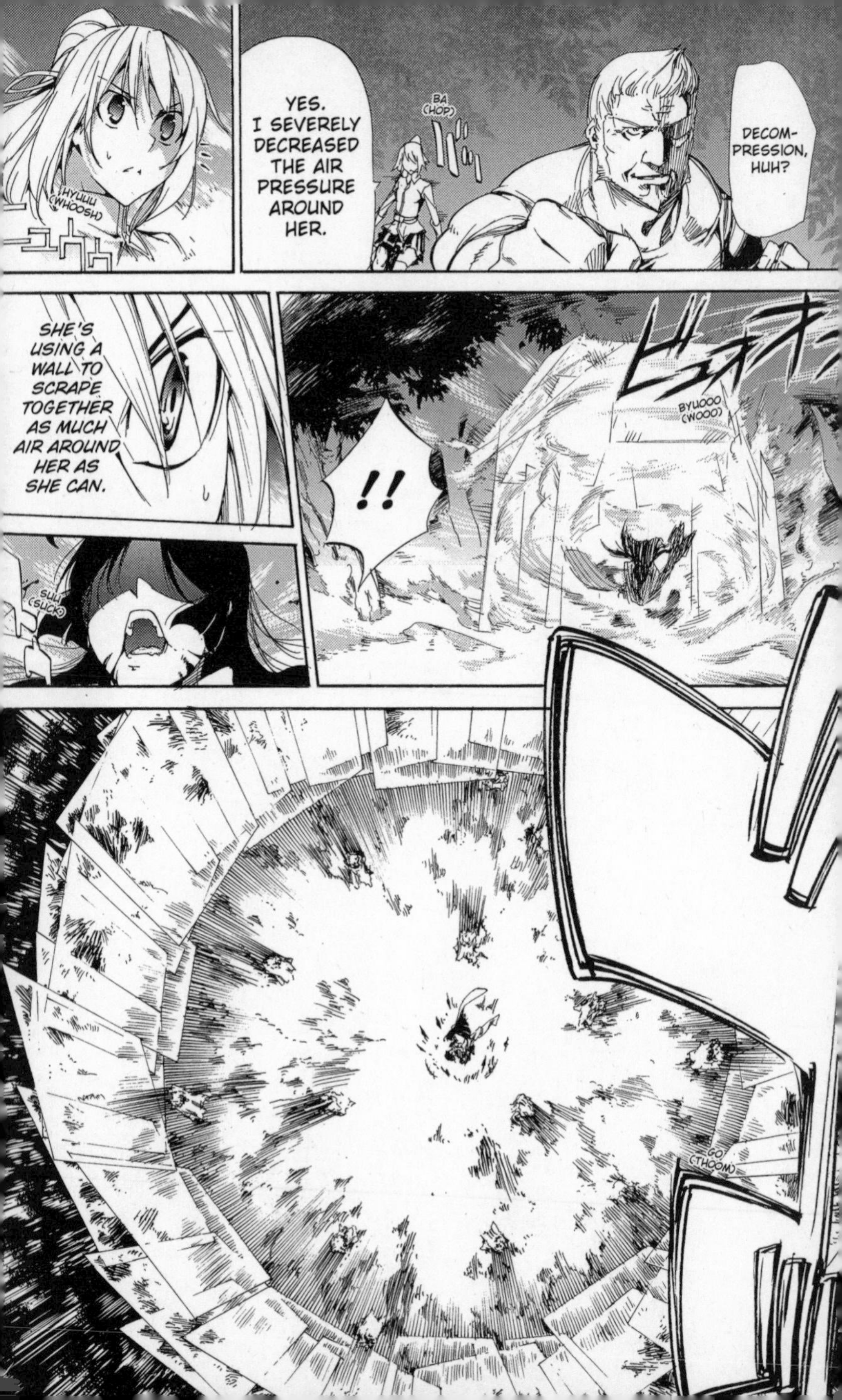
DECOM-PRESSION, HUH?
BA (HOP)
YES. I SEVERELY DECREASED THE AIR PRESSURE AROUND HER.
HYUUU (WHOOSH)
BYUOOO (WOOO)
!!
SHE'S USING A WALL TO SCRAPE TOGETHER AS MUCH AIR AROUND HER AS SHE CAN.
SUU (SUCK)
GO (THOOM)

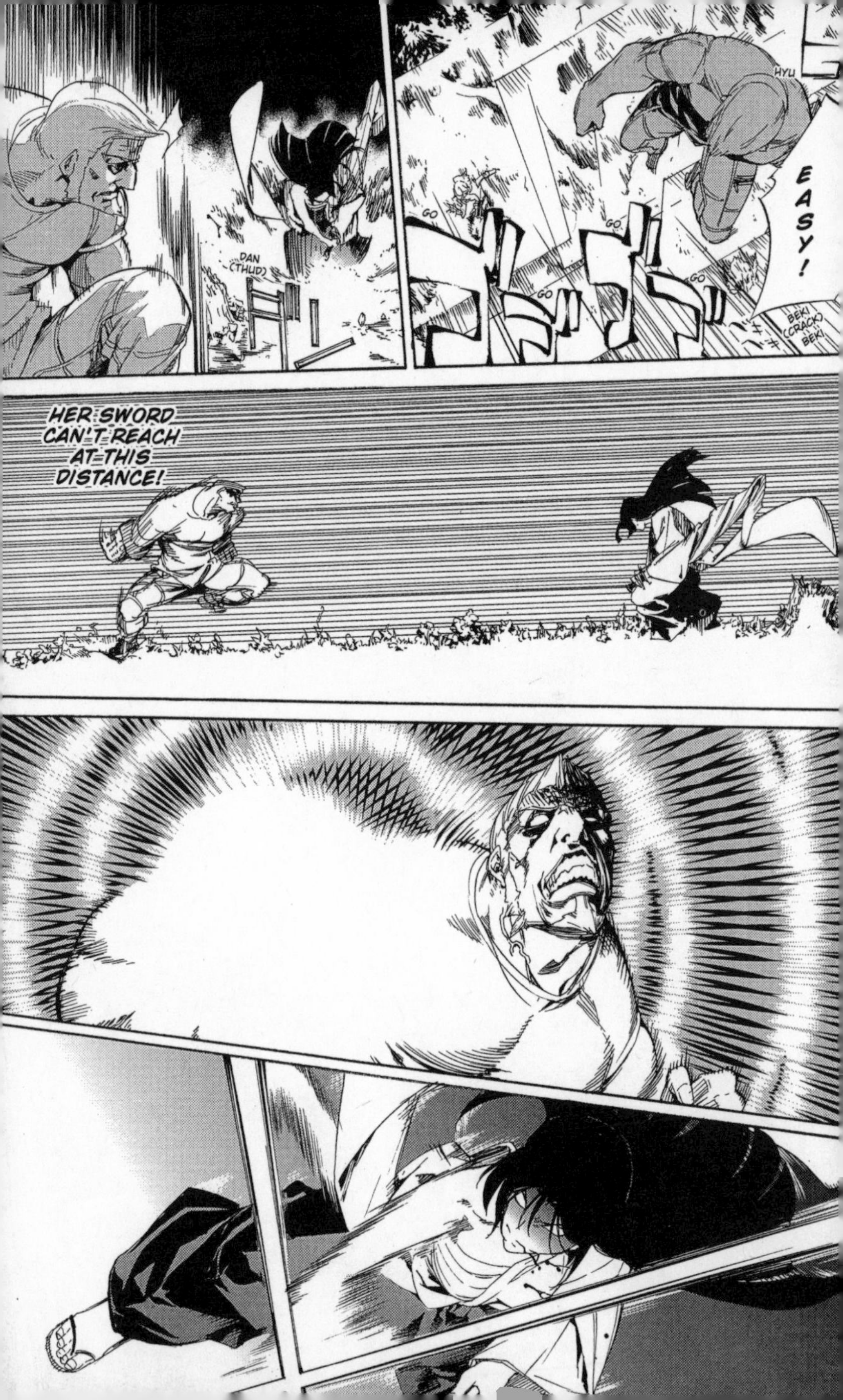
HYU
EASY!
GO
GO
GO
GO
BEKI (CRACK) BEKI
DAN (THUD)
HER SWORD CAN'T REACH AT THIS DISTANCE!

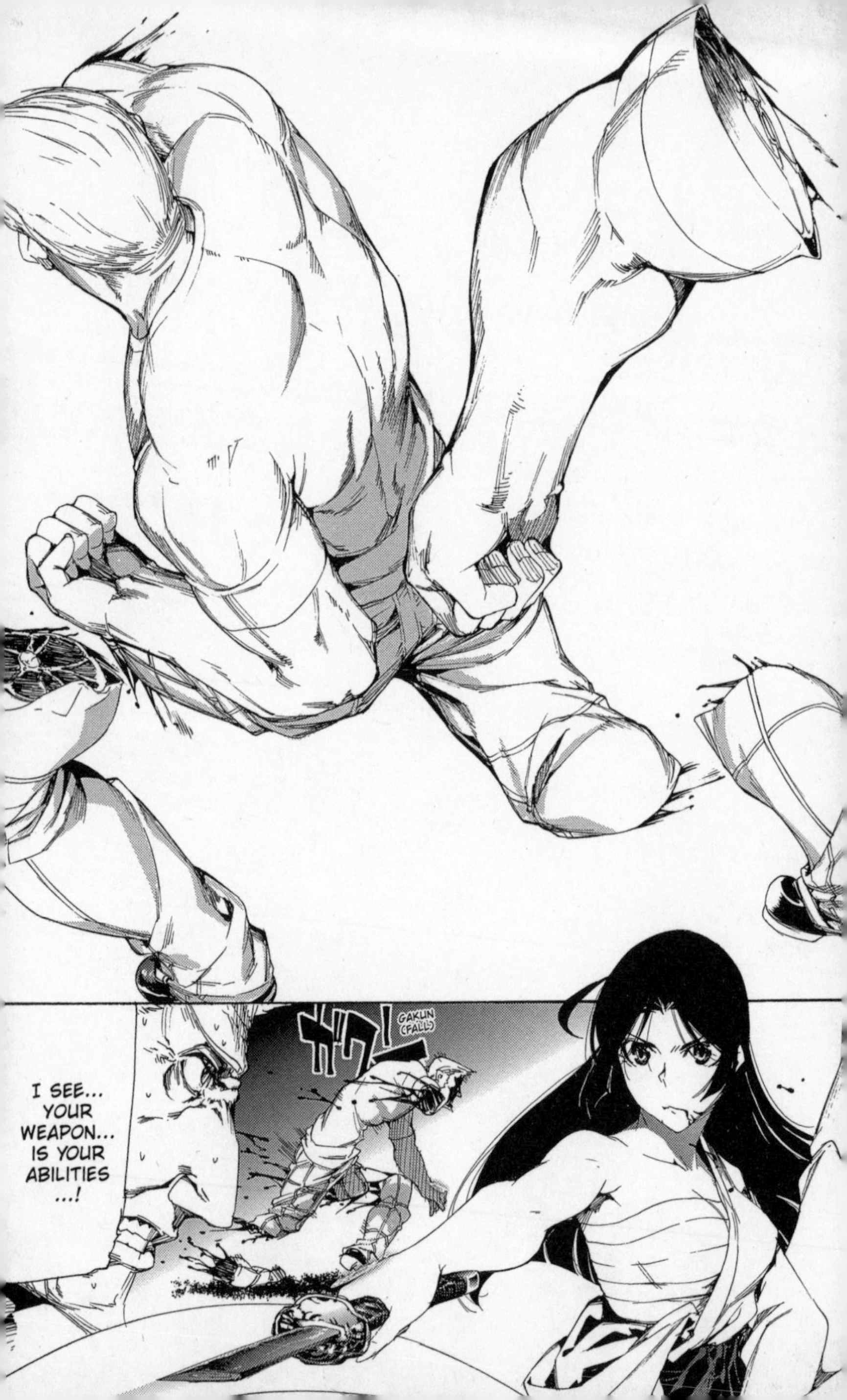
GAKUN (FALL)
I SEE... YOUR WEAPON... IS YOUR ABILITIES ...!

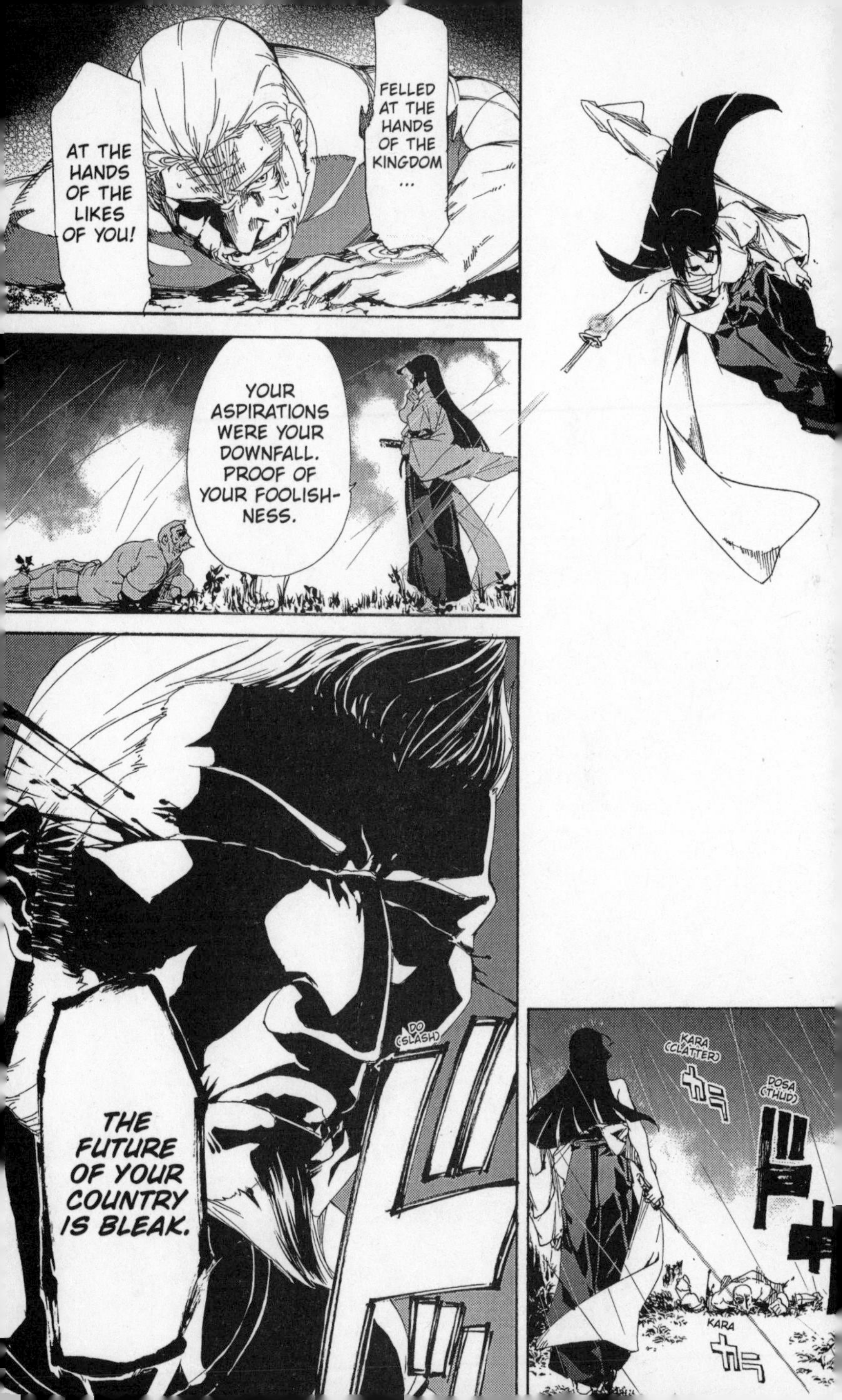
FELLED AT THE HANDS OF THE KINGDOM ...
AT THE HANDS OF THE LIKES OF YOU!
YOUR ASPIRATIONS WERE YOUR DOWNFALL. PROOF OF YOUR FOOLISH-NESS.
DO (SLASH)
THE FUTURE OF YOUR COUNTRY IS BLEAK.
KARA (CLATTER)
DOSA (THUD)
KARA

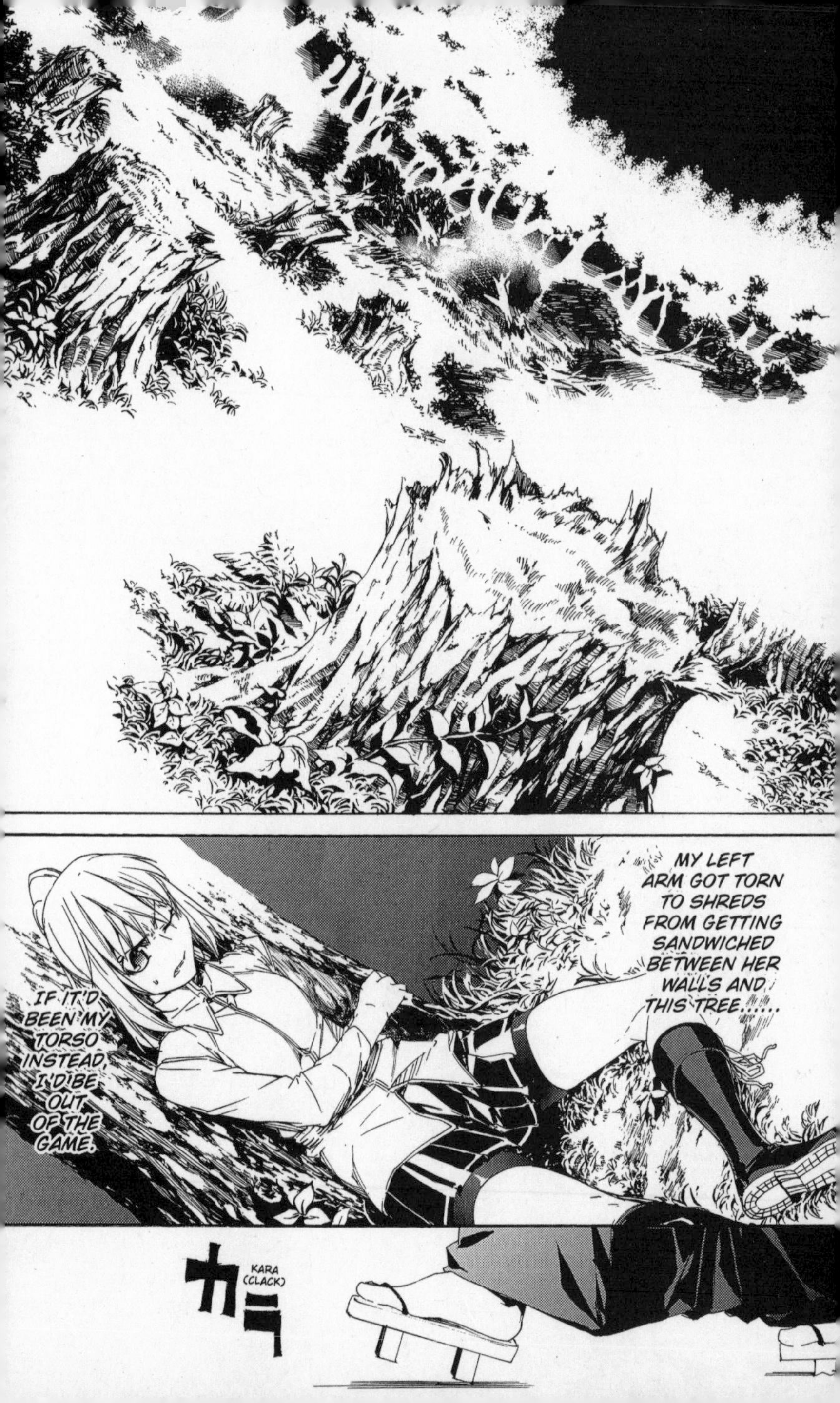
MY LEFT ARM GOT TORN TO SHREDS FROM GETTING SANDWICHED BETWEEN HER WALLS AND THIS TREE......
IF IT'D BEEN MY TORSO INSTEAD, I'D BE OUT OF THE GAME.
カラ
KARA (CLACK)

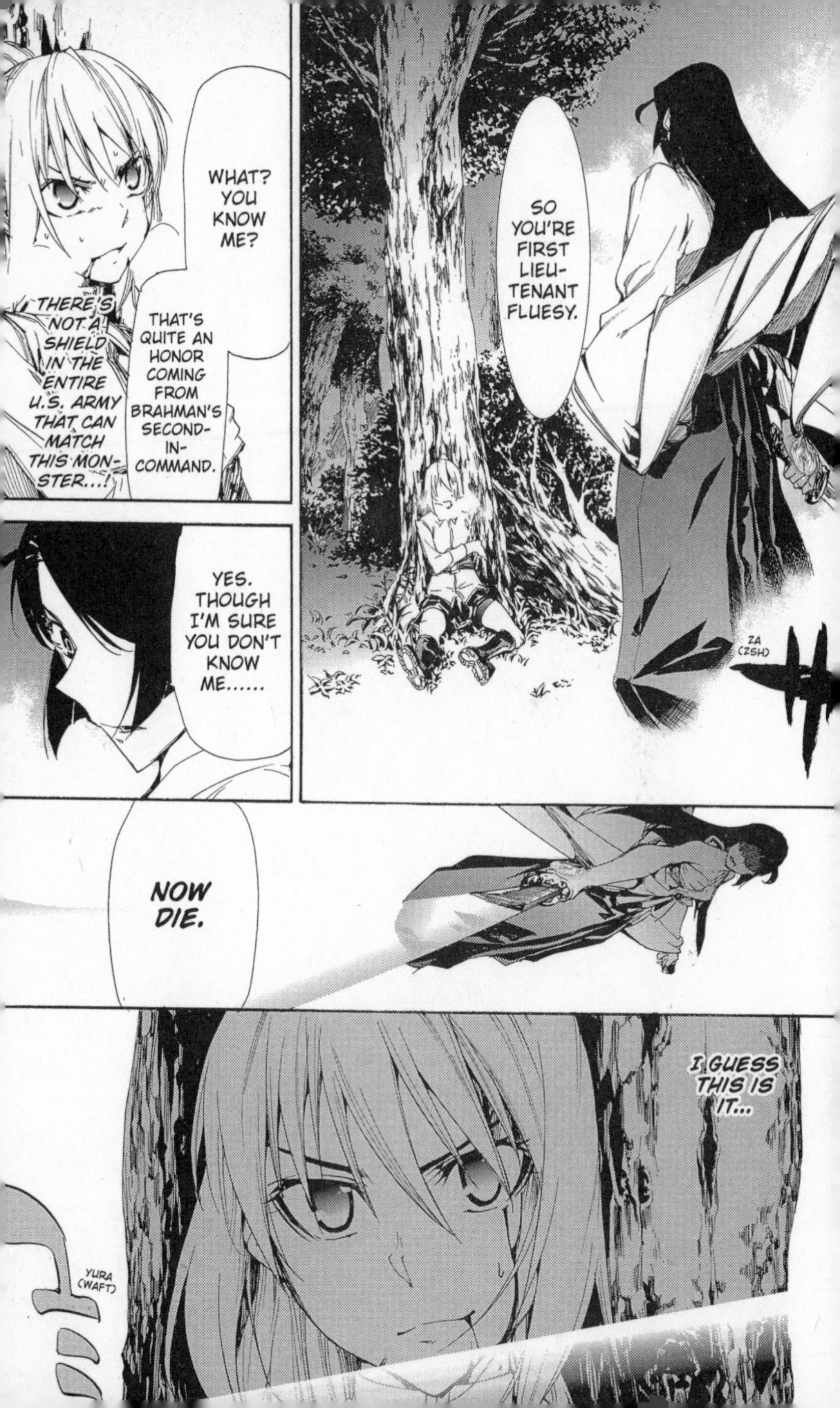
SO YOU'RE FIRST LIEU-TENANT FLUESY.
ZA (ZSH)
WHAT? YOU KNOW ME?
THAT'S QUITE AN HONOR COMING FROM BRAHMAN'S SECOND-IN-COMMAND.
THERE'S NOT A SHIELD IN THE ENTIRE U.S. ARMY THAT CAN MATCH THIS MON-STER...!
YES. THOUGH I'M SURE YOU DON'T KNOW ME......
NOW DIE.
I GUESS THIS IS IT...
YURA (WAFT)

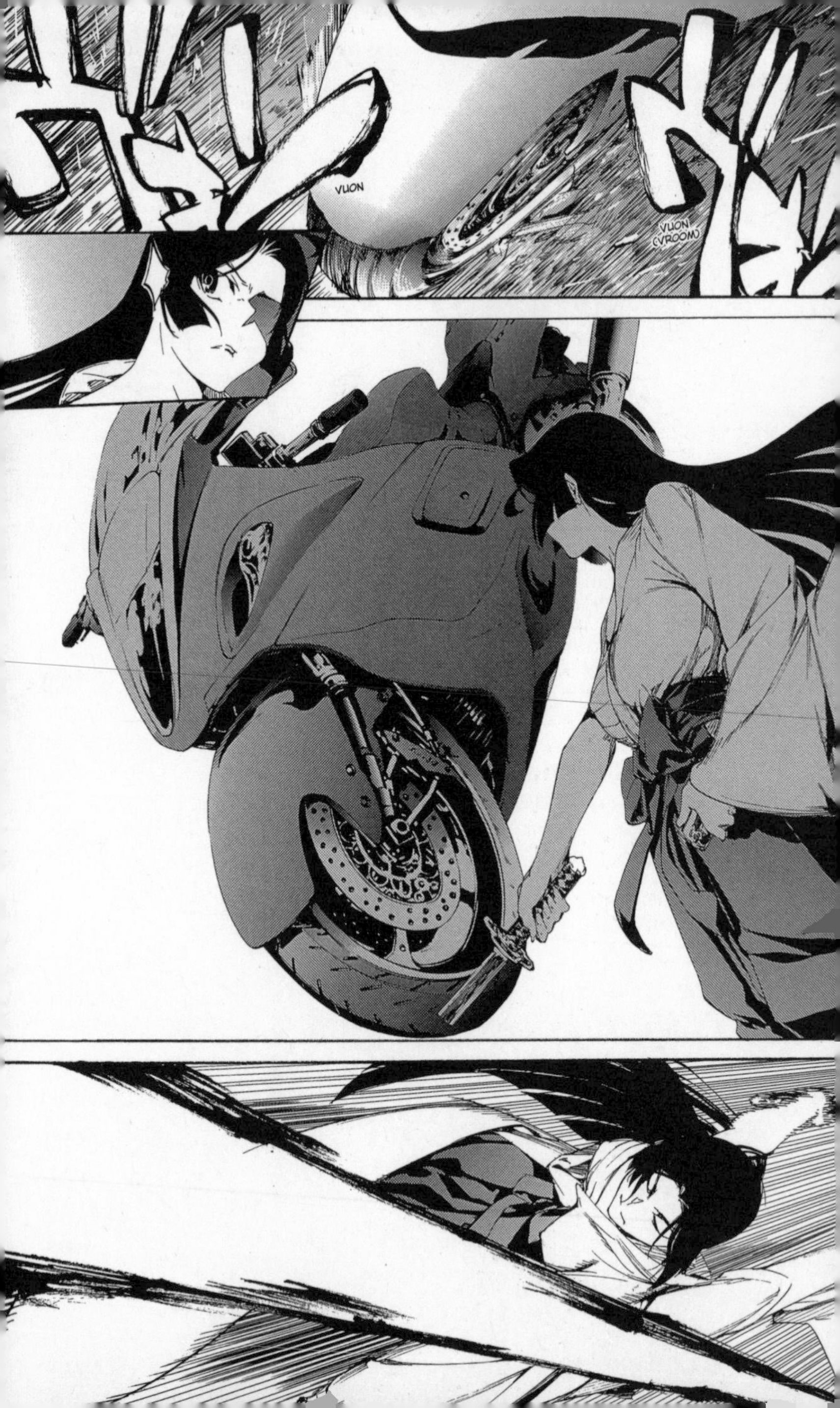
VUON
(VROOM)
VUON

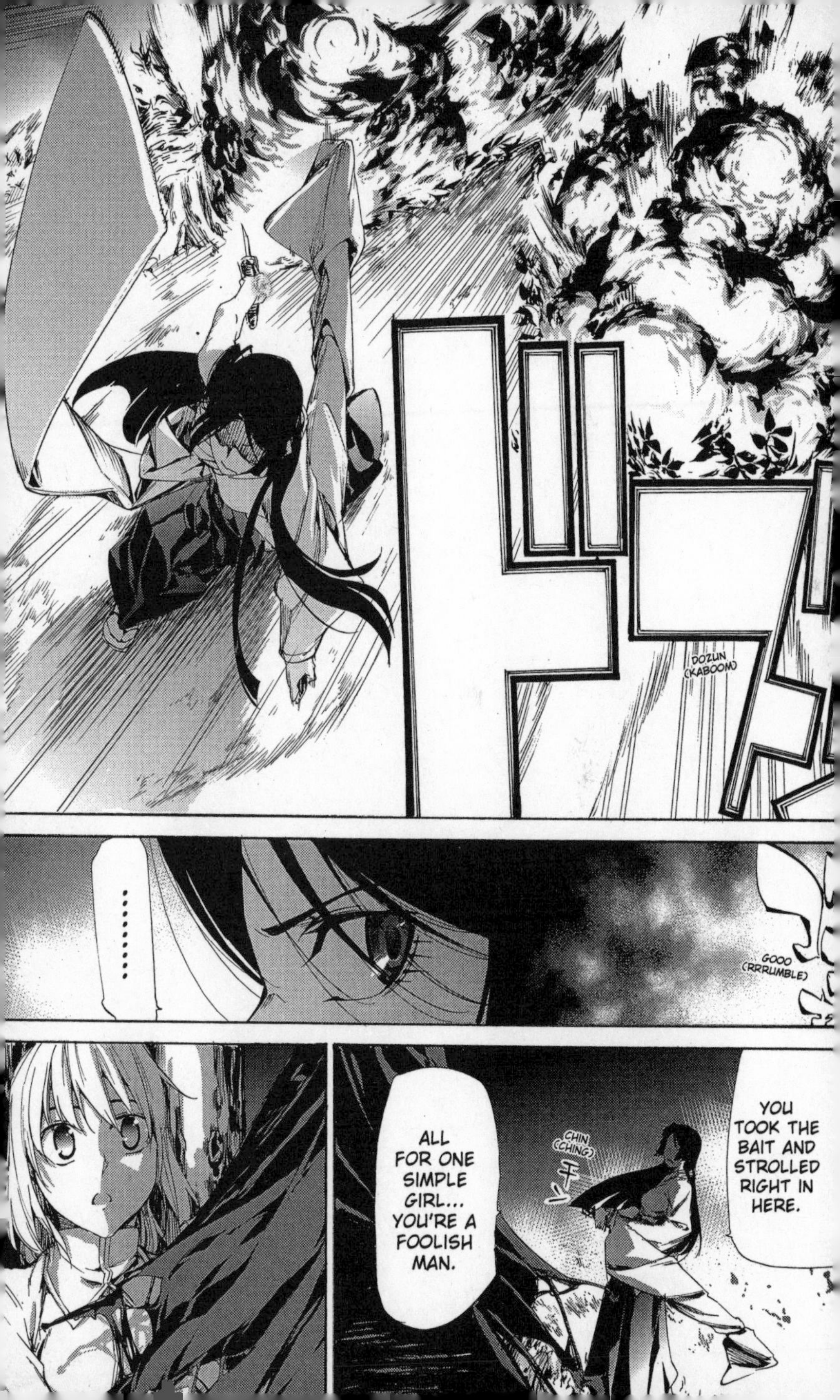
DOZUN (KABOOM)
GOOO (RRRUMBLE)
......
YOU TOOK THE BAIT AND STROLLED RIGHT IN HERE.
CHIN (CHING)
ALL FOR ONE SIMPLE GIRL... YOU'RE A FOOLISH MAN.

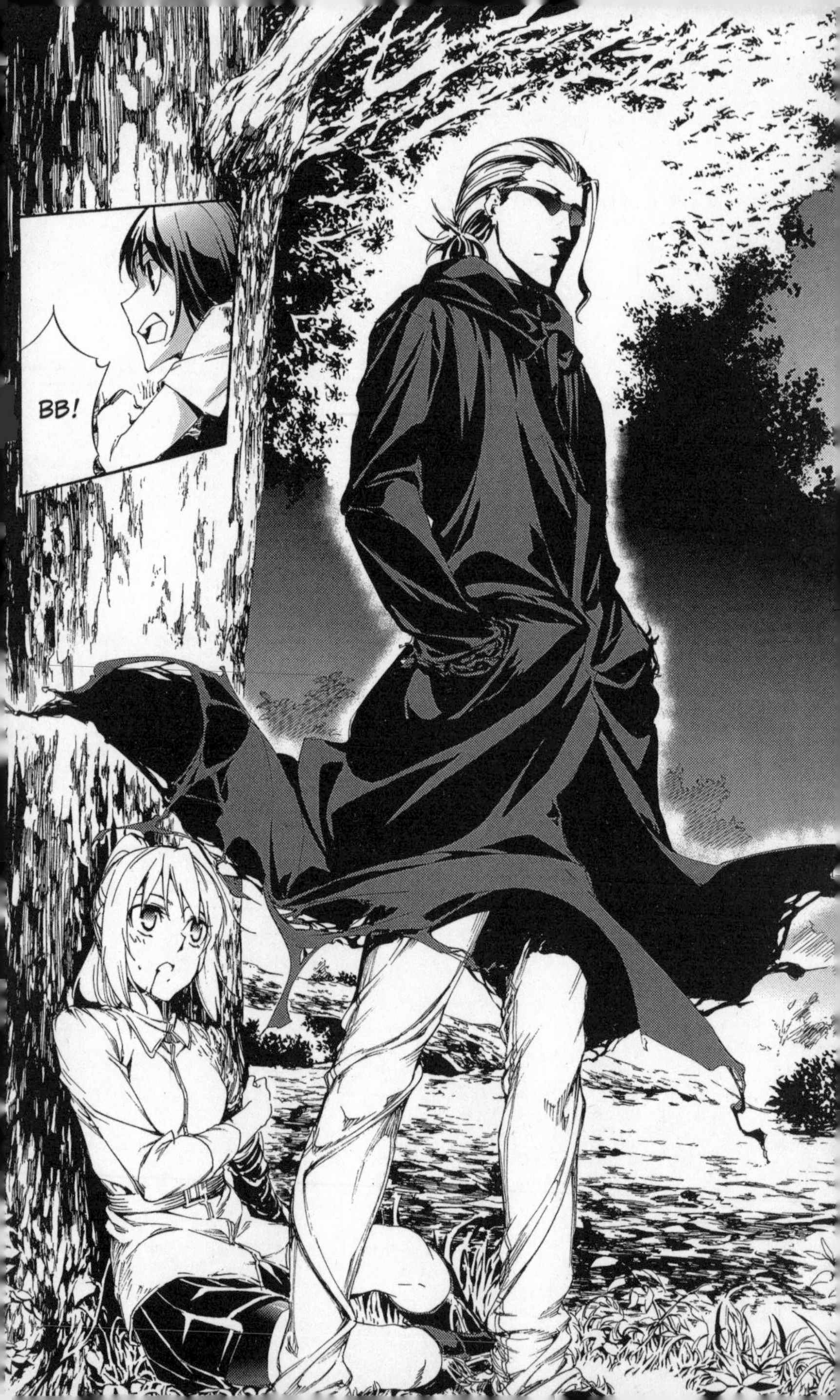
BB!

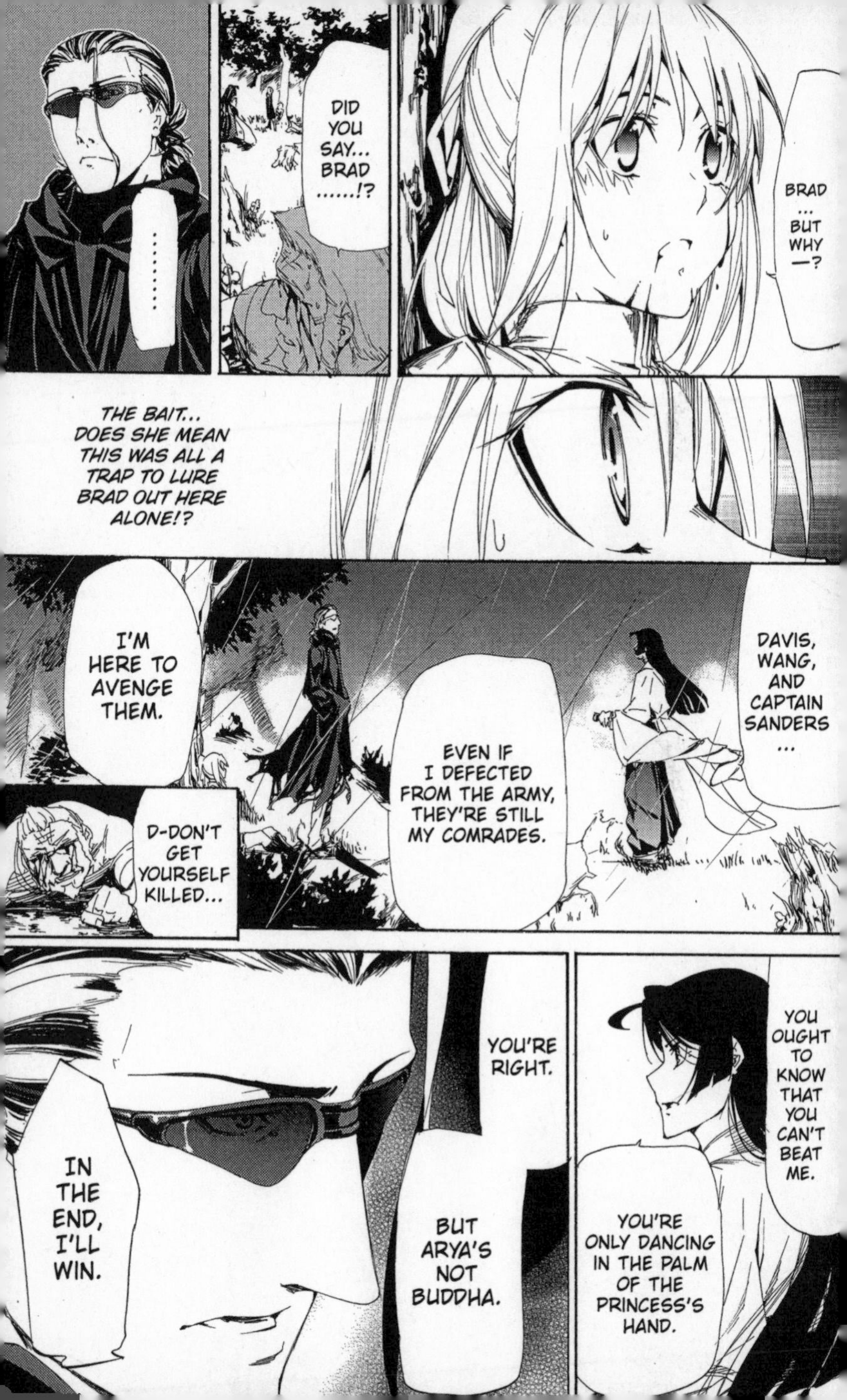
BRAD ... BUT WHY —?
DID YOU SAY... BRAD ......!?
......
THE BAIT... DOES SHE MEAN THIS WAS ALL A TRAP TO LURE BRAD OUT HERE ALONE!?
DAVIS, WANG, AND CAPTAIN SANDERS ...
EVEN IF I DEFECTED FROM THE ARMY, THEY'RE STILL MY COMRADES.
I'M HERE TO AVENGE THEM.
D-DON'T GET YOURSELF KILLED...
YOU OUGHT TO KNOW THAT YOU CAN'T BEAT ME.
YOU'RE ONLY DANCING IN THE PALM OF THE PRINCESS'S HAND.
YOU'RE RIGHT.
BUT ARYA'S NOT BUDDHA.
IN THE END, I'LL WIN.

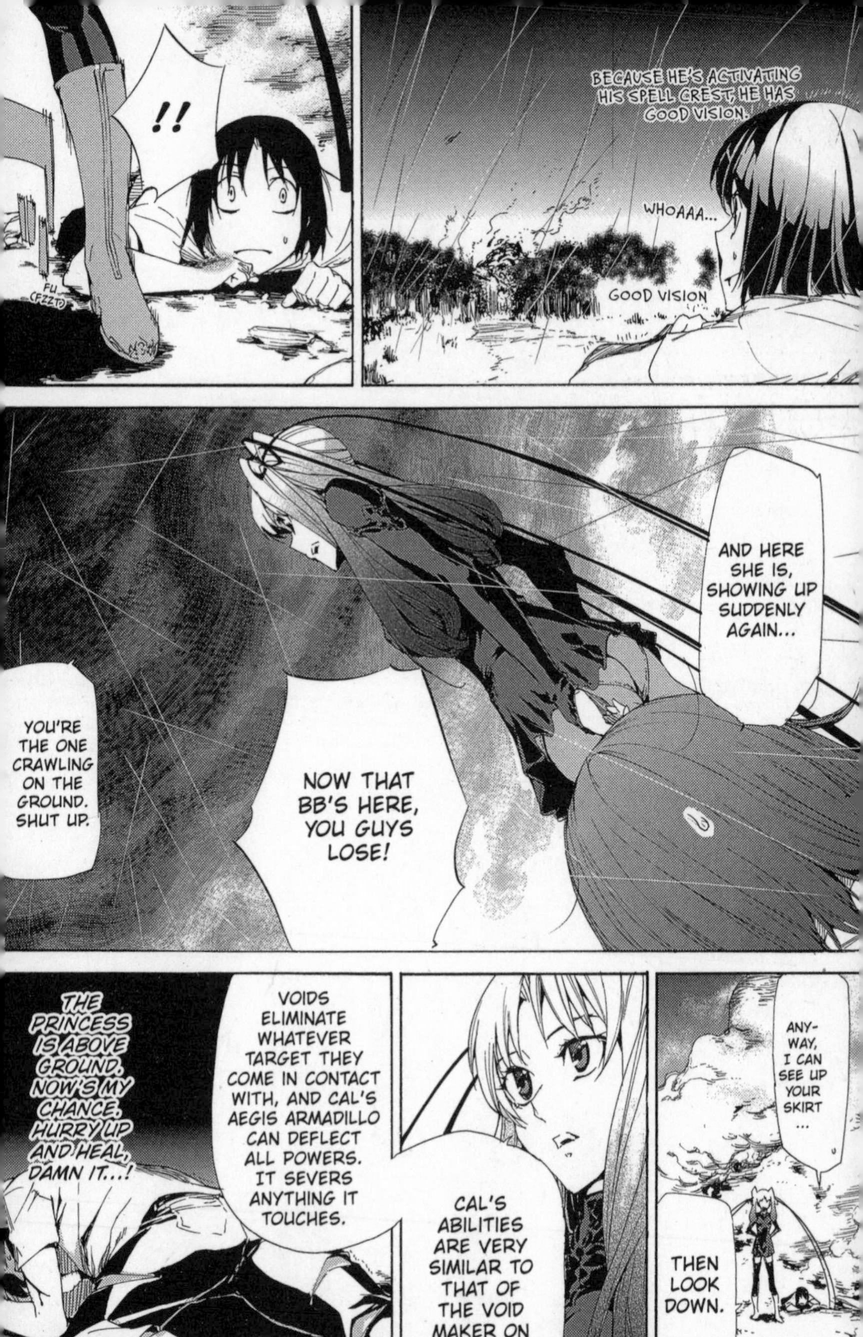
BECAUSE HE'S ACTIVATING HIS SPELL CREST, HE HAS GOOD VISION.
WHOAAA...
GOOD VISION
!!
FU (FZZT)
AND HERE SHE IS, SHOWING UP SUDDENLY AGAIN...
NOW THAT BB'S HERE, YOU GUYS LOSE!
YOU'RE THE ONE CRAWLING ON THE GROUND. SHUT UP.
ANY-WAY, I CAN SEE UP YOUR SKIRT...
THEN LOOK DOWN.
CAL'S ABILITIES ARE VERY SIMILAR TO THAT OF THE VOID MAKER ON THE FIELD.
VOIDS ELIMINATE WHATEVER TARGET THEY COME IN CONTACT WITH, AND CAL'S AEGIS ARMADILLO CAN DEFLECT ALL POWERS. IT SEVERS ANYTHING IT TOUCHES.
THE PRINCESS IS ABOVE GROUND. NOW'S MY CHANCE. HURRY UP AND HEAL, DAMN IT...!

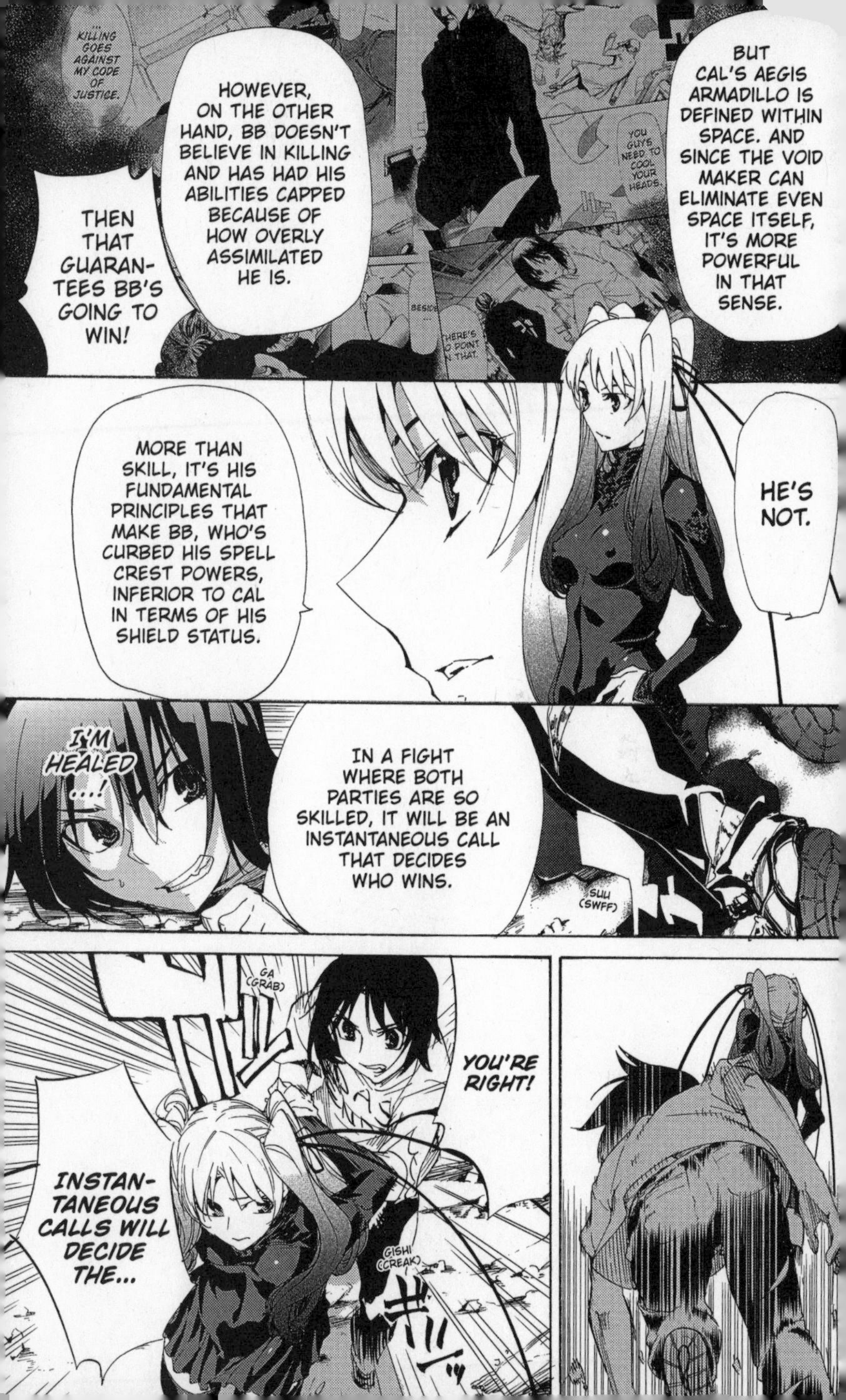
BUT CAL'S AEGIS ARMADILLO IS DEFINED WITHIN SPACE. AND SINCE THE VOID MAKER CAN ELIMINATE EVEN SPACE ITSELF, IT'S MORE POWERFUL IN THAT SENSE.
YOU GUYS NEED TO COOL YOUR HEADS.
HOWEVER, ON THE OTHER HAND, BB DOESN'T BELIEVE IN KILLING AND HAS HAD HIS ABILITIES CAPPED BECAUSE OF HOW OVERLY ASSIMILATED HE IS.
...KILLING GOES AGAINST MY CODE OF JUSTICE.
THEN THAT GUARANTEES BB'S GOING TO WIN!
HE'S NOT.
MORE THAN SKILL, IT'S HIS FUNDAMENTAL PRINCIPLES THAT MAKE BB, WHO'S CURBED HIS SPELL CREST POWERS, INFERIOR TO CAL IN TERMS OF HIS SHIELD STATUS.
SUU (SWFF)
IN A FIGHT WHERE BOTH PARTIES ARE SO SKILLED, IT WILL BE AN INSTANTANEOUS CALL THAT DECIDES WHO WINS.
I'M HEALED ...!
YOU'RE RIGHT!
GA (GRAB)
GISHI (CREAK)
INSTAN-TANEOUS CALLS WILL DECIDE THE...

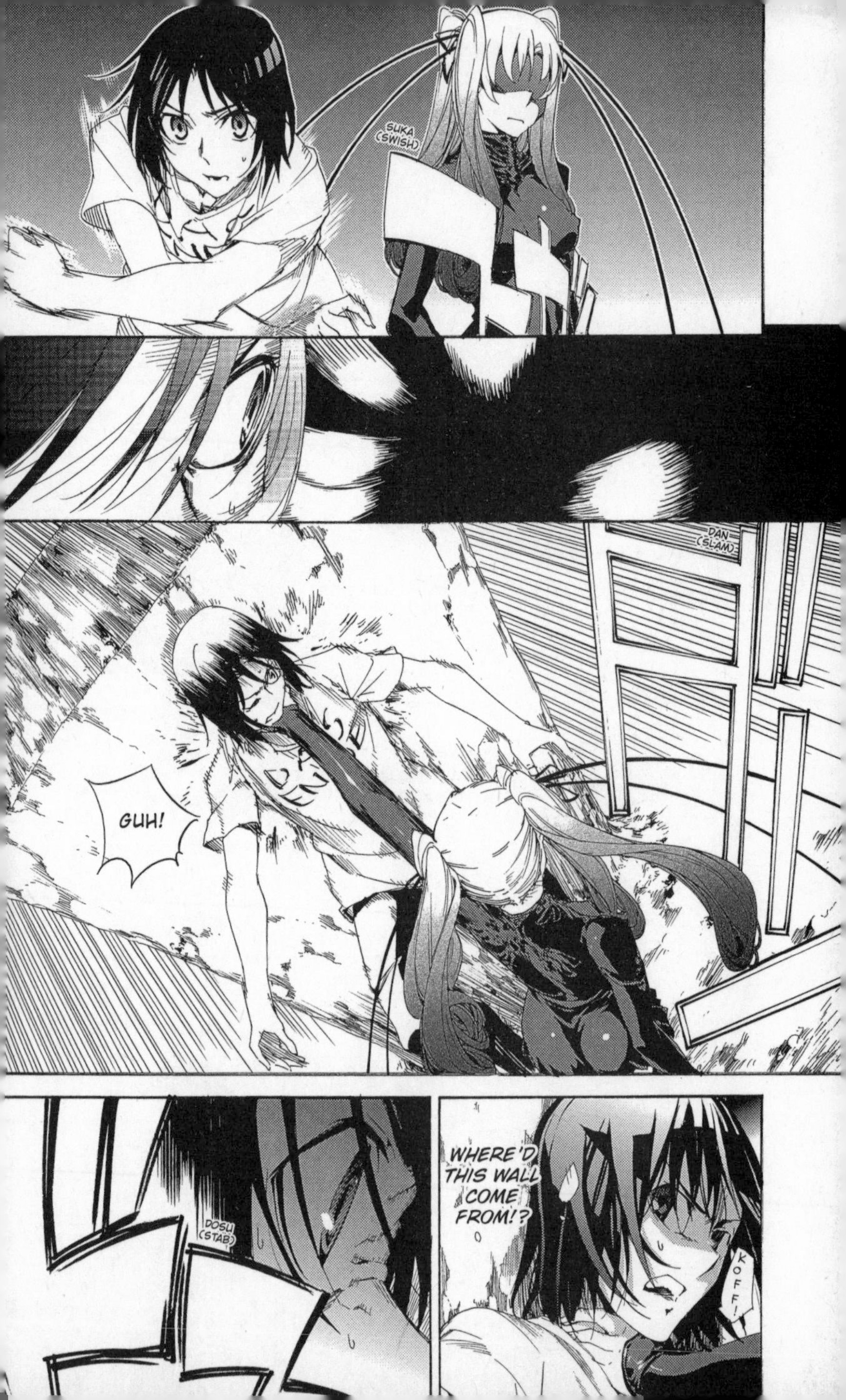
SUKA (SWISH)
DAN (SLAM)
GUH!
WHERE'D THIS WALL COME FROM!?
KOFF!
DOSU (STAB)

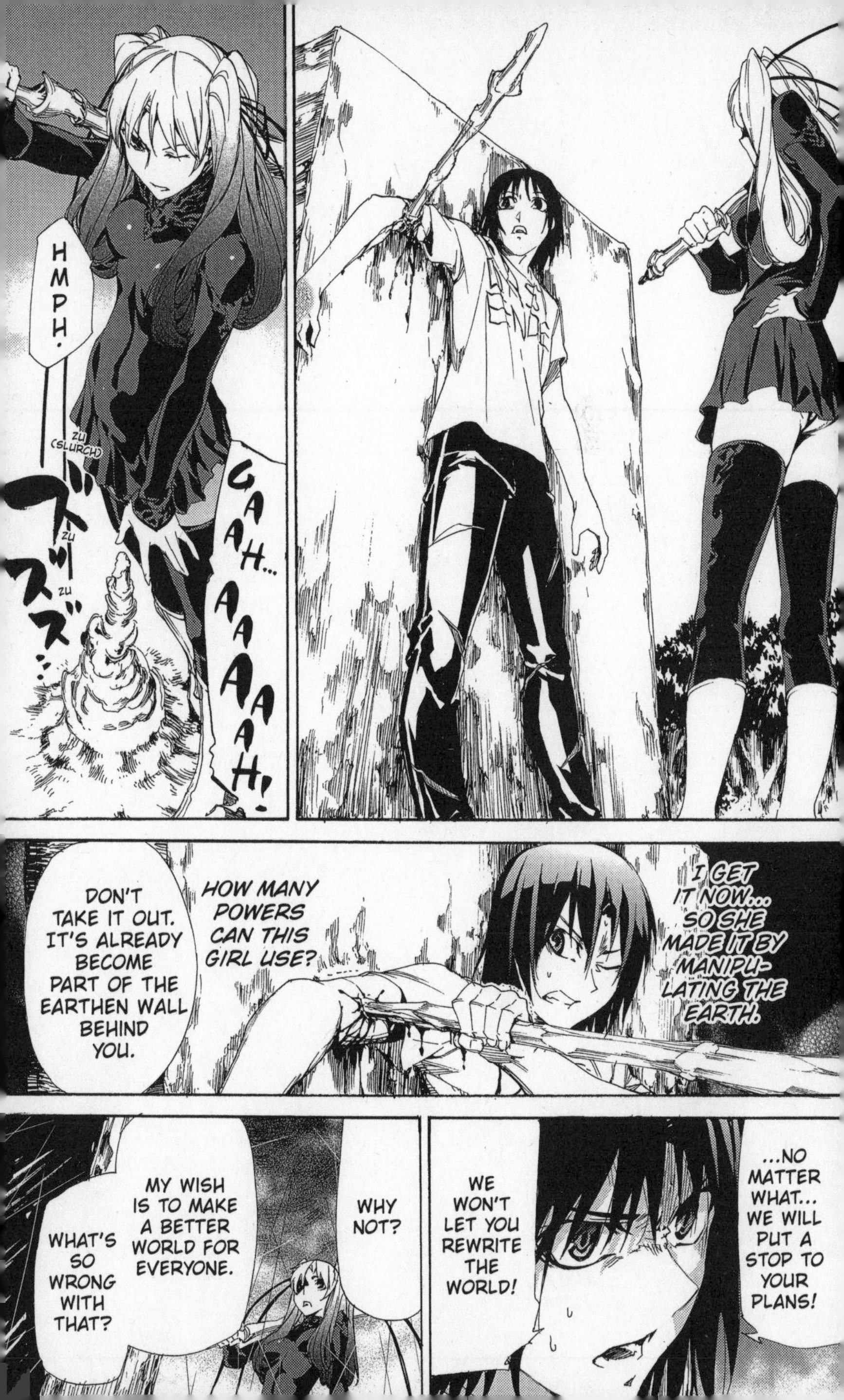
HMPH.
ZU (SLURCH)
ズッズズッ
ZU
ZU
GAAH... AAAAAAAH!
I GET IT NOW... SO SHE MADE IT BY MANIPU-LATING THE EARTH.
HOW MANY POWERS CAN THIS GIRL USE?
DON'T TAKE IT OUT. IT'S ALREADY BECOME PART OF THE EARTHEN WALL BEHIND YOU.
...NO MATTER WHAT... WE WILL PUT A STOP TO YOUR PLANS!
WE WON'T LET YOU REWRITE THE WORLD!
WHY NOT?
MY WISH IS TO MAKE A BETTER WORLD FOR EVERYONE.
WHAT'S SO WRONG WITH THAT?

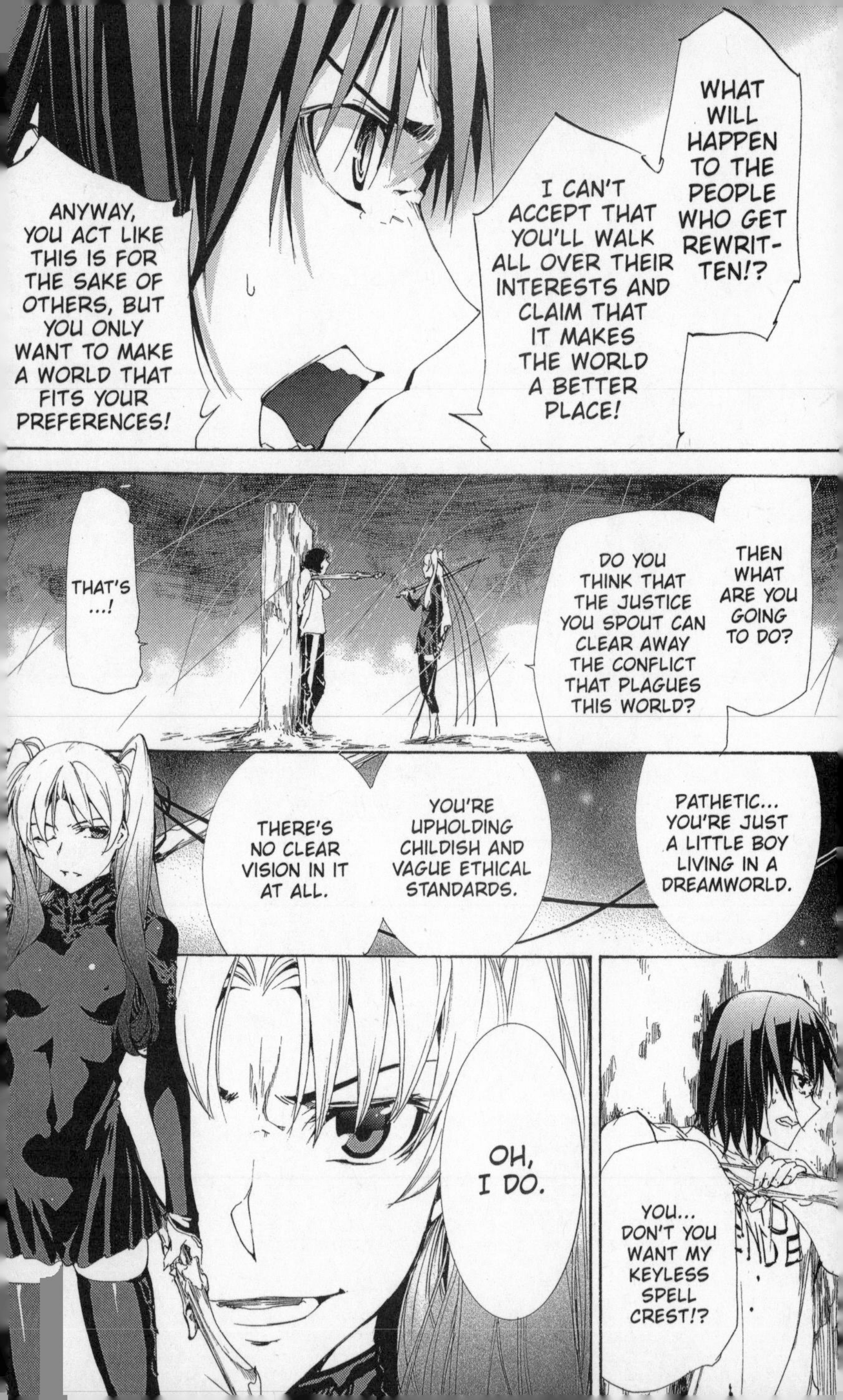
WHAT WILL HAPPEN TO THE PEOPLE WHO GET REWRIT-TEN!?
I CAN'T ACCEPT THAT YOU'LL WALK ALL OVER THEIR INTERESTS AND CLAIM THAT IT MAKES THE WORLD A BETTER PLACE!
ANYWAY, YOU ACT LIKE THIS IS FOR THE SAKE OF OTHERS, BUT YOU ONLY WANT TO MAKE A WORLD THAT FITS YOUR PREFERENCES!
THEN WHAT ARE YOU GOING TO DO?
DO YOU THINK THAT THE JUSTICE YOU SPOUT CAN CLEAR AWAY THE CONFLICT THAT PLAGUES THIS WORLD?
THAT'S ...!
PATHETIC... YOU'RE JUST A LITTLE BOY LIVING IN A DREAMWORLD.
YOU'RE UPHOLDING CHILDISH AND VAGUE ETHICAL STANDARDS.
THERE'S NO CLEAR VISION IN IT AT ALL.
YOU... DON'T YOU WANT MY KEYLESS SPELL CREST!?
OH, I DO.

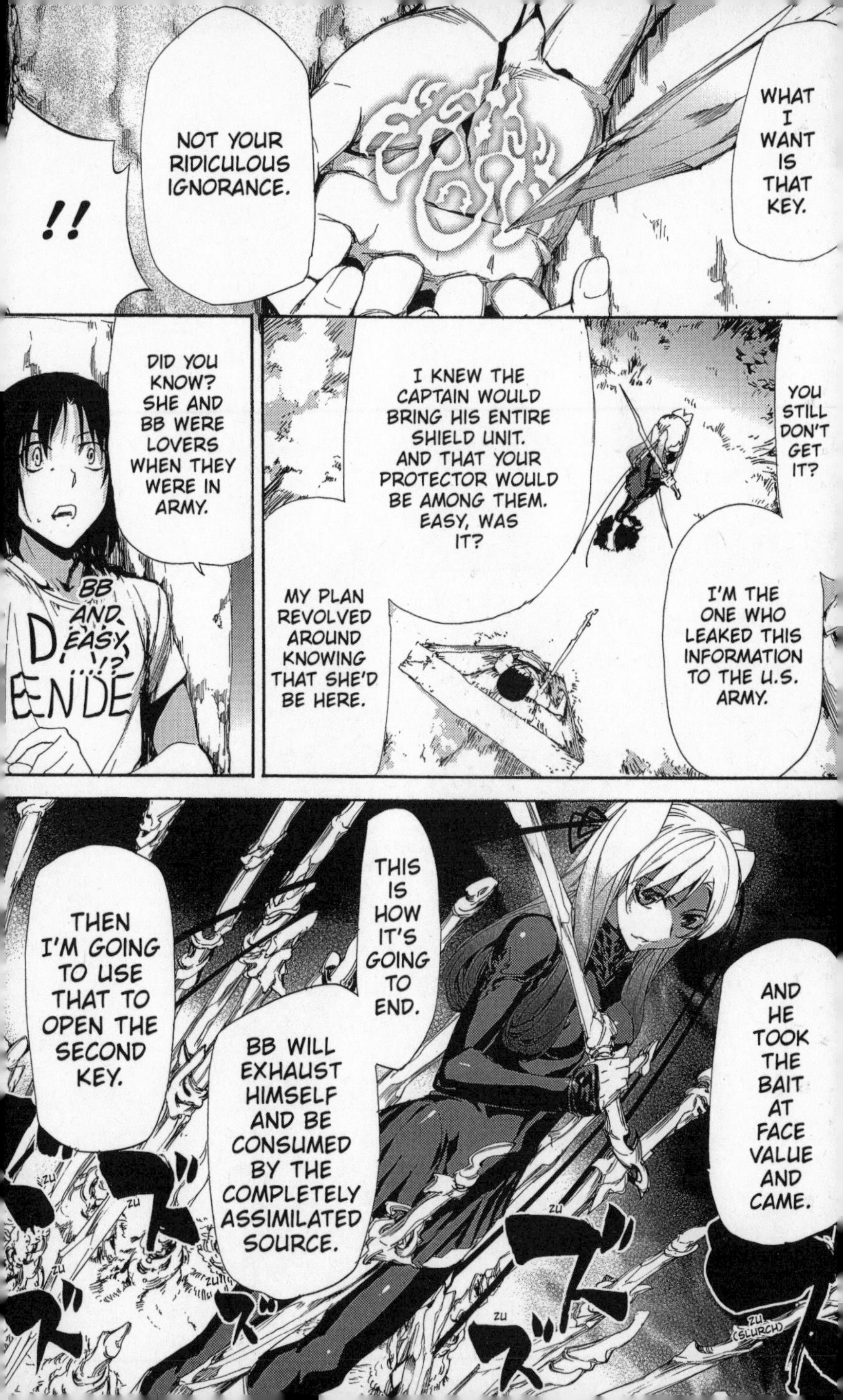

WHAT I WANT IS THAT KEY.
NOT YOUR RIDICULOUS IGNORANCE.
!!
YOU STILL DON'T GET IT?
I'M THE ONE WHO LEAKED THIS INFORMATION TO THE U.S. ARMY.
I KNEW THE CAPTAIN WOULD BRING HIS ENTIRE SHIELD UNIT. AND THAT YOUR PROTECTOR WOULD BE AMONG THEM. EASY, WAS IT?
MY PLAN REVOLVED AROUND KNOWING THAT SHE'D BE HERE.
DID YOU KNOW? SHE AND BB WERE LOVERS WHEN THEY WERE IN ARMY.
BB AND EASY ...!?
AND HE TOOK THE BAIT AT FACE VALUE AND CAME.
THIS IS HOW IT'S GOING TO END.
BB WILL EXHAUST HIMSELF AND BE CONSUMED BY THE COMPLETELY ASSIMILATED SOURCE.
THEN I'M GOING TO USE THAT TO OPEN THE SECOND KEY.
ZU (SLURCH)
ZU
ZU
ZU
ZU
ZU

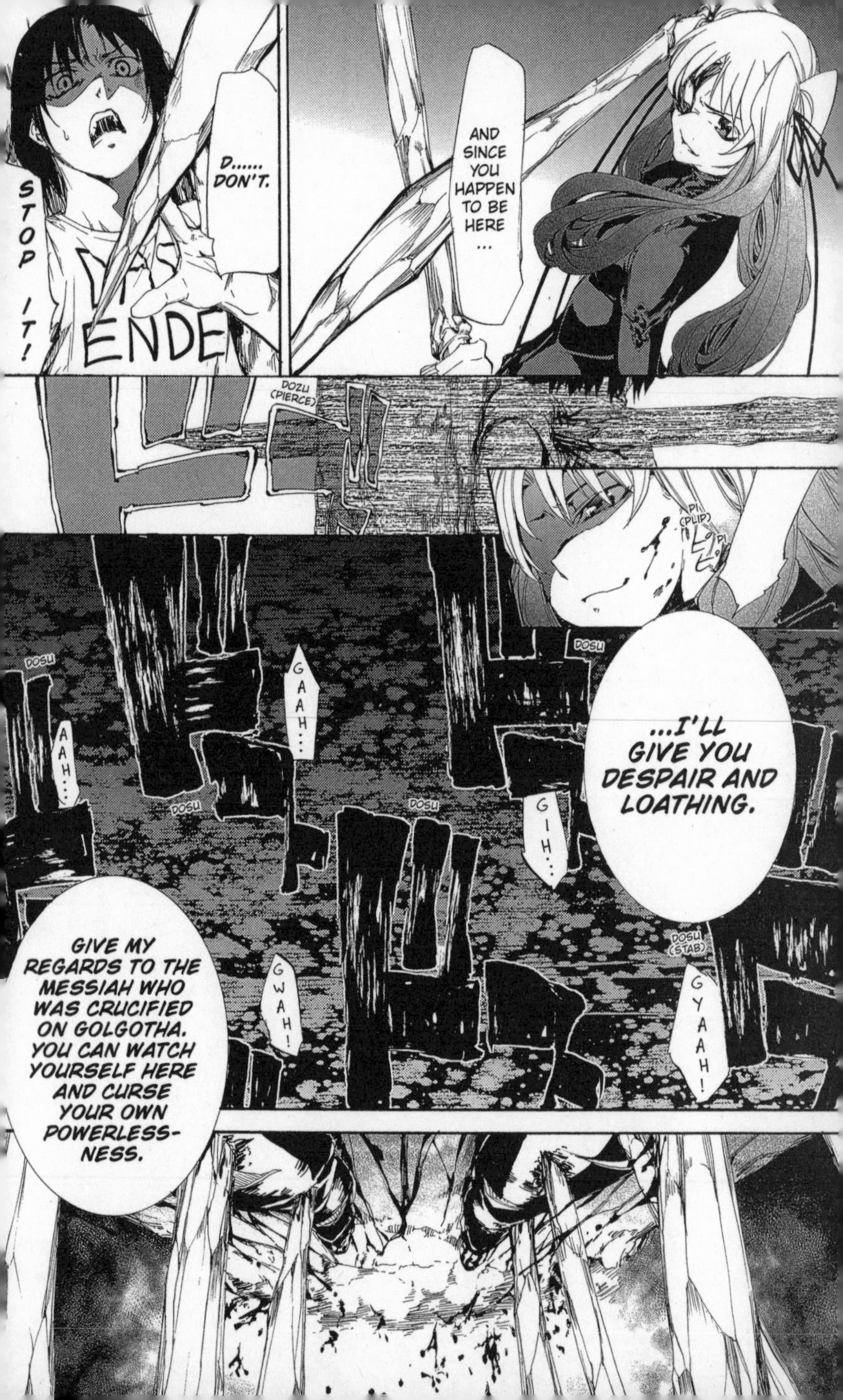
AND SINCE YOU HAPPEN TO BE HERE ...
D...... DON'T.
STOP IT!
ENDE
DOZU (PIERCE)
PI (PLIP)
PI
...I'LL GIVE YOU DESPAIR AND LOATHING.
DOSU
GIH...
DOSU (STAB)
GYAAH!
DOSU
GAAH...
DOSU
DOSU
AAH...
GWAH!
GIVE MY REGARDS TO THE MESSIAH WHO WAS CRUCIFIED ON GOLGOTHA. YOU CAN WATCH YOURSELF HERE AND CURSE YOUR OWN POWERLESS-NESS.

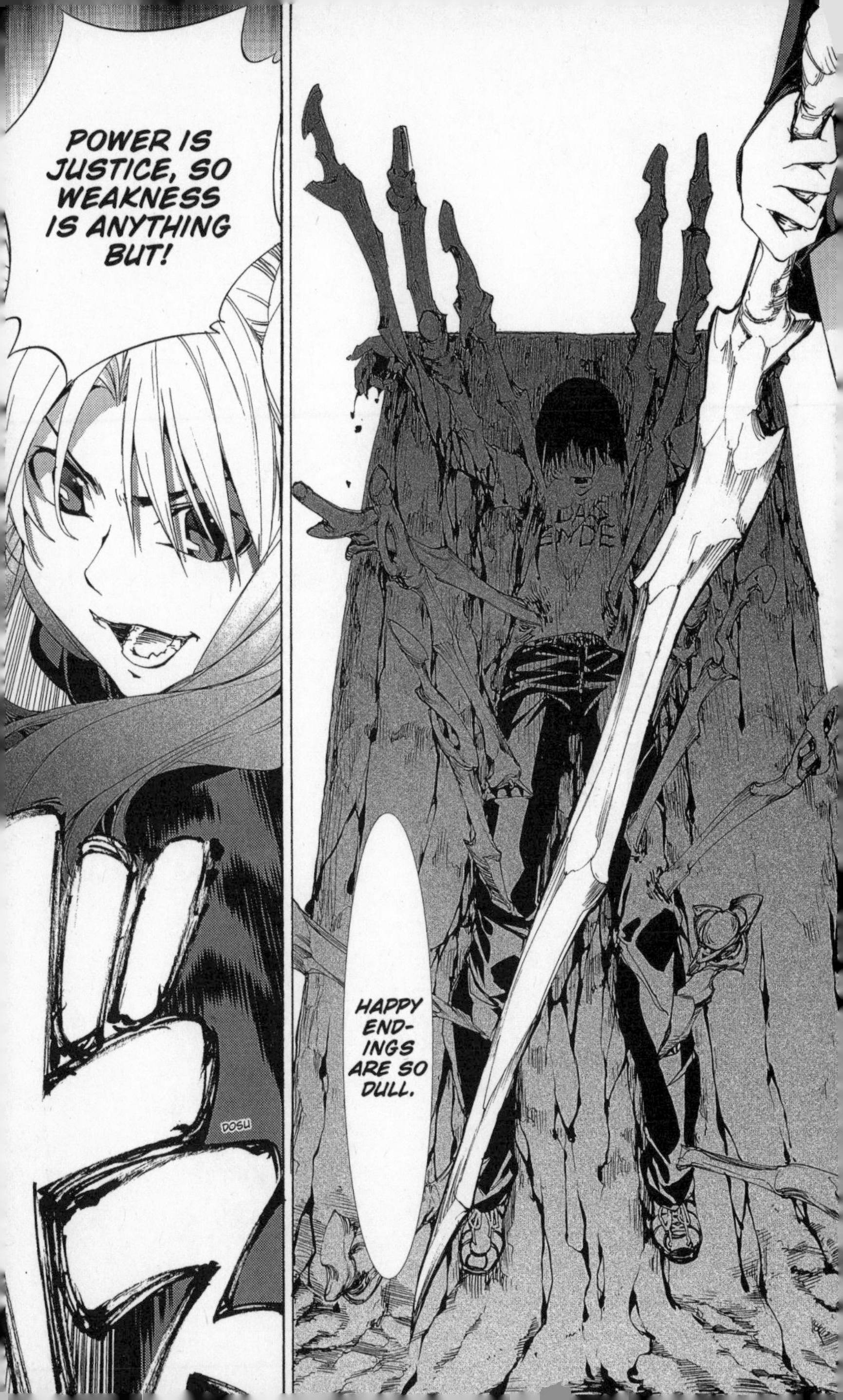
HAPPY END-INGS ARE SO DULL.
POWER IS JUSTICE, SO WEAKNESS IS ANYTHING BUT!
DOSU

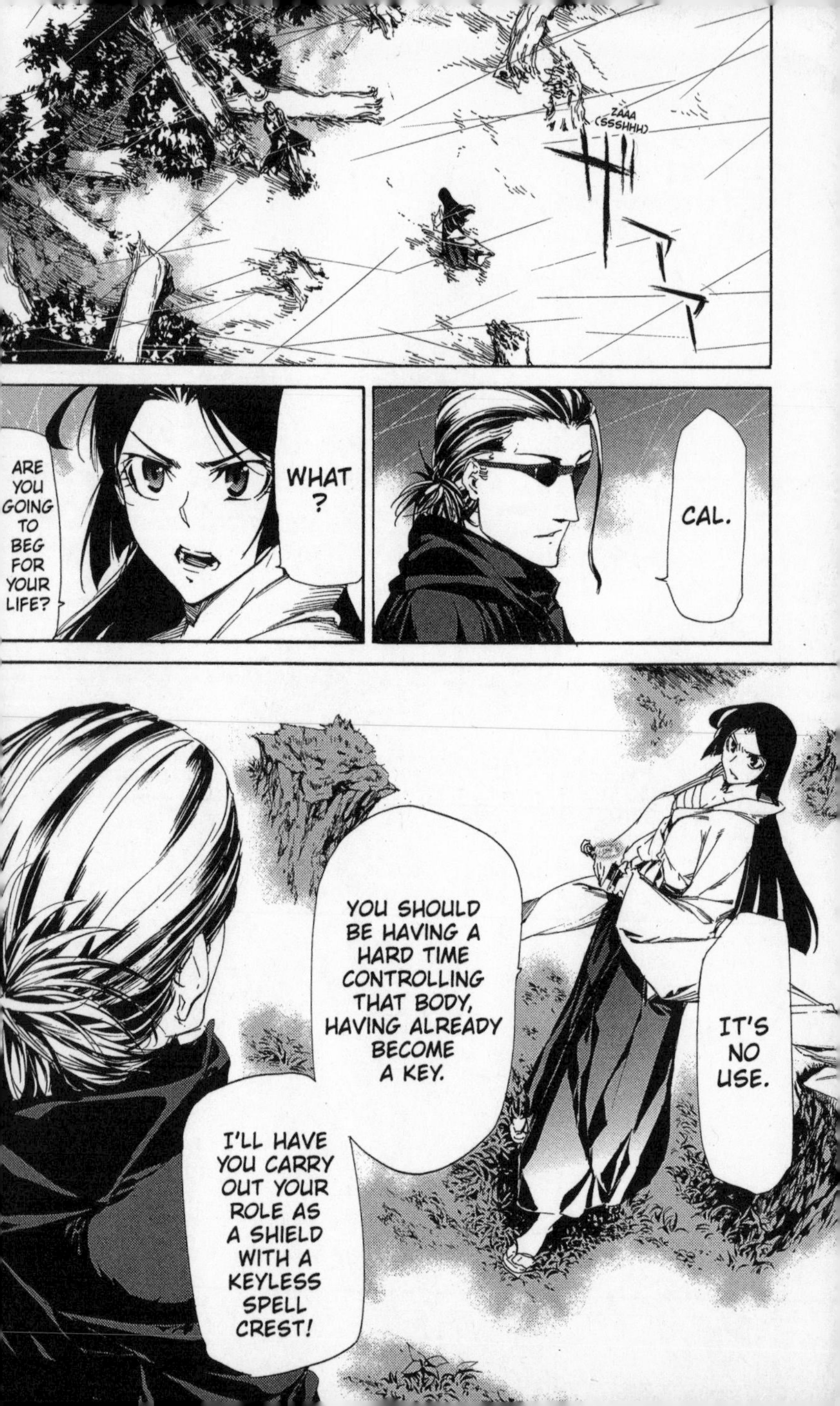
ZAAA (SSSHHH)
CAL.
WHAT?
ARE YOU GOING TO BEG FOR YOUR LIFE?
IT'S NO USE.
YOU SHOULD BE HAVING A HARD TIME CONTROLLING THAT BODY, HAVING ALREADY BECOME A KEY.
I'LL HAVE YOU CARRY OUT YOUR ROLE AS A SHIELD WITH A KEYLESS SPELL CREST!

YOU'RE
IN LOVE
WITH ME.

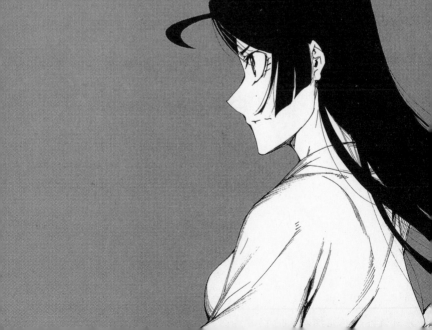

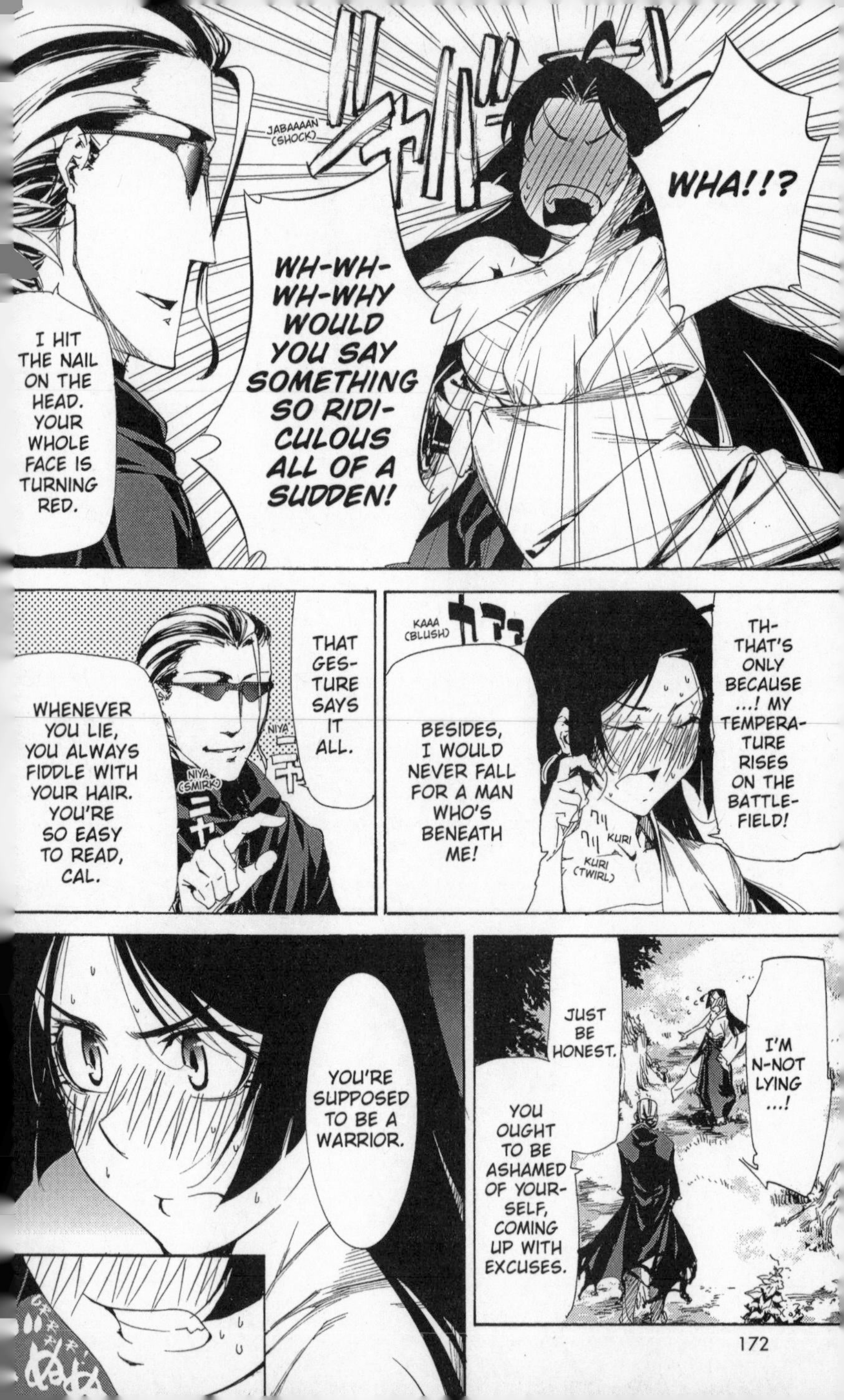
WHA!!?
JABAAAAN (SHOCK)
WH-WH-WH-WHY WOULD YOU SAY SOMETHING SO RIDICULOUS ALL OF A SUDDEN!
I HIT THE NAIL ON THE HEAD. YOUR WHOLE FACE IS TURNING RED.
KAAA (BLUSH)
TH-THAT'S ONLY BECAUSE ...! MY TEMPERATURE RISES ON THE BATTLEFIELD!
BESIDES, I WOULD NEVER FALL FOR A MAN WHO'S BENEATH ME!
KURI KURI (TWIRL)
THAT GESTURE SAYS IT ALL.
NIYA NIYA (SMIRK)
WHENEVER YOU LIE, YOU ALWAYS FIDDLE WITH YOUR HAIR. YOU'RE SO EASY TO READ, CAL.
I'M N-NOT LYING ...!
JUST BE HONEST.
YOU OUGHT TO BE ASHAMED OF YOURSELF, COMING UP WITH EXCUSES.
YOU'RE SUPPOSED TO BE A WARRIOR.

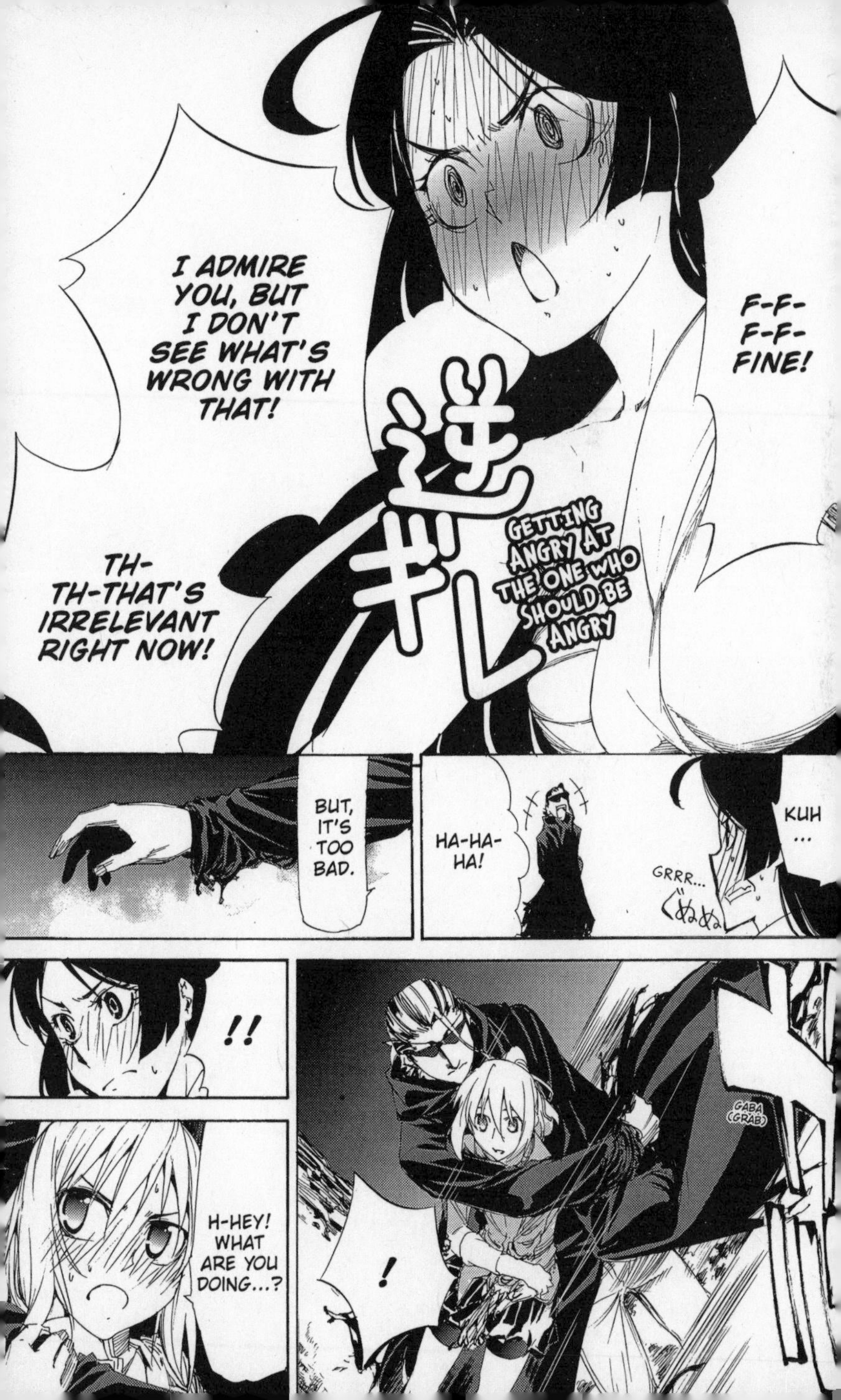
F-F-F-F-FINE!
I ADMIRE YOU, BUT I DON'T SEE WHAT'S WRONG WITH THAT!
逆ギレ
GETTING ANGRY AT THE ONE WHO SHOULD BE ANGRY
TH-TH-THAT'S IRRELEVANT RIGHT NOW!
KUH ...
GRRR... くぬぬ
HA-HA-HA!
BUT, IT'S TOO BAD.
GABA (GRAB)
!
!!
H-HEY! WHAT ARE YOU DOING...?

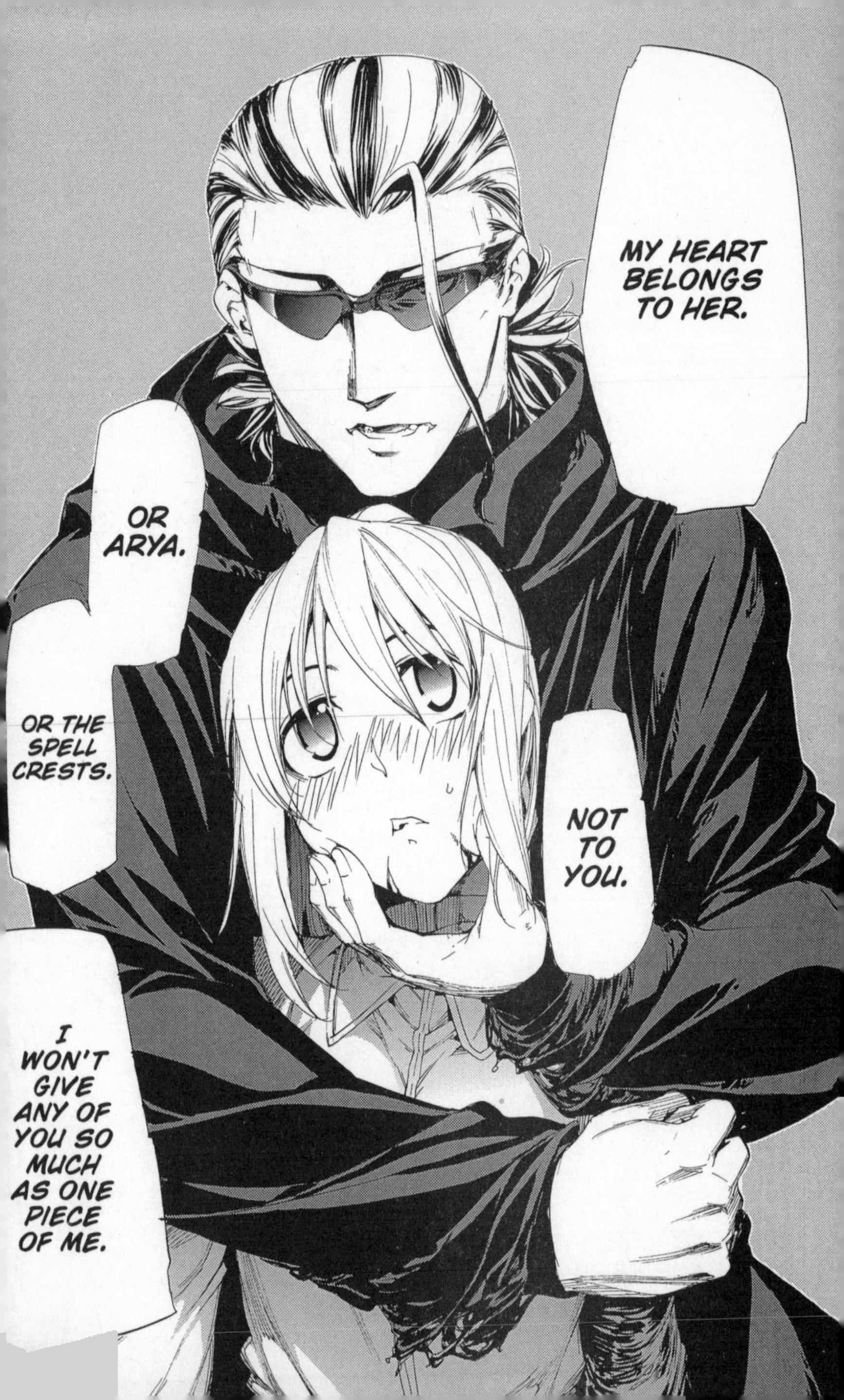
MY HEART BELONGS TO HER.
NOT TO YOU.
OR ARYA.
OR THE SPELL CRESTS.
I WON'T GIVE ANY OF YOU SO MUCH AS ONE PIECE OF ME.

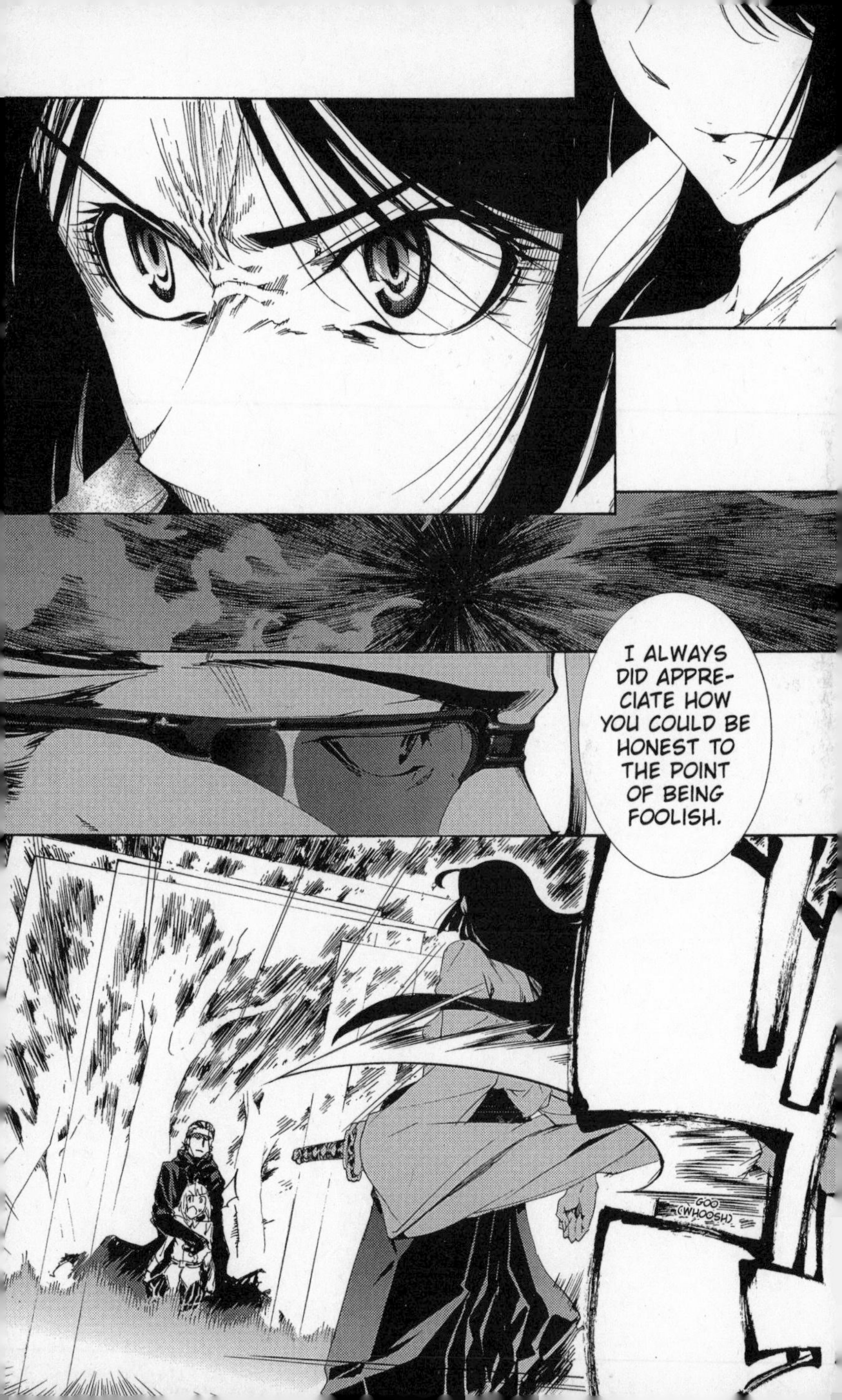
I ALWAYS DID APPRECIATE HOW YOU COULD BE HONEST TO THE POINT OF BEING FOOLISH.
GOO (WHOOSH)

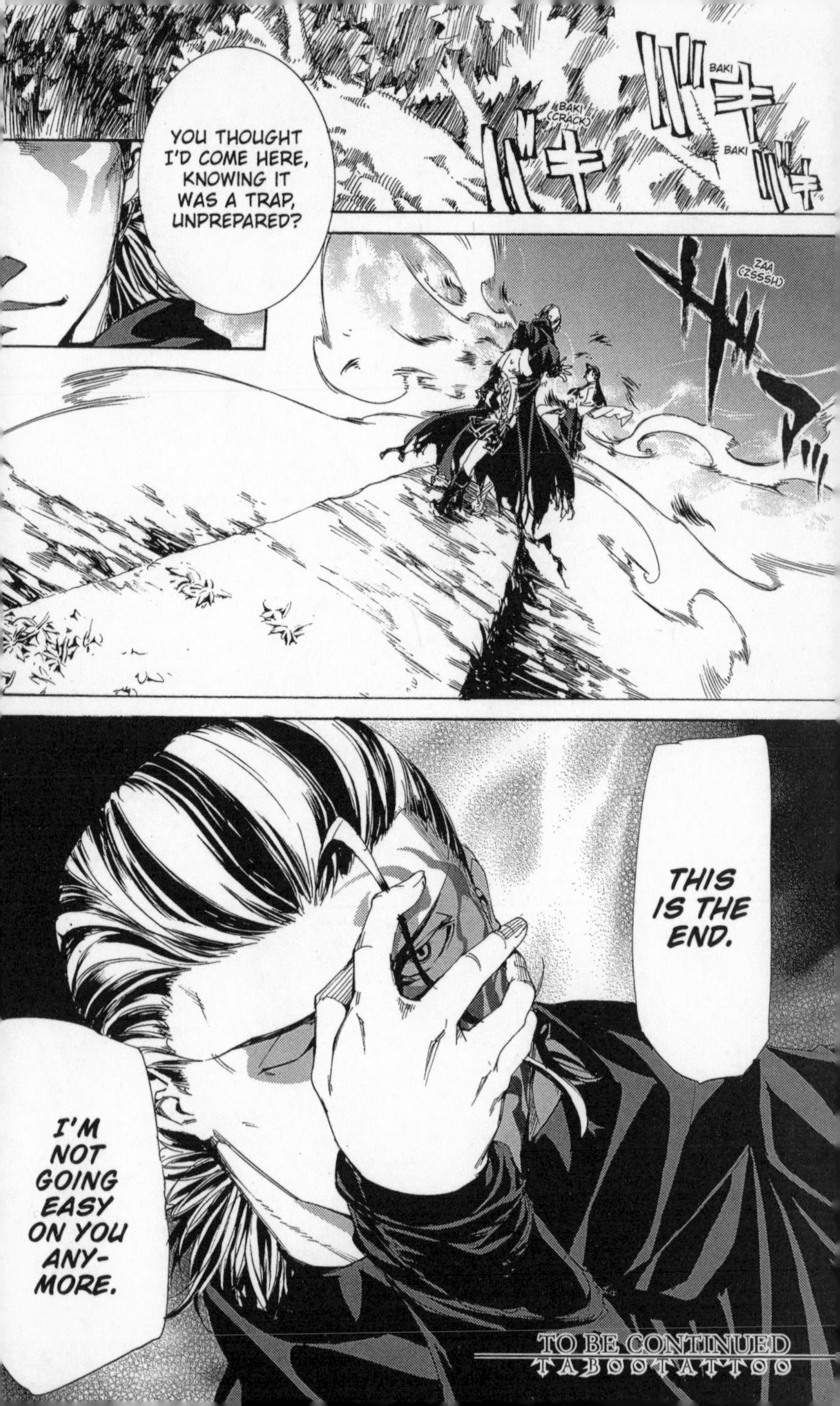
BAKI
BAKI (CRACK)
BAKI
YOU THOUGHT I'D COME HERE, KNOWING IT WAS A TRAP, UNPREPARED?
ZAA (ZSSSH)
THIS IS THE END.
I'M NOT GOING EASY ON YOU ANY-MORE.
TO BE CONTINUED
TABOOTATTOO

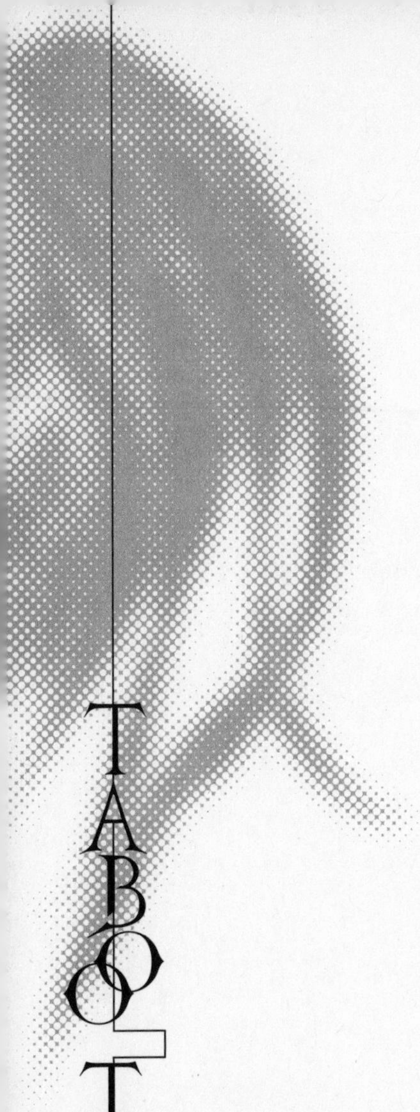

TABOO TATTOO

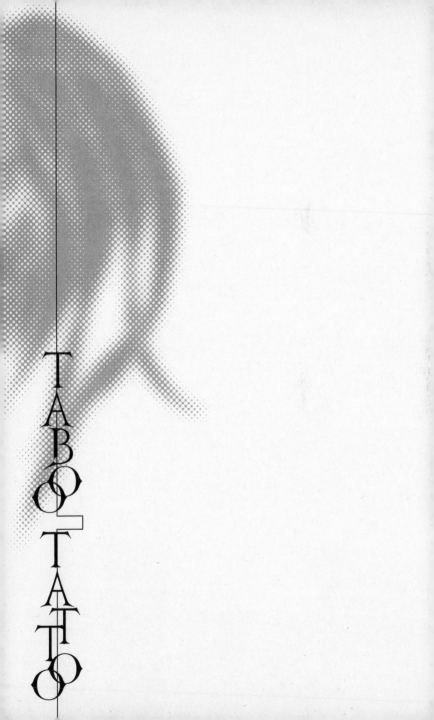

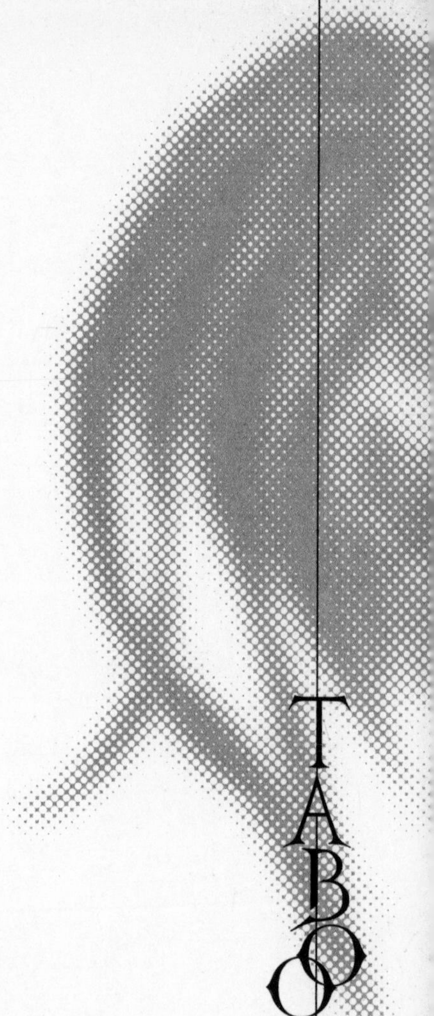

TABOO TATTOO

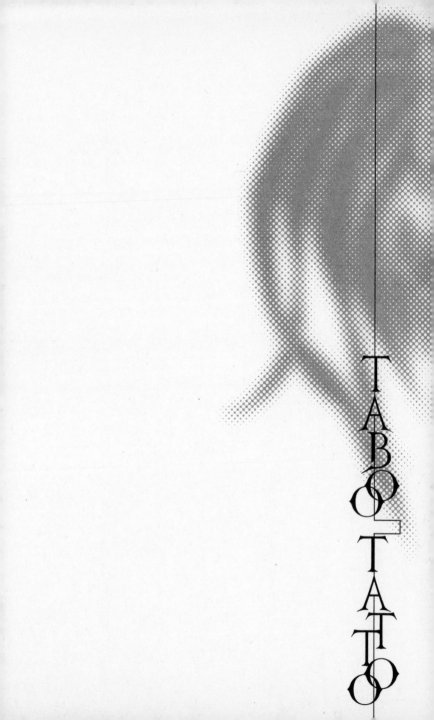

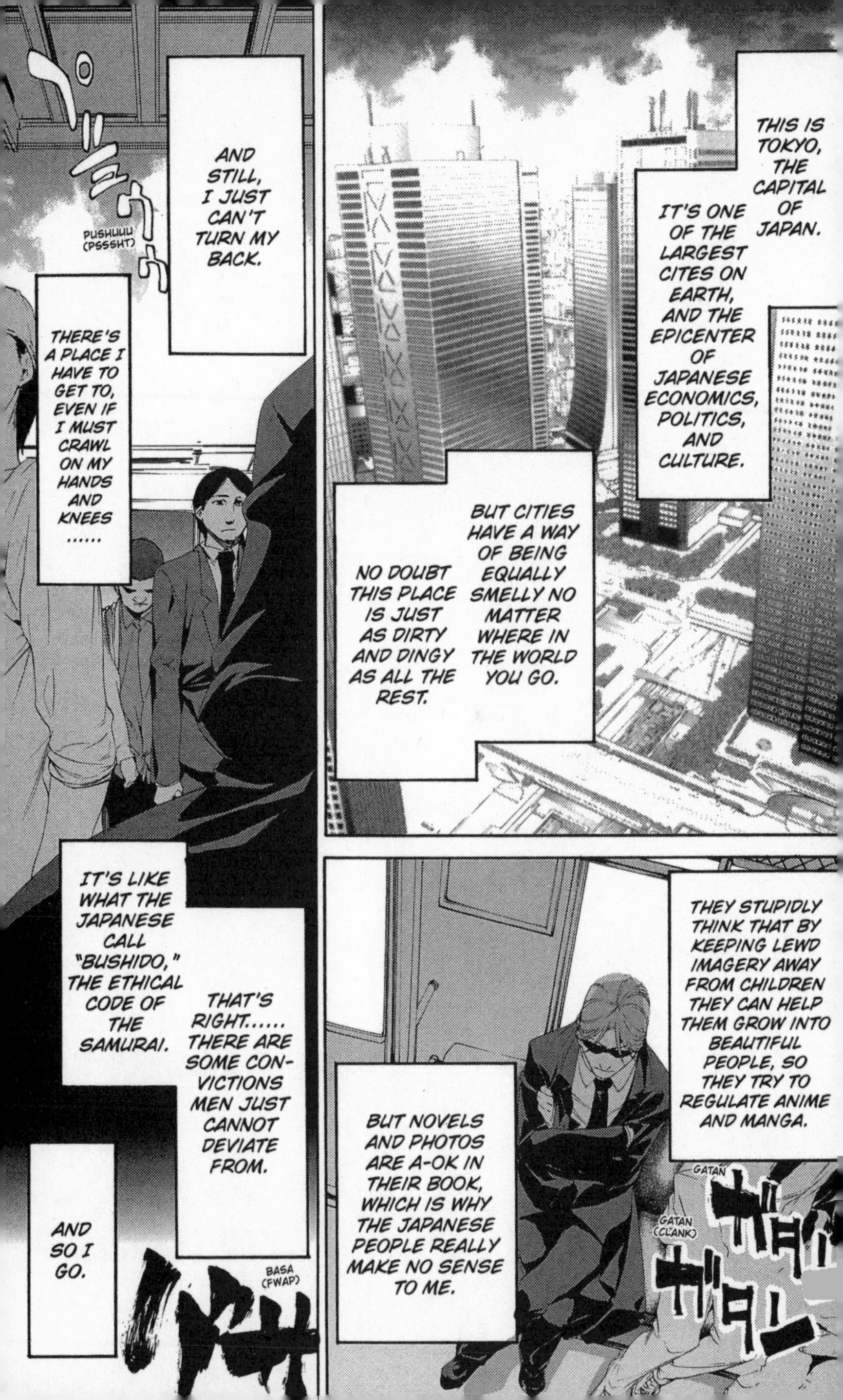
THIS IS TOKYO, THE CAPITAL OF JAPAN.
IT'S ONE OF THE LARGEST CITES ON EARTH, AND THE EPICENTER OF JAPANESE ECONOMICS, POLITICS, AND CULTURE.
BUT CITIES HAVE A WAY OF BEING EQUALLY SMELLY NO MATTER WHERE IN THE WORLD YOU GO.
NO DOUBT THIS PLACE IS JUST AS DIRTY AND DINGY AS ALL THE REST.
AND STILL, I JUST CAN'T TURN MY BACK.
PUSHUUU (PSSSHT)
THERE'S A PLACE I HAVE TO GET TO, EVEN IF I MUST CRAWL ON MY HANDS AND KNEES ......
THEY STUPIDLY THINK THAT BY KEEPING LEWD IMAGERY AWAY FROM CHILDREN THEY CAN HELP THEM GROW INTO BEAUTIFUL PEOPLE, SO THEY TRY TO REGULATE ANIME AND MANGA.
GATAN
GATAN (CLANK)
BUT NOVELS AND PHOTOS ARE A-OK IN THEIR BOOK, WHICH IS WHY THE JAPANESE PEOPLE REALLY MAKE NO SENSE TO ME.
THAT'S RIGHT...... THERE ARE SOME CON-VICTIONS MEN JUST CANNOT DEVIATE FROM.
IT'S LIKE WHAT THE JAPANESE CALL "BUSHIDO," THE ETHICAL CODE OF THE SAMURAI.
AND SO I GO.
BASA (FWAP)

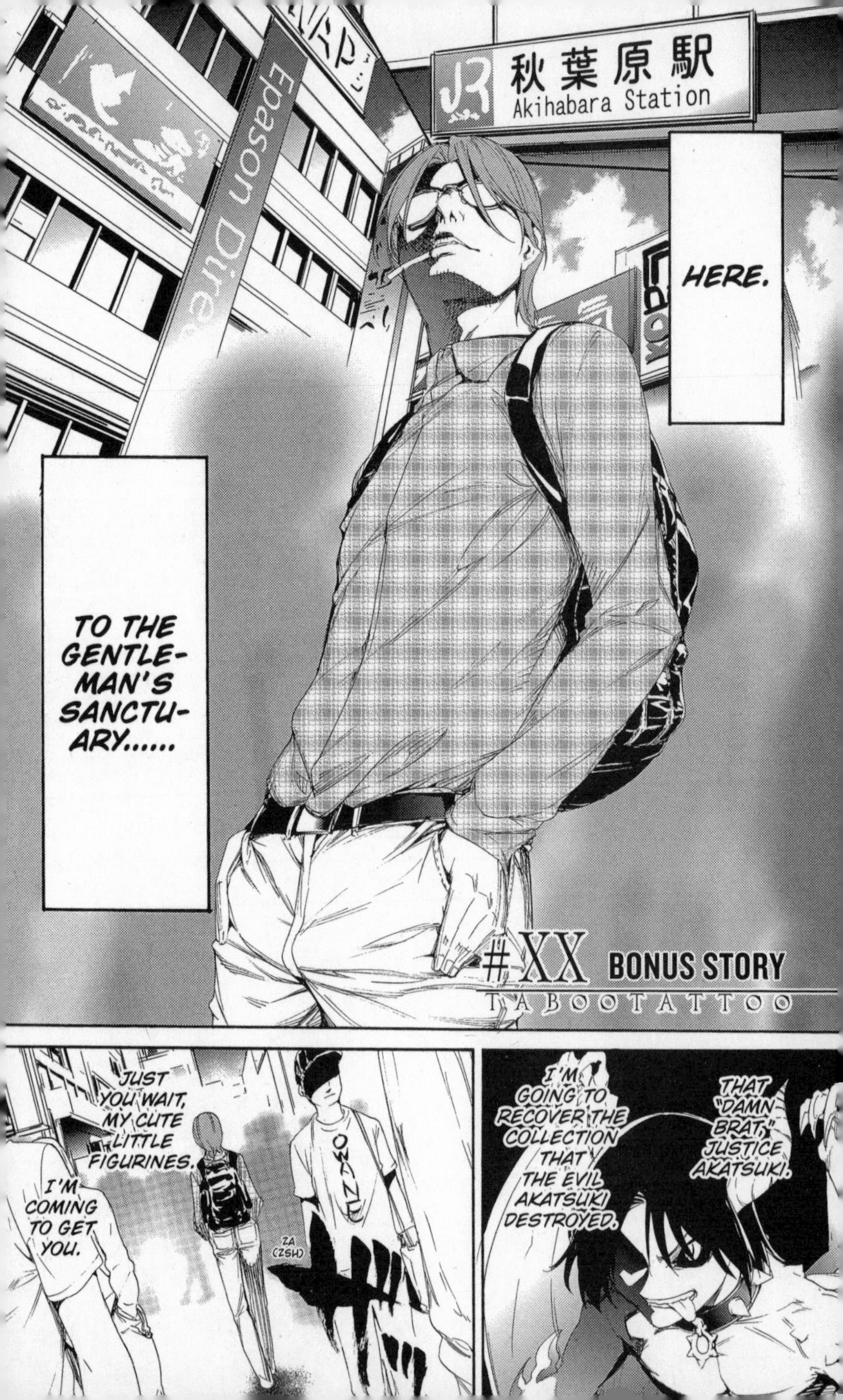
秋葉原駅
Akihabara Station
Epason Dire
HERE.
TO THE GENTLEMAN'S SANCTUARY......
#XX BONUS STORY
TABOOTATTOO
THAT "DAMN BRAT," JUSTICE AKATSUKI.
I'M GOING TO RECOVER THE COLLECTION THAT THE EVIL AKATSUKI DESTROYED.
JUST YOU WAIT, MY CUTE LITTLE FIGURINES.
I'M COMING TO GET YOU.
ZA (ZSH)

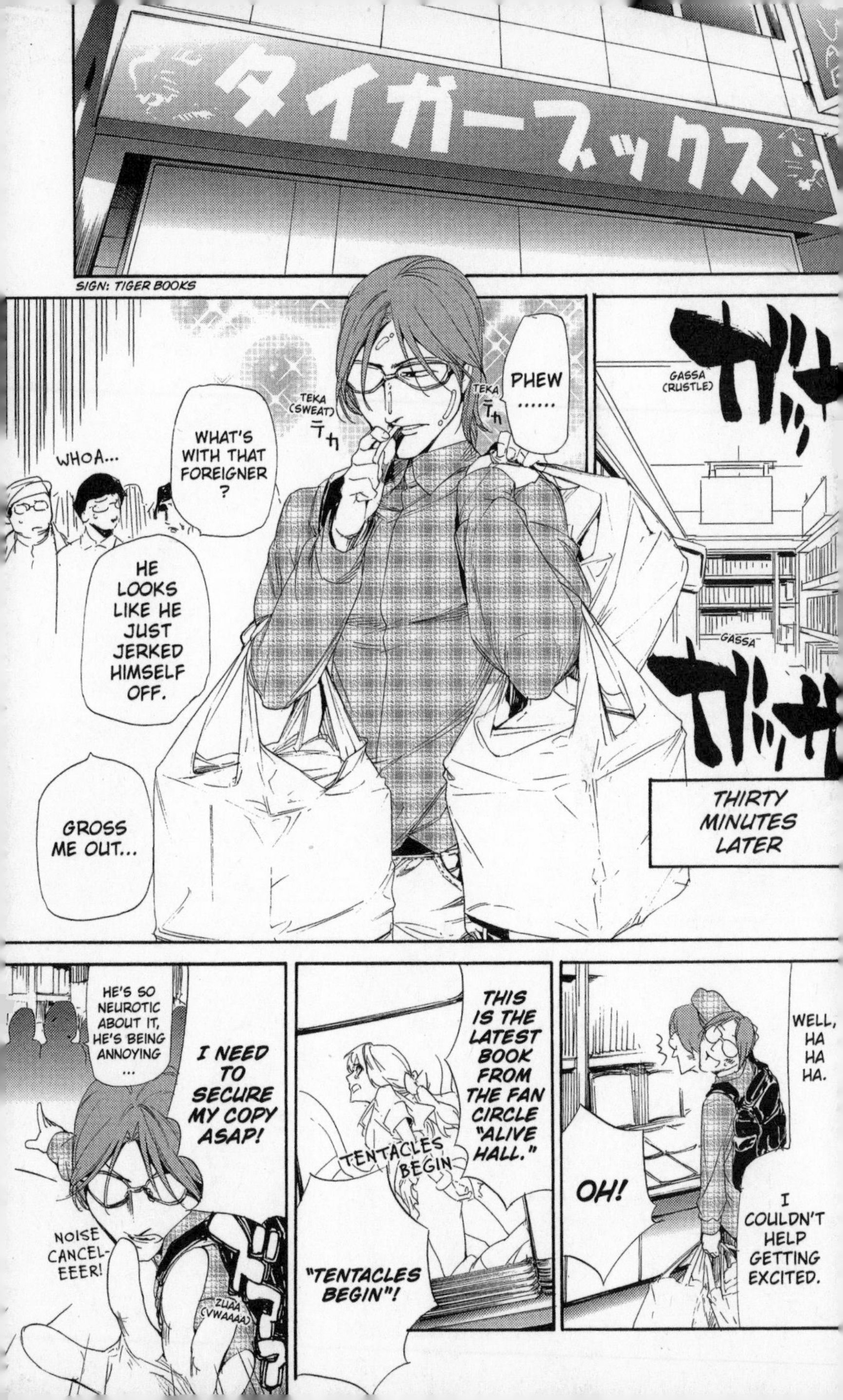

タイガーブックス
SIGN: TIGER BOOKS
GASSA (RUSTLE)
GASSA
THIRTY MINUTES LATER
PHEW ......
TEKA
TEKA (SWEAT)
WHAT'S WITH THAT FOREIGNER?
WHOA...
HE LOOKS LIKE HE JUST JERKED HIMSELF OFF.
GROSS ME OUT...
WELL, HA HA HA.
I COULDN'T HELP GETTING EXCITED.
OH!
THIS IS THE LATEST BOOK FROM THE FAN CIRCLE "ALIVE HALL."
TENTACLES BEGIN
"TENTACLES BEGIN"!
HE'S SO NEUROTIC ABOUT IT, HE'S BEING ANNOYING ...
I NEED TO SECURE MY COPY ASAP!
NOISE CANCEL-EEER!
ZUAA (VWAAAA)

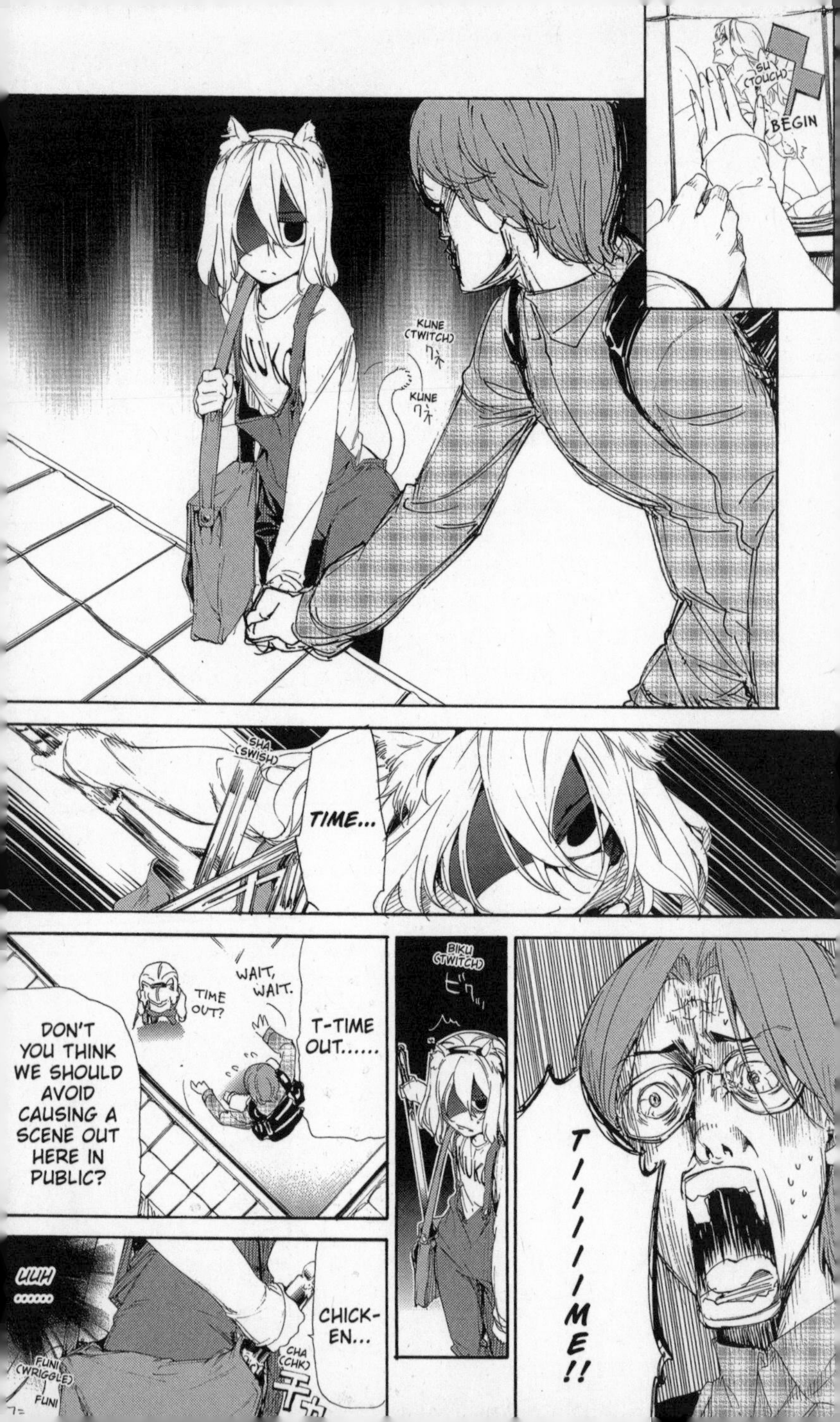
SUY (TOUCH)
BEGIN
KUNE (TWITCH) クネ
KUNE クネ
SHA (SWISH)
TIME...
TIIIIIME!!
BIKU (TWITCH) ビクッ
T-TIME OUT......
WAIT, WAIT.
TIME OUT?
DON'T YOU THINK WE SHOULD AVOID CAUSING A SCENE OUT HERE IN PUBLIC?
CHICK-EN...
CHA (CHK)
UUH ......
FUNI (WRIGGLE) FUNI

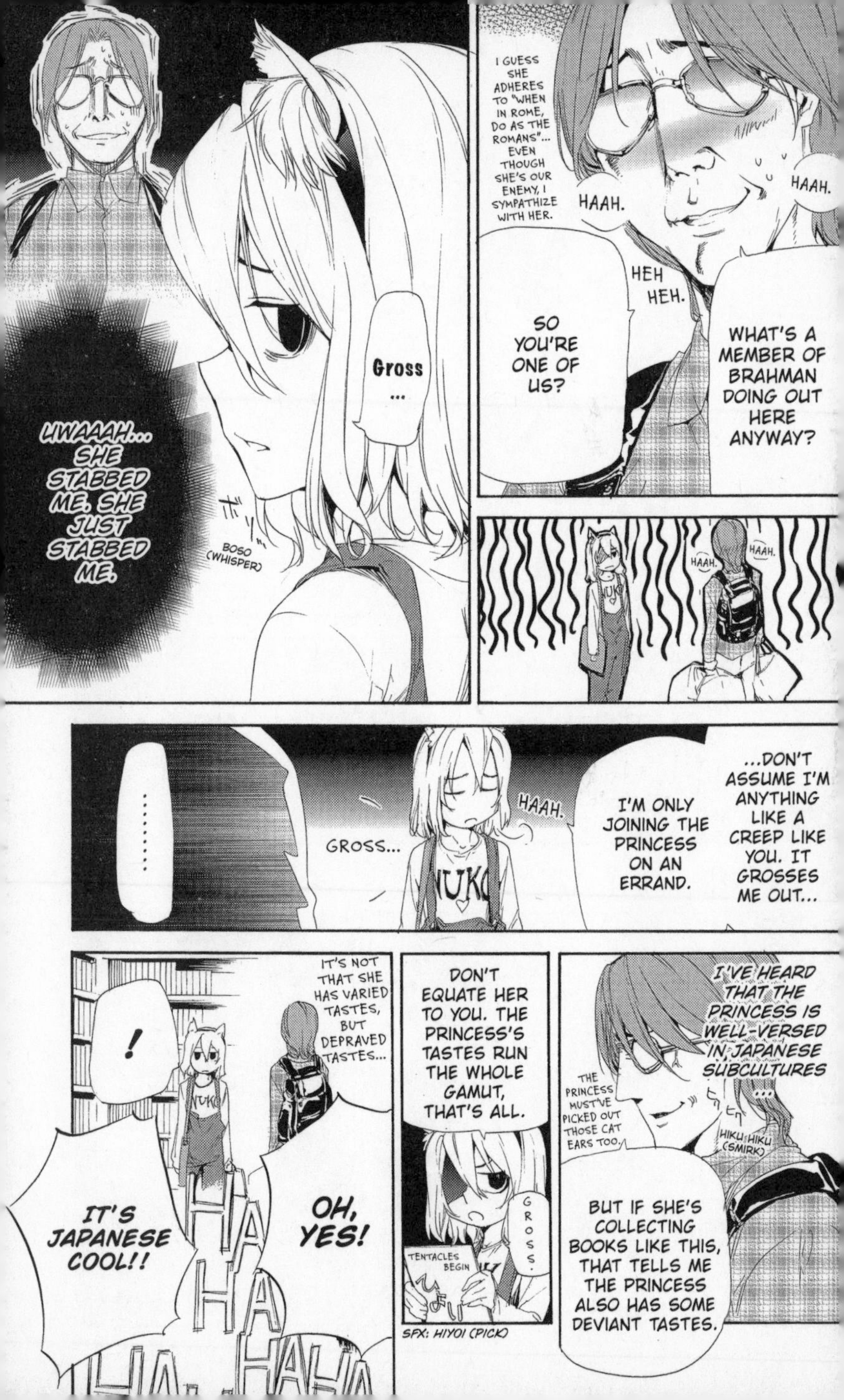
HAAH.
WHAT'S A MEMBER OF BRAHMAN DOING OUT HERE ANYWAY?
HEH HEH.
SO YOU'RE ONE OF US?
I GUESS SHE ADHERES TO "WHEN IN ROME, DO AS THE ROMANS"... EVEN THOUGH SHE'S OUR ENEMY, I SYMPATHIZE WITH HER.
HAAH.
HAAH.
HAAH.
Gross...
BOSO (WHISPER)
UWAAAH... SHE STABBED ME. SHE JUST STABBED ME.
...DON'T ASSUME I'M ANYTHING LIKE A CREEP LIKE YOU. IT GROSSES ME OUT...
I'M ONLY JOINING THE PRINCESS ON AN ERRAND.
HAAH.
GROSS...
....
I'VE HEARD THAT THE PRINCESS IS WELL-VERSED IN JAPANESE SUBCULTURES...
HIKU HIKU (SMIRK)
THE PRINCESS MUST'VE PICKED OUT THOSE CAT EARS TOO.
BUT IF SHE'S COLLECTING BOOKS LIKE THIS, THAT TELLS ME THE PRINCESS ALSO HAS SOME DEVIANT TASTES.
DON'T EQUATE HER TO YOU. THE PRINCESS'S TASTES RUN THE WHOLE GAMUT, THAT'S ALL.
GROSS.
TENTACLES BEGIN
SFX: HIYOI (PICK)
IT'S NOT THAT SHE HAS VARIED TASTES, BUT DEPRAVED TASTES...
!
OH, YES!
IT'S JAPANESE COOL!!
HA HA HA HA HAHA

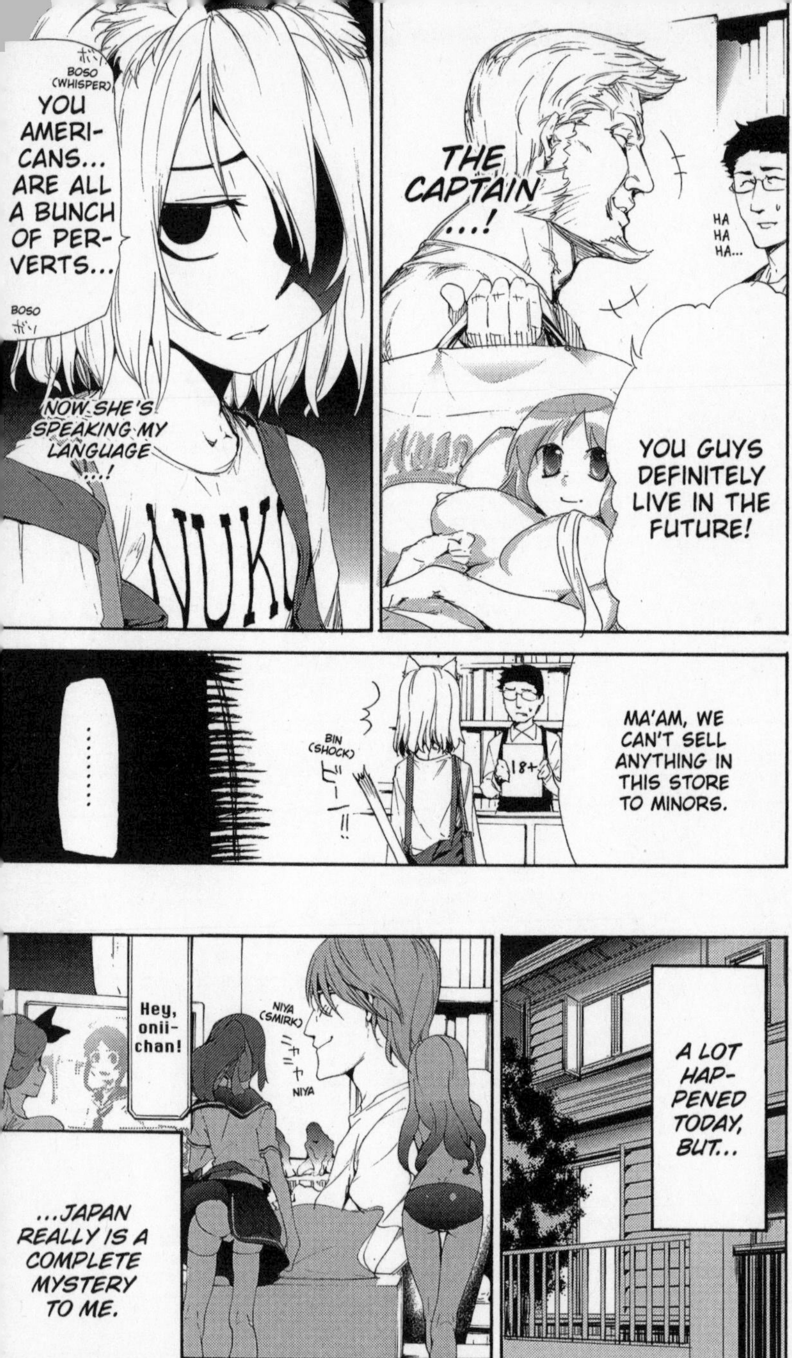
THE CAPTAIN...!
HA HA HA...
YOU GUYS DEFINITELY LIVE IN THE FUTURE!
ボソッ BOSO (WHISPER)
YOU AMERICANS... ARE ALL A BUNCH OF PERVERTS...
BOSO ボソッ
NOW SHE'S SPEAKING MY LANGUAGE...!
MA'AM, WE CAN'T SELL ANYTHING IN THIS STORE TO MINORS.
18+
BIN (SHOCK)
ビー!!
....
A LOT HAPPENED TODAY, BUT...
Hey, onii-chan!
NIYA (SMIRK)
ニヤニヤ
NIYA
...JAPAN REALLY IS A COMPLETE MYSTERY TO ME.

AFTERWORD

I'M...

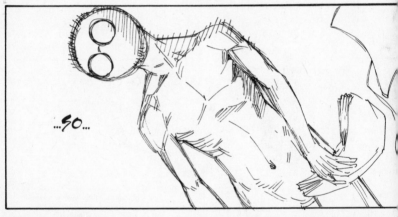

...SO...

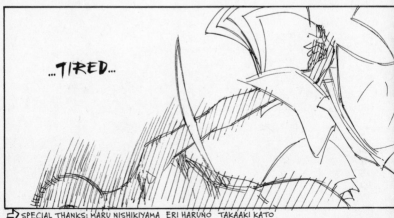

...TIRED...

⇨ SPECIAL THANKS: MARU NISHIKIYAMA   ERI HARUNO   TAKAAKI KATO
          #15~17   #18.19   #18

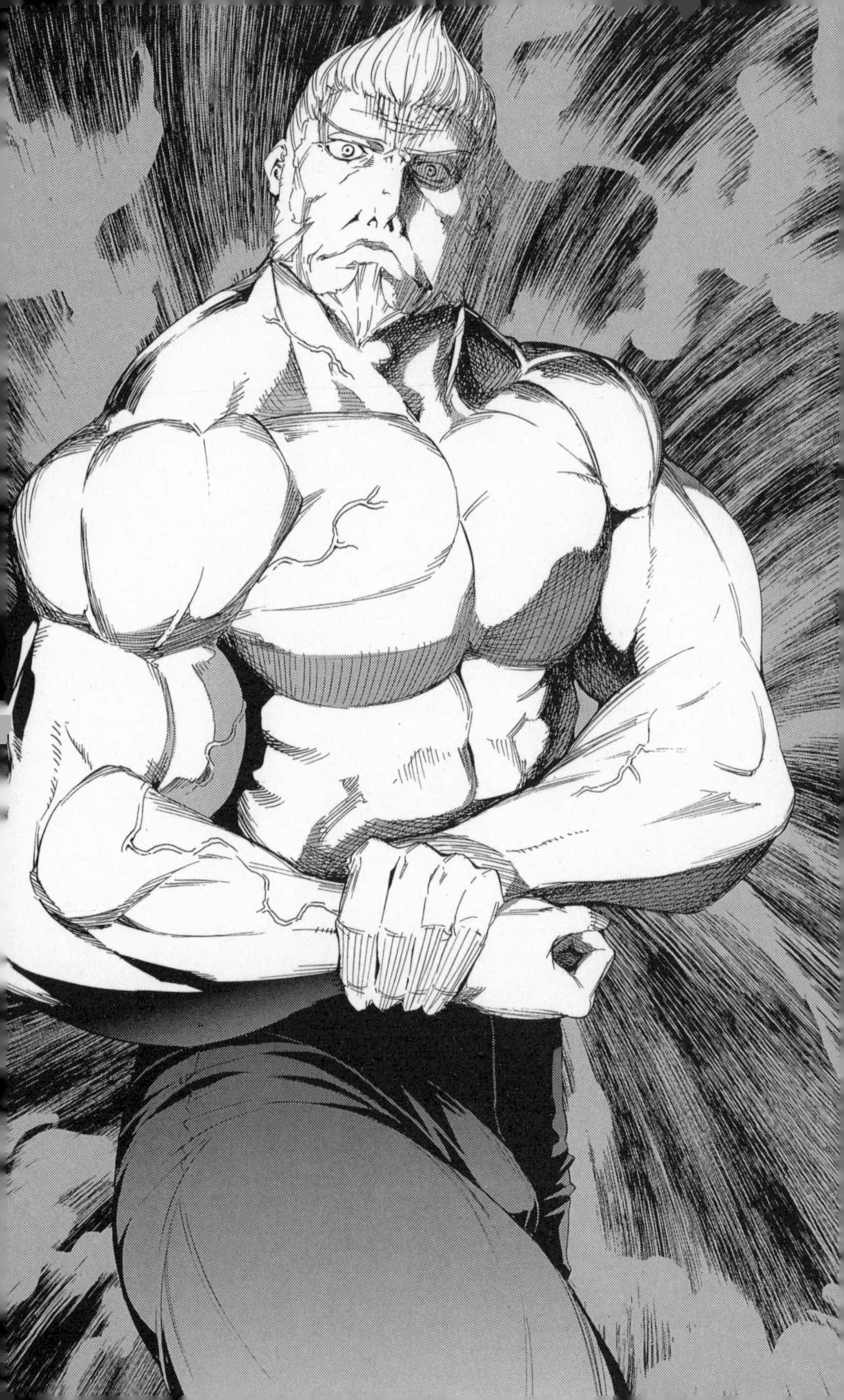

UNDERDOGS

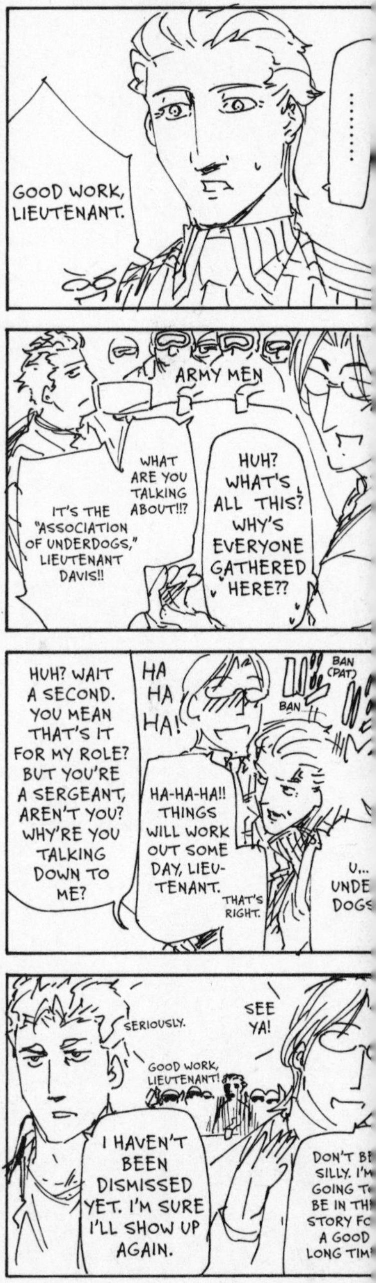
……
GOOD WORK, LIEUTENANT.
ARMY MEN
HUH? WHAT'S ALL THIS? WHY'S EVERYONE GATHERED HERE??
WHAT ARE YOU TALKING ABOUT!!?
IT'S THE "ASSOCIATION OF UNDERDOGS," LIEUTENANT DAVIS!!
BAN (PAT)
BAN
U... UNDE DOGS
HA HA HA!
HA-HA-HA!! THINGS WILL WORK OUT SOME DAY, LIEU-TENANT.
THAT'S RIGHT.
HUH? WAIT A SECOND. YOU MEAN THAT'S IT FOR MY ROLE? BUT YOU'RE A SERGEANT, AREN'T YOU? WHY'RE YOU TALKING DOWN TO ME?
SEE YA!
SERIOUSLY.
GOOD WORK, LIEUTENANT!
DON'T BE SILLY. I'M GOING T BE IN TH STORY FO A GOOD LONG TIM
I HAVEN'T BEEN DISMISSED YET. I'M SURE I'LL SHOW UP AGAIN.

WAR

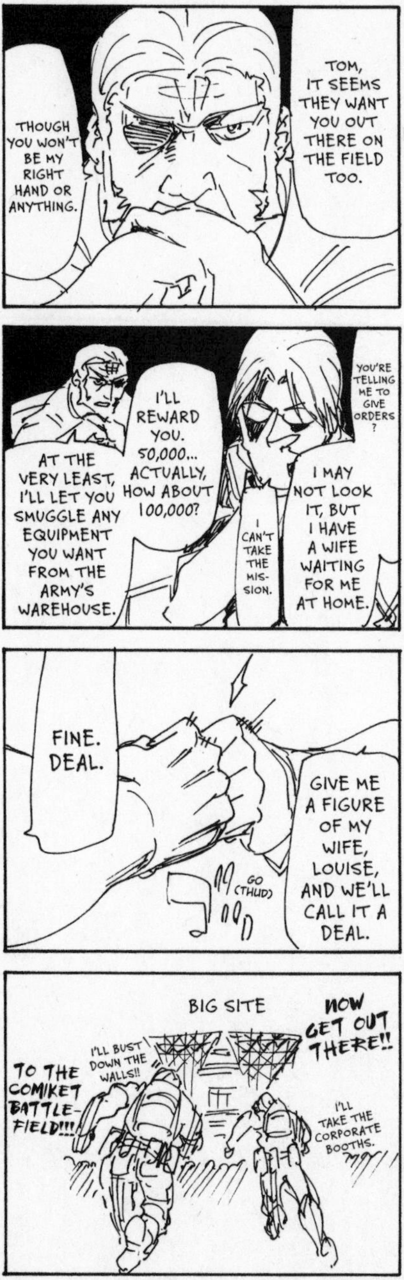
TOM, IT SEEMS THEY WANT YOU OUT THERE ON THE FIELD TOO.
THOUGH YOU WON'T BE MY RIGHT HAND OR ANYTHING.
YOU'RE TELLING ME TO GIVE ORDERS?
I MAY NOT LOOK IT, BUT I HAVE A WIFE WAITING FOR ME AT HOME.
I CAN'T TAKE THE MIS-SION.
I'LL REWARD YOU. 50,000... ACTUALLY, HOW ABOUT 100,000?
AT THE VERY LEAST, I'LL LET YOU SMUGGLE ANY EQUIPMENT YOU WANT FROM THE ARMY'S WAREHOUSE.
GIVE ME A FIGURE OF MY WIFE, LOUISE, AND WE'LL CALL IT A DEAL.
GO (THUD)
FINE. DEAL.
NOW GET OUT THERE!!
BIG SITE
I'LL TAKE THE CORPORATE BOOTHS.
I'LL BUST DOWN THE WALLS!!
TO THE COMIKET BATTLE-FIELD!!!

IT WRONG TO TRY TO PICK UP GIRLS A DUNGEON?, VOL. 1–5

A would-be hero turns damsel in distress in this hilarious send-up of sword-and-sorcery tropes.

MANGA ADAPTATION AVAILABLE NOW!

s It Wrong to Try to Pick Up Girls n a Dungeon? © Fujino Omori / 5B Creative Corp.

ANOTHER

The spine-chilling horror novel that took Japan by storm is now available in print for the first time in English—in a gorgeous hardcover edition.

MANGA ADAPTATION AVAILABLE NOW!

Another © Yukito Ayatsuji 2009/ KADOKAWA CORPORATION, Tokyo

CERTAIN MAGICAL INDEX, VOL. 1–6

ence and magic collide as Japan's st popular light novel franchise kes its English-language debut.

NGA ADAPTATION AVAILABLE NOW!

CERTAIN MAGICAL INDEX © KAZUMA KAMACHI LUSTRATION: KIYOTAKA HAIMURA ADOKAWA CORPORATION ASCII MEDIA WORKS

VISIT YENPRESS.COM TO CHECK OUT ALL THE TITLES IN OUR NEW LIGHT NOVEL INITIATIVE AND...

GET YOUR YEN ON!

www.YenPress.com

HAVE YOU BEEN TURNED ON TO LIGHT NOVELS YET?

IN STORES NOW!

SWORD ART ONLINE, VOL. 1–7
SWORD ART ONLINE, PROGRESSIVE 1–3

The chart-topping light novel series that spawned the explosively popular anime and manga adaptations!

MANGA ADAPTATION AVAILABLE NOW!

SWORD ART ONLINE © REKI KAWAHARA ILLUSTRATION: abec
KADOKAWA CORPORATION ASCII MEDIA WORKS

ACCEL WORLD, VOL. 1–6

Prepare to accelerate with an action-packed cyber-thriller from the bestselling author of *Sword Art Online*.

MANGA ADAPTATION AVAILABLE NOW!

ACCEL WORLD © REKI KAWAHARA ILLUSTRATION: HIMA
KADOKAWA CORPORATION ASCII MEDIA WORKS

SPICE AND WOLF, VOL. 1–17

A disgruntled goddess joins a traveling merchant in this light novel series that inspired the *New York Times* bestselling manga.

MANGA ADAPTATION AVAILABLE NOW!

SPICE AND WOLF © ISUNA HASEKURA ILLUSTRATION: JYUU AYAKU
KADOKAWA CORPORATION ASCII MEDIA WORKS

PRESENTING THE LATEST SERIES FROM

JUN MOCHIZUKI

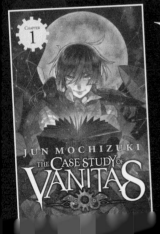

THE CASE STUDY OF VANITAS

READ THE CHAPTERS AT THE SAME TIME AS JAPAN!

AVAILABLE NOW WORLDWIDE WHEREVER E-BOOKS ARE SOLD!

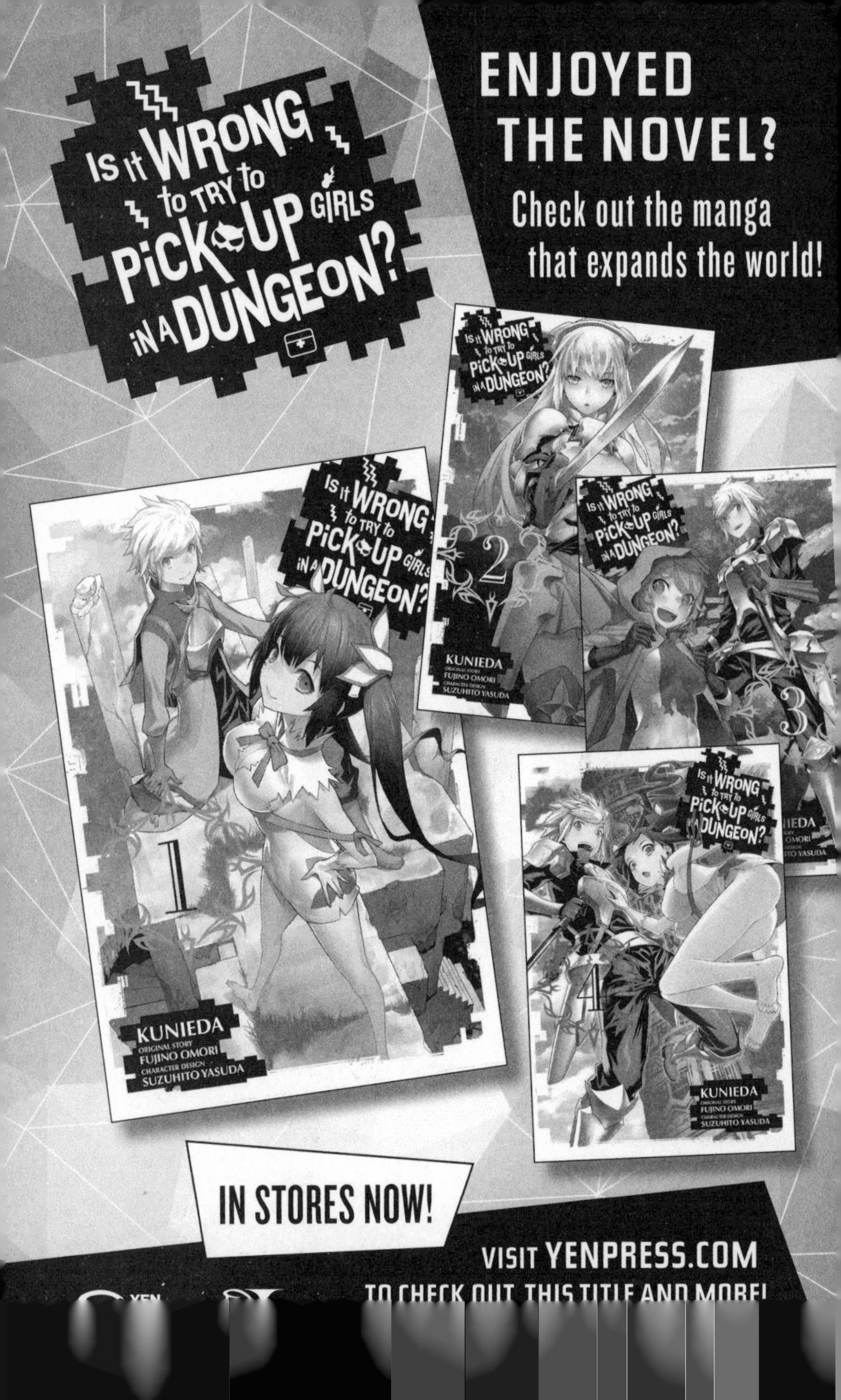
ENJOYED THE NOVEL?
Check out the manga that expands the world!
Is it WRONG to TRY to PiCK-UP GIRLS iN A DUNGEON?
KUNIEDA
ORIGINAL STORY FUJINO OMORI
CHARACTER DESIGN SUZUHITO YASUDA
IN STORES NOW!
VISIT YENPRESS.COM
TO CHECK OUT THIS TITLE AND MORE!

THE CHART-TOPPING SERIES
THAT SPAWNED THE EXPLOSIVELY POPULAR ANIME ADAPTATIONS!

SWORD ART ONLINE, VOL. 1-7
LIGHT NOVEL SERIES
SWORD ART ONLINE © REKI KAWAHARA
KADOKAWA CORPORATION ASCII MEDIA WORKS

SWORD ART ONLINE, PROGRESSIVE, VOL. 1-3
LIGHT NOVEL SERIES
SWORD ART ONLINE: PROGRESSIVE © REKI KAWAHARA
KADOKAWA CORPORATION ASCII MEDIA WORKS

SWORD ART ONLINE, PROGRESSIVE, VOL. 1-4
MANGA SERIES
SWORD ART ONLINE: PROGRESSIVE
© REKI KAWAHARA / KISEKI HIMURA
KADOKAWA CORPORATION ASCII MEDIA WORKS

SWORD ART ONLINE, VOL. 1-7
MANGA SERIES
SWORD ART ONLINE: AINCRAD
REKI KAWAHARA / TAMAKO NAKAMURA
OKAWA CORPORATION ASCII MEDIA WORKS

SWORD ART ONLINE, GIRLS' OPS, VOL. 1-2
MANGA SERIES
SWORD ART ONLINE: GIRLS' OPS
© REKI KAWAHARA / NEKO NEKOBYOU
KADOKAWA CORPORATION ASCII MEDIA WORKS

VISIT YENPRESS.COM
TO CHECK OUT ALL THESE TITLES AND MORE!

▶▶▶ PREPARE TO ACCELERATE

WITH AN ACTION-PACKED CYBER-THRILLER FROM
THE BESTSELLING AUTHOR OF *SWORD ART ONLINE*!

ACCEL WORLD, VOL. 1-6
LIGHT NOVEL SERIES

ACCEL WORLD, VOL. 1-6
MANGA SERIES

VISIT **YENPRESS.COM**
TO CHECK OUT THESE TITLES AND MORE!

ACCEL WORLD (manga) © REKI KAWAHARA / HIROYUKI AIGAMO   ACCEL WORLD (novel) © REKI KAWAHARA   ILLUSTRATION: HIMA

TABOO TATTOO

by SHINJIRO

Translation: Christine Dashiell • Lettering: Phil Christie

This book is a work of fiction. Names, characters, places, and incidents are the product of the author's imagination or are used fictitiously. Any resemblance to actual events, locales, or persons, living or dead, is coincidental.

TABOO TATTOO
© Shinjiro 2011
First published in Japan in 2011 by KADOKAWA CORPORATION. English translation rights reserved by Yen Press, LLC under the license from KADOKAWA CORPORATION, Tokyo through TUTTLE-MORI AGENCY, Inc., Tokyo.

English translation © 2016 by Yen Press, LLC

Yen Press, LLC supports the right to free expression and the value of copyright. The purpose of copyright is to encourage writers and artists to produce the creative works that enrich our culture.

The scanning, uploading, and distribution of this book without permission is a theft of the author's intellectual property. If you would like permission to use material from the book (other than for review purposes), please contact the publisher. Thank you for your support of the author's rights.

Yen Press
1290 Avenue of the Americas
New York, NY 10104

Visit us at yenpress.com
facebook.com/yenpress
twitter.com/yenpress
yenpress.tumblr.com
instagram.com/yenpress

First Yen Press Edition: October 2016

Yen Press is an imprint of Yen Press, LLC.
The Yen Press name and logo are trademarks of Yen Press, LLC.

The publisher is not responsible for websites (or their content) that are not owned by the publisher.

Library of Congress Control Number: 2015952591

ISBNs: 978-0-316-31055-0 (paperback)
978-0-316-31056-7 (ebook)
978-0-316-31057-4 (app)

10 9 8 7 6 5 4 3 2 1

BVG

Printed in the United States of America